I often listen to children's music with my kid. They're all such fun and lively songs. But sometimes, at certain moments, I become teary-eyed.

Songs composed by grown-ups for children...they have none of the usual stiffness or formality. Their only goal is to touch children's hearts. Songs like these celebrate our wishes for the little people, tinged with an adult's gentleness, sadness and nostalgia for bygone days.

–Hiroyuki Asada, 2012

Hiroyuki Asada made his debut in *Monthly Shonen Jump* in 1986. He's best known for his basketball manga *I'll*. He's a contributor to artist Range Murata's quarterly manga anthology *Robot*. *Tegami Bachi: Letter Bee* is his most recent series.

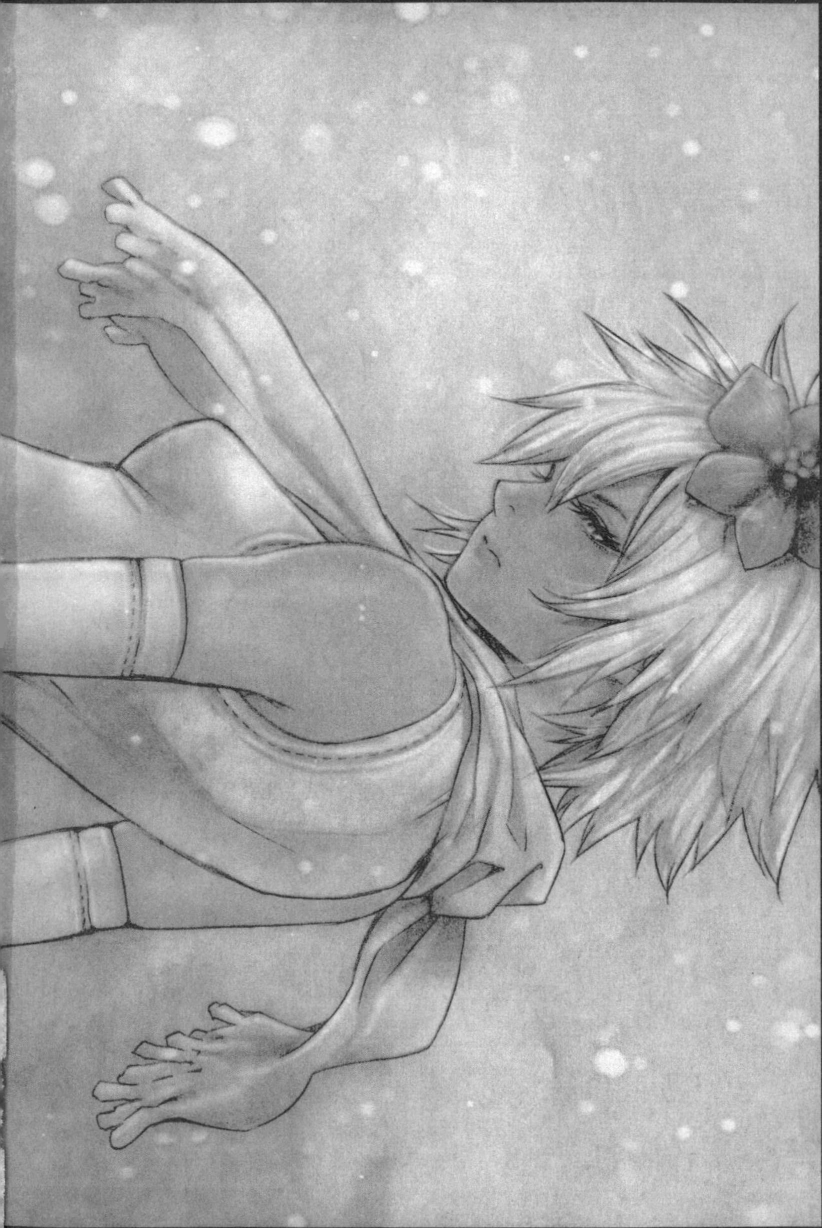

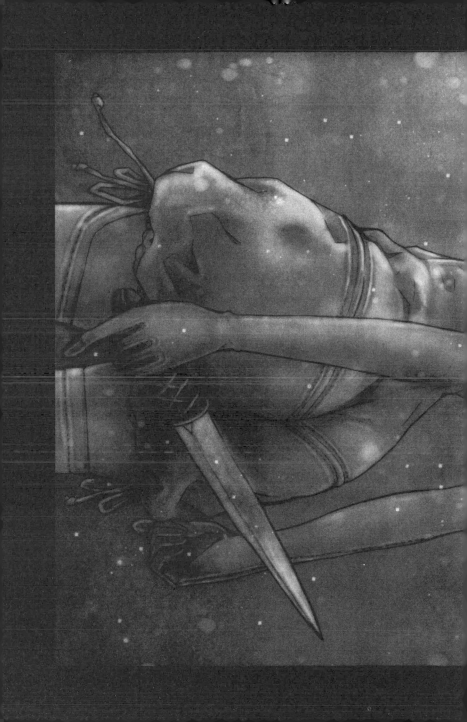

Tegami Bachi
LETTER · BEE

Volume 15

SHONEN JUMP Manga Edition

Story and Art by Hiroyuki Asada

English Adaptation/Rich Amtower
Translation/JN Productions
Touch-up & Lettering/Annaliese Christman
Design/Amy Martin
Editor/Shaenon K. Garrity

TEGAMIBACHI © 2006 by Hiroyuki Asada. All rights reserved.
First published in Japan in 2006 by SHUEISHA Inc., Tokyo. English
translation rights arranged by SHUEISHA Inc.

The stories, characters and incidents mentioned in this publication are
entirely fictional.

Printed in Canada

Published by VIZ Media, LLC
P.O. Box 77010
San Francisco, CA 94107

10 9 8 7 6 5 4 3 2 1
First printing, November 2013

www.viz.com

THE WORLD'S
MOST POPULAR MANGA

www.shonenjump.com

Tegami Bachi
LETTER · BEE

VOLUME 15

TO THE
LITTLE PEOPLE

STORY AND ART BY
HIROYUKI ASADA

This is a country known as Amberground, where night never ends.

Its capital, Akatsuki, is illuminated by a man-made sun. The farther one strays from the capital, the weaker the light. The Yuusari region is cast in twilight; the Yodaka region survives only on pale moonlight.

Letter Bee Gauche Suede and young Lag Seeing meet in the Yodaka region— a postal worker and the "letter" he must deliver. In their short time together, they form a fast friendship, but when the journey ends, each departs down his own path. Gauche longs to become Head Bee, while Lag himself wants to be a Letter Bee, like Gauche.

In time, Lag becomes a Letter Bee. But Gauche has lost his *heart* and become a Marauder named Noir, working for the rebel organization Reverse.

After a harsh battle, the Bees defeat Cabernet, an enormously powerful Gaichuu, with help from Noir and a temporarily mature Niche. In the midst of battle, Lag enters Noir's *heart* and finds a message left there by his mother, Anne. Following the directions in the message, Lag returns to the village where he grew up to learn the truth about Amberground...

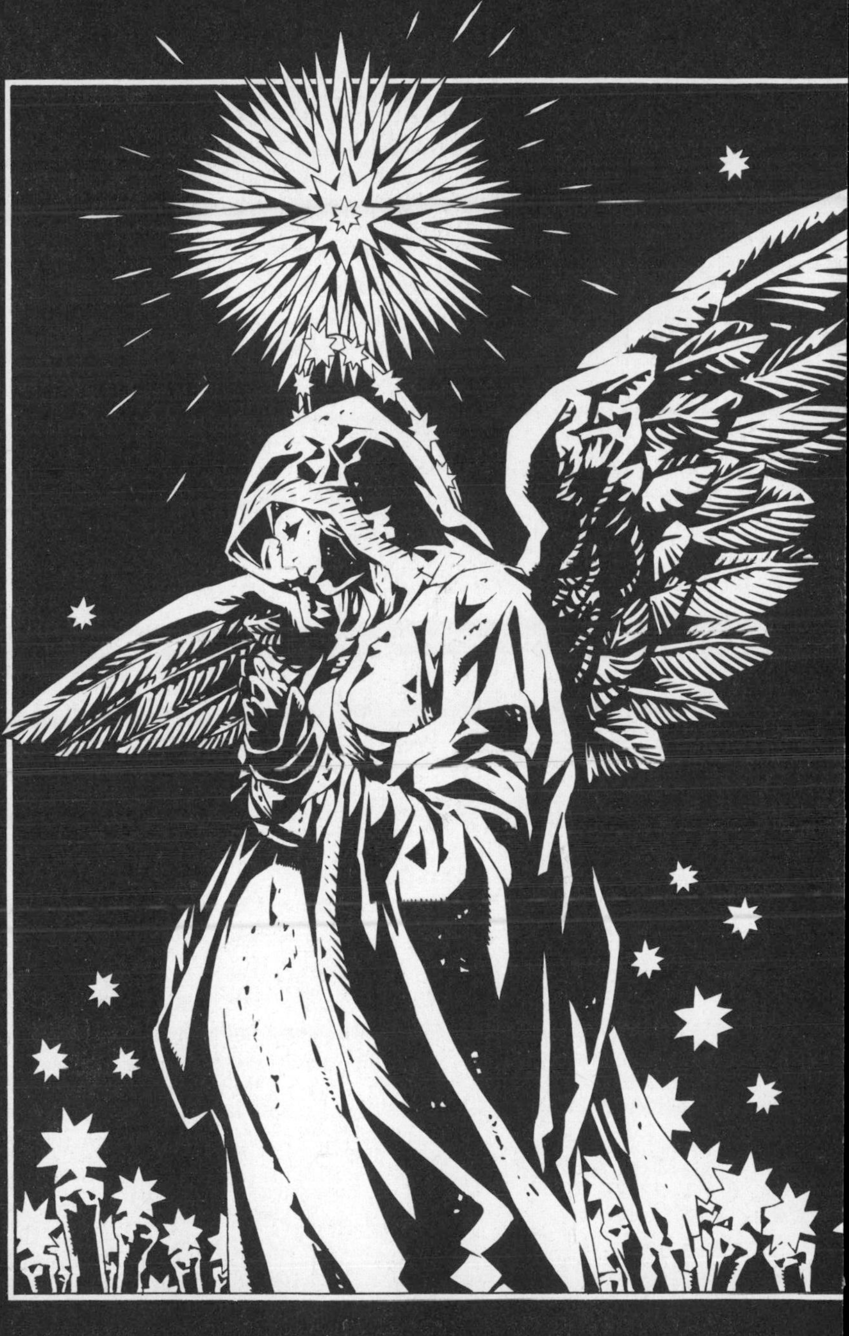

List of Characters

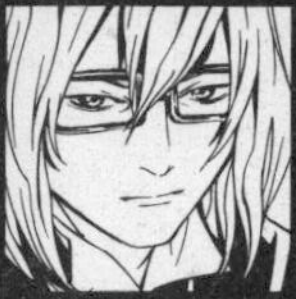

LARGO LLOYD
Ex-Beehive Director

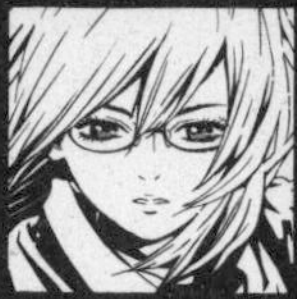

ARIA LINK
Section Chief of the Dead Letter Office

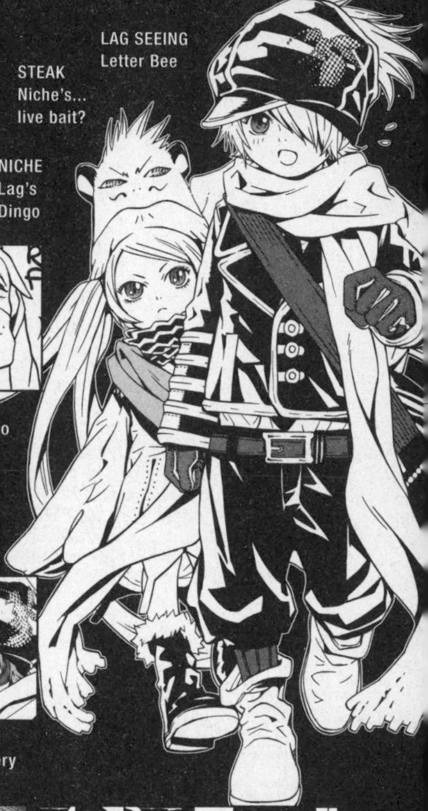

LAG SEEING
Letter Bee

STEAK
Niche's... live bait?

NICHE
Lag's Dingo

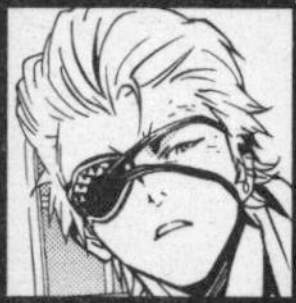

DR. THUNDERLAND, JR.
Member of the AG Biological Science Advisory Board, Third Division and head doctor at the Beehive

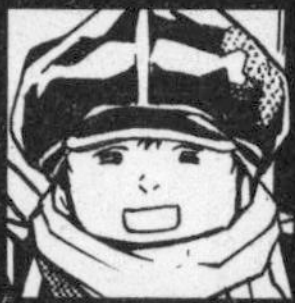

CONNOR KLUFF
Letter Bee

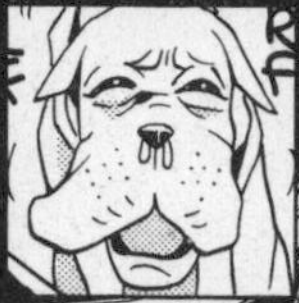

GUS
Connor's Dingo

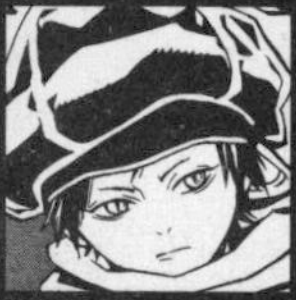

ZAZIE
Letter Bee

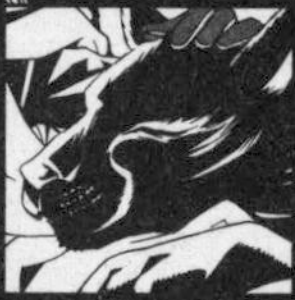

WASIOLKA
Zazie's Dingo

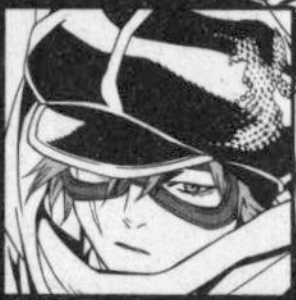

JIGGY PEPPER
Express Delivery Letter Bee

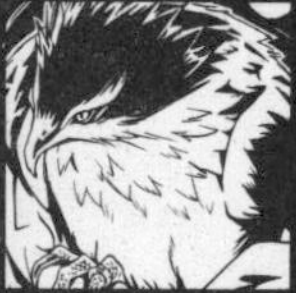

HARRY
Jiggy's Dingo

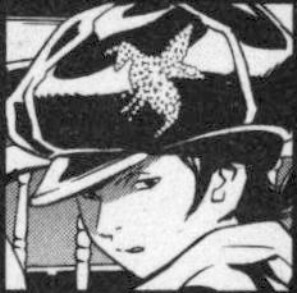

MOC SULLIVAN
Letter Bee

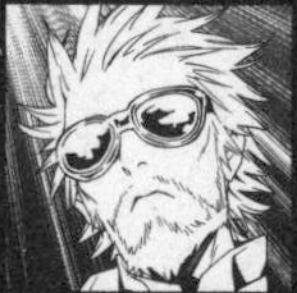

CHALYBS GARRARD
Inspector and ex-Letter Bee

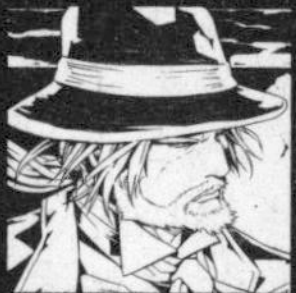

HAZEL VALENTINE
Inspector and Garrard's ex-Dingo

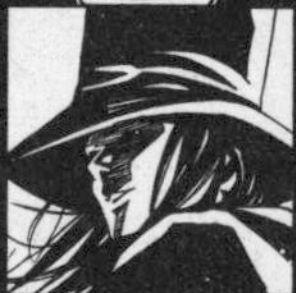

LAWRENCE
The ringleader of Reverse

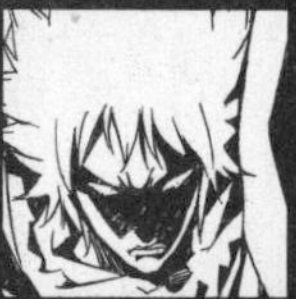

ZEAL
Marauder for Reverse

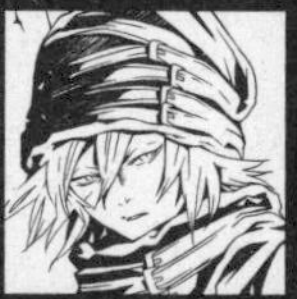

NOIR (FORMERLY GAUCHE SUEDE)
Marauder for Reverse and an ex–Letter Bee

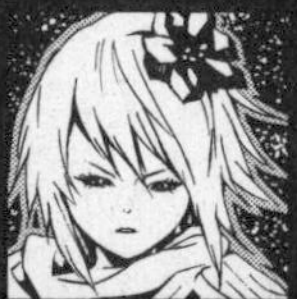

RODA
Noir's Dingo

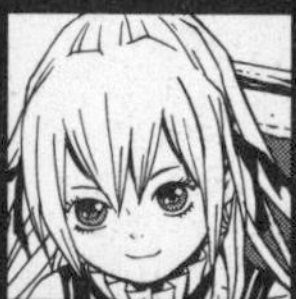

SYLVETTE SUEDE
Gauche's Sister

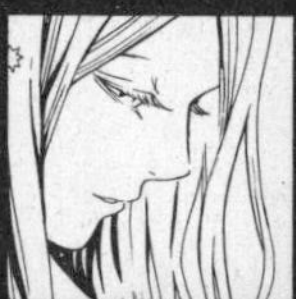

ANNE SEEING
Lag's Mother (Missing)

Tegami Bachi

LETTER · BEE

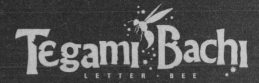

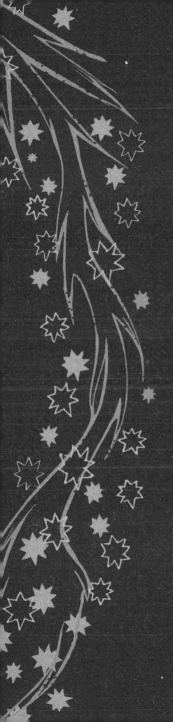

VOLUME 15

To the Little People

In all things...

the heart must take precedence.

The heart rules over all things...

...and all things come from the heart.

—THE SCRIPTURES OF AMBERGROUND, 1st verse

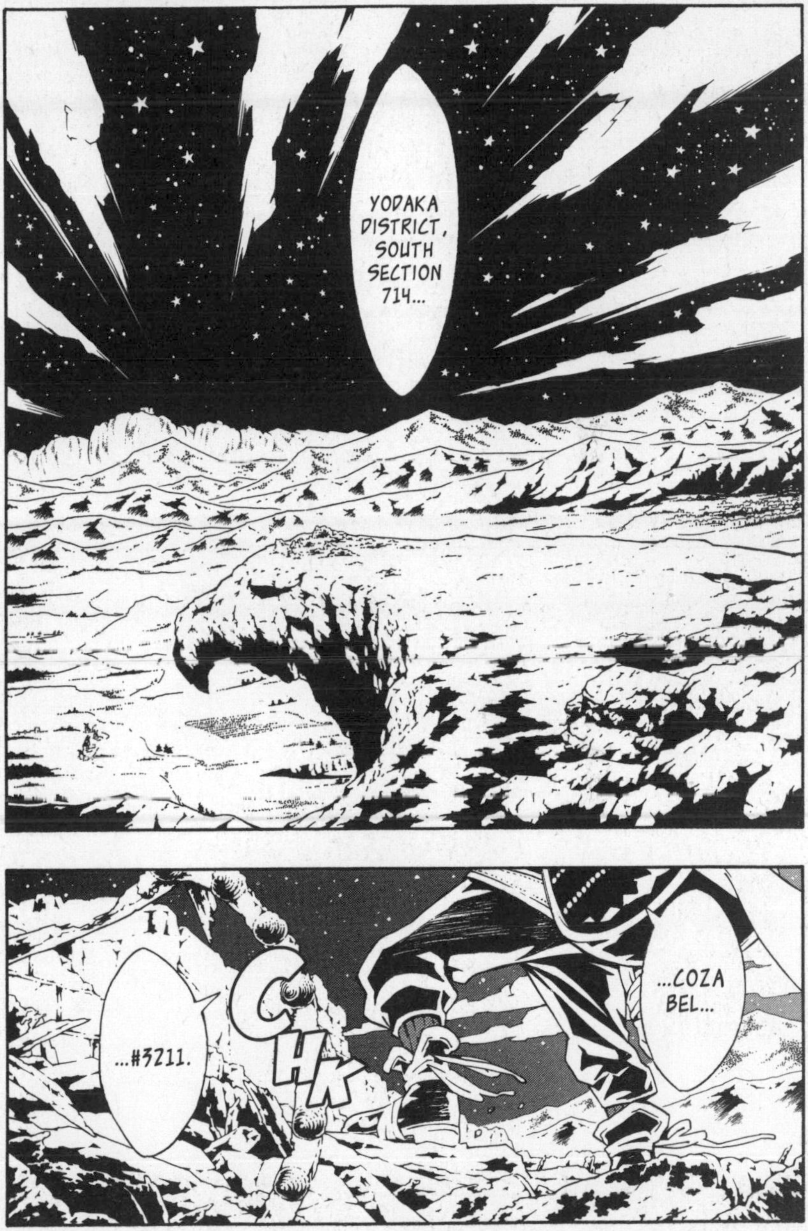
YODAKA DISTRICT, SOUTH SECTION 714...
...COZA BEL...
CHK
...#3211.

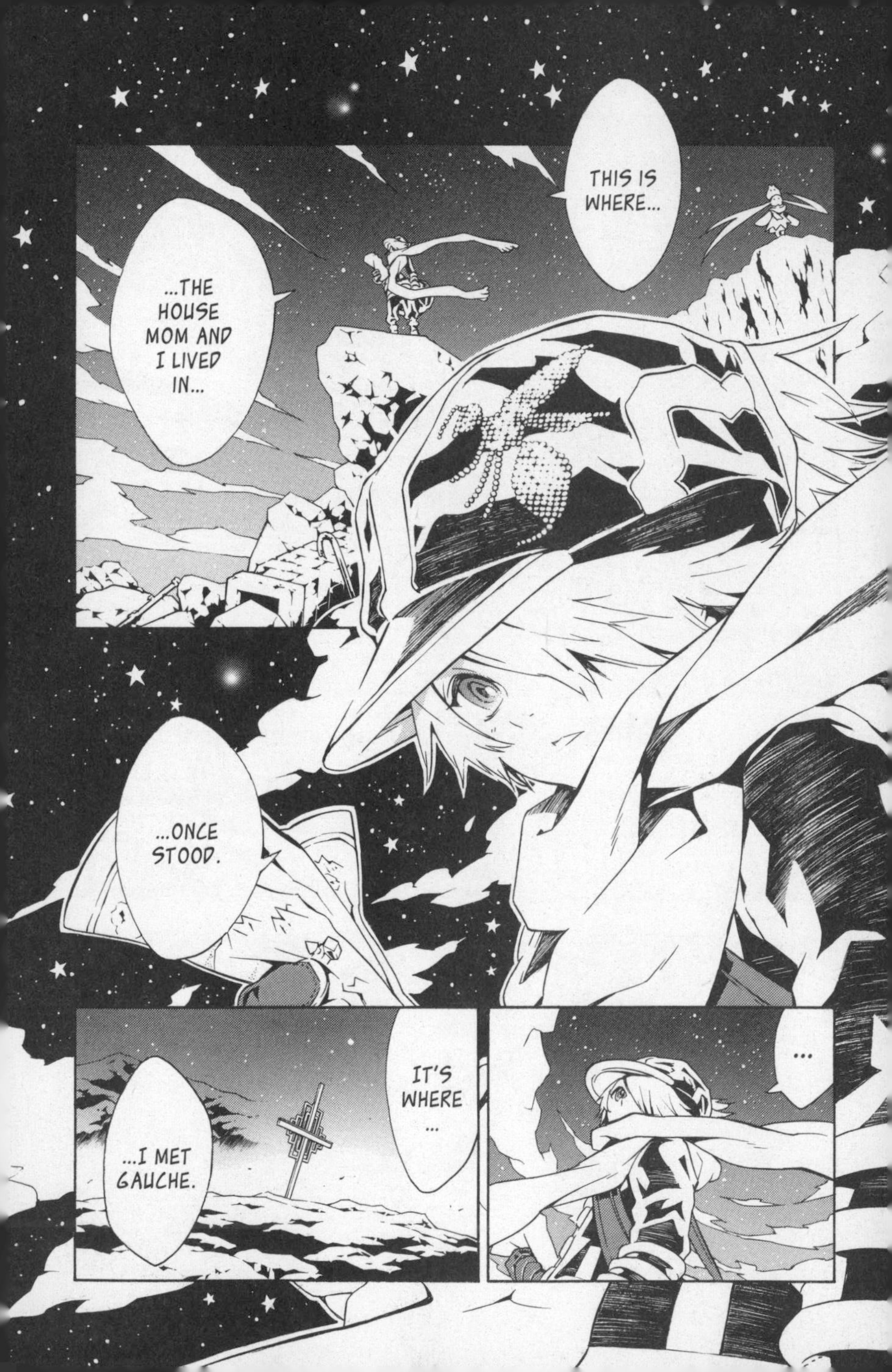
THIS IS WHERE...
...THE HOUSE MOM AND I LIVED IN...
...ONCE STOOD.
...
IT'S WHERE ...
...I MET GAUCHE.

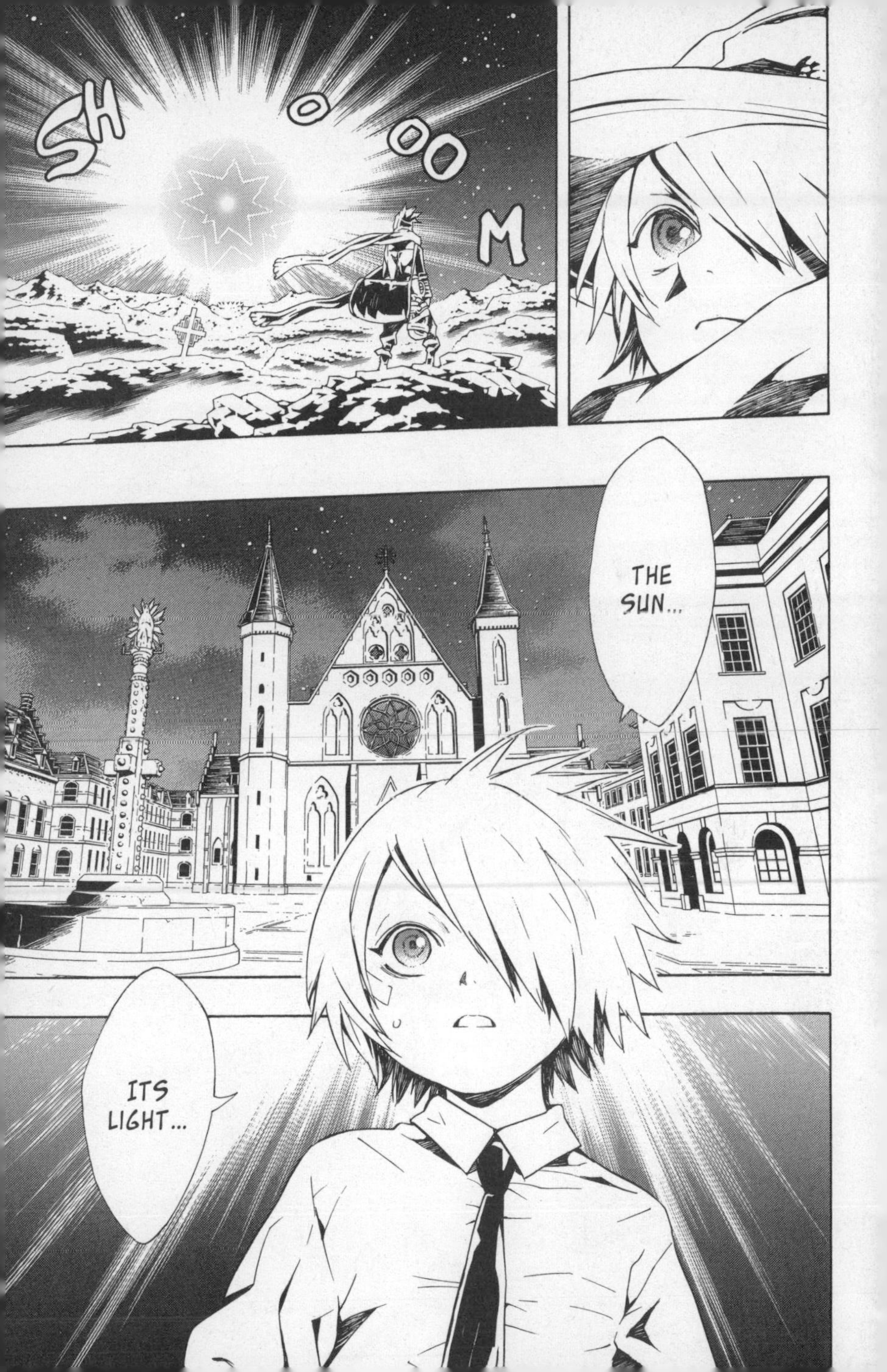
SHOOOM
THE SUN...
ITS LIGHT...

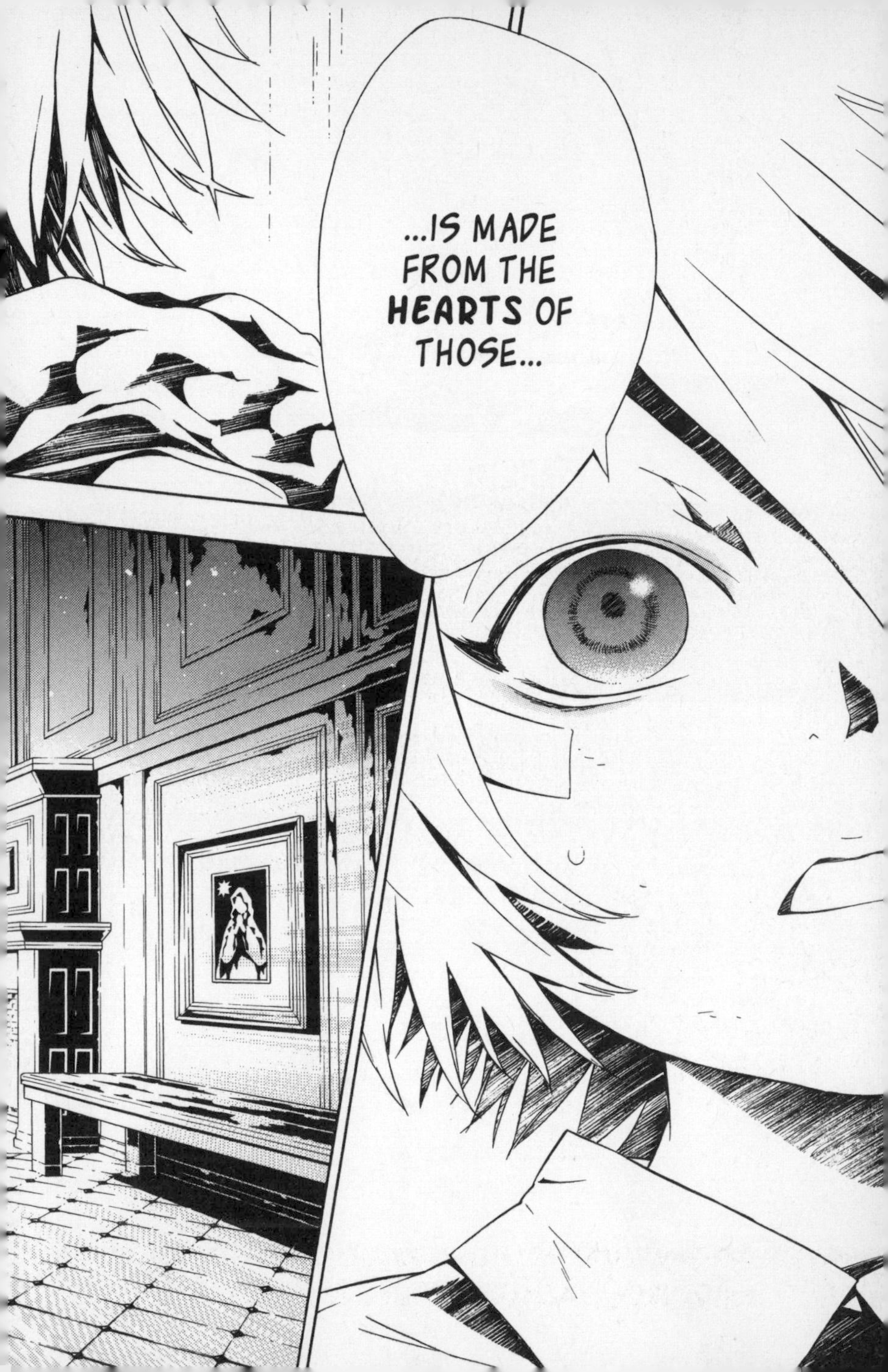
...IS MADE FROM THE HEARTS OF THOSE...

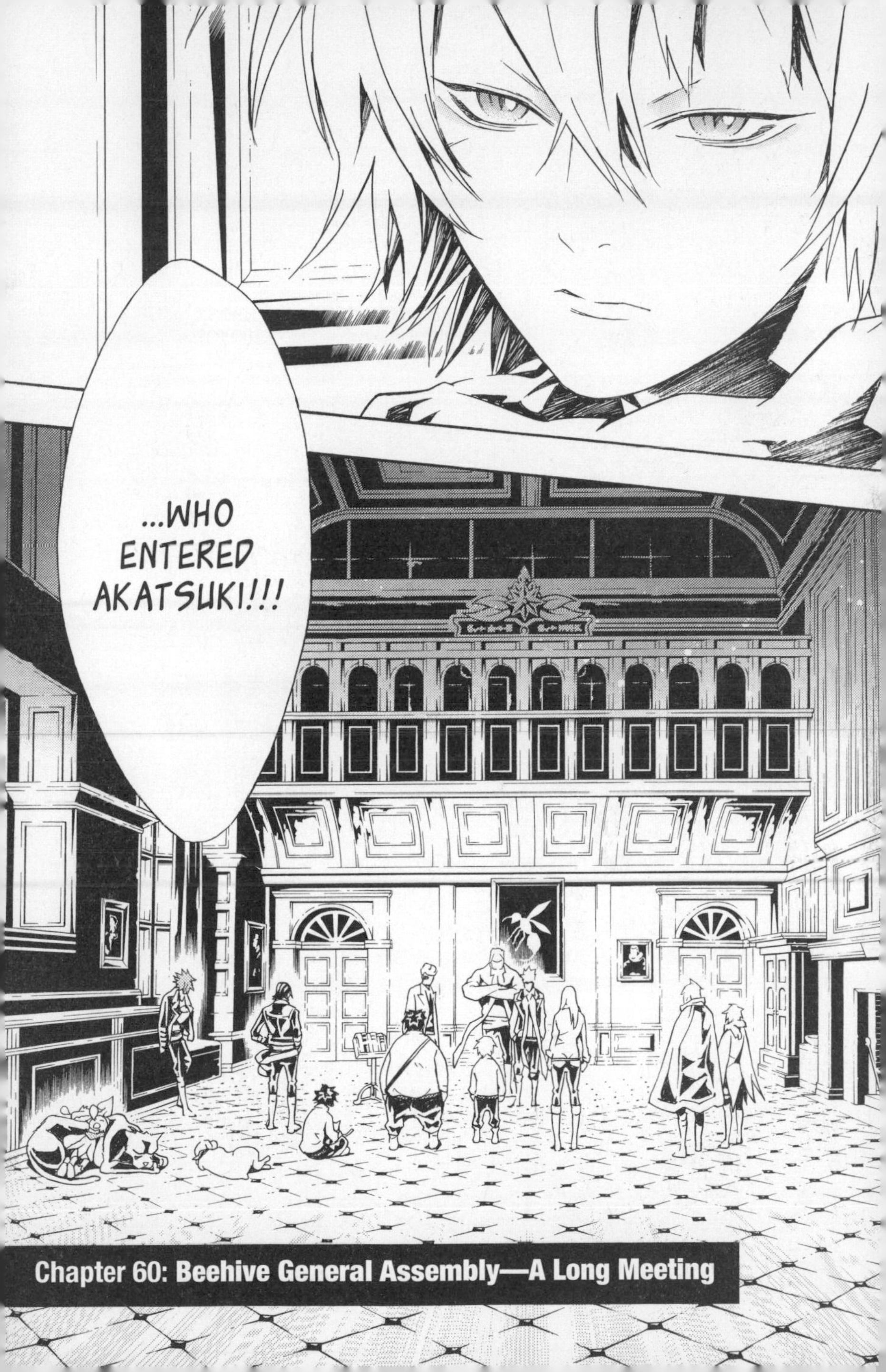
...WHO ENTERED AKATSUKI!!!

Chapter 60: Beehive General Assembly—A Long Meeting

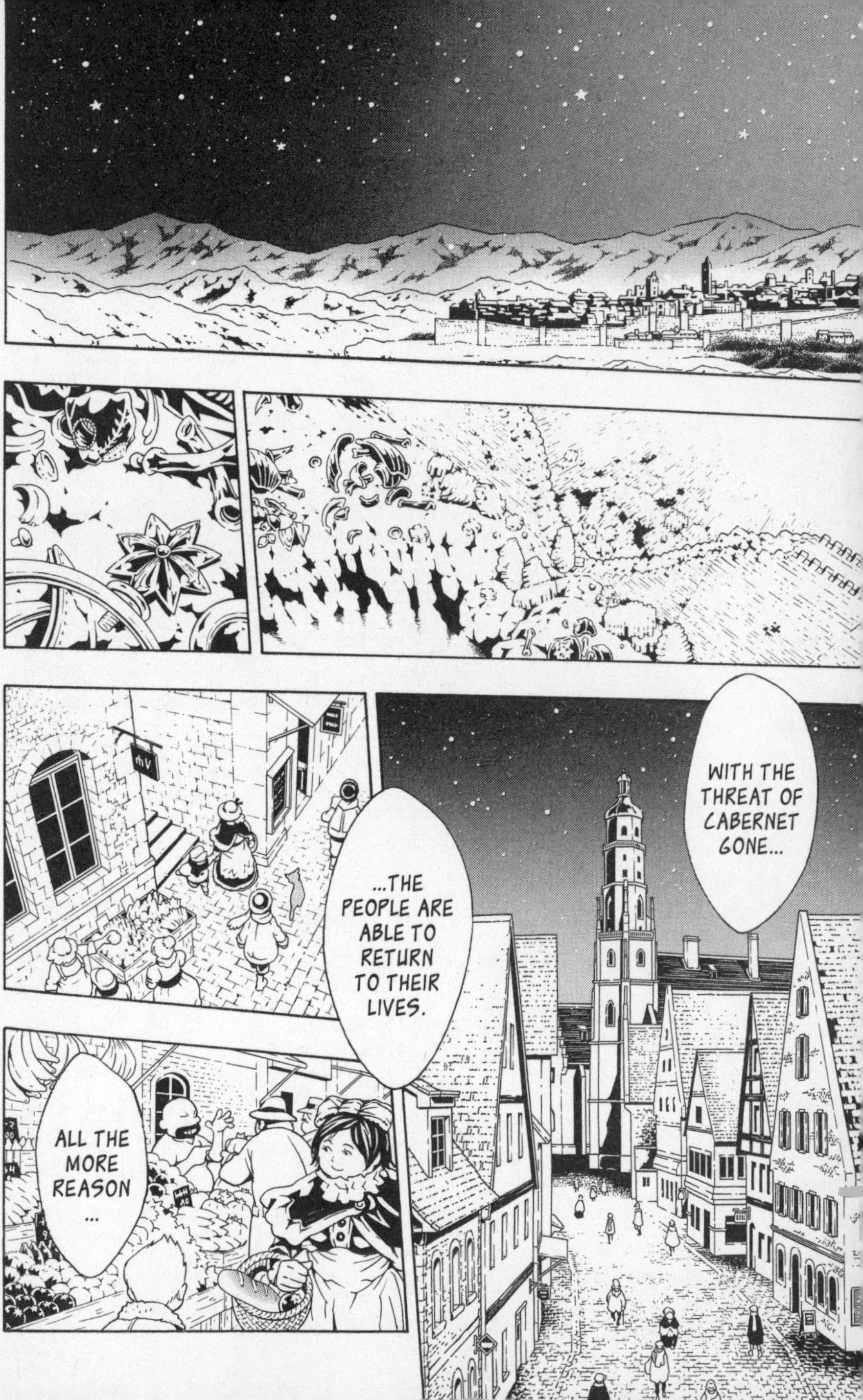
WITH THE THREAT OF CABERNET GONE...
...THE PEOPLE ARE ABLE TO RETURN TO THEIR LIVES.
ALL THE MORE REASON ...

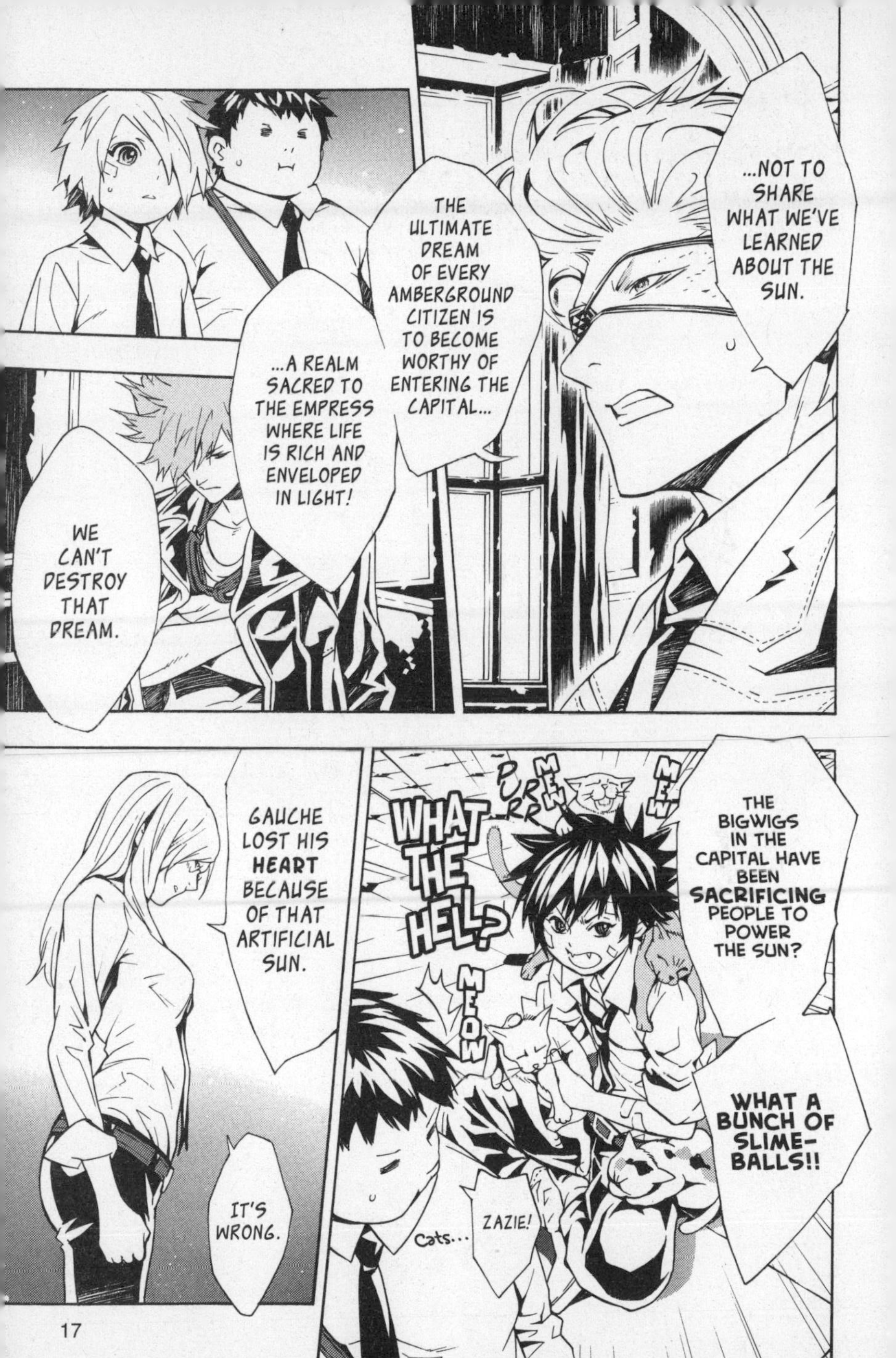
...NOT TO SHARE WHAT WE'VE LEARNED ABOUT THE SUN.
THE ULTIMATE DREAM OF EVERY AMBERGROUND CITIZEN IS TO BECOME WORTHY OF ENTERING THE CAPITAL...
...A REALM SACRED TO THE EMPRESS WHERE LIFE IS RICH AND ENVELOPED IN LIGHT!
WE CAN'T DESTROY THAT DREAM.
THE BIGWIGS IN THE CAPITAL HAVE BEEN SACRIFICING PEOPLE TO POWER THE SUN?
MEW
MEW
PURRR
WHAT THE HELL?
MEOW
WHAT A BUNCH OF SLIME-BALLS!!
ZAZIE!
Cats...
GAUCHE LOST HIS HEART BECAUSE OF THAT ARTIFICIAL SUN.
IT'S WRONG.

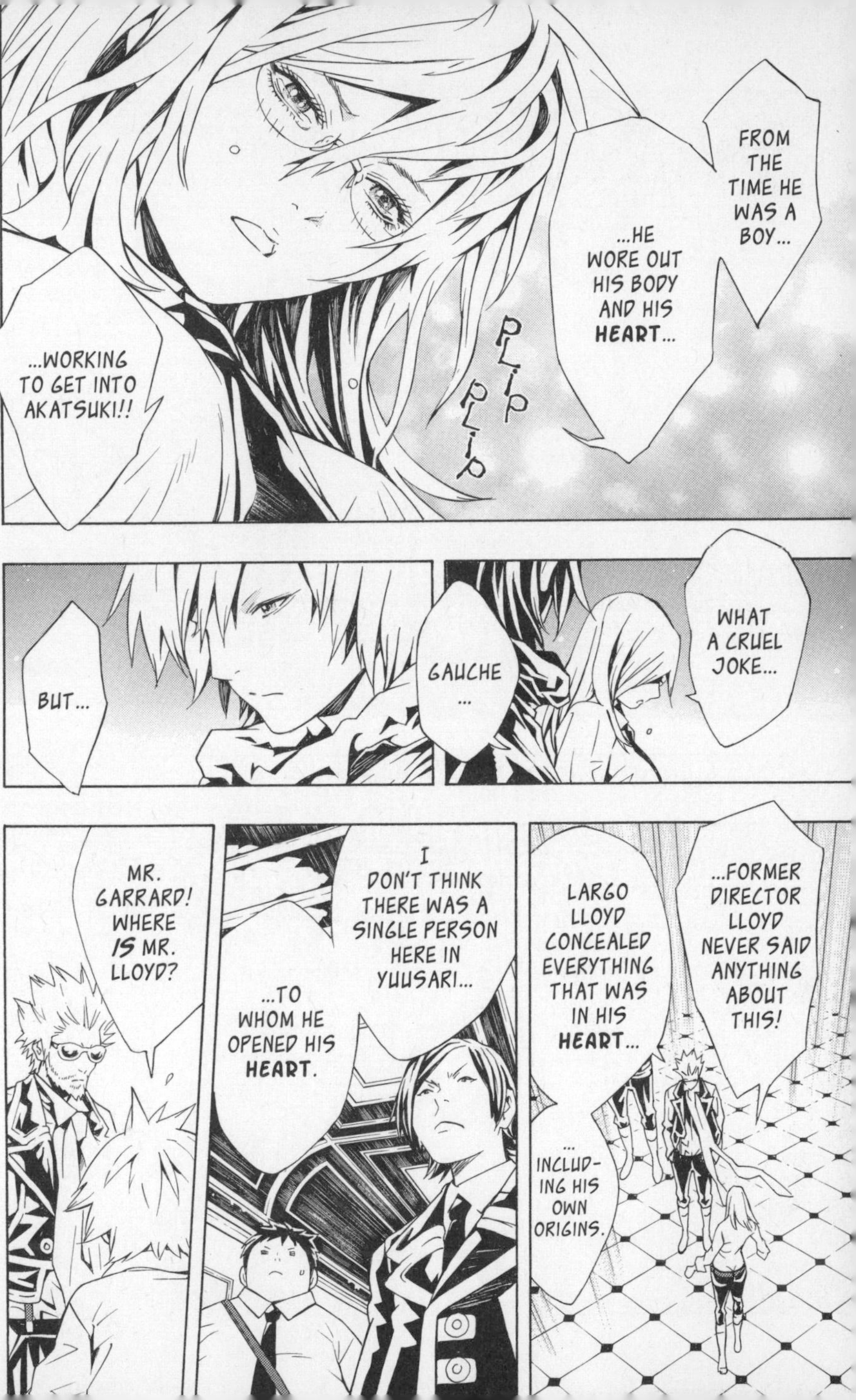
FROM THE TIME HE WAS A BOY...
...HE WORE OUT HIS BODY AND HIS **HEART**...
PLIP PLIP
...WORKING TO GET INTO AKATSUKI!!
WHAT A CRUEL JOKE...
GAUCHE ...
BUT...
...FORMER DIRECTOR LLOYD NEVER SAID ANYTHING ABOUT THIS!
LARGO LLOYD CONCEALED EVERYTHING THAT WAS IN HIS **HEART**...
... INCLUDING HIS OWN ORIGINS.
I DON'T THINK THERE WAS A SINGLE PERSON HERE IN YUUSARI...
...TO WHOM HE OPENED HIS **HEART**.
MR. GARRARD! WHERE *IS* MR. LLOYD?

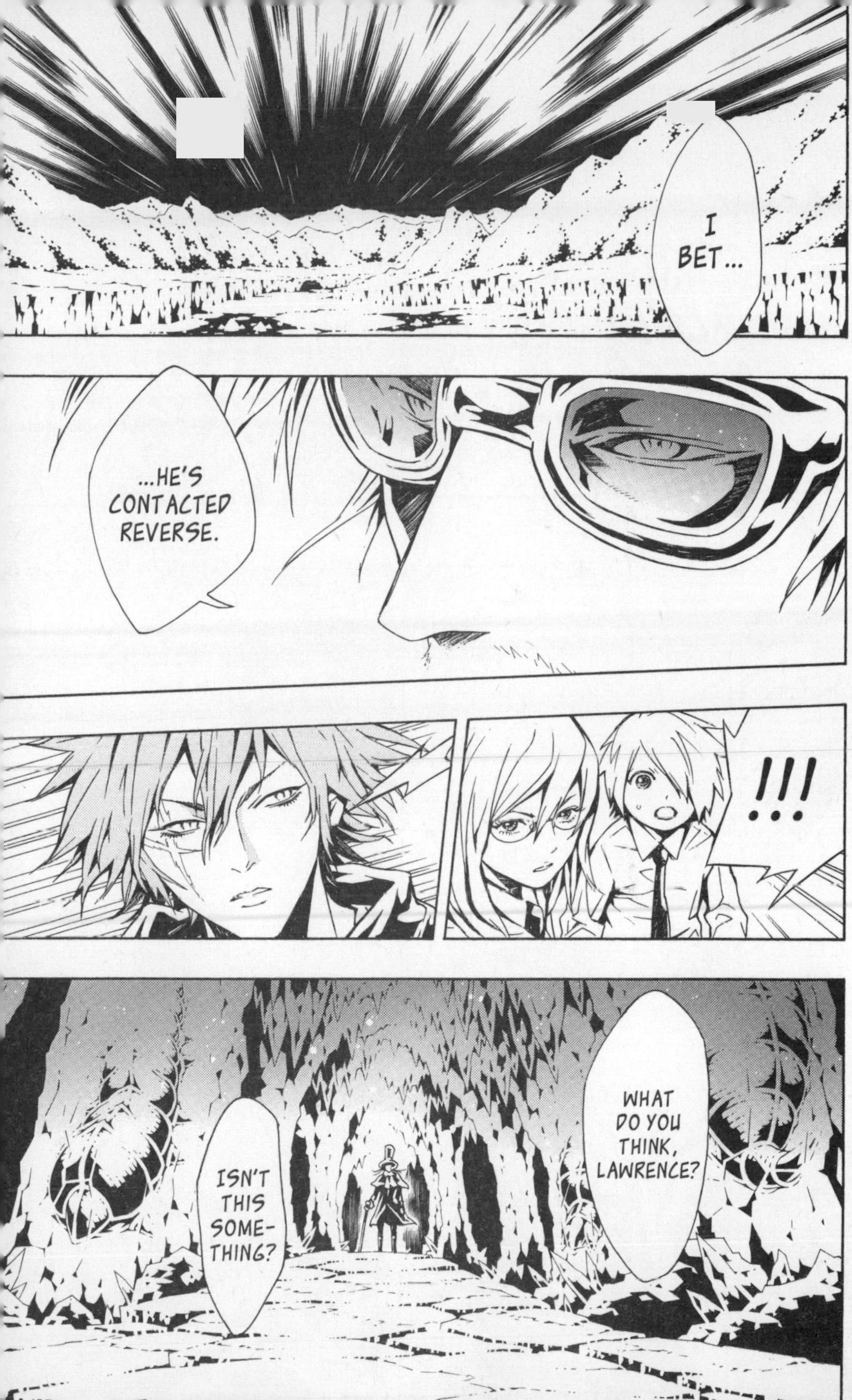
I BET...
...HE'S CONTACTED REVERSE.
!!!
WHAT DO YOU THINK, LAWRENCE?
ISN'T THIS SOMETHING?

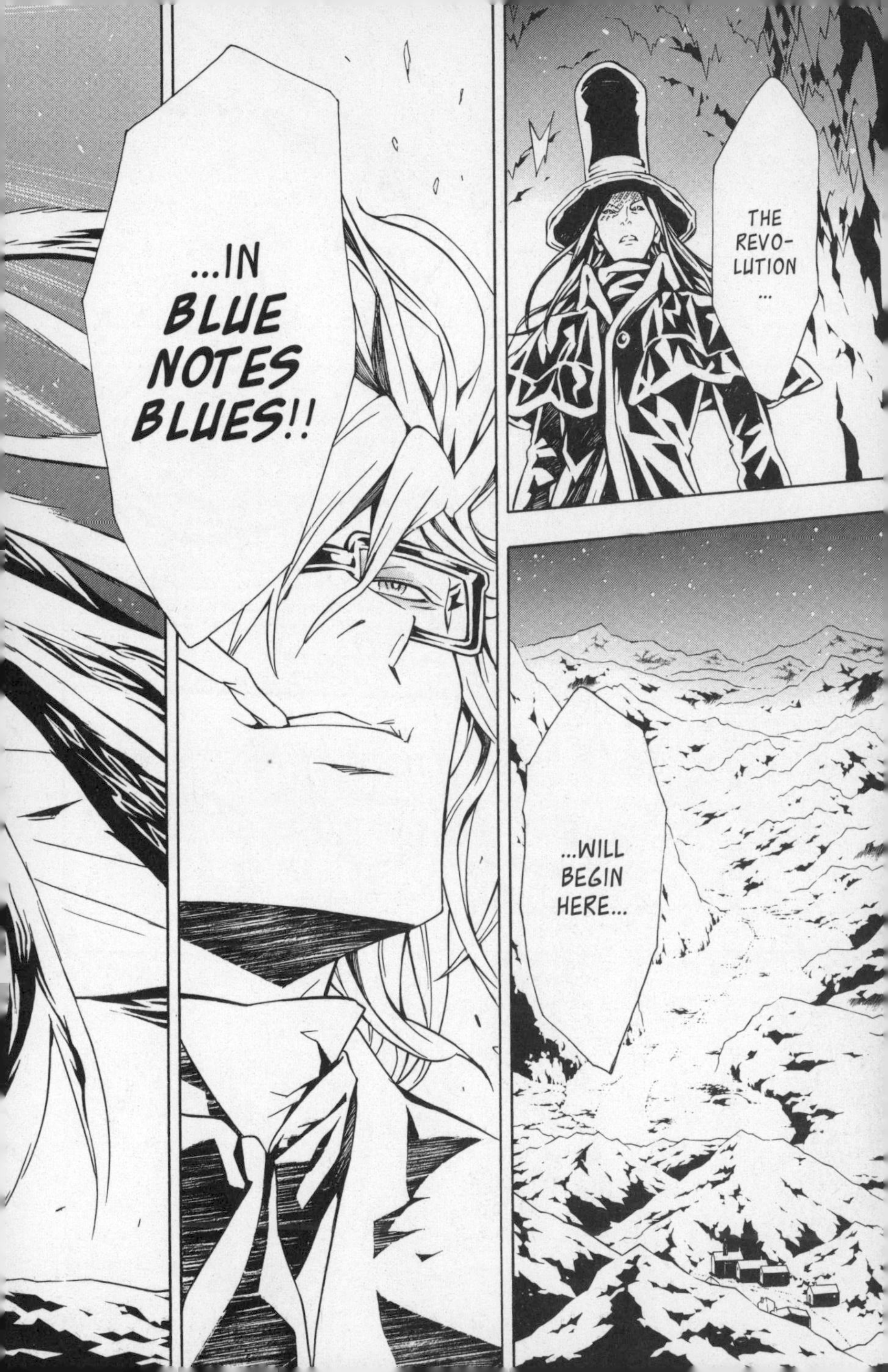
THE REVO-
LUTION
...
...WILL
BEGIN
HERE...
...IN
BLUE
NOTES
BLUES!!

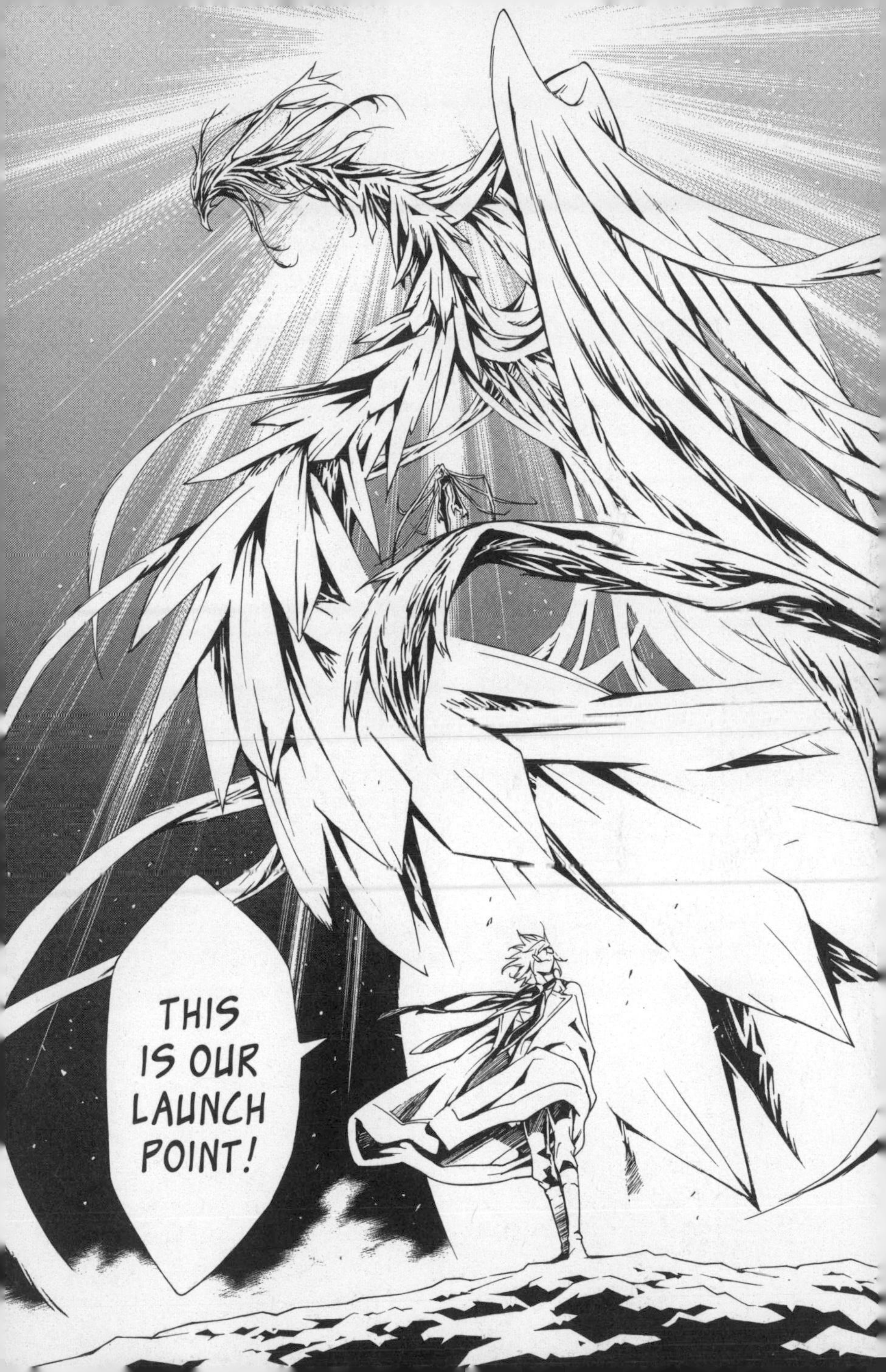
THIS IS OUR LAUNCH POINT!

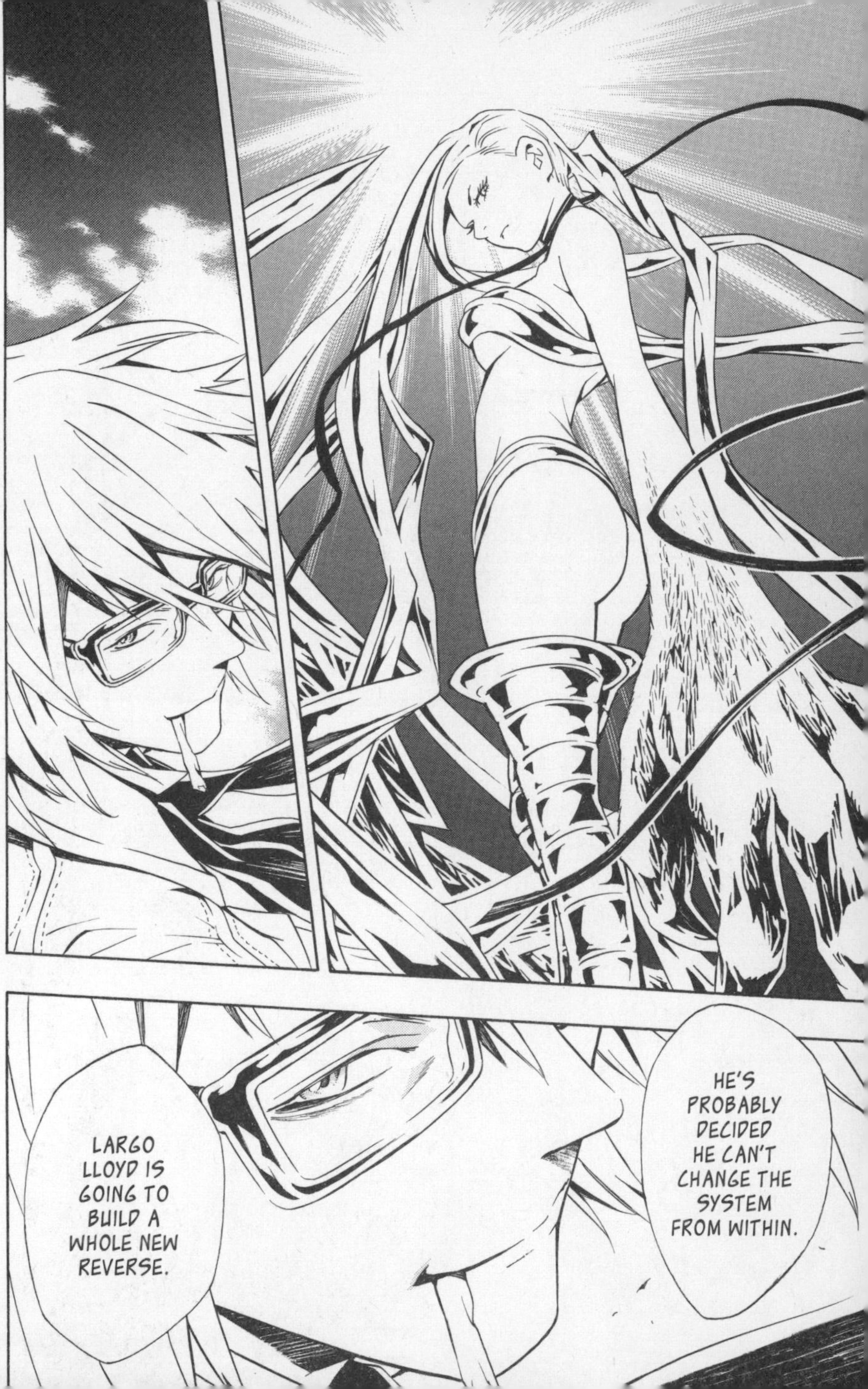
HE'S PROBABLY DECIDED HE CAN'T CHANGE THE SYSTEM FROM WITHIN.
LARGO LLOYD IS GOING TO BUILD A WHOLE NEW REVERSE.

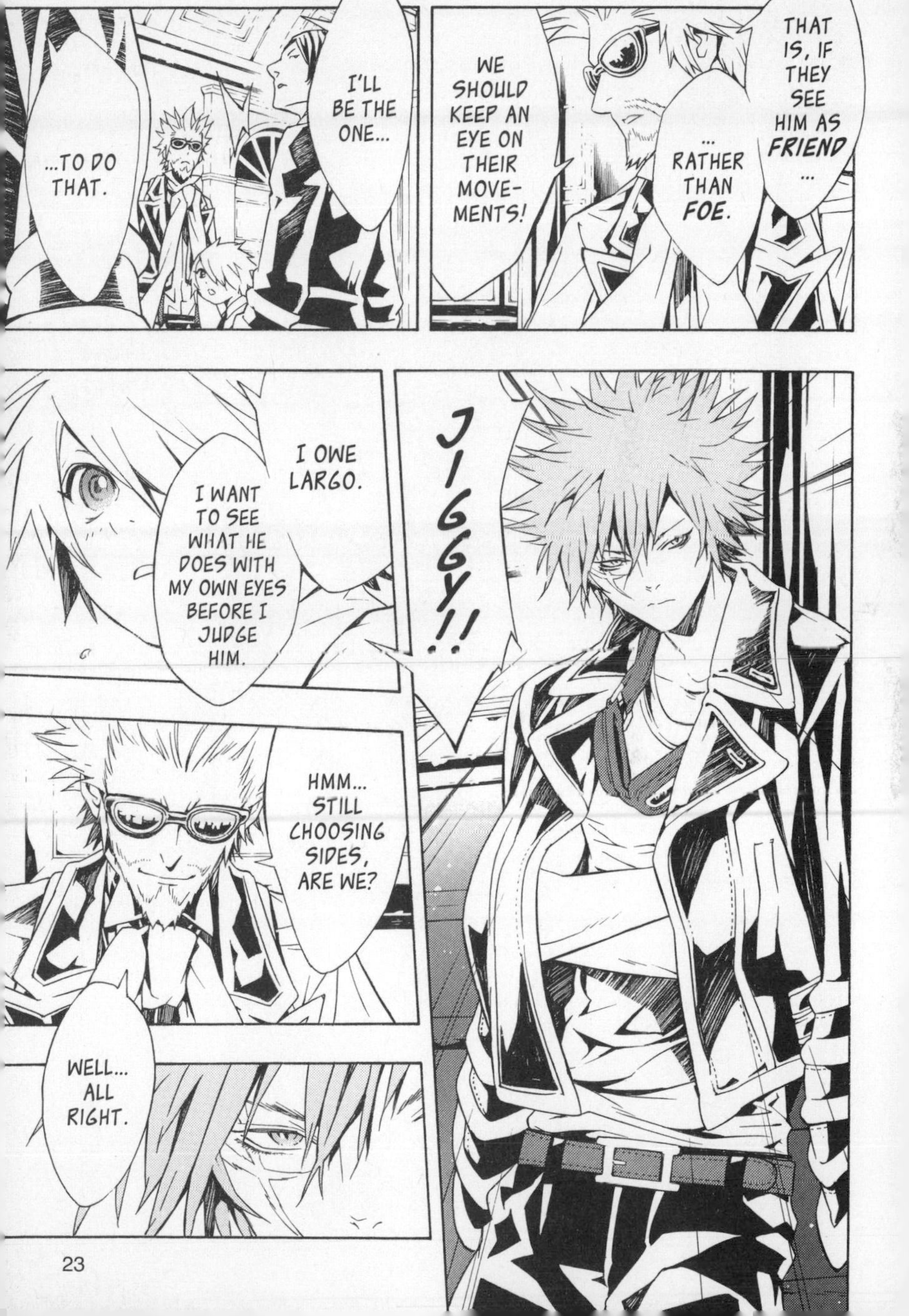
THAT IS, IF THEY SEE HIM AS FRIEND...
...RATHER THAN FOE.
WE SHOULD KEEP AN EYE ON THEIR MOVEMENTS!
I'LL BE THE ONE...
...TO DO THAT.
JIGGY!!
I OWE LARGO.
I WANT TO SEE WHAT HE DOES WITH MY OWN EYES BEFORE I JUDGE HIM.
HMM... STILL CHOOSING SIDES, ARE WE?
WELL... ALL RIGHT.

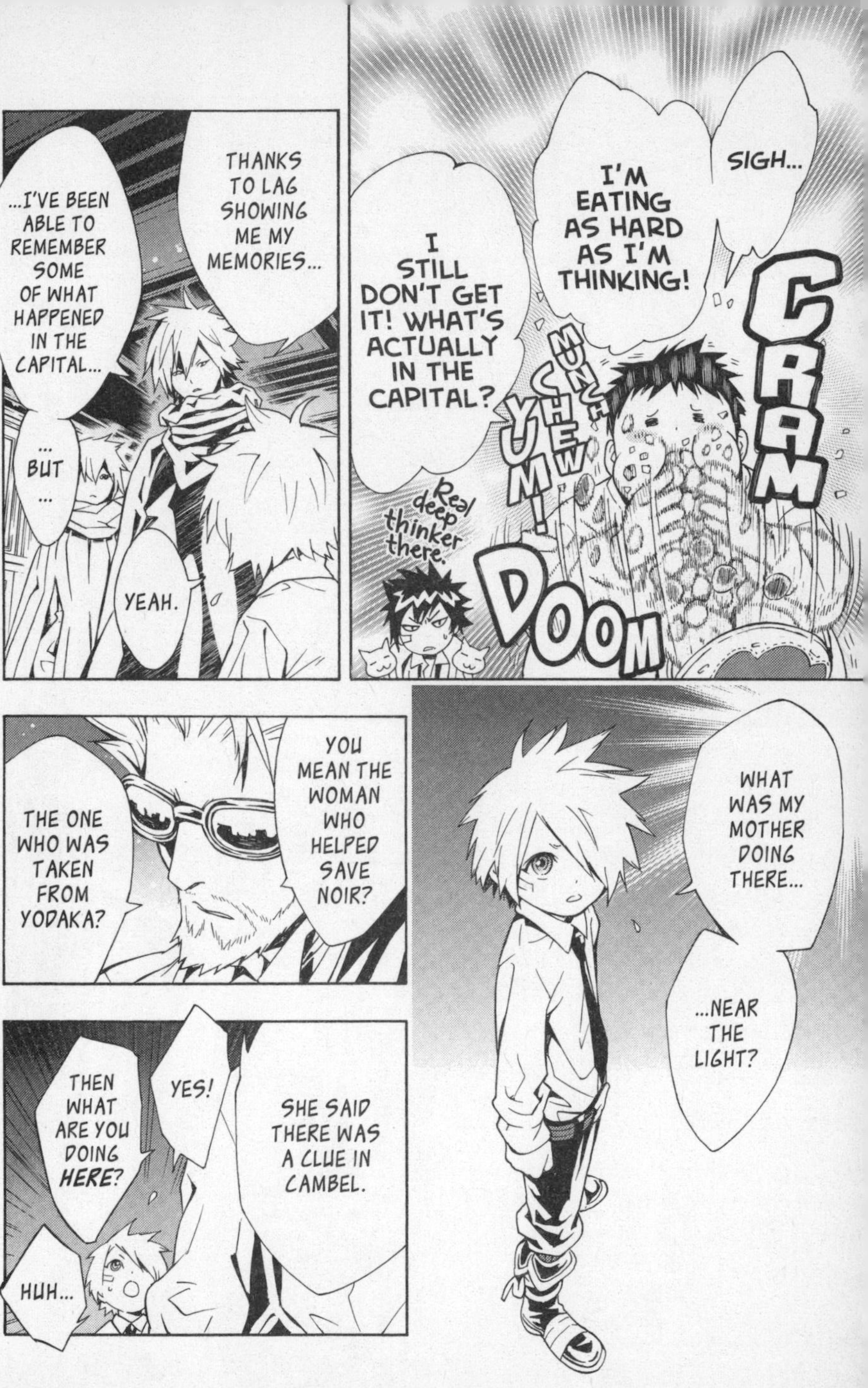
SIGH...
I'M EATING AS HARD AS I'M THINKING!
CRAM
I STILL DON'T GET IT! WHAT'S ACTUALLY IN THE CAPITAL?
MUNCH
CHEW
YUM!
Real deep thinker there.
DOOM
THANKS TO LAG SHOWING ME MY MEMORIES...
...I'VE BEEN ABLE TO REMEMBER SOME OF WHAT HAPPENED IN THE CAPITAL...
...BUT...
YEAH.
WHAT WAS MY MOTHER DOING THERE...
...NEAR THE LIGHT?
YOU MEAN THE WOMAN WHO HELPED SAVE NOIR?
THE ONE WHO WAS TAKEN FROM YODAKA?
YES!
SHE SAID THERE WAS A CLUE IN CAMBEL.
THEN WHAT ARE YOU DOING *HERE*?
HUH...

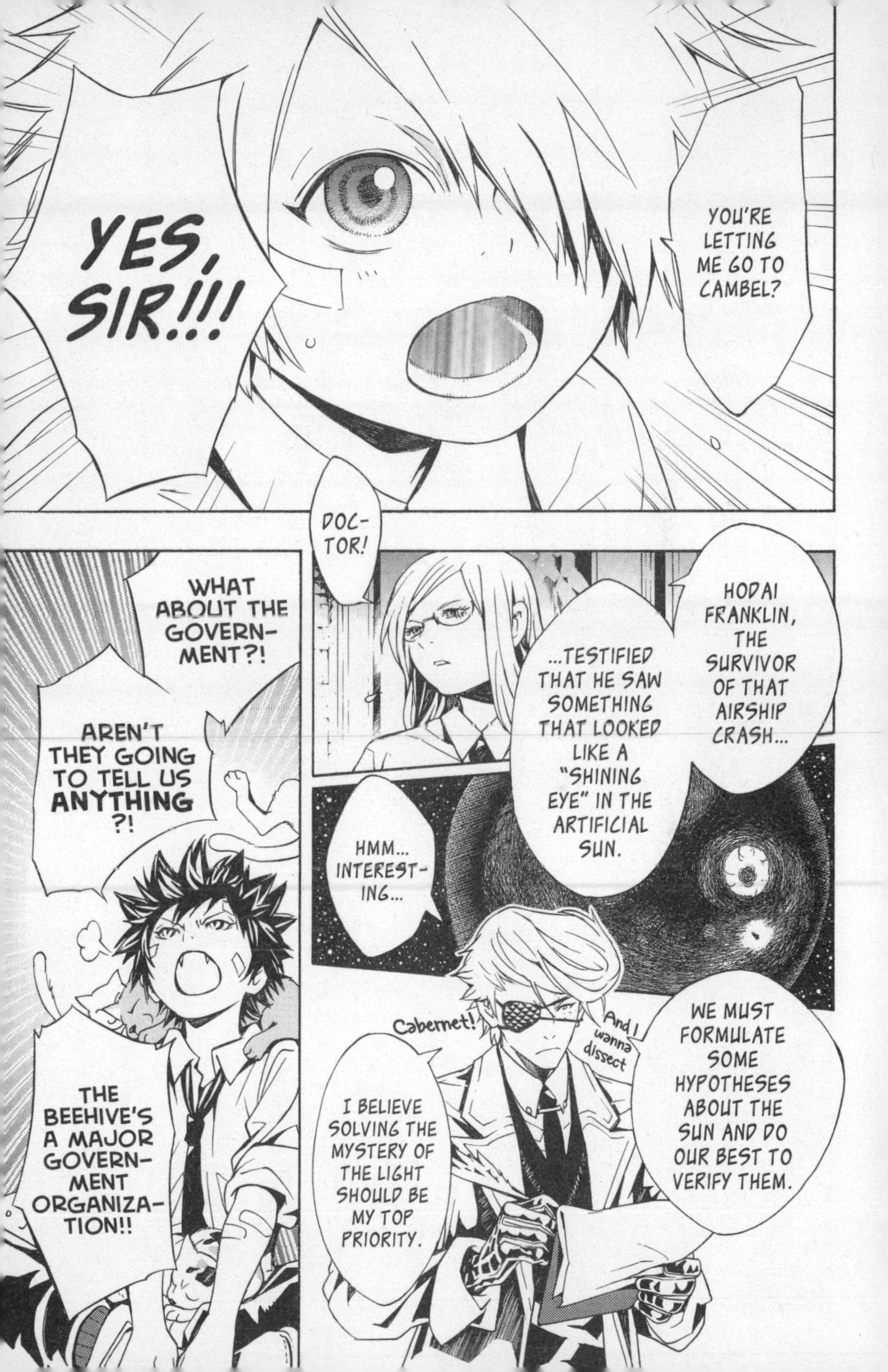
YOU'RE LETTING ME GO TO CAMBEL?
YES, SIR!!!
DOC-TOR!
HODAI FRANKLIN, THE SURVIVOR OF THAT AIRSHIP CRASH...
...TESTIFIED THAT HE SAW SOMETHING THAT LOOKED LIKE A "SHINING EYE" IN THE ARTIFICIAL SUN.
HMM... INTEREST-ING...
WE MUST FORMULATE SOME HYPOTHESES ABOUT THE SUN AND DO OUR BEST TO VERIFY THEM.
And I wanna dissect
Cabernet!
I BELIEVE SOLVING THE MYSTERY OF THE LIGHT SHOULD BE MY TOP PRIORITY.
WHAT ABOUT THE GOVERN-MENT?!
AREN'T THEY GOING TO TELL US ANYTHING?!
THE BEEHIVE'S A MAJOR GOVERN-MENT ORGANIZA-TION!!

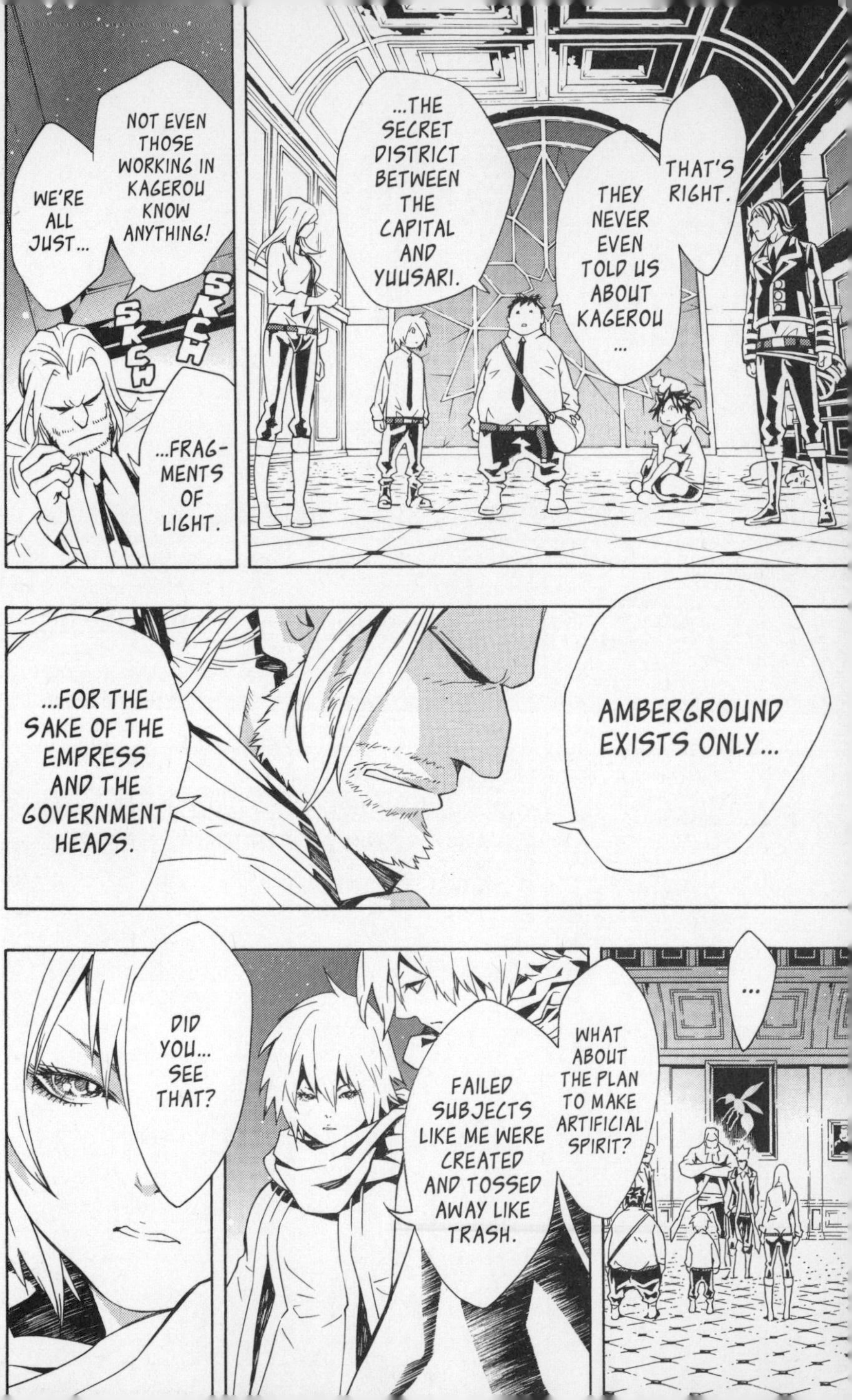
THAT'S RIGHT.
THEY NEVER EVEN TOLD US ABOUT KAGEROU...
...THE SECRET DISTRICT BETWEEN THE CAPITAL AND YUUSARI.
NOT EVEN THOSE WORKING IN KAGEROU KNOW ANYTHING!
WE'RE ALL JUST...
SKCH SKCH
...FRAG-MENTS OF LIGHT.
AMBERGROUND EXISTS ONLY...
...FOR THE SAKE OF THE EMPRESS AND THE GOVERNMENT HEADS.
...
WHAT ABOUT THE PLAN TO MAKE ARTIFICIAL SPIRIT?
FAILED SUBJECTS LIKE ME WERE CREATED AND TOSSED AWAY LIKE TRASH.
DID YOU... SEE THAT?

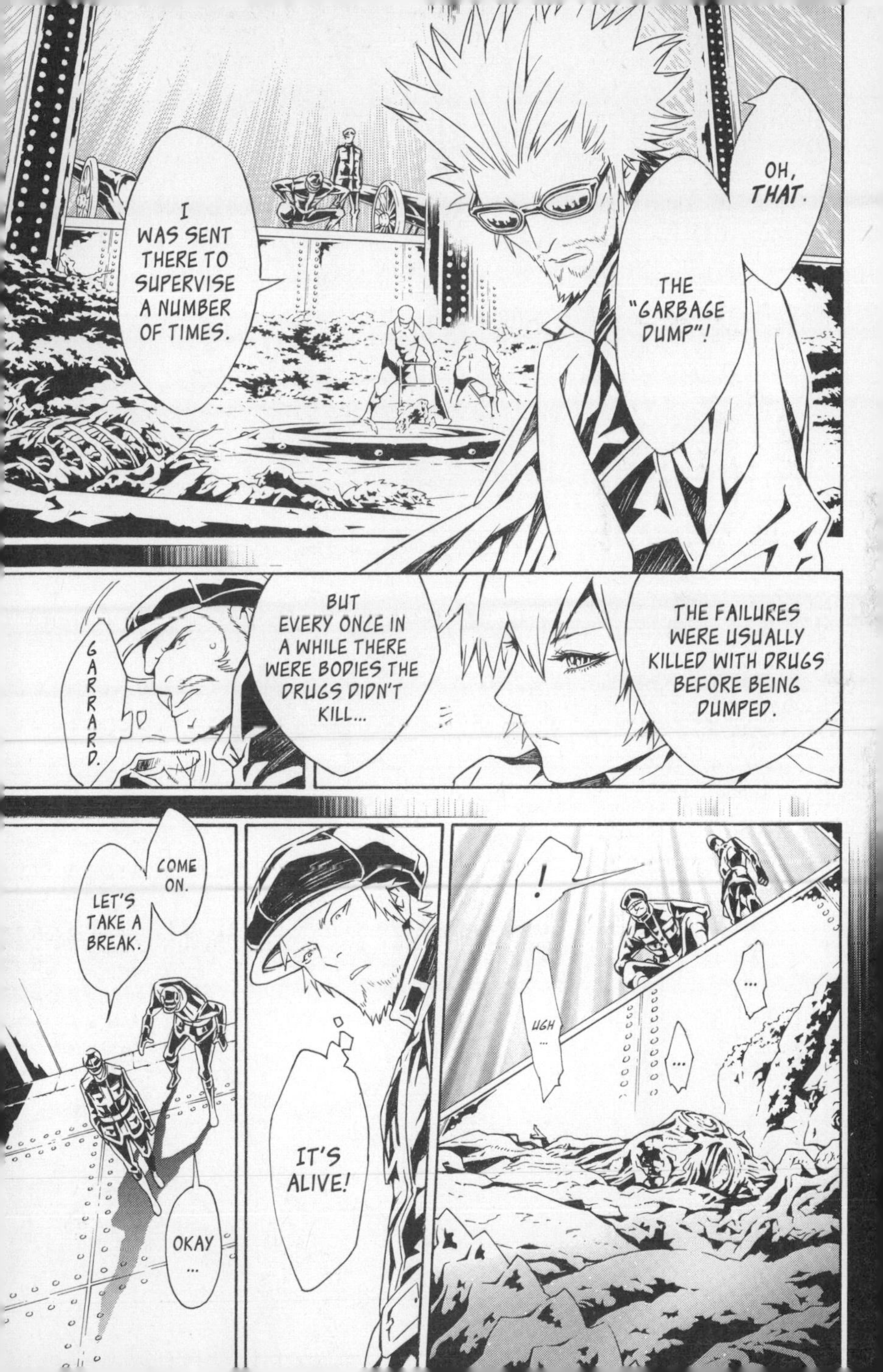
OH, THAT.
THE "GARBAGE DUMP"!
I WAS SENT THERE TO SUPERVISE A NUMBER OF TIMES.
THE FAILURES WERE USUALLY KILLED WITH DRUGS BEFORE BEING DUMPED.
BUT EVERY ONCE IN A WHILE THERE WERE BODIES THE DRUGS DIDN'T KILL...
GARRARD.
!
...
UGH...
...
IT'S ALIVE!
COME ON.
LET'S TAKE A BREAK.
OKAY...

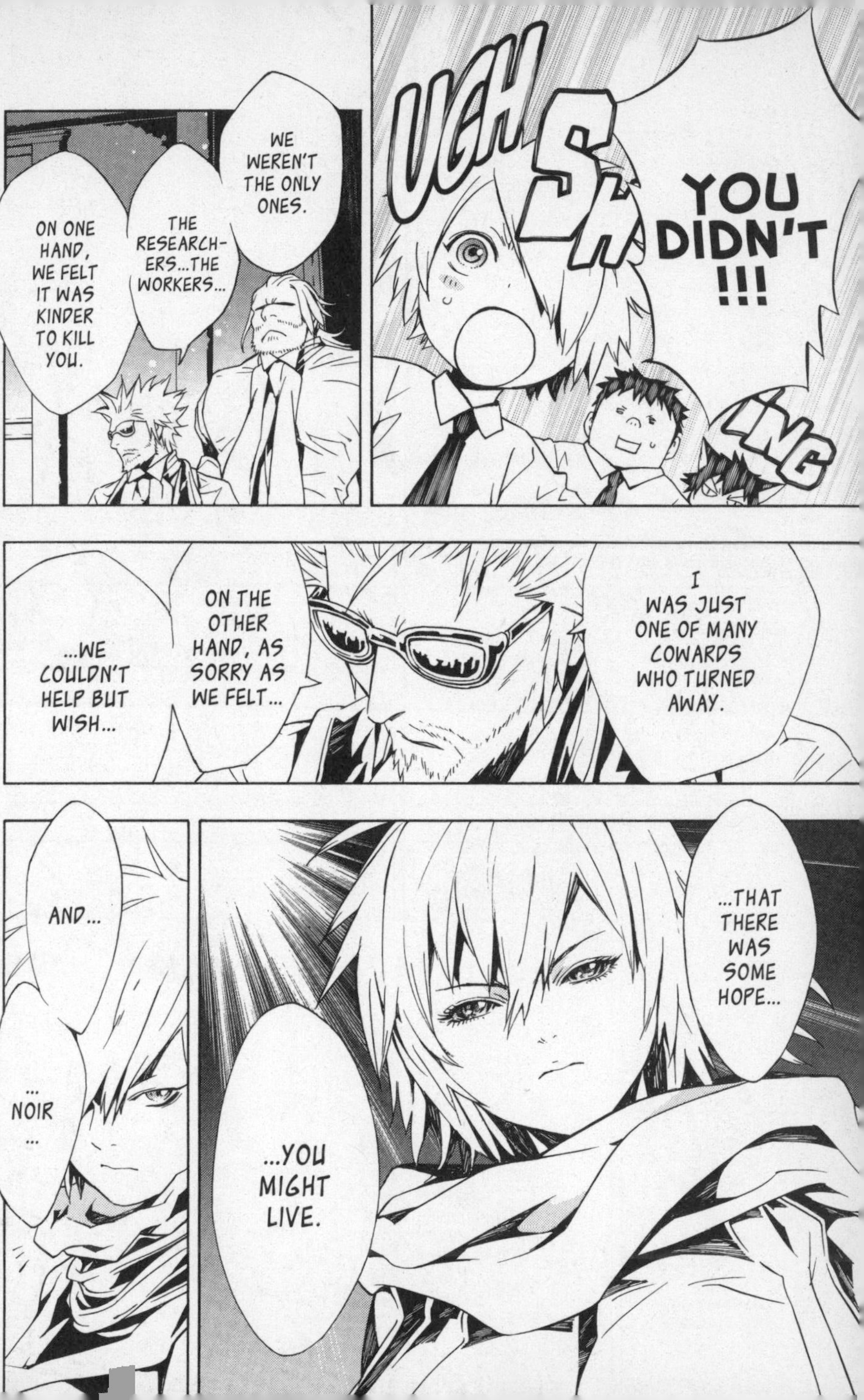
YOU DIDN'T !!!
UGH
SH
ING
WE WEREN'T THE ONLY ONES.
THE RESEARCHERS...THE WORKERS...
ON ONE HAND, WE FELT IT WAS KINDER TO KILL YOU.
I WAS JUST ONE OF MANY COWARDS WHO TURNED AWAY.
ON THE OTHER HAND, AS SORRY AS WE FELT...
...WE COULDN'T HELP BUT WISH...
...THAT THERE WAS SOME HOPE...
...YOU MIGHT LIVE.
AND...
... NOIR ...

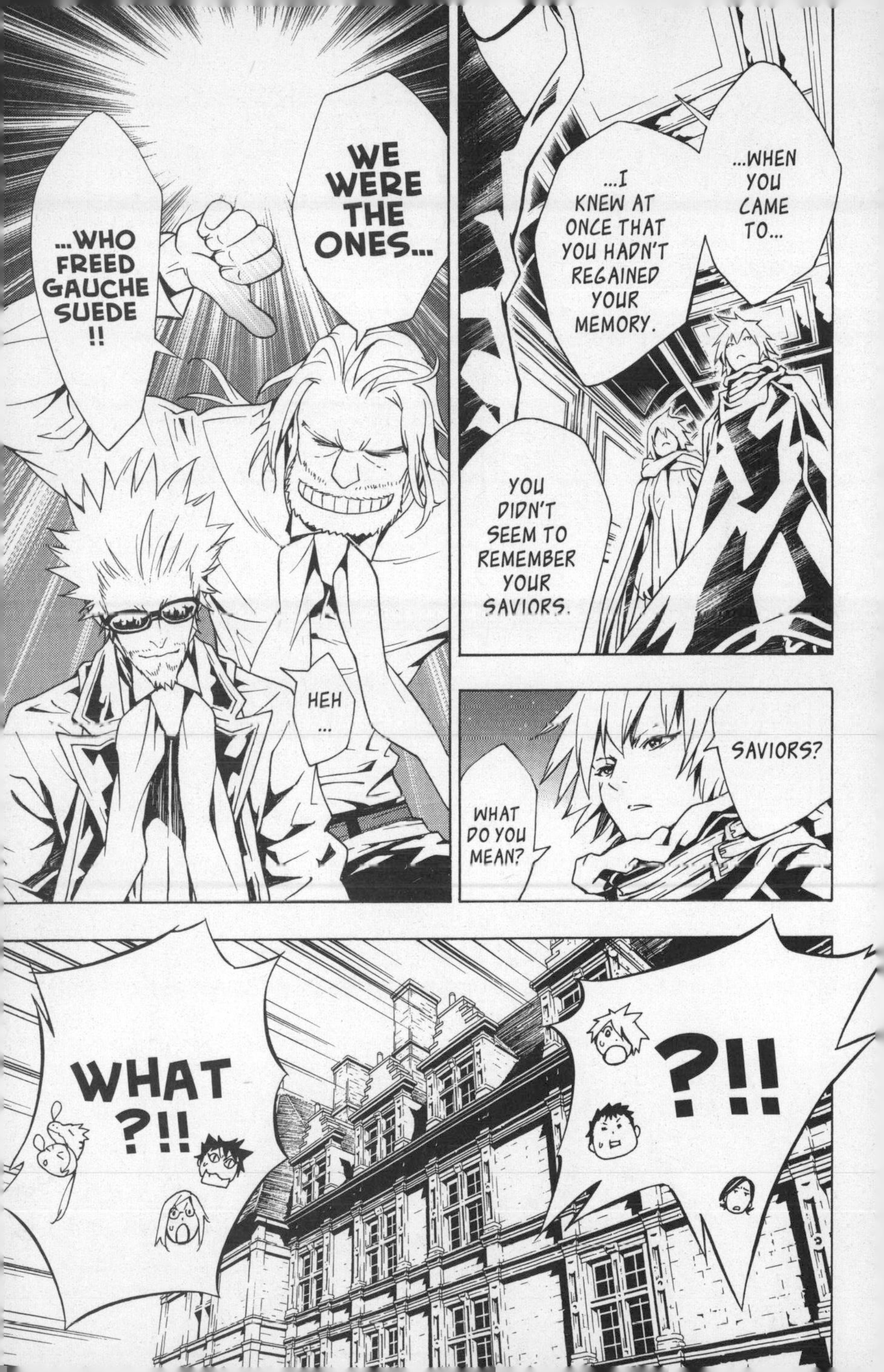
...WHEN YOU CAME TO...
...I KNEW AT ONCE THAT YOU HADN'T REGAINED YOUR MEMORY.
YOU DIDN'T SEEM TO REMEMBER YOUR SAVIORS.
SAVIORS?
WHAT DO YOU MEAN?
WE WERE THE ONES...
...WHO FREED GAUCHE SUEDE !!
HEH ...
?!!
WHAT ?!!

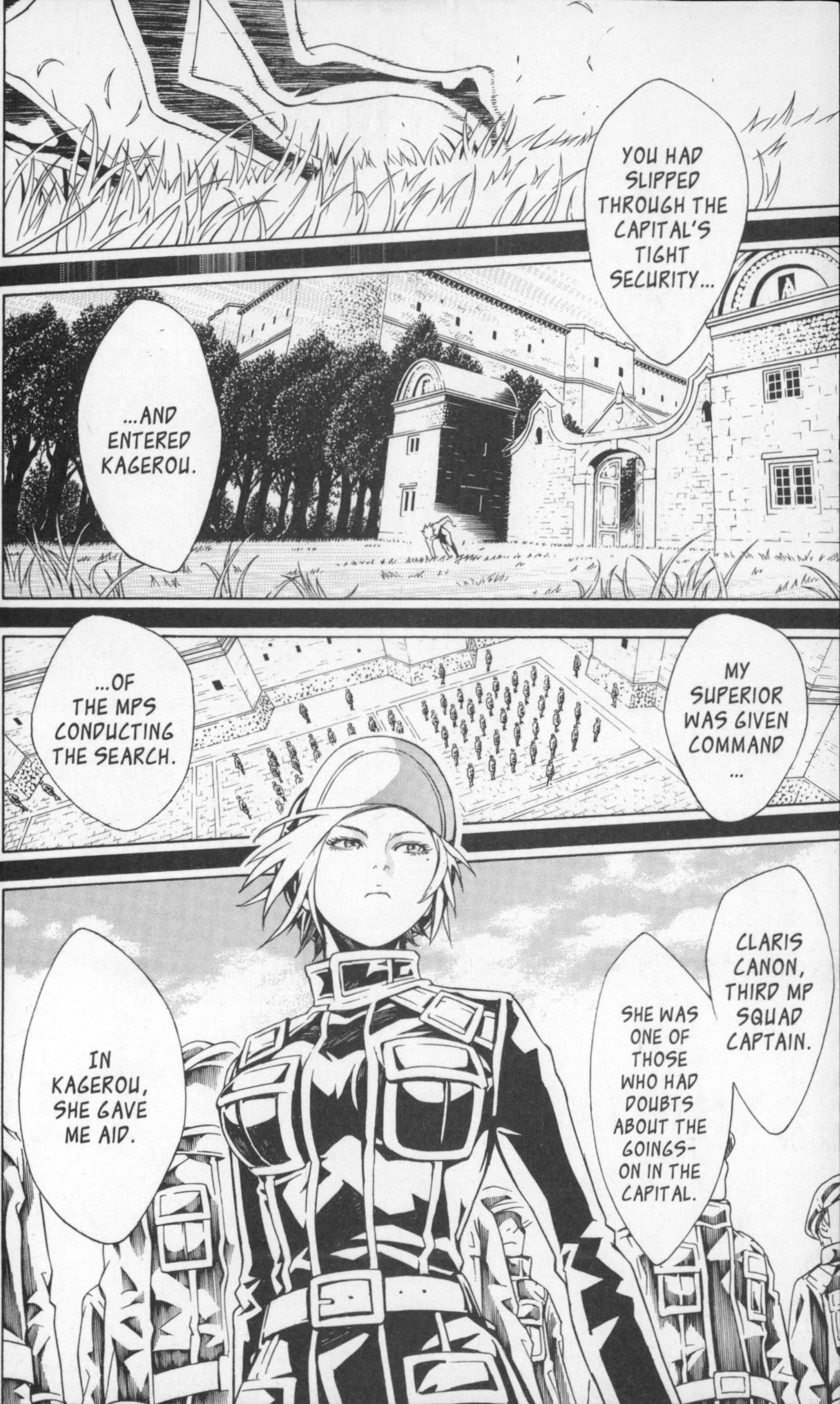
YOU HAD SLIPPED THROUGH THE CAPITAL'S TIGHT SECURITY...
...AND ENTERED KAGEROU.
MY SUPERIOR WAS GIVEN COMMAND ...
...OF THE MPS CONDUCTING THE SEARCH.
CLARIS CANON, THIRD MP SQUAD CAPTAIN.
SHE WAS ONE OF THOSE WHO HAD DOUBTS ABOUT THE GOINGS-ON IN THE CAPITAL.
IN KAGEROU, SHE GAVE ME AID.

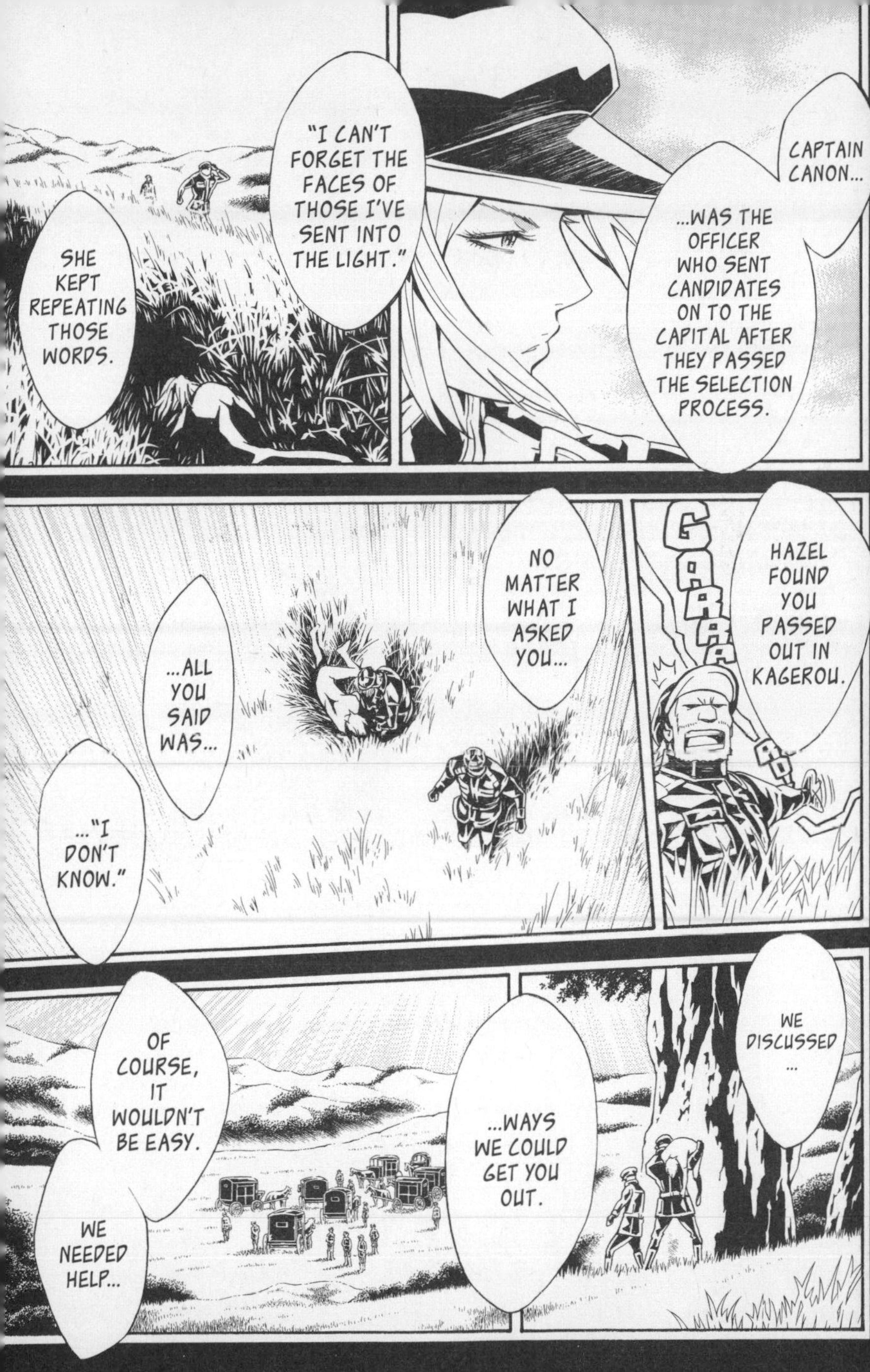
CAPTAIN CANON...
...WAS THE OFFICER WHO SENT CANDIDATES ON TO THE CAPITAL AFTER THEY PASSED THE SELECTION PROCESS.
"I CAN'T FORGET THE FACES OF THOSE I'VE SENT INTO THE LIGHT."
SHE KEPT REPEATING THOSE WORDS.
HAZEL FOUND YOU PASSED OUT IN KAGEROU.
NO MATTER WHAT I ASKED YOU...
...ALL YOU SAID WAS...
..."I DON'T KNOW."
WE DISCUSSED ...
...WAYS WE COULD GET YOU OUT.
OF COURSE, IT WOULDN'T BE EASY.
WE NEEDED HELP...

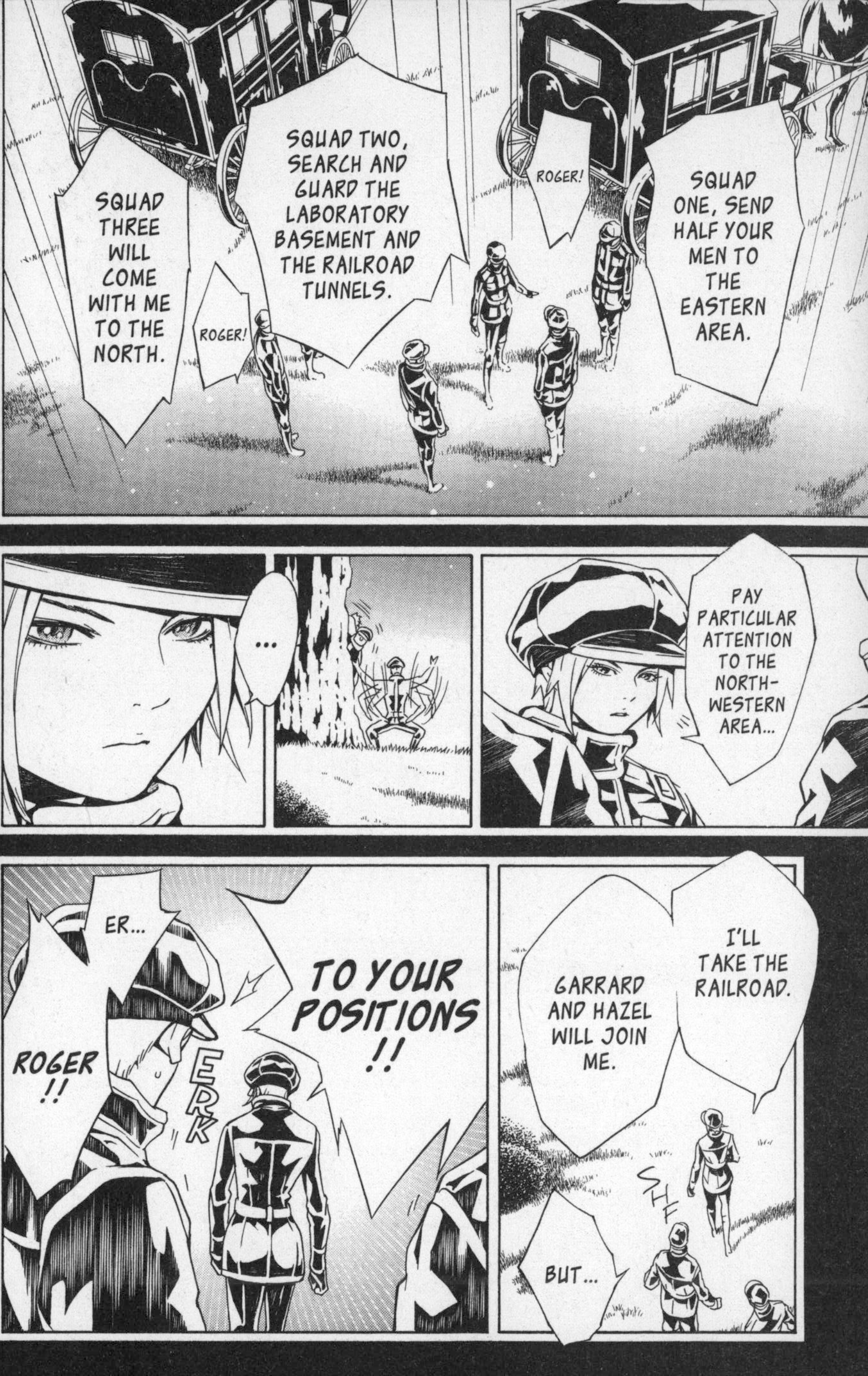
SQUAD ONE, SEND HALF YOUR MEN TO THE EASTERN AREA.
ROGER!
SQUAD TWO, SEARCH AND GUARD THE LABORATORY BASEMENT AND THE RAILROAD TUNNELS.
ROGER!
SQUAD THREE WILL COME WITH ME TO THE NORTH.
PAY PARTICULAR ATTENTION TO THE NORTH-WESTERN AREA...
...
I'LL TAKE THE RAILROAD.
GARRARD AND HAZEL WILL JOIN ME.
SHF
BUT...
TO YOUR POSITIONS!!
ER...
ERK
ROGER!!

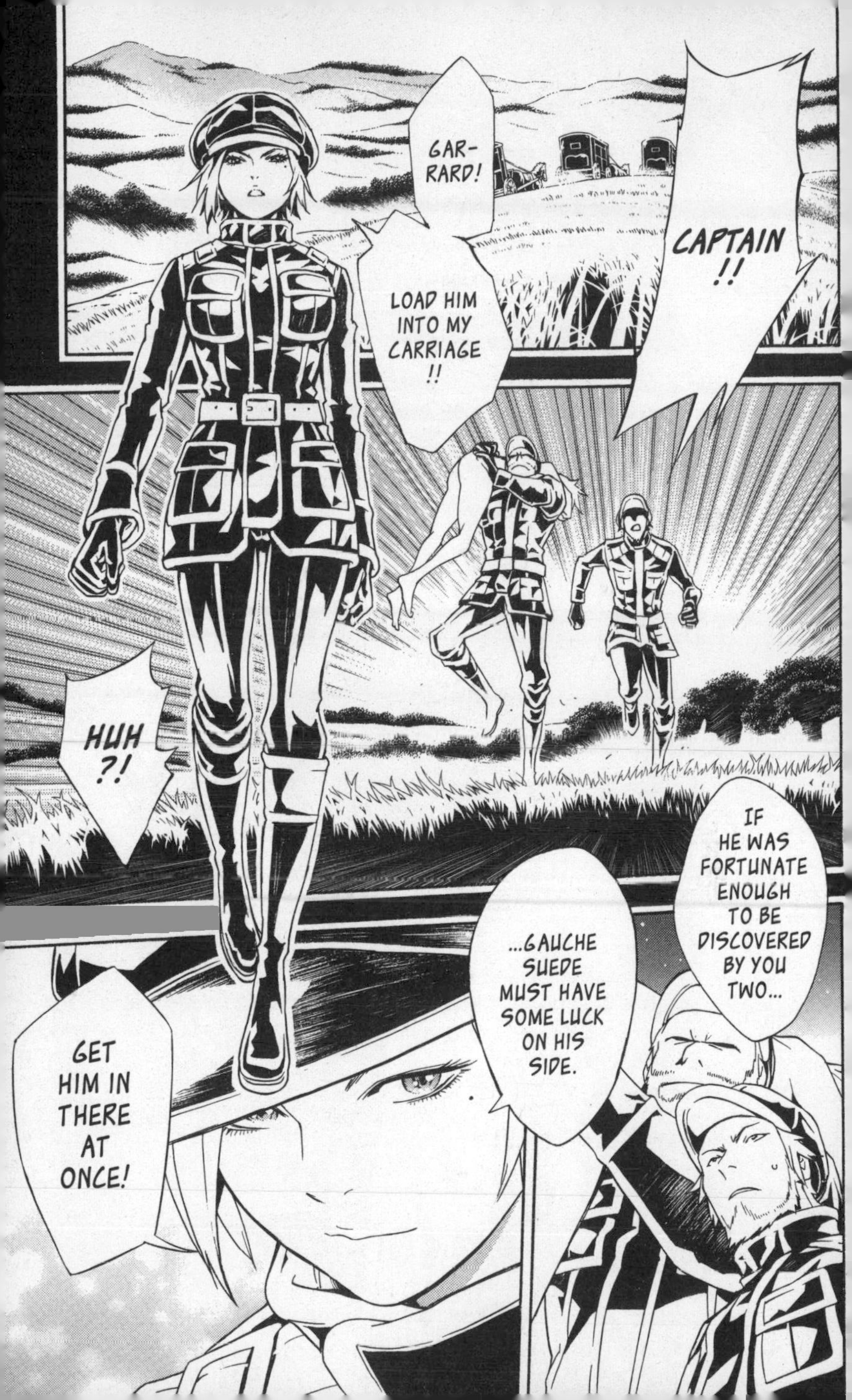
CAPTAIN !!
GAR-RARD!
LOAD HIM INTO MY CARRIAGE !!
HUH ?!
IF HE WAS FORTUNATE ENOUGH TO BE DISCOVERED BY YOU TWO...
...GAUCHE SUEDE MUST HAVE SOME LUCK ON HIS SIDE.
GET HIM IN THERE AT ONCE!

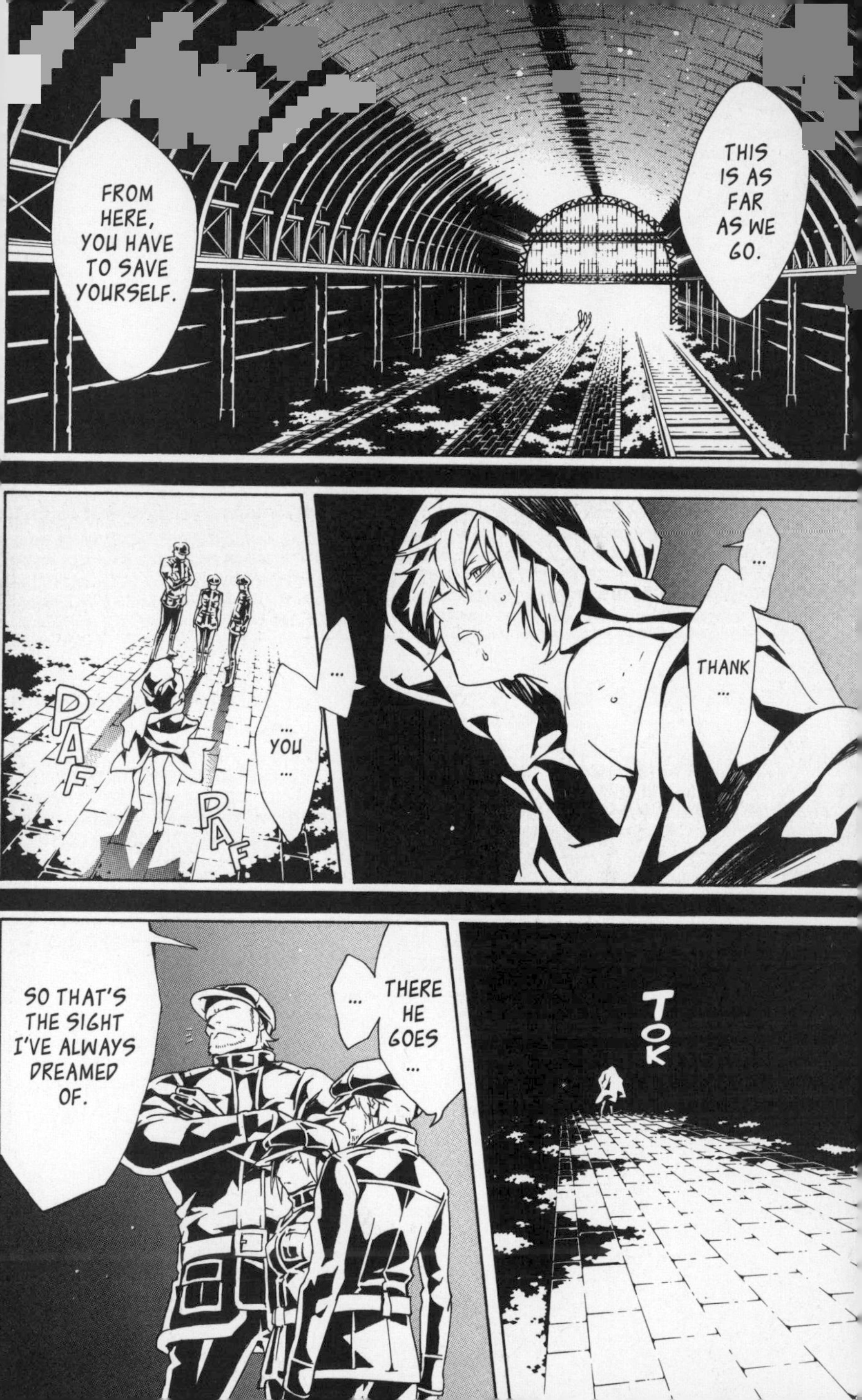
THIS IS AS FAR AS WE GO.
FROM HERE, YOU HAVE TO SAVE YOURSELF.
...
THANK ...
...
... YOU ...
PAF
PAF
TOK
... THERE HE GOES ...
SO THAT'S THE SIGHT I'VE ALWAYS DREAMED OF.

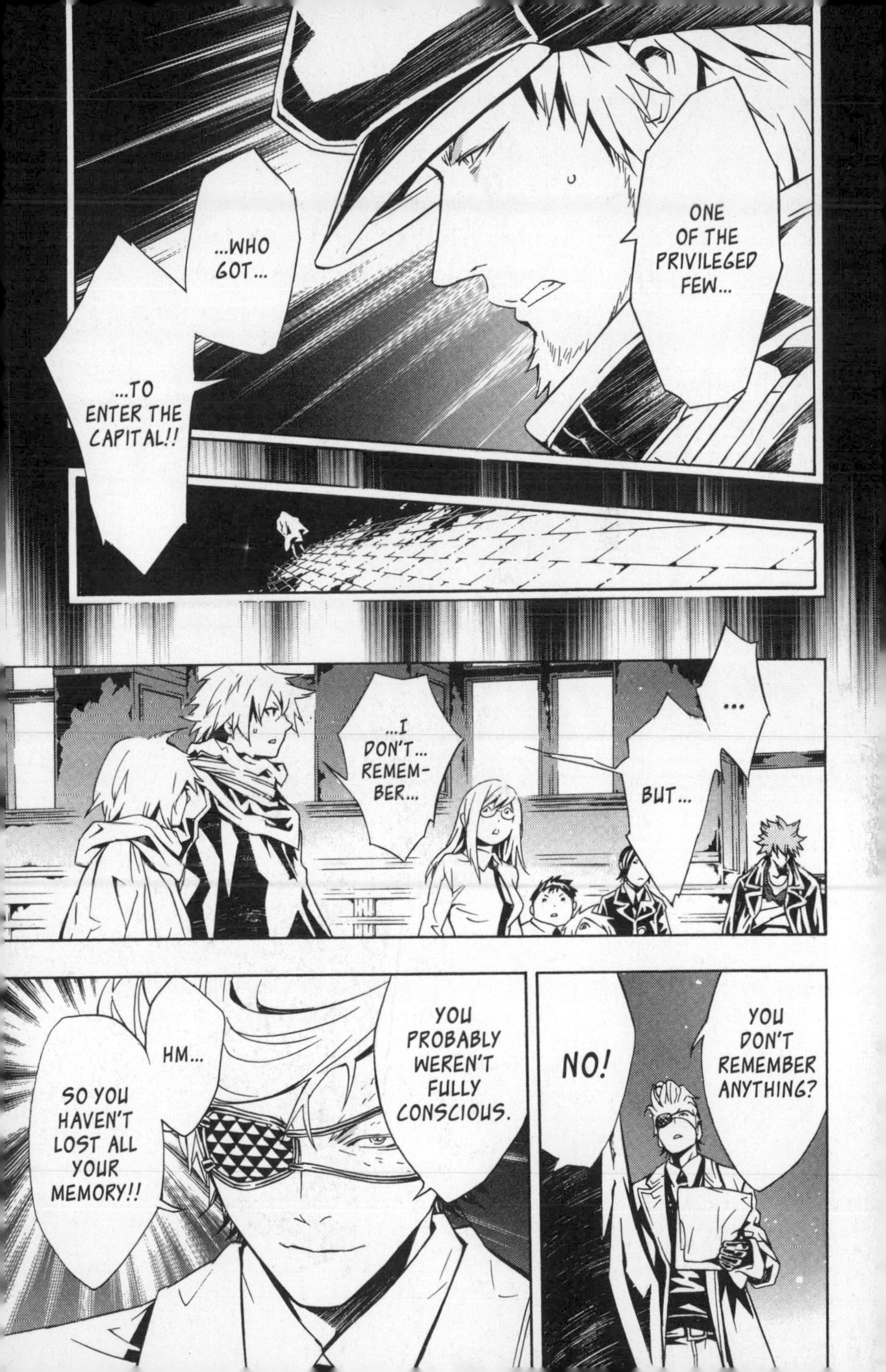
ONE OF THE PRIVILEGED FEW...
...WHO GOT...
...TO ENTER THE CAPITAL!!
... BUT...
...I DON'T... REMEMBER...
YOU DON'T REMEMBER ANYTHING?
NO!
YOU PROBABLY WEREN'T FULLY CONSCIOUS.
HM...
SO YOU HAVEN'T LOST ALL YOUR MEMORY!!

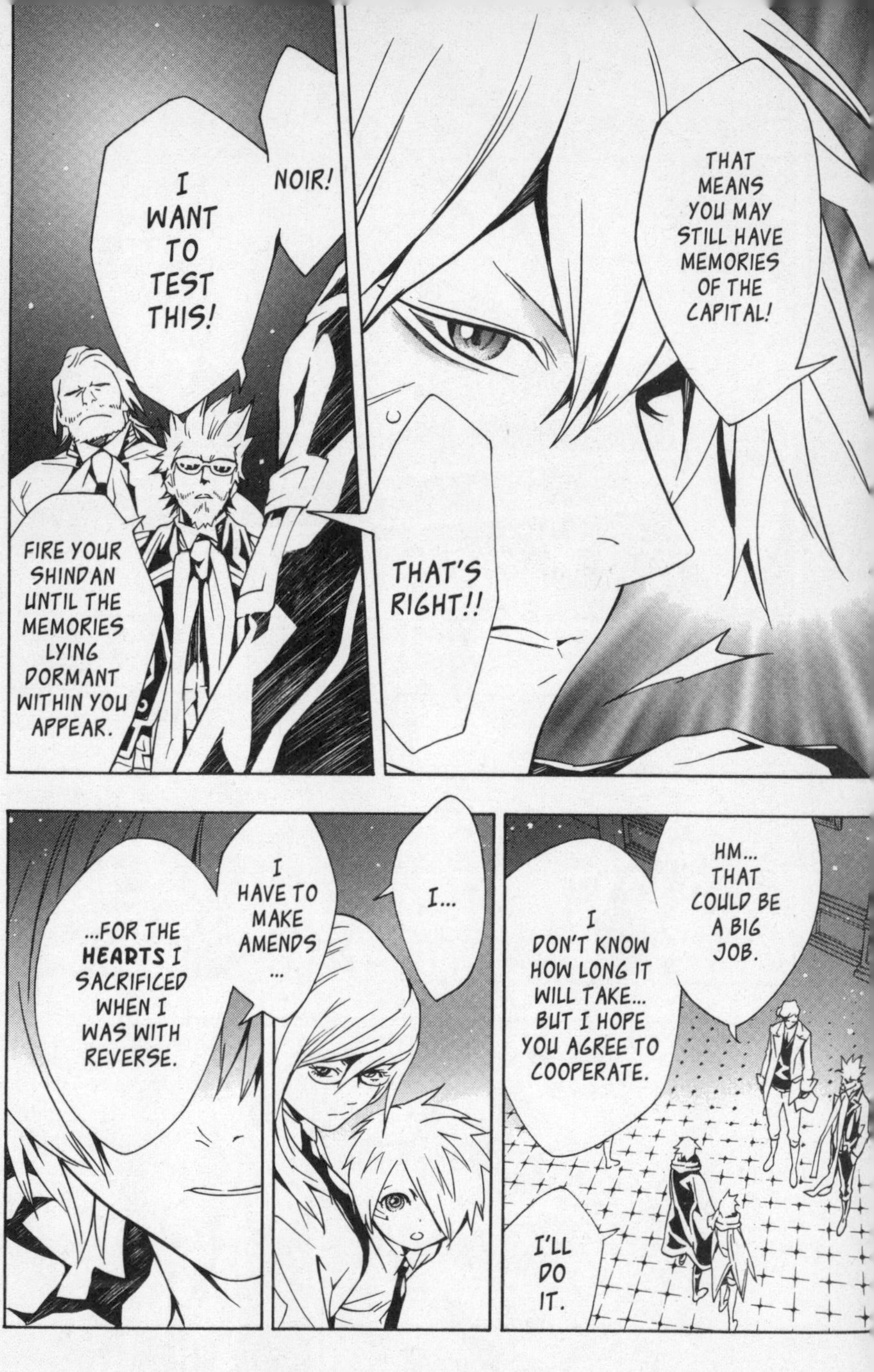
THAT MEANS YOU MAY STILL HAVE MEMORIES OF THE CAPITAL!
NOIR!
I WANT TO TEST THIS!
THAT'S RIGHT!!
FIRE YOUR SHINDAN UNTIL THE MEMORIES LYING DORMANT WITHIN YOU APPEAR.
HM... THAT COULD BE A BIG JOB.
I DON'T KNOW HOW LONG IT WILL TAKE... BUT I HOPE YOU AGREE TO COOPERATE.
I'LL DO IT.
I...
I HAVE TO MAKE AMENDS...
...FOR THE HEARTS I SACRIFICED WHEN I WAS WITH REVERSE.

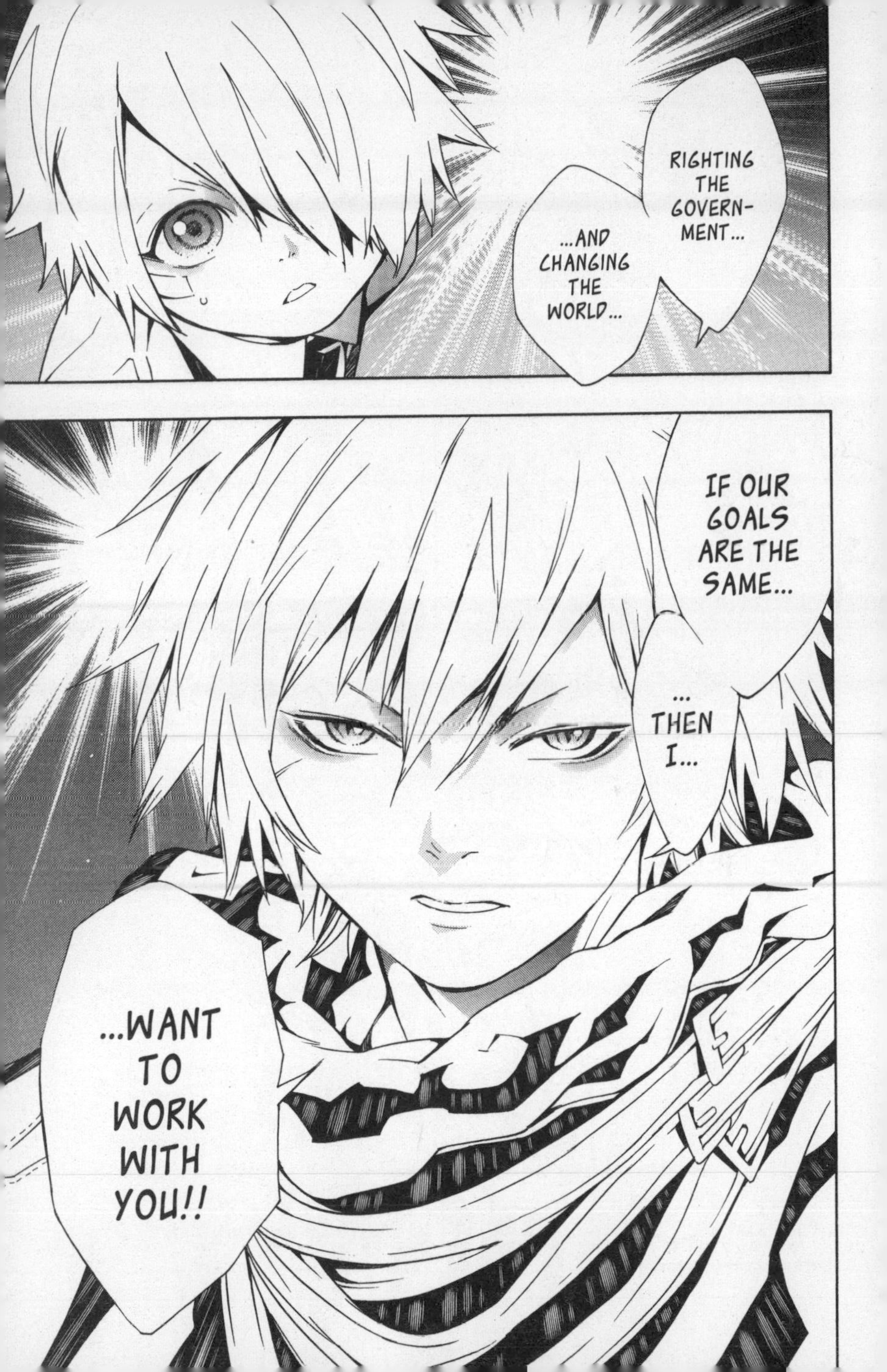
RIGHTING THE GOVERN-MENT...
...AND CHANGING THE WORLD...
IF OUR GOALS ARE THE SAME...
...THEN I...
...WANT TO WORK WITH YOU!!

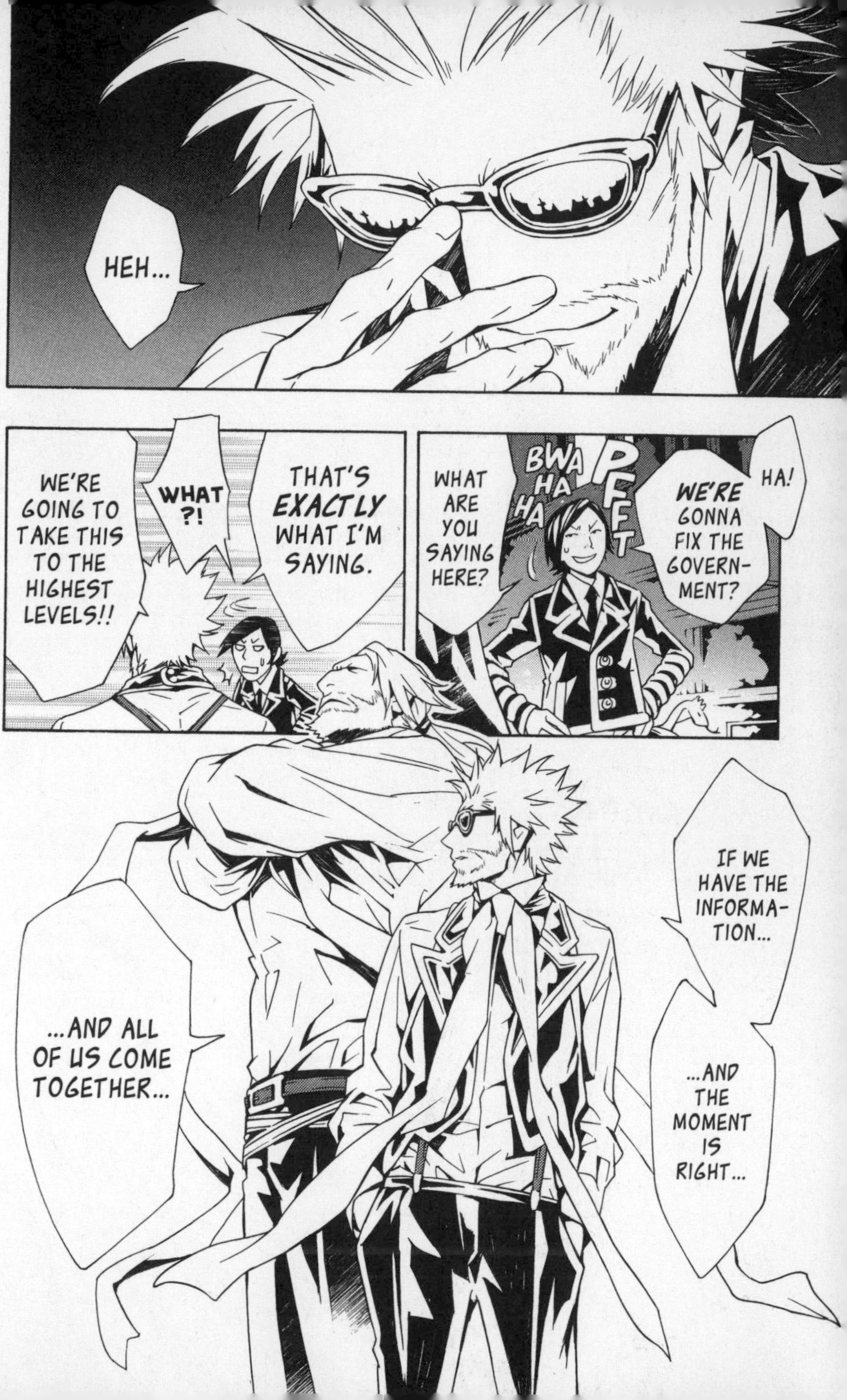
HEH...
HA!
WE'RE GONNA FIX THE GOVERN-MENT?
PFFT
BWA HA HA HA
WHAT ARE YOU SAYING HERE?
THAT'S EXACTLY WHAT I'M SAYING.
WHAT?!
WE'RE GOING TO TAKE THIS TO THE HIGHEST LEVELS!!
IF WE HAVE THE INFORMA-TION...
...AND THE MOMENT IS RIGHT...
...AND ALL OF US COME TOGETHER...

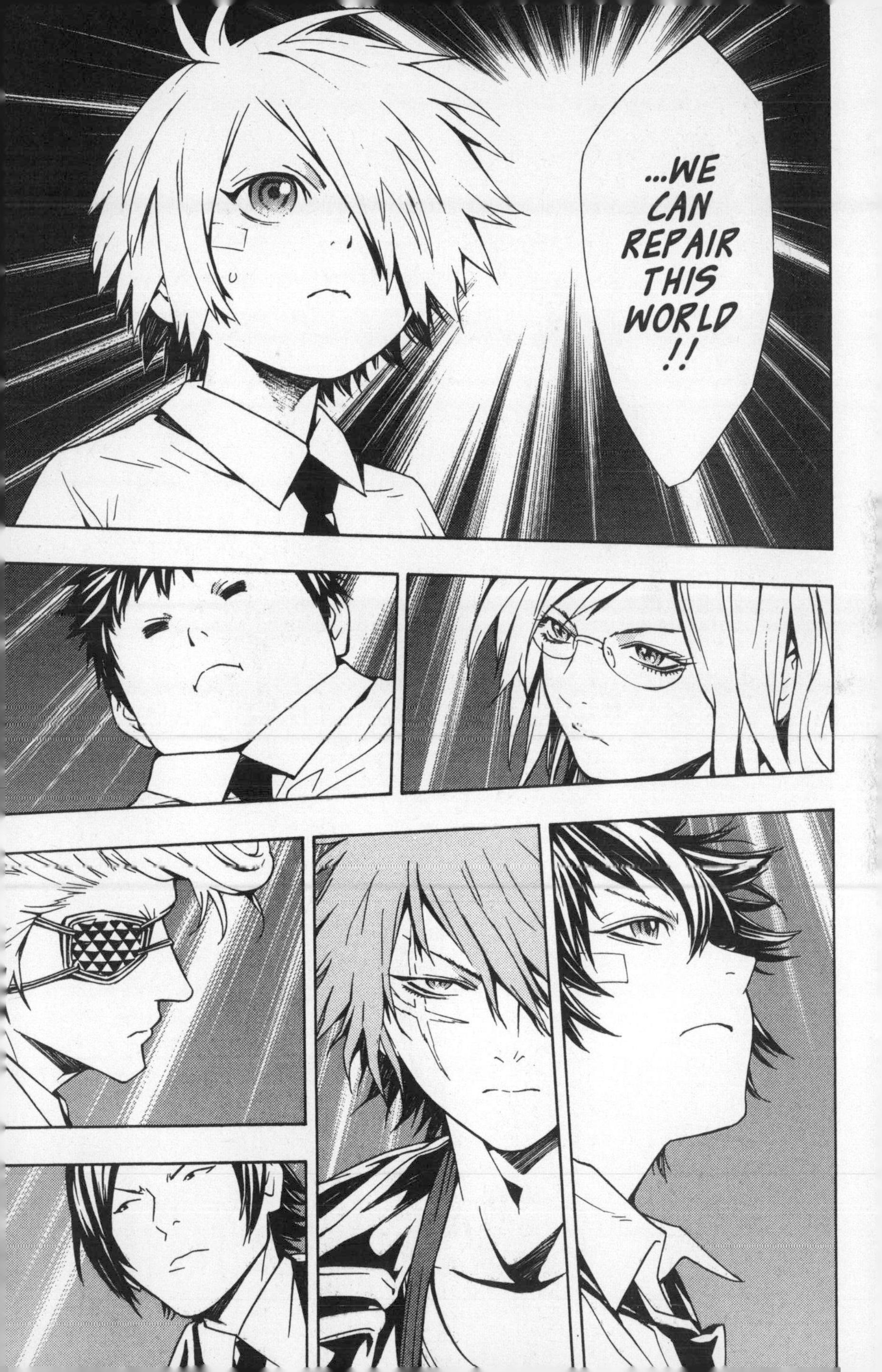
...WE CAN REPAIR THIS WORLD!!

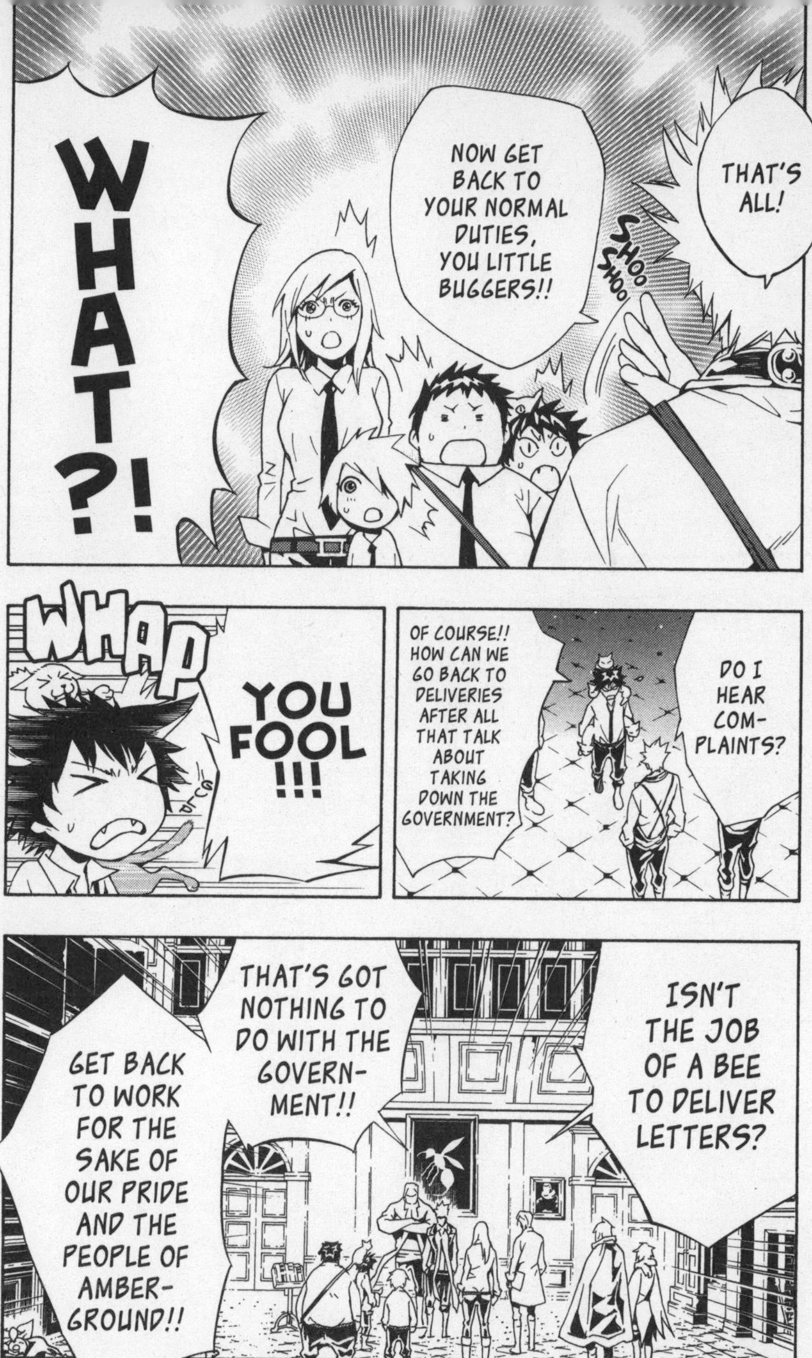
THAT'S ALL!
SHOO SHOO
NOW GET BACK TO YOUR NORMAL DUTIES, YOU LITTLE BUGGERS!!
WHAT?!
DO I HEAR COM-PLAINTS?
OF COURSE!! HOW CAN WE GO BACK TO DELIVERIES AFTER ALL THAT TALK ABOUT TAKING DOWN THE GOVERNMENT?
WHAP
YOU FOOL!!!
ISN'T THE JOB OF A BEE TO DELIVER LETTERS?
THAT'S GOT NOTHING TO DO WITH THE GOVERN-MENT!!
GET BACK TO WORK FOR THE SAKE OF OUR PRIDE AND THE PEOPLE OF AMBER-GROUND!!

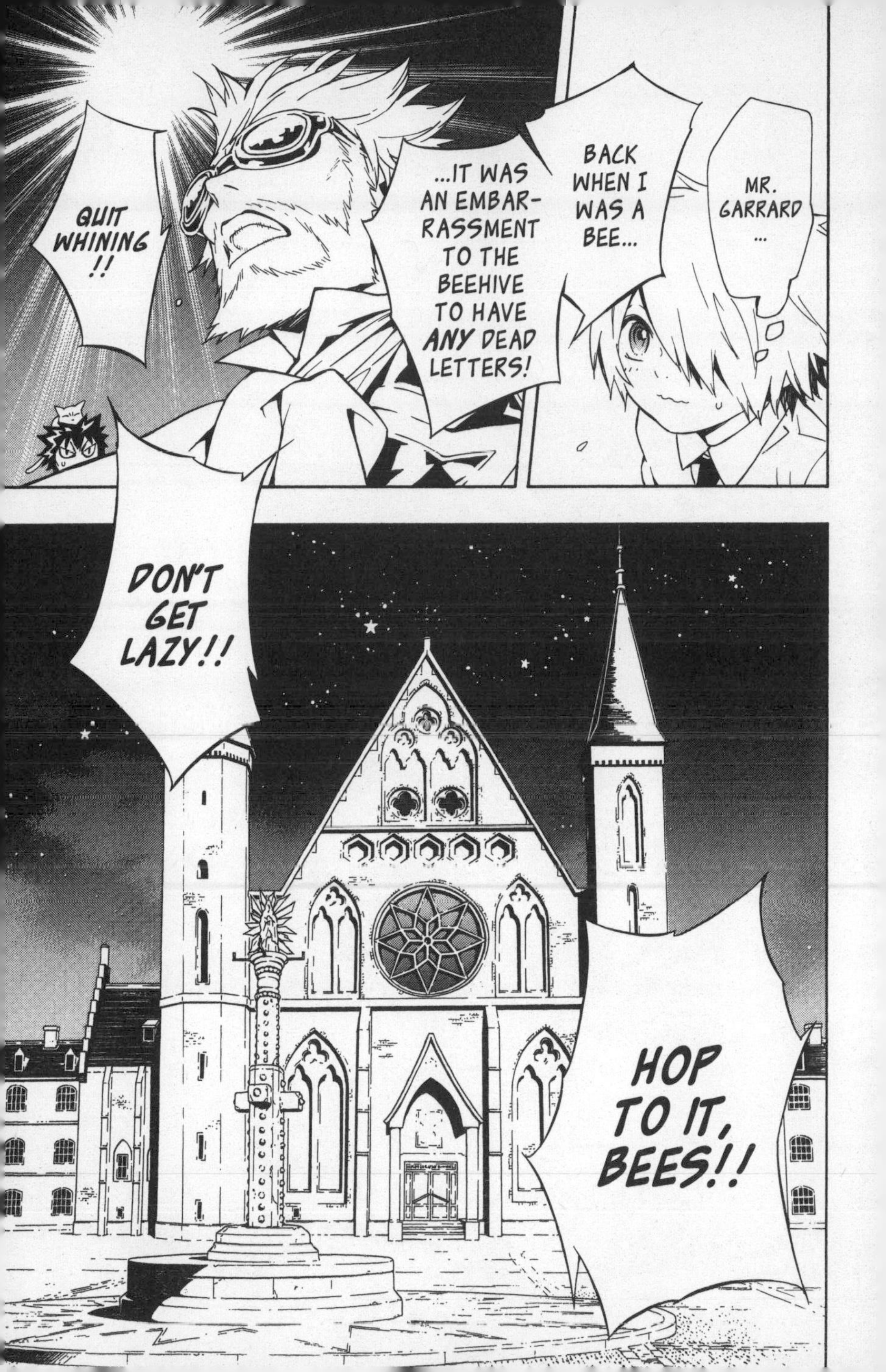
MR. GARRARD ...
BACK WHEN I WAS A BEE...
...IT WAS AN EMBAR-RASSMENT TO THE BEEHIVE TO HAVE *ANY* DEAD LETTERS!
QUIT WHINING!!
DON'T GET LAZY!!
HOP TO IT, BEES!!

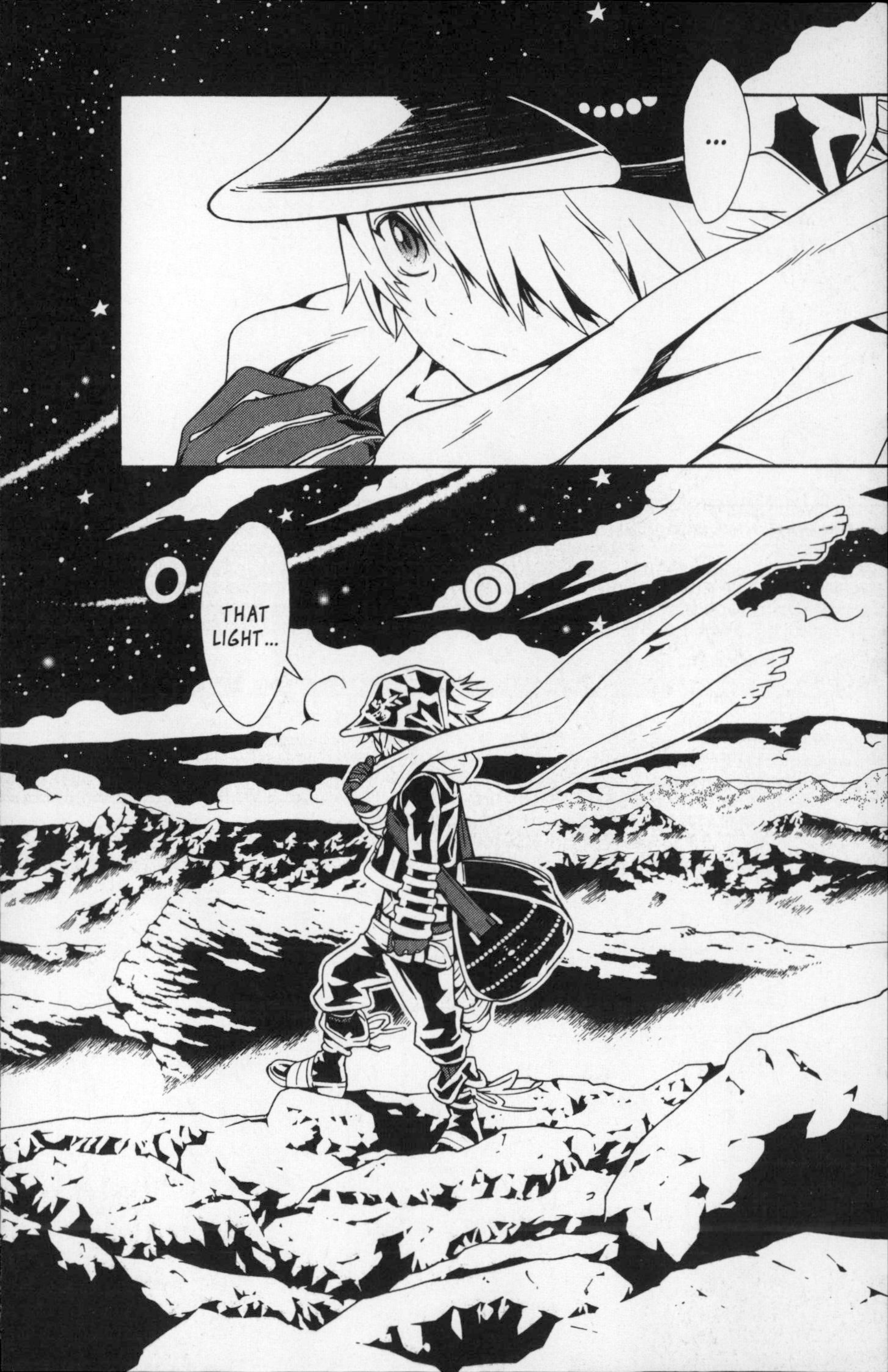
...
THAT LIGHT...

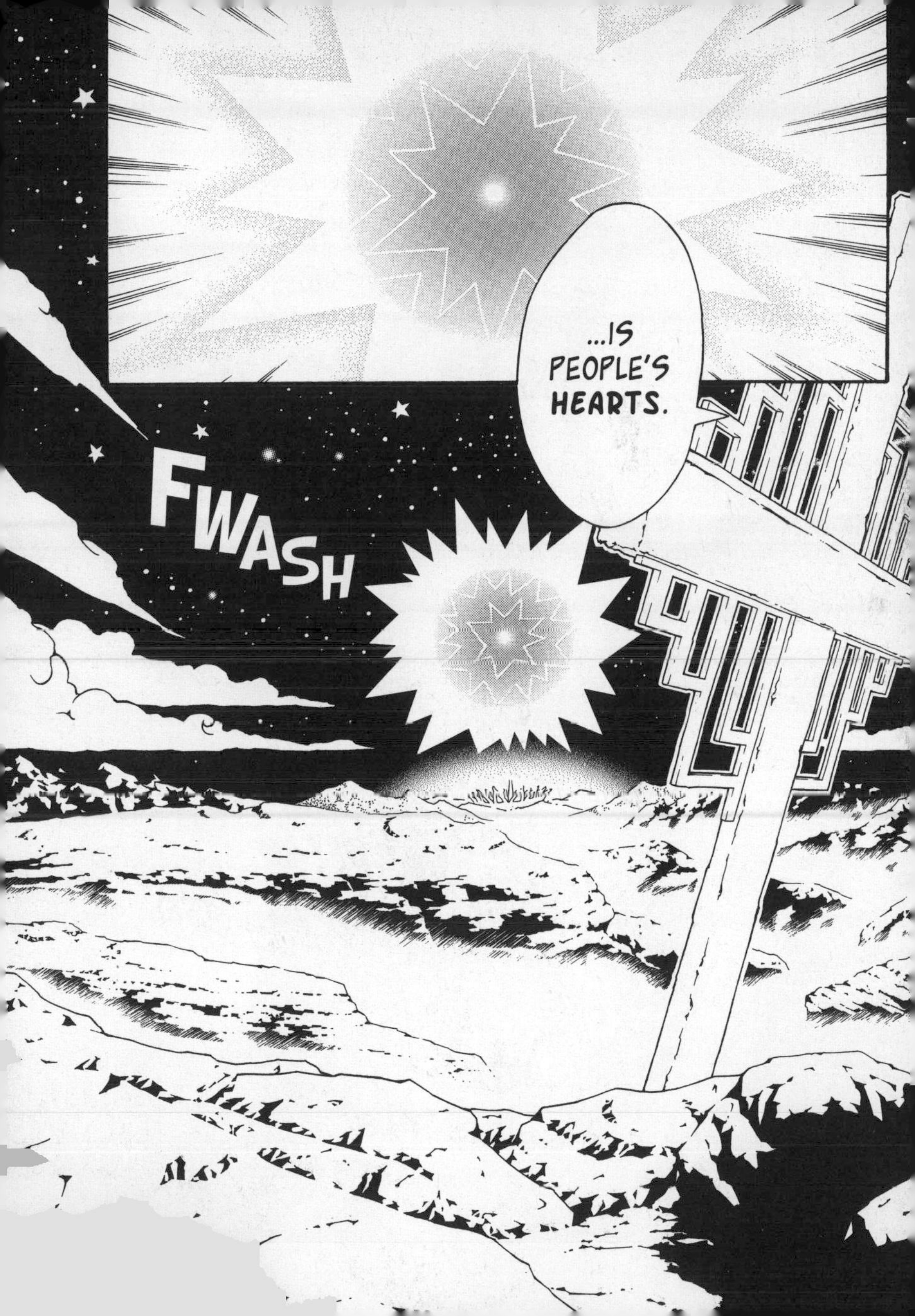
...IS PEOPLE'S HEARTS.
FWASH

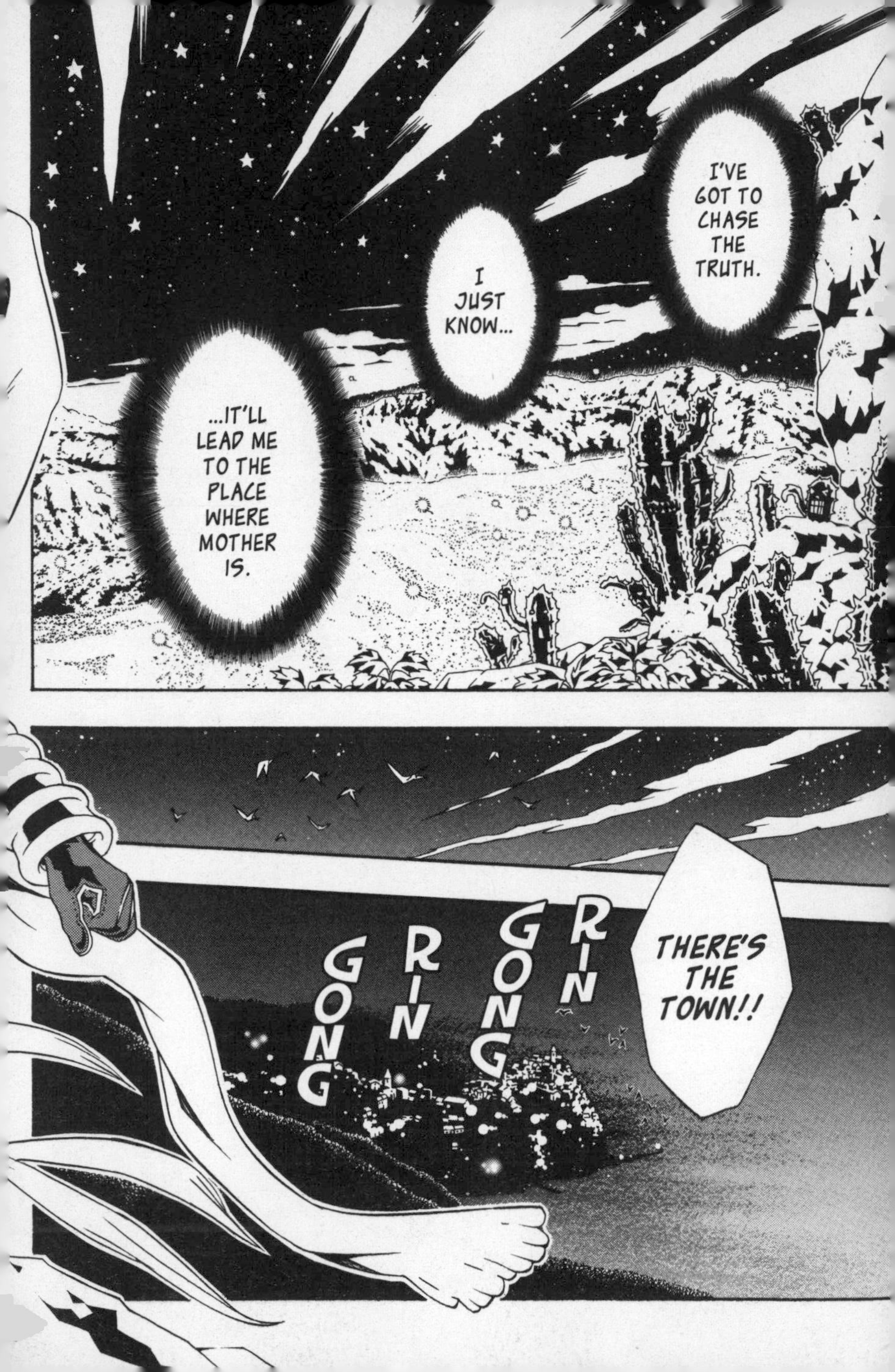
I'VE GOT TO CHASE THE TRUTH.
I JUST KNOW...
...IT'LL LEAD ME TO THE PLACE WHERE MOTHER IS.
THERE'S THE TOWN!!
RIN
GONG
RIN
GONG

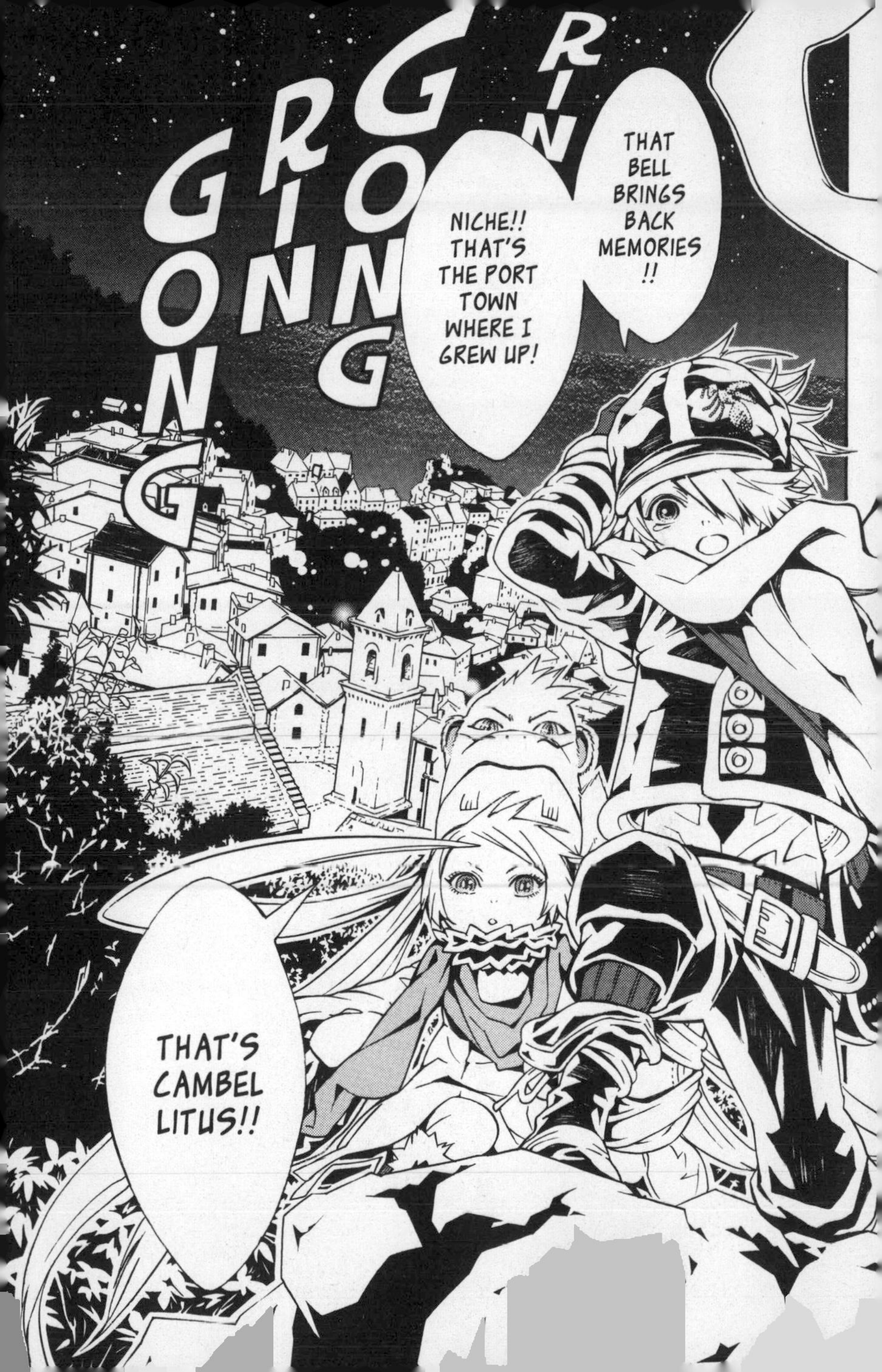
RIN
GONG
RIN
GONG
THAT BELL BRINGS BACK MEMORIES!!
NICHE!! THAT'S THE PORT TOWN WHERE I GREW UP!
THAT'S CAMBEL LITUS!!

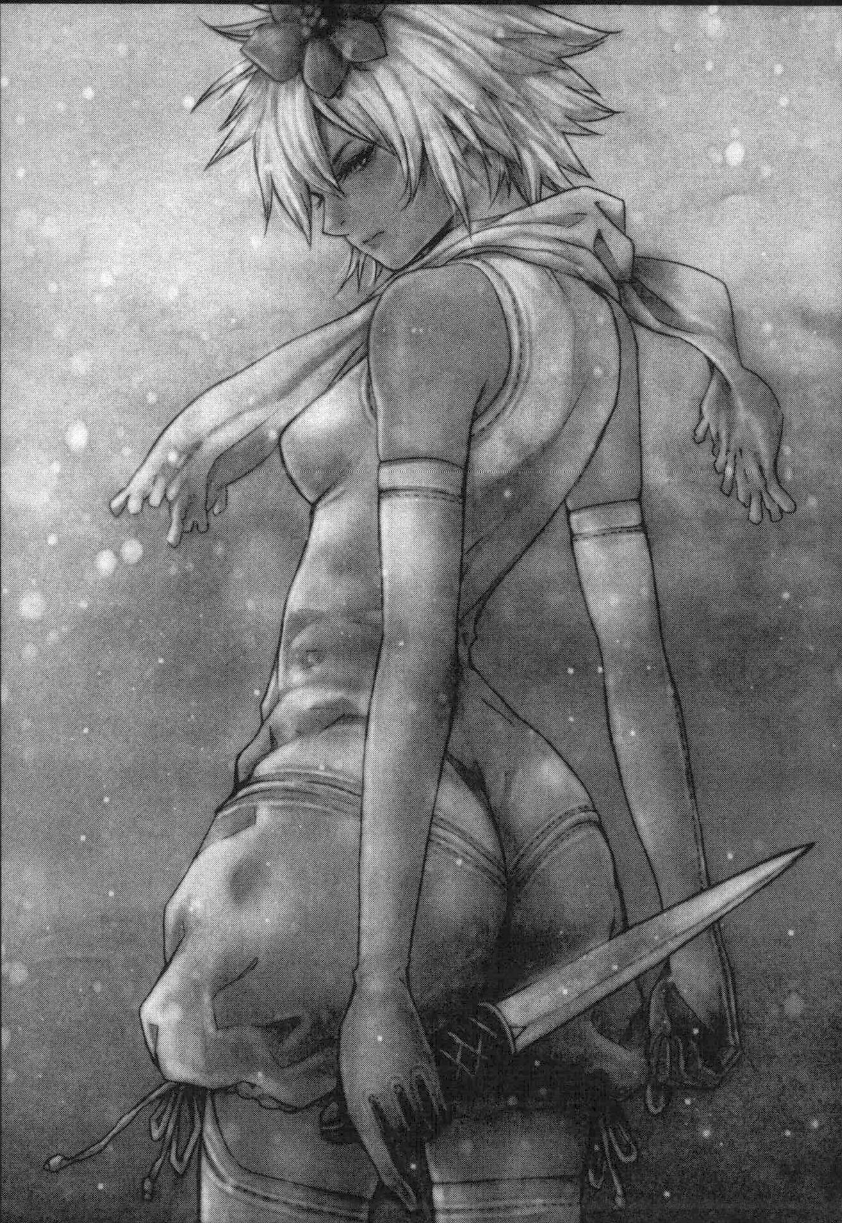

Chapter 61: Not Quite Human

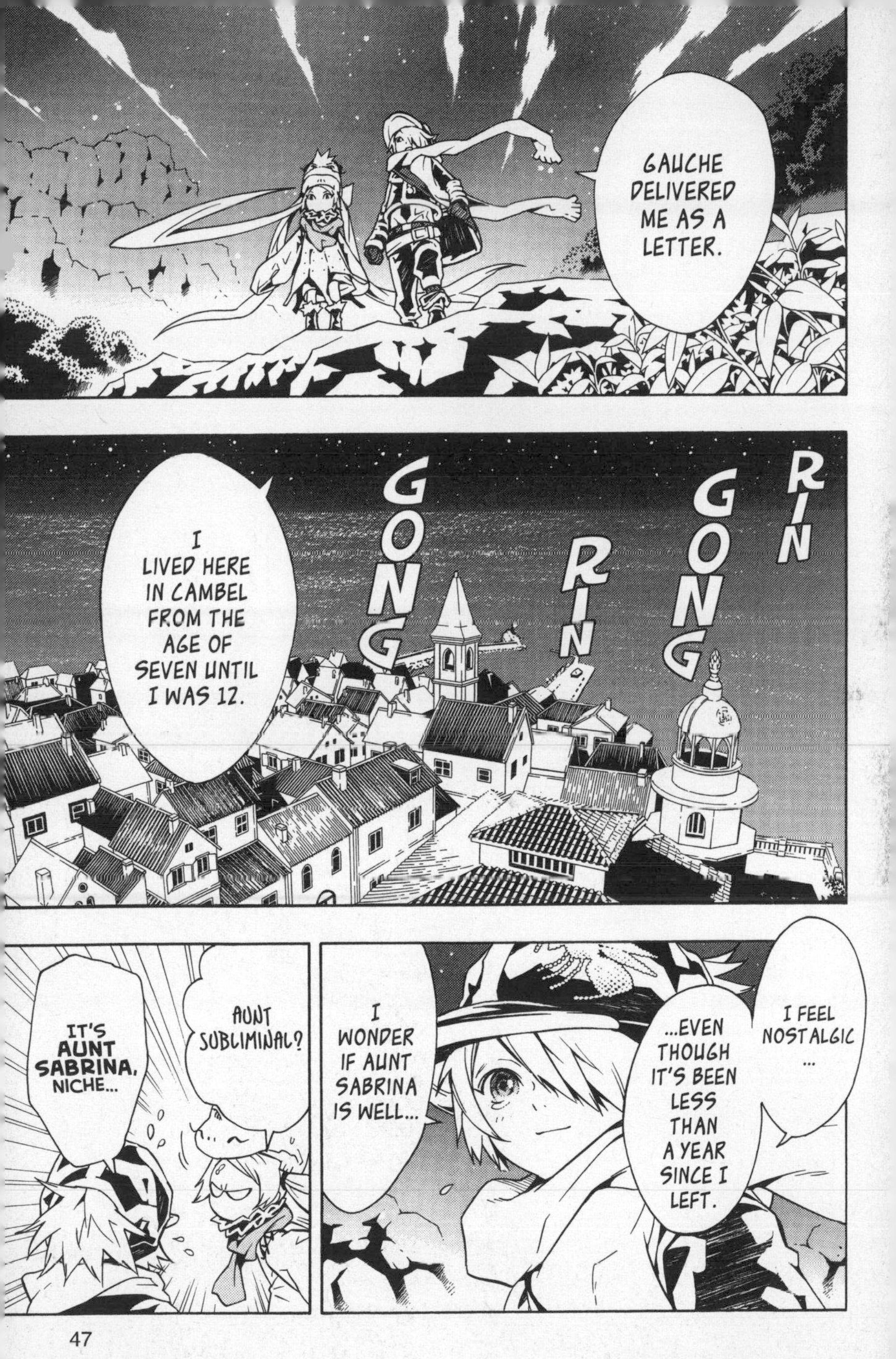
GAUCHE DELIVERED ME AS A LETTER.
RIN
GONG
RIN
GONG
I LIVED HERE IN CAMBEL FROM THE AGE OF SEVEN UNTIL I WAS 12.
I FEEL NOSTALGIC ...
...EVEN THOUGH IT'S BEEN LESS THAN A YEAR SINCE I LEFT.
I WONDER IF AUNT SABRINA IS WELL...
AUNT SUBLIMINAL?
IT'S AUNT SABRINA, NICHE...

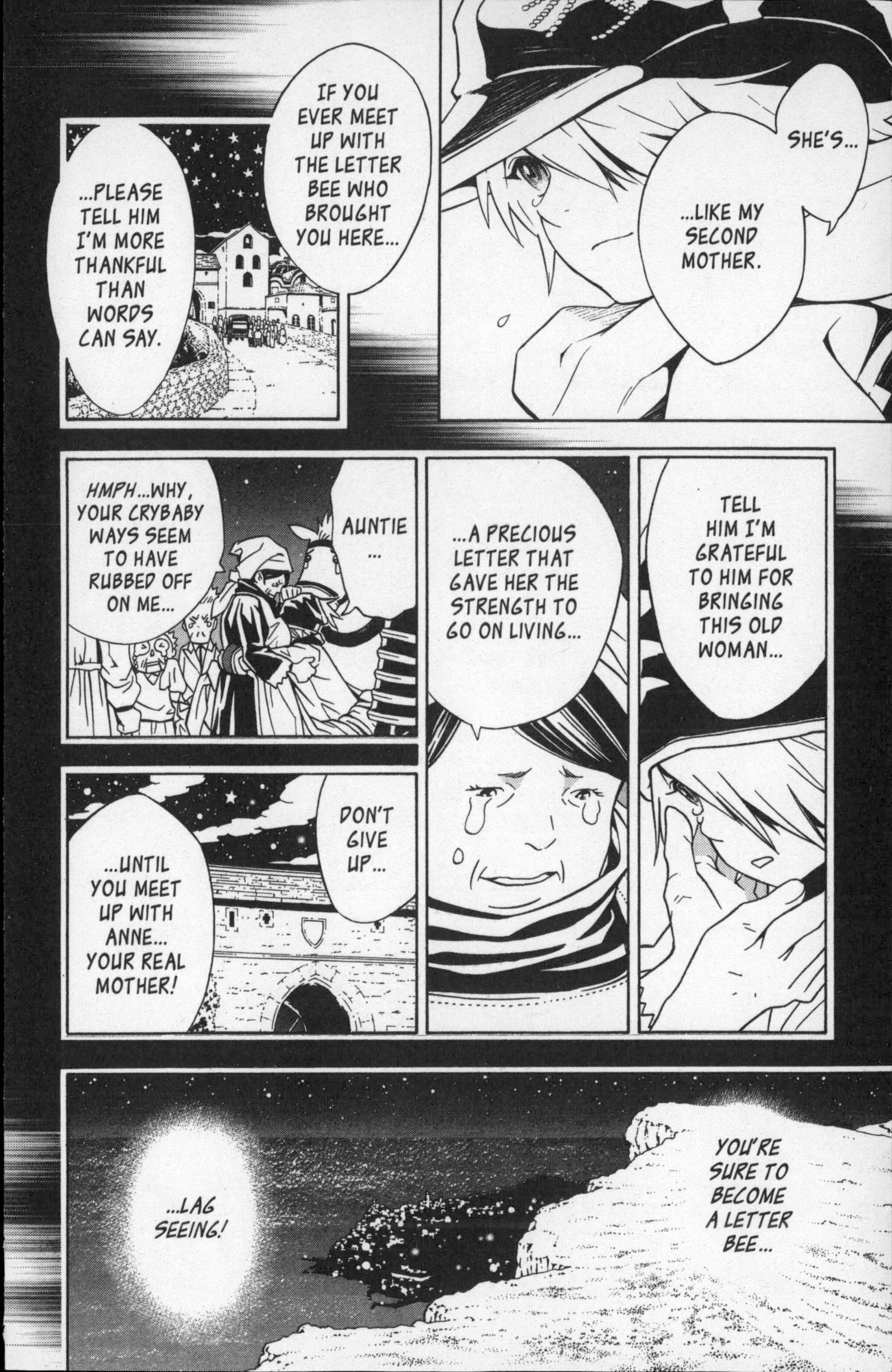
SHE'S...
...LIKE MY SECOND MOTHER.
IF YOU EVER MEET UP WITH THE LETTER BEE WHO BROUGHT YOU HERE...
...PLEASE TELL HIM I'M MORE THANKFUL THAN WORDS CAN SAY.
TELL HIM I'M GRATEFUL TO HIM FOR BRINGING THIS OLD WOMAN...
...A PRECIOUS LETTER THAT GAVE HER THE STRENGTH TO GO ON LIVING...
AUNTIE ...
HMPH...WHY, YOUR CRYBABY WAYS SEEM TO HAVE RUBBED OFF ON ME...
DON'T GIVE UP...
...UNTIL YOU MEET UP WITH ANNE... YOUR REAL MOTHER!
YOU'RE SURE TO BECOME A LETTER BEE...
...LAG SEEING!

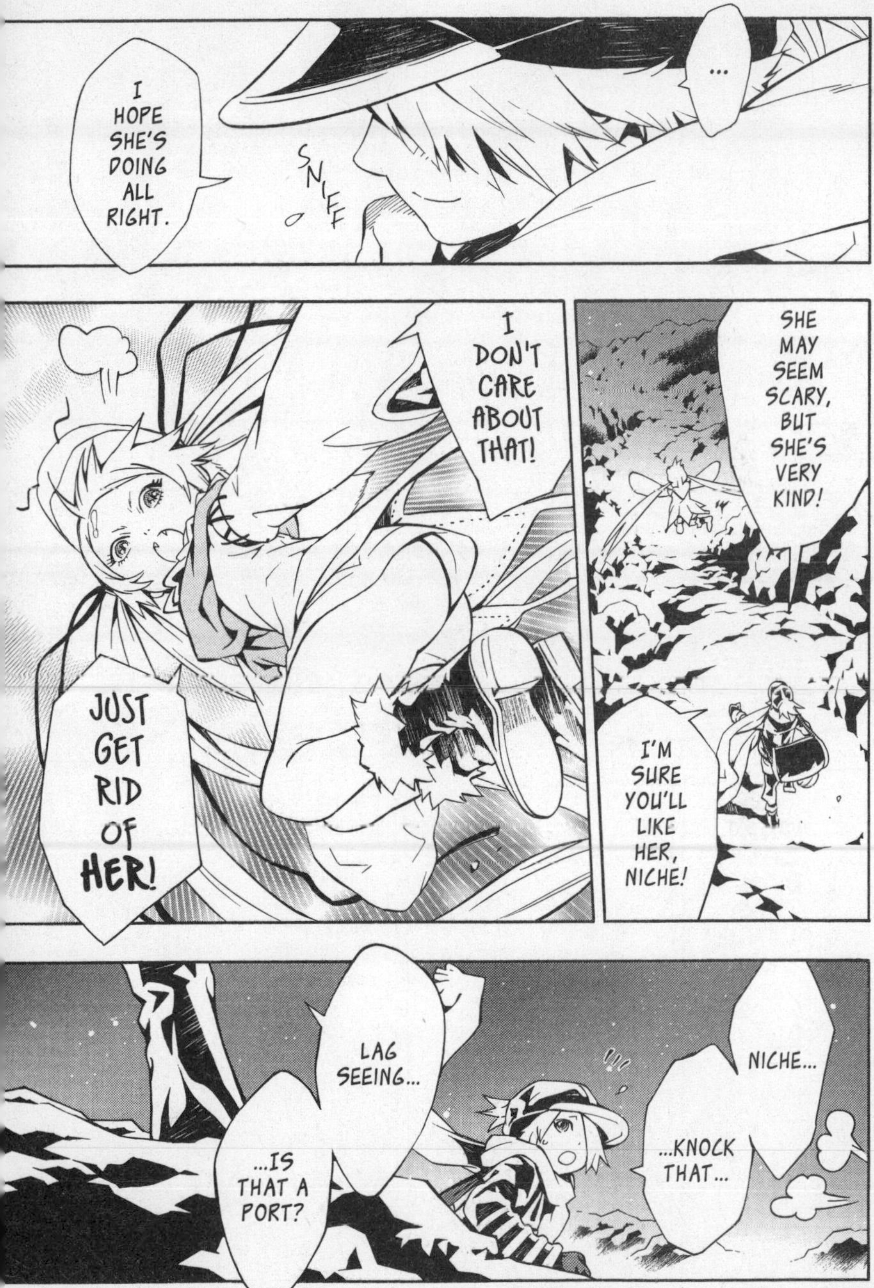
...
I HOPE SHE'S DOING ALL RIGHT.
SNIFF
SHE MAY SEEM SCARY, BUT SHE'S VERY KIND!
I'M SURE YOU'LL LIKE HER, NICHE!
I DON'T CARE ABOUT THAT!
JUST GET RID OF HER!
NICHE...
...KNOCK THAT...
LAG SEEING...
...IS THAT A PORT?

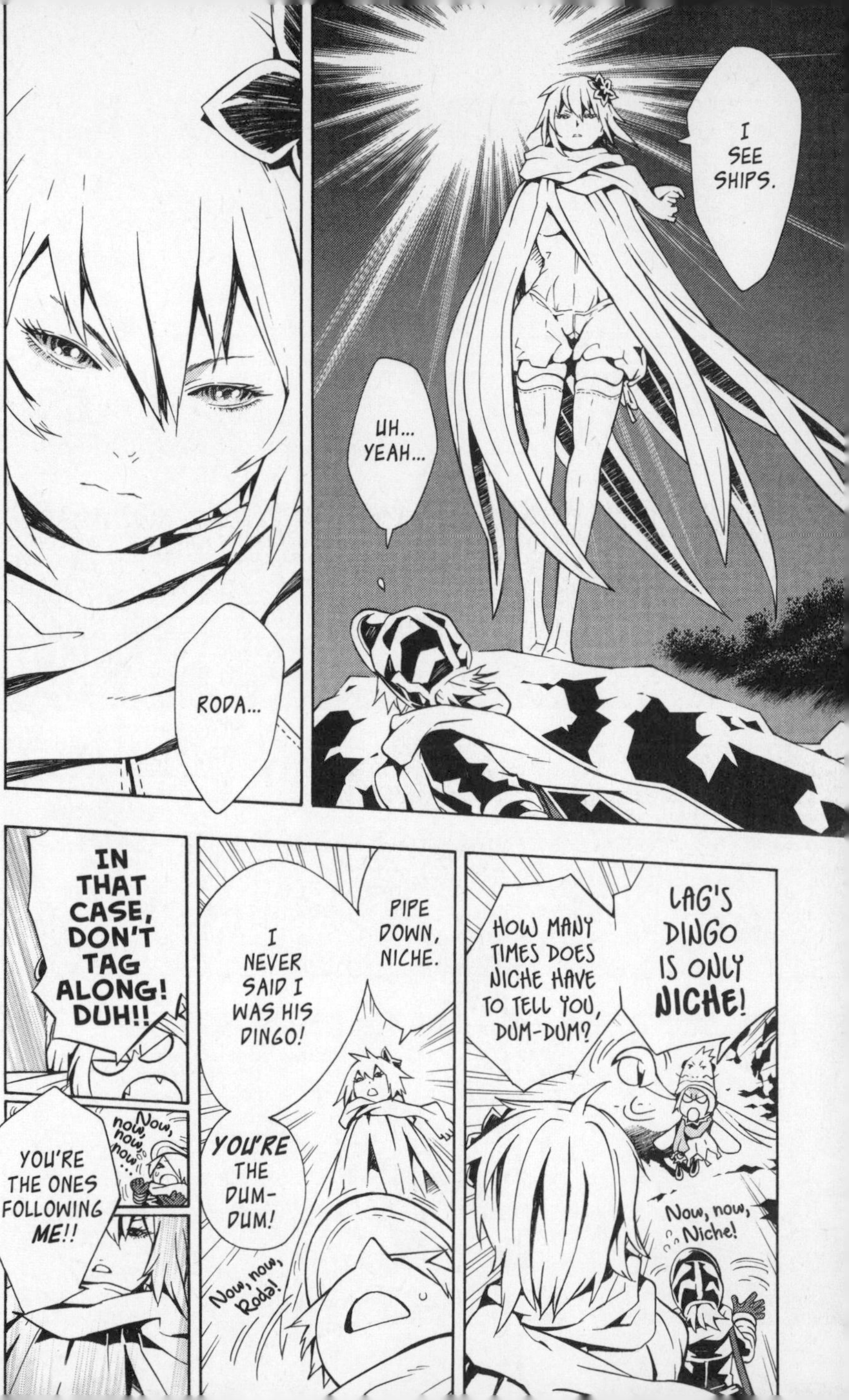
I SEE SHIPS.
UH... YEAH...
RODA...
LAG'S DINGO IS ONLY NICHE!
HOW MANY TIMES DOES NICHE HAVE TO TELL YOU, DUM-DUM?
Now, now, Niche!
PIPE DOWN, NICHE.
I NEVER SAID I WAS HIS DINGO!
YOU'RE THE DUM-DUM!
Now, now, Roda!
IN THAT CASE, DON'T TAG ALONG! DUH!!
Now, now, now, now...
YOU'RE THE ONES FOLLOWING ME!!

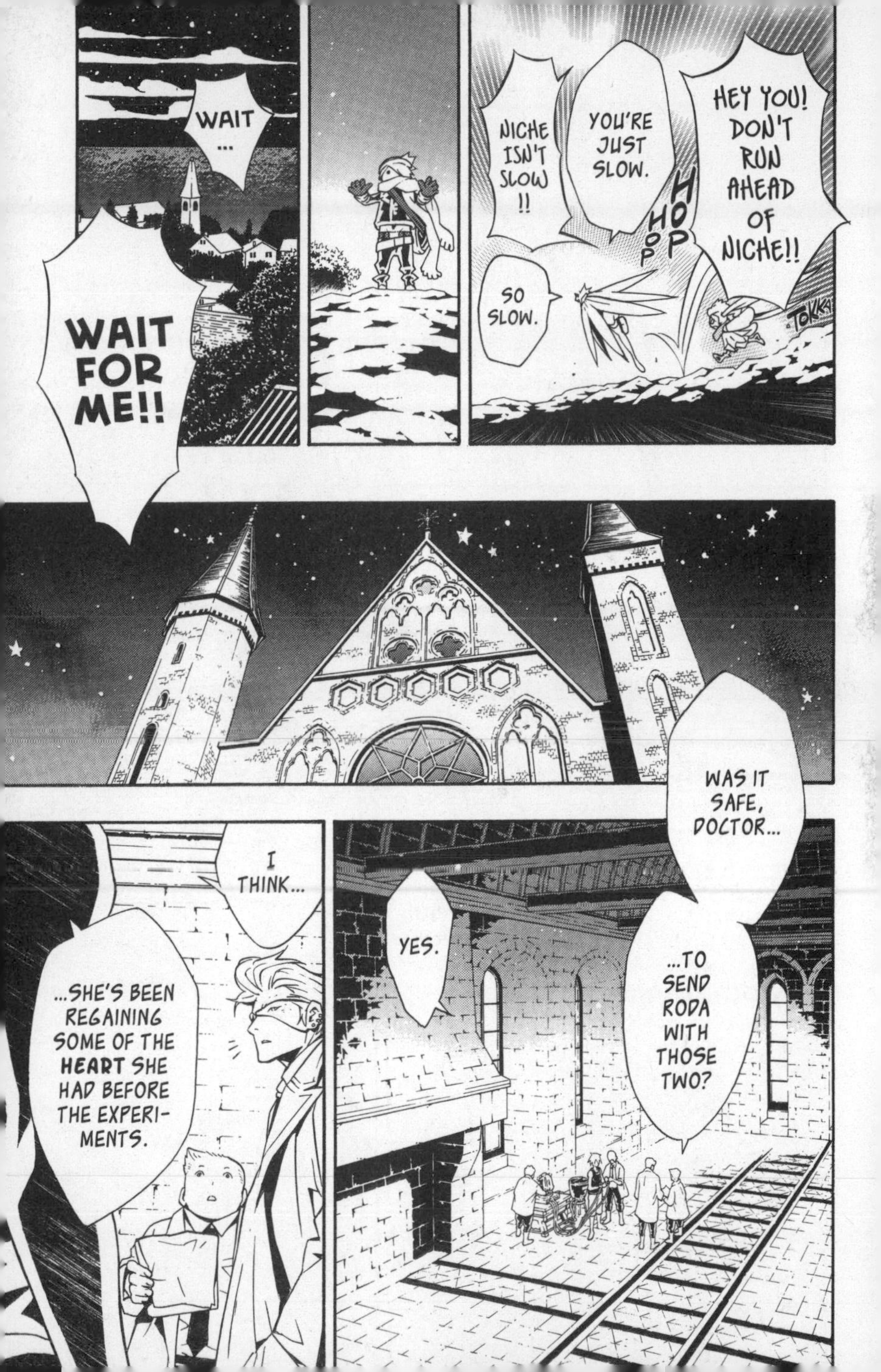
HEY YOU! DON'T RUN AHEAD OF NICHE!!
YOU'RE JUST SLOW.
NICHE ISN'T SLOW !!
HOP HOP HOP
TOKKA
SO SLOW.
WAIT ...
WAIT FOR ME!!
WAS IT SAFE, DOCTOR...
...TO SEND RODA WITH THOSE TWO?
YES.
I THINK...
...SHE'S BEEN REGAINING SOME OF THE **HEART** SHE HAD BEFORE THE EXPERI-MENTS.

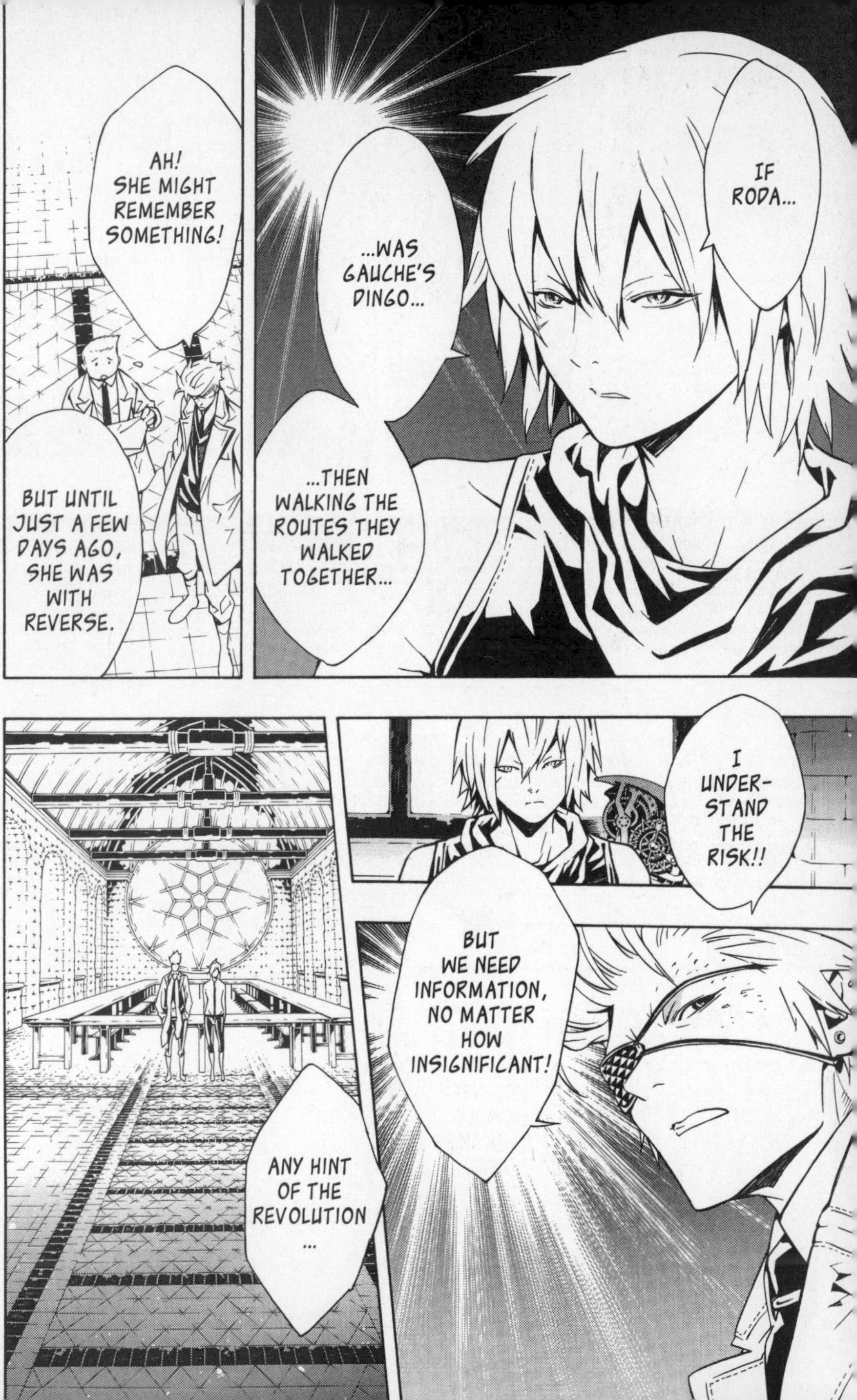
IF RODA...
...WAS GAUCHE'S DINGO...
...THEN WALKING THE ROUTES THEY WALKED TOGETHER...
AH! SHE MIGHT REMEMBER SOMETHING!
BUT UNTIL JUST A FEW DAYS AGO, SHE WAS WITH REVERSE.
I UNDER-STAND THE RISK!!
BUT WE NEED INFORMATION, NO MATTER HOW INSIGNIFICANT!
ANY HINT OF THE REVOLUTION ...

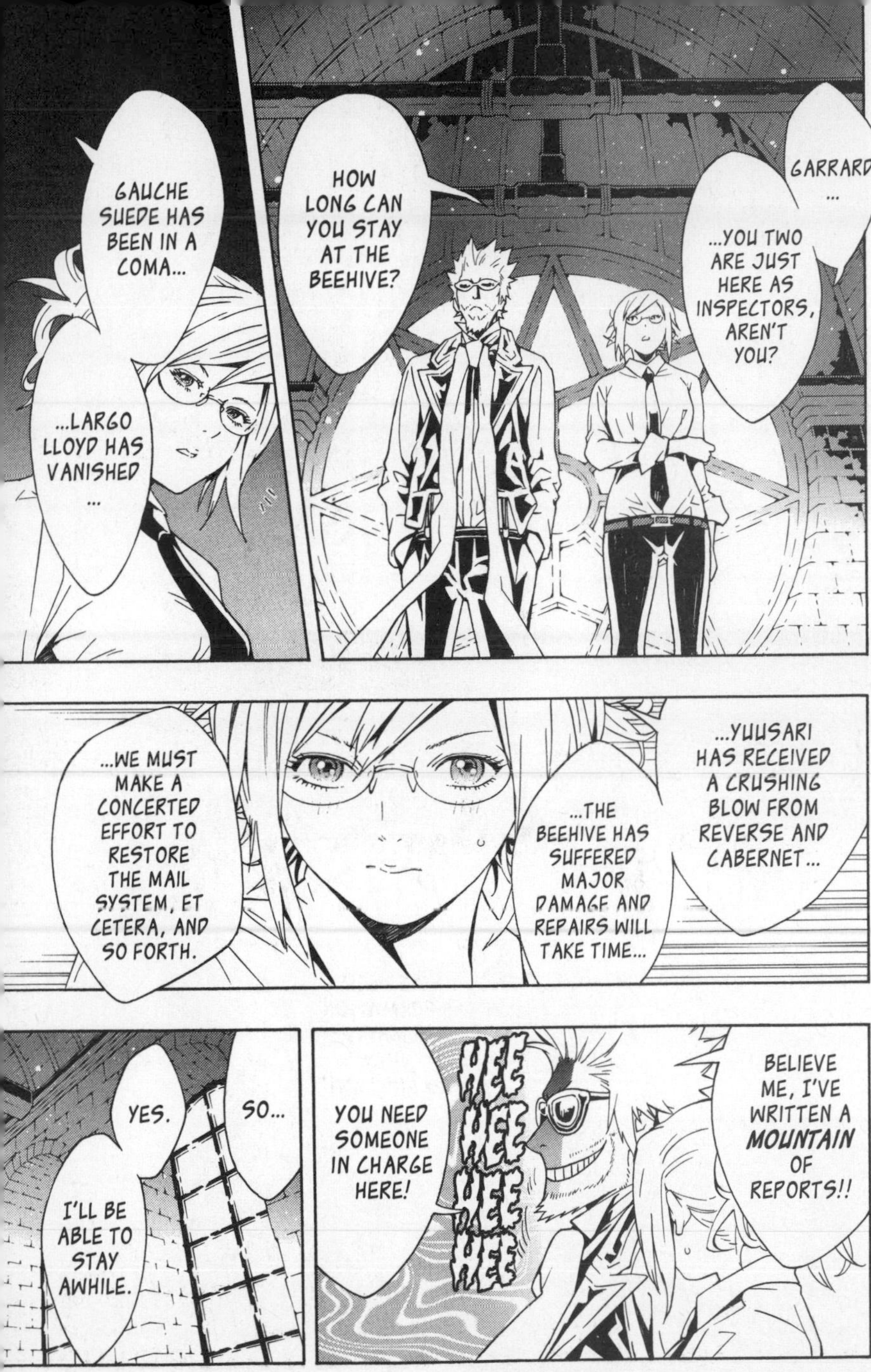
GARRARD ...
...YOU TWO ARE JUST HERE AS INSPECTORS, AREN'T YOU?
HOW LONG CAN YOU STAY AT THE BEEHIVE?
GAUCHE SUEDE HAS BEEN IN A COMA...
...LARGO LLOYD HAS VANISHED ...
...YUUSARI HAS RECEIVED A CRUSHING BLOW FROM REVERSE AND CABERNET...
...THE BEEHIVE HAS SUFFERED MAJOR DAMAGE AND REPAIRS WILL TAKE TIME...
...WE MUST MAKE A CONCERTED EFFORT TO RESTORE THE MAIL SYSTEM, ET CETERA, AND SO FORTH.
BELIEVE ME, I'VE WRITTEN A *MOUNTAIN* OF REPORTS!!
HEE HEE HEE HEE
YOU NEED SOMEONE IN CHARGE HERE!
SO...
YES.
I'LL BE ABLE TO STAY AWHILE.

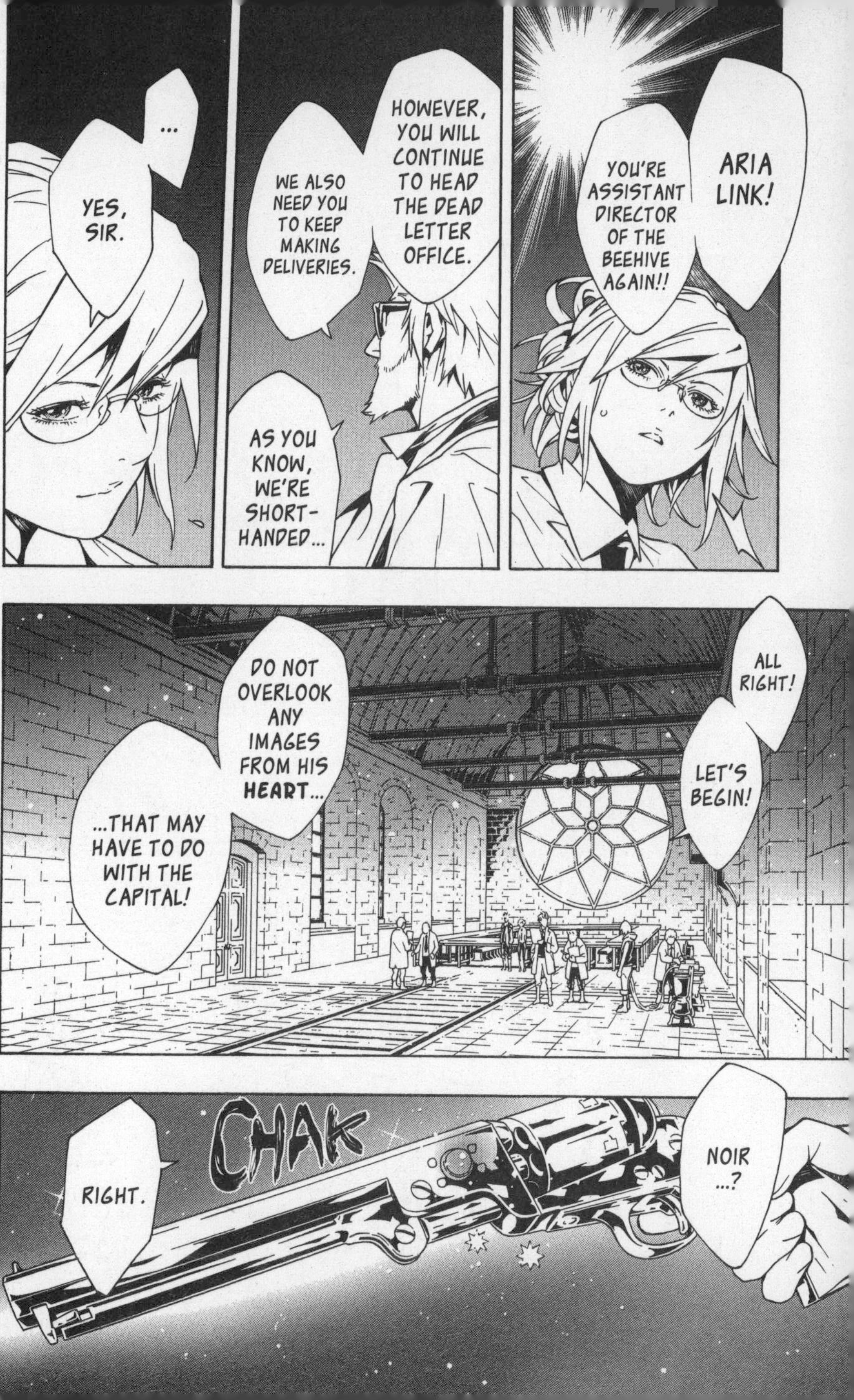
ARIA LINK!
YOU'RE ASSISTANT DIRECTOR OF THE BEEHIVE AGAIN!!
HOWEVER, YOU WILL CONTINUE TO HEAD THE DEAD LETTER OFFICE.
WE ALSO NEED YOU TO KEEP MAKING DELIVERIES.
AS YOU KNOW, WE'RE SHORT-HANDED...
...
YES, SIR.
ALL RIGHT!
LET'S BEGIN!
DO NOT OVERLOOK ANY IMAGES FROM HIS **HEART**...
...THAT MAY HAVE TO DO WITH THE CAPITAL!
NOIR ...?
CHAK
RIGHT.

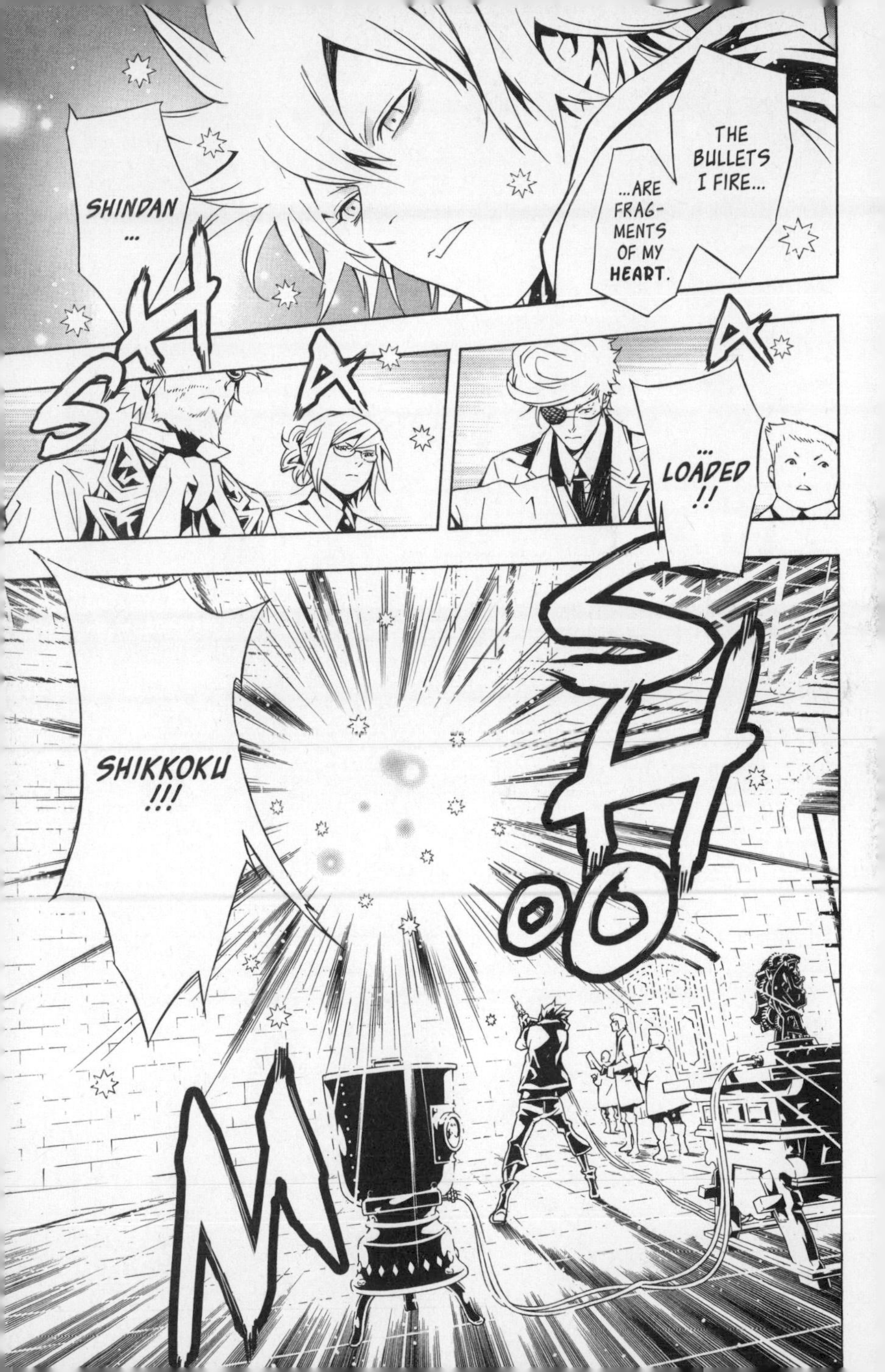
THE BULLETS I FIRE...
...ARE FRAG-MENTS OF MY HEART.
SHINDAN ...
SHA
... LOADED !!
SHIKKOKU !!!
SHOOM

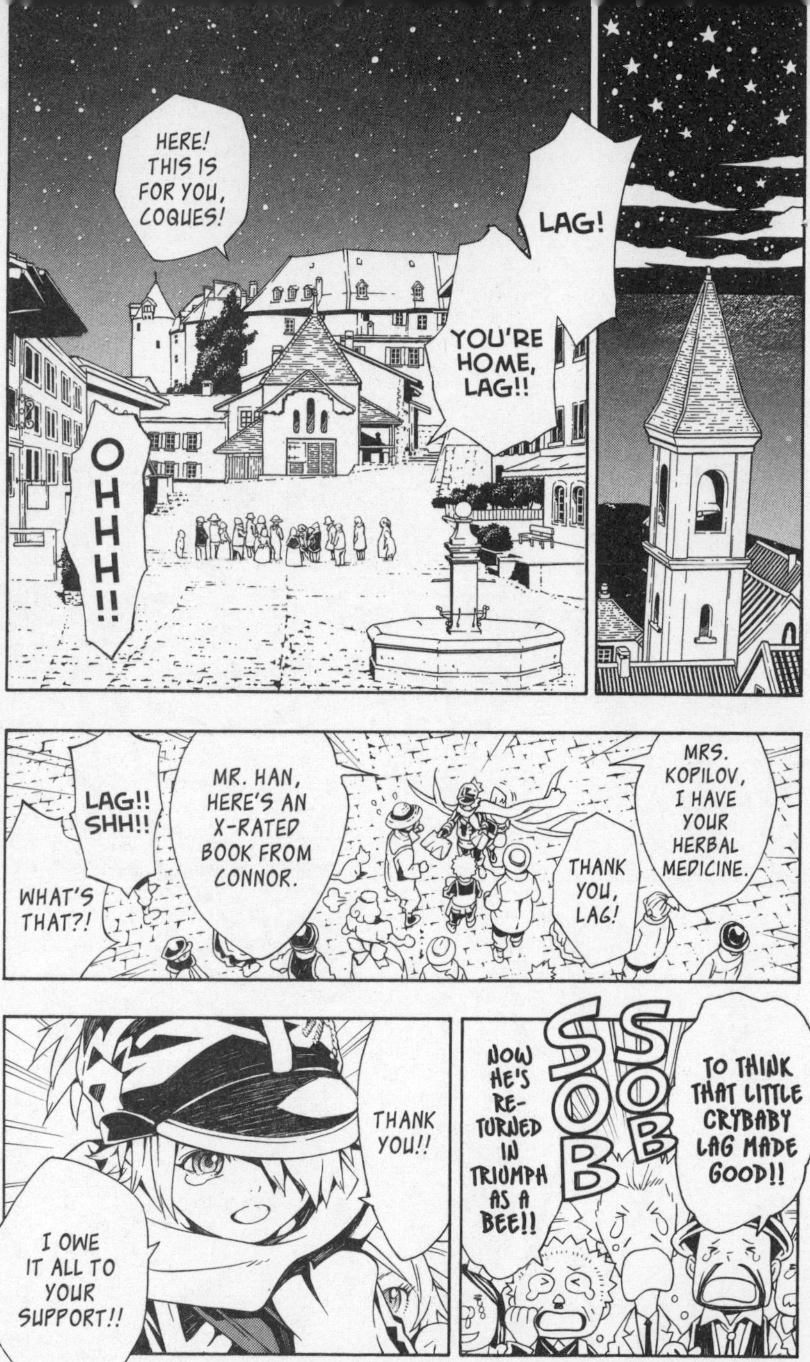

LAG!
YOU'RE HOME, LAG!!
HERE! THIS IS FOR YOU, COQUES!
OHHHH!!
MRS. KOPILOV, I HAVE YOUR HERBAL MEDICINE.
THANK YOU, LAG!
MR. HAN, HERE'S AN X-RATED BOOK FROM CONNOR.
LAG!! SHH!!
WHAT'S THAT?!
TO THINK THAT LITTLE CRYBABY LAG MADE GOOD!!
SOB SOB
NOW HE'S RE-TURNED IN TRIUMPH AS A BEE!!
THANK YOU!!
I OWE IT ALL TO YOUR SUPPORT!!

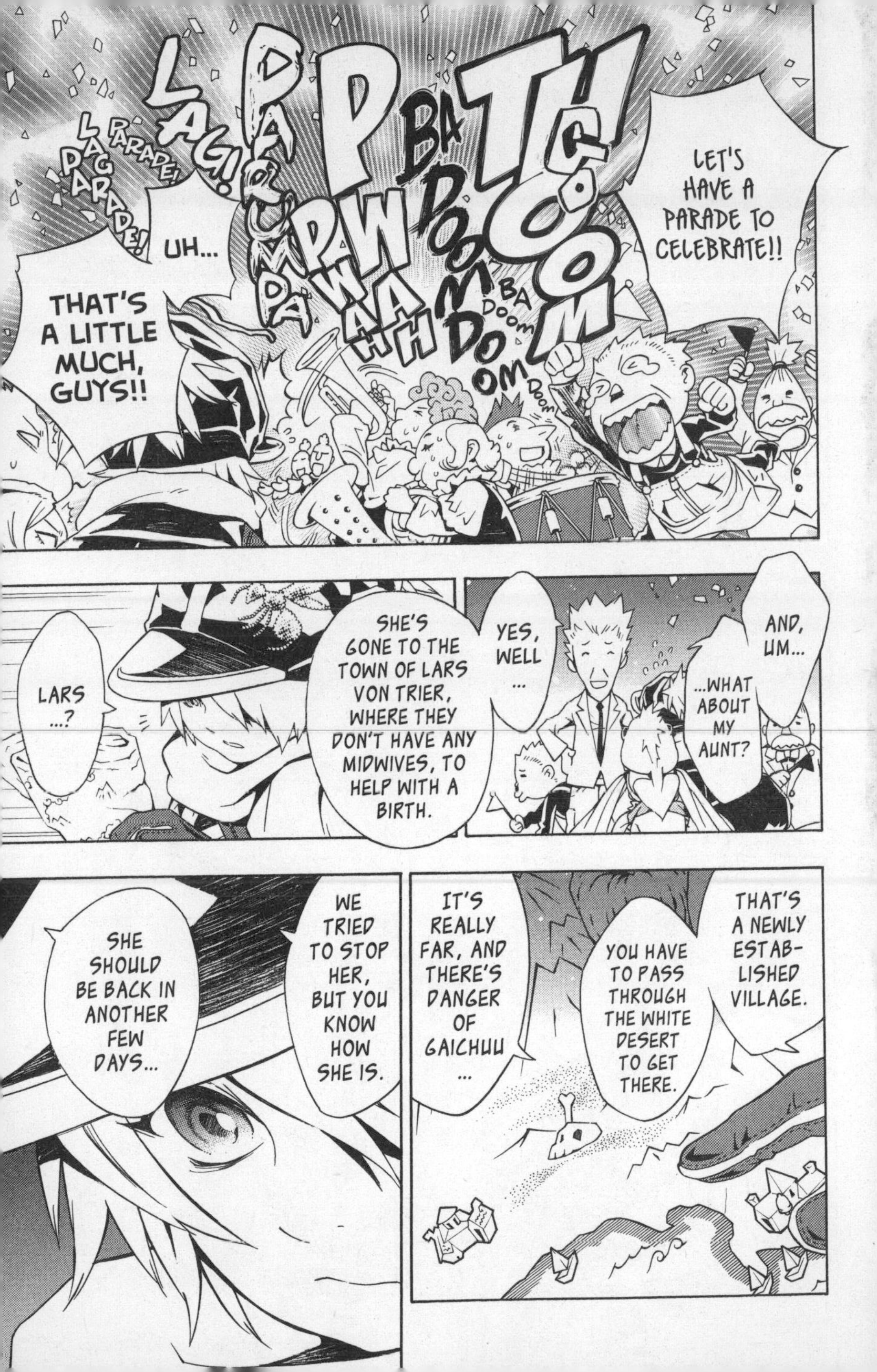
LET'S HAVE A PARADE TO CELEBRATE!!
BA DOOM
PARADE! PARADE!
UH...
THAT'S A LITTLE MUCH, GUYS!!
AND, UM...
...WHAT ABOUT MY AUNT?
YES, WELL ...
SHE'S GONE TO THE TOWN OF LARS VON TRIER, WHERE THEY DON'T HAVE ANY MIDWIVES, TO HELP WITH A BIRTH.
LARS ...?
THAT'S A NEWLY ESTAB-LISHED VILLAGE.
YOU HAVE TO PASS THROUGH THE WHITE DESERT TO GET THERE.
IT'S REALLY FAR, AND THERE'S DANGER OF GAICHUU ...
WE TRIED TO STOP HER, BUT YOU KNOW HOW SHE IS.
SHE SHOULD BE BACK IN ANOTHER FEW DAYS...

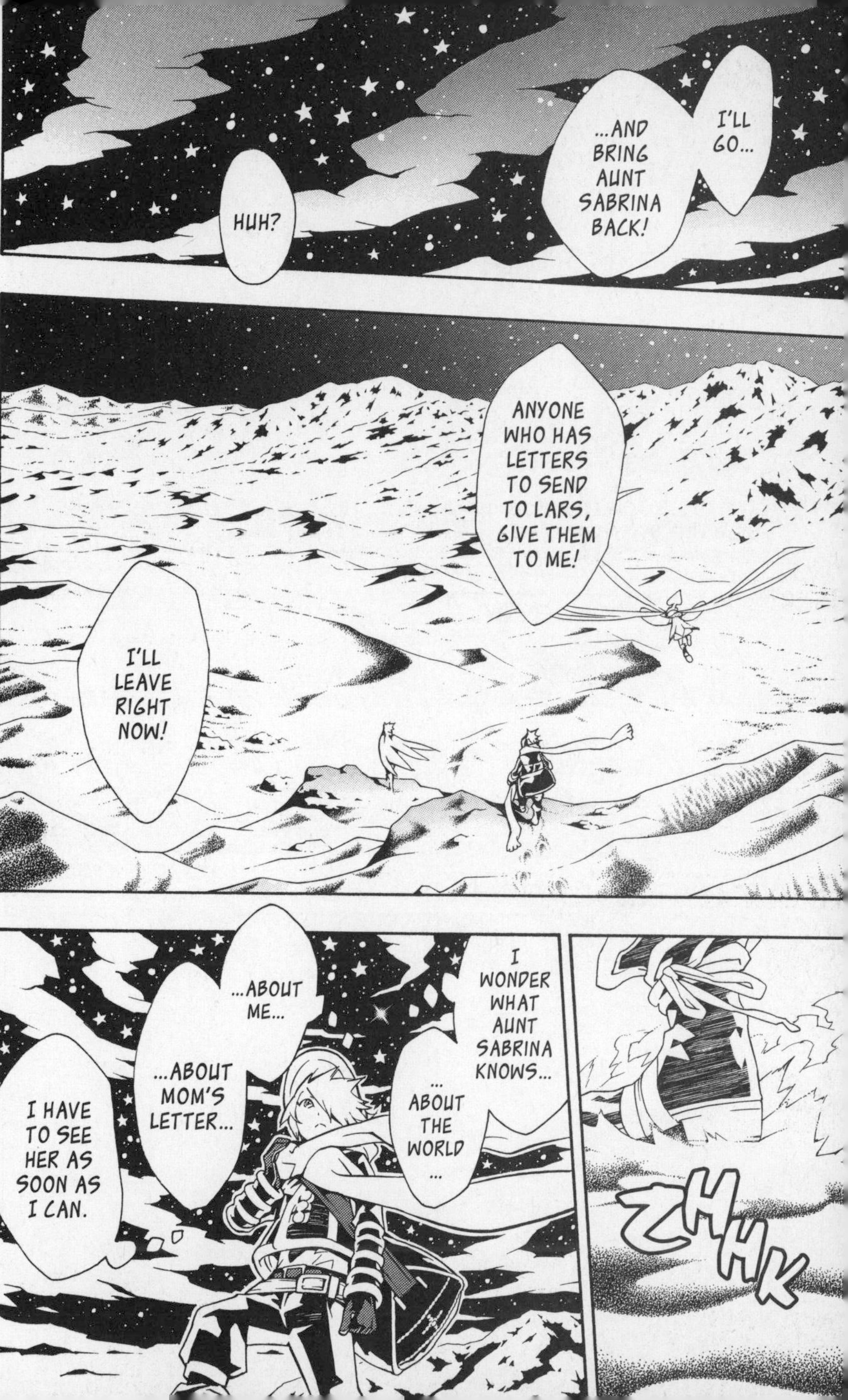
I'LL GO...
...AND BRING AUNT SABRINA BACK!
HUH?
ANYONE WHO HAS LETTERS TO SEND TO LARS, GIVE THEM TO ME!
I'LL LEAVE RIGHT NOW!
ZHHK
I WONDER WHAT AUNT SABRINA KNOWS...
...ABOUT THE WORLD...
...ABOUT ME...
...ABOUT MOM'S LETTER...
I HAVE TO SEE HER AS SOON AS I CAN.

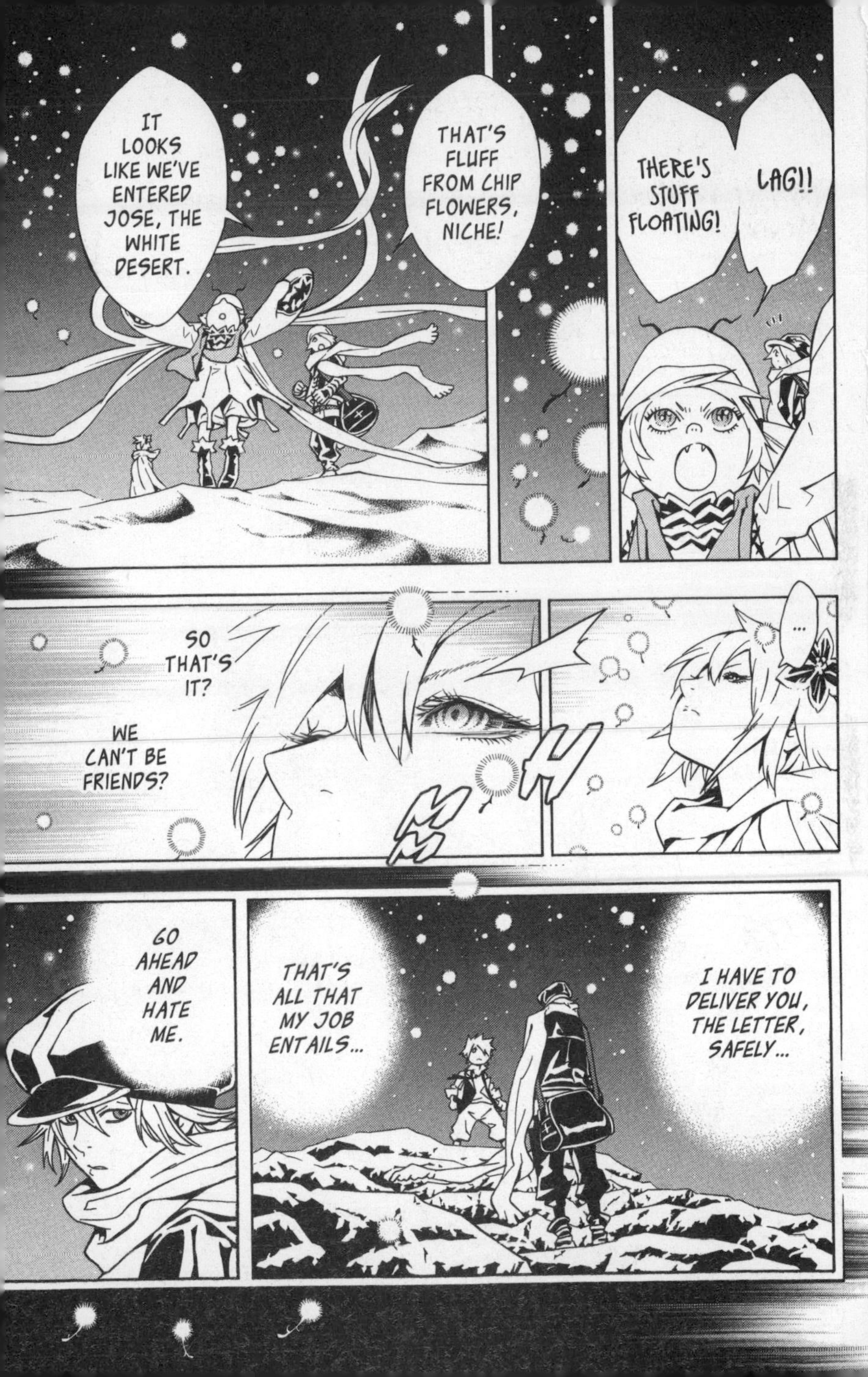
LAG!!
THERE'S STUFF FLOATING!
THAT'S FLUFF FROM CHIP FLOWERS, NICHE!
IT LOOKS LIKE WE'VE ENTERED JOSE, THE WHITE DESERT.
...
SO THAT'S IT?
WE CAN'T BE FRIENDS?
I HAVE TO DELIVER YOU, THE LETTER, SAFELY...
THAT'S ALL THAT MY JOB ENTAILS...
GO AHEAD AND HATE ME.

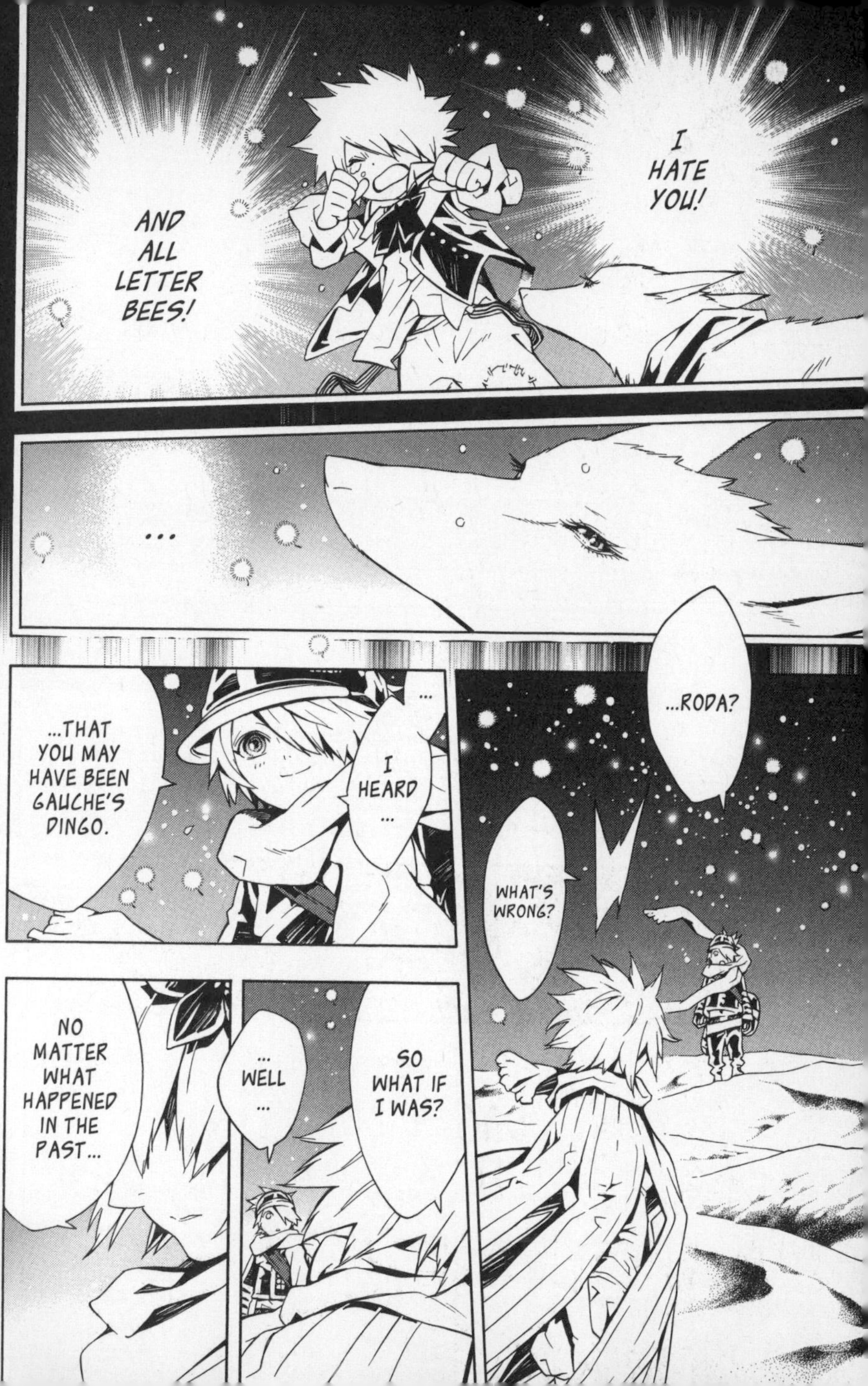

I HATE YOU!
AND ALL LETTER BEES!
...
...RODA?
WHAT'S WRONG?
... I HEARD ...
...THAT YOU MAY HAVE BEEN GAUCHE'S DINGO.
SO WHAT IF I WAS?
... WELL ...
NO MATTER WHAT HAPPENED IN THE PAST...

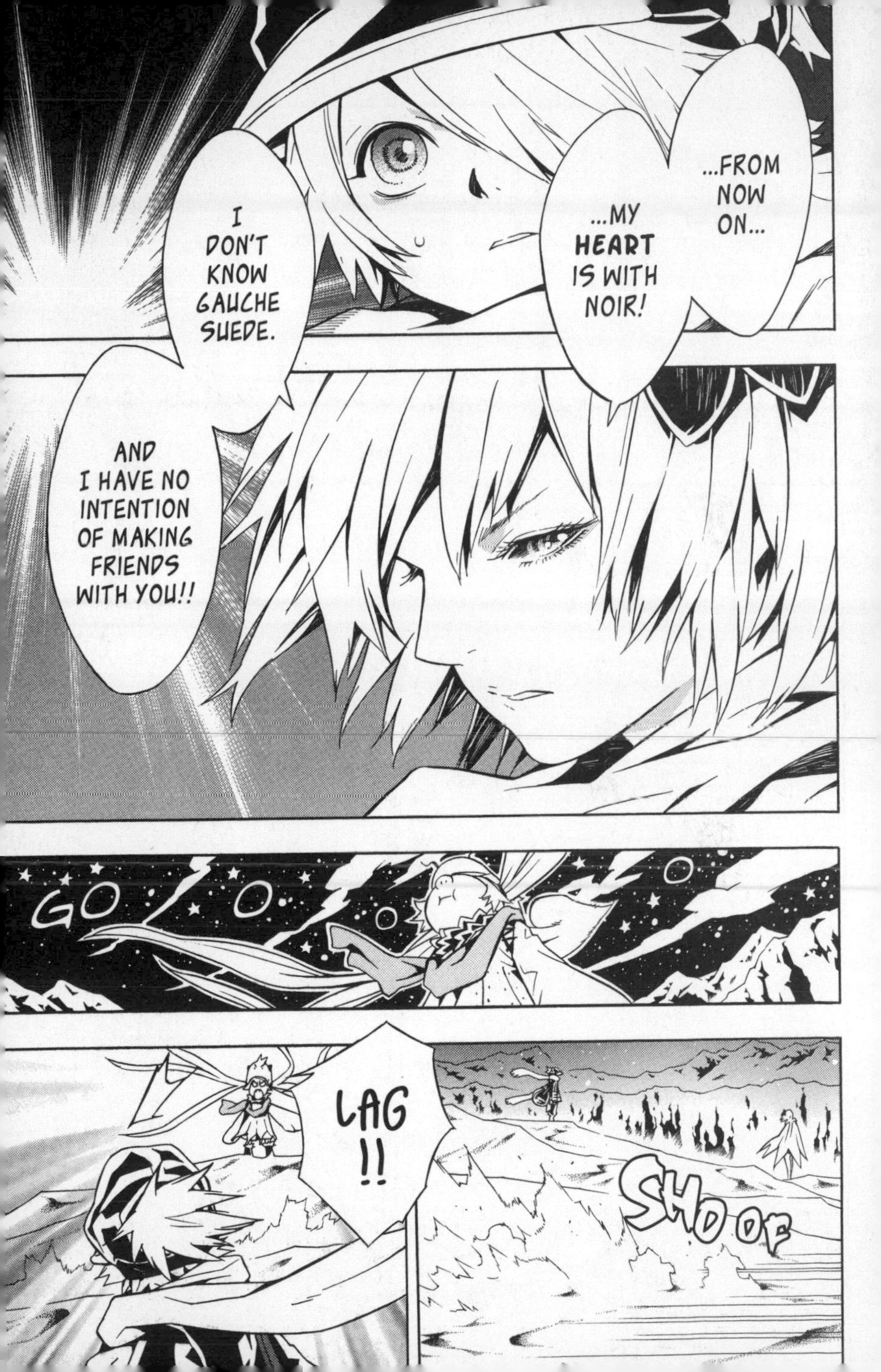
...FROM NOW ON...
...MY **HEART** IS WITH NOIR!
I DON'T KNOW GAUCHE SUEDE.
AND I HAVE NO INTENTION OF MAKING FRIENDS WITH YOU!!
GO O
LAG !!
SHOOF

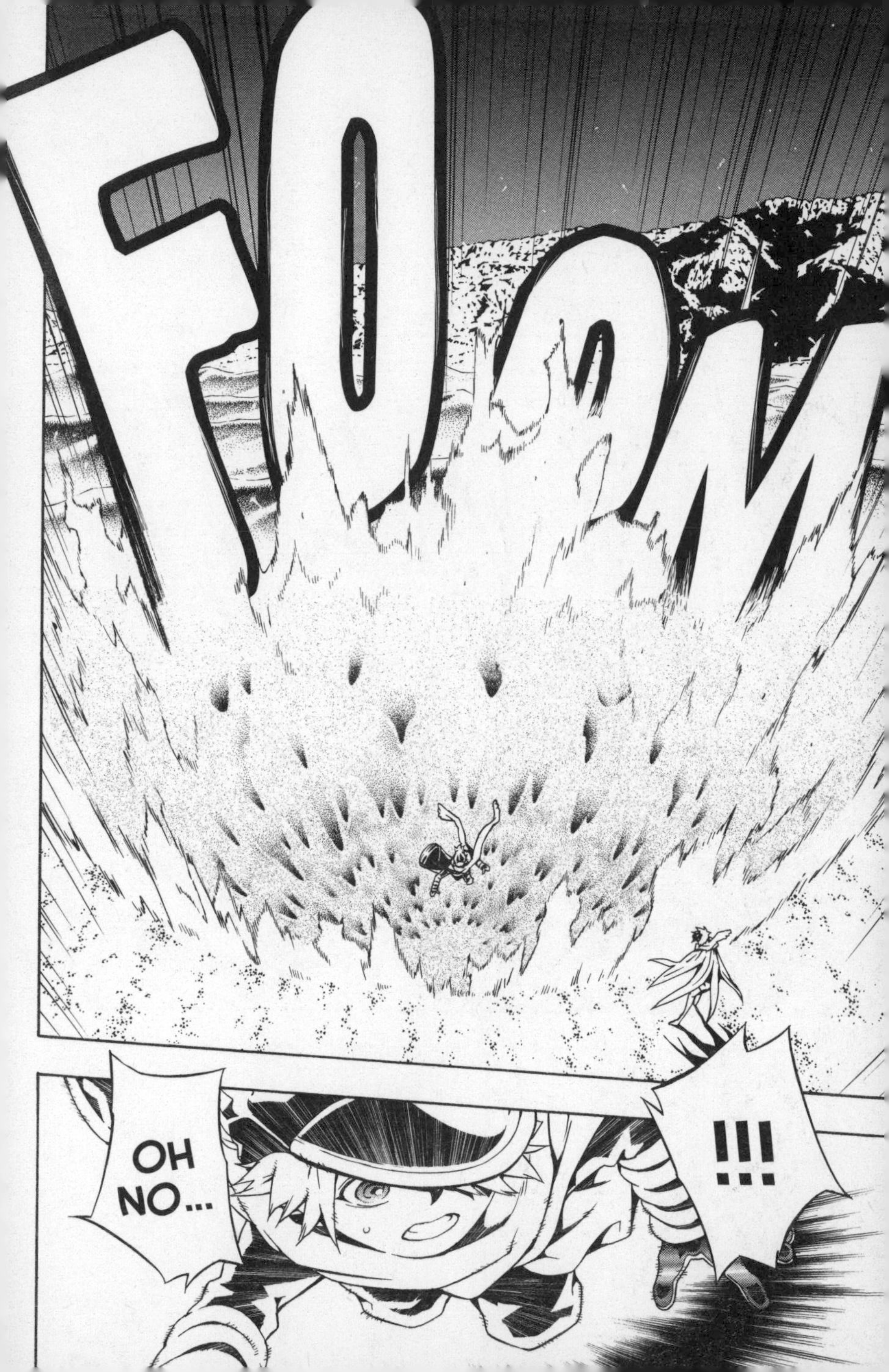
FOOM
!!!
OH NO...

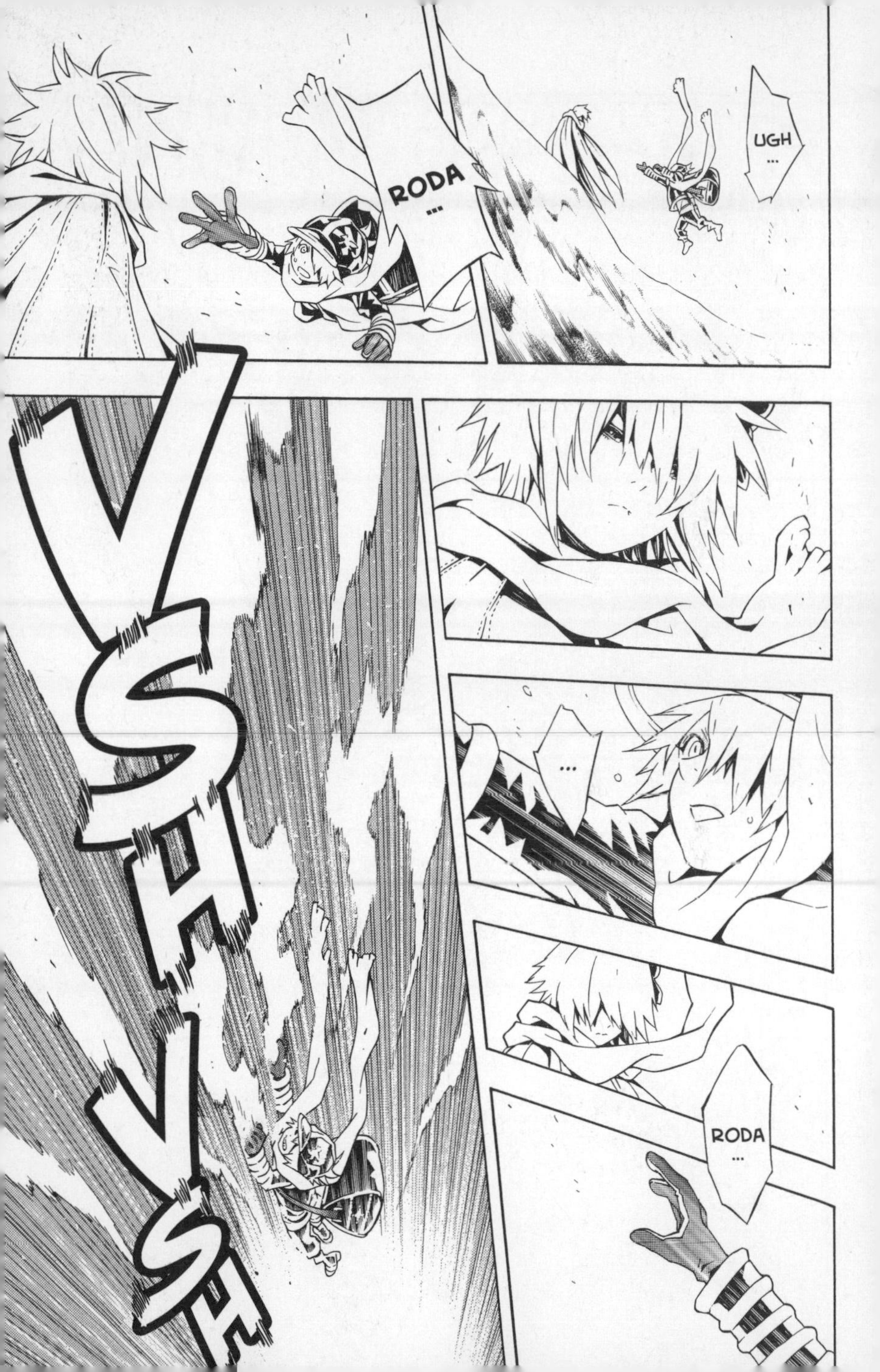
UGH ...
RODA ...
VSH
...
RODA ...
VSH

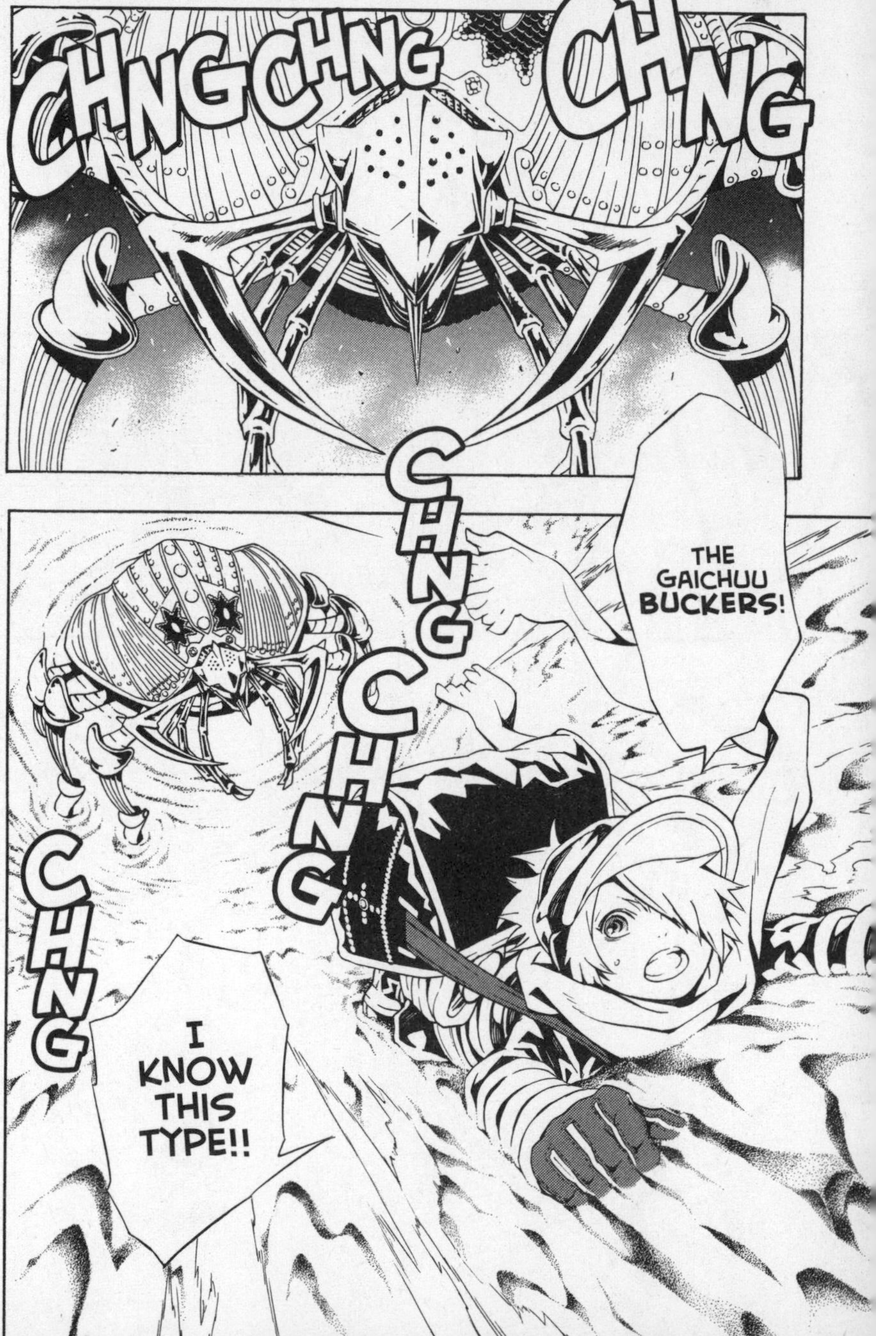
CHNG
CHNGCHNG
THE GAICHUU BUCKERS!
CHNG
CHNG
CHNG
I KNOW THIS TYPE!!

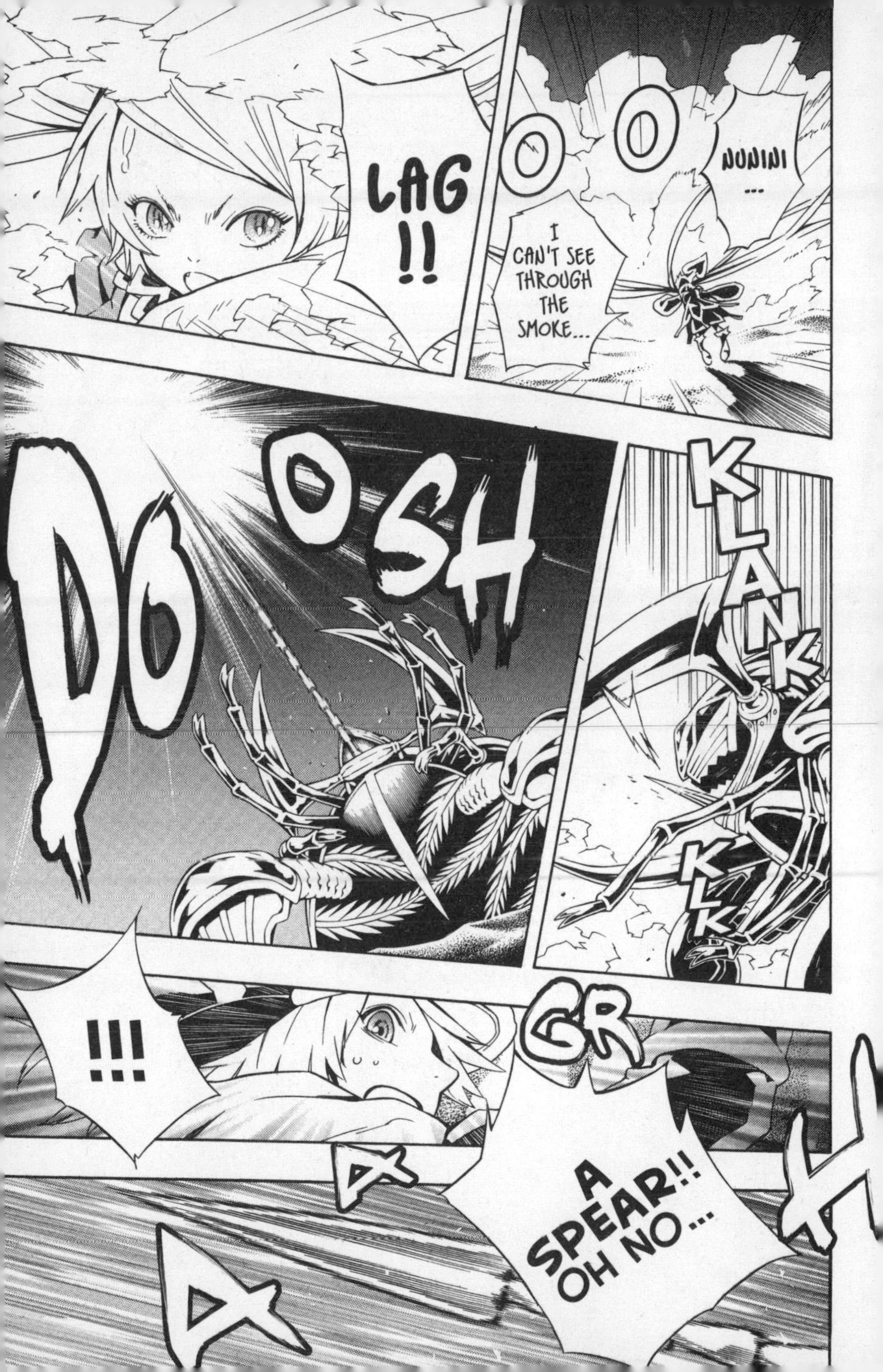
NUNINI ...
OO
I CAN'T SEE THROUGH THE SMOKE...
LAG!!
KLANK
KLK
DOOSH
GR
!!!
A SPEAR!! OH NO...

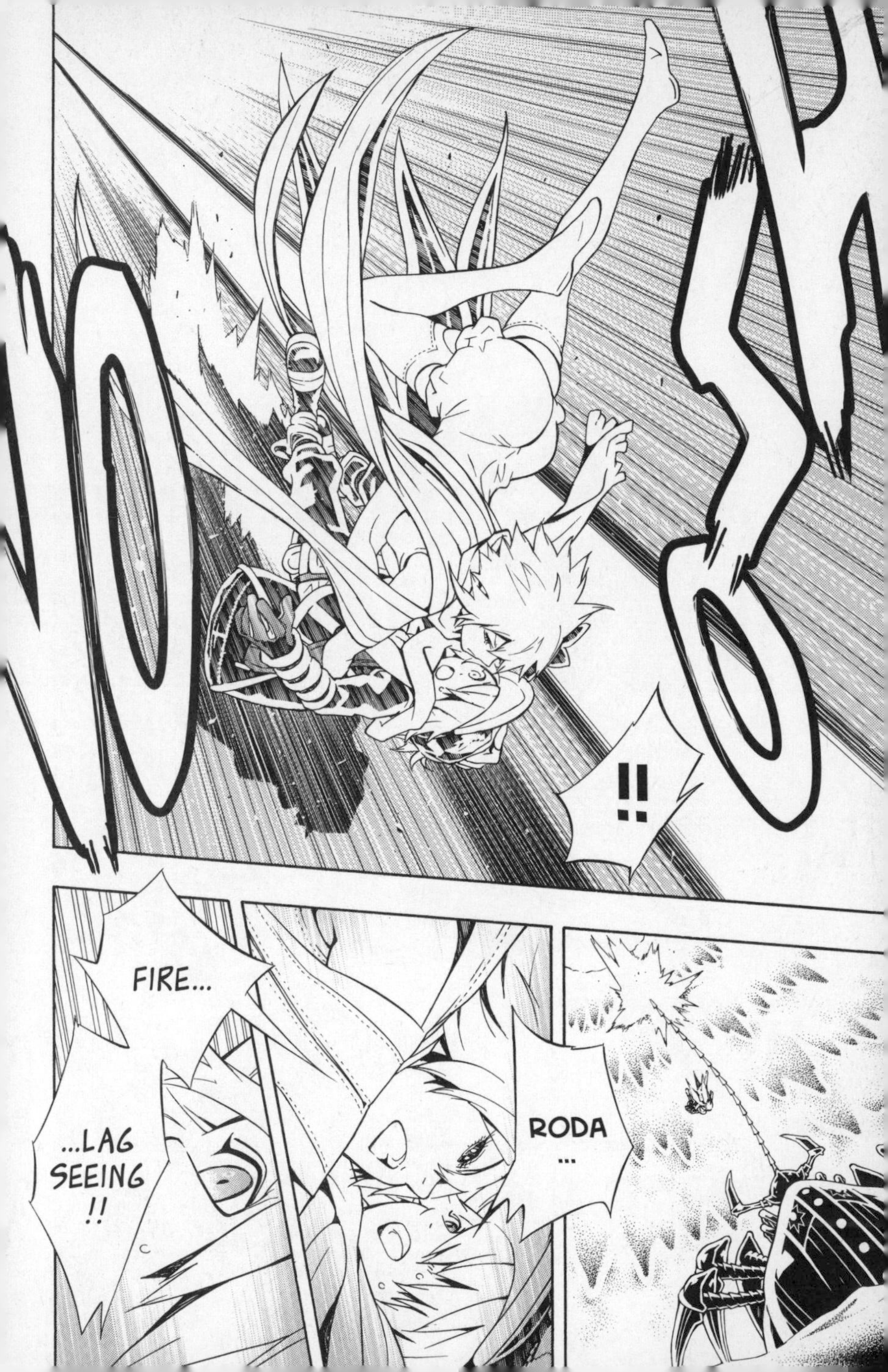
!!
RODA
...
FIRE...
...LAG SEEING !!

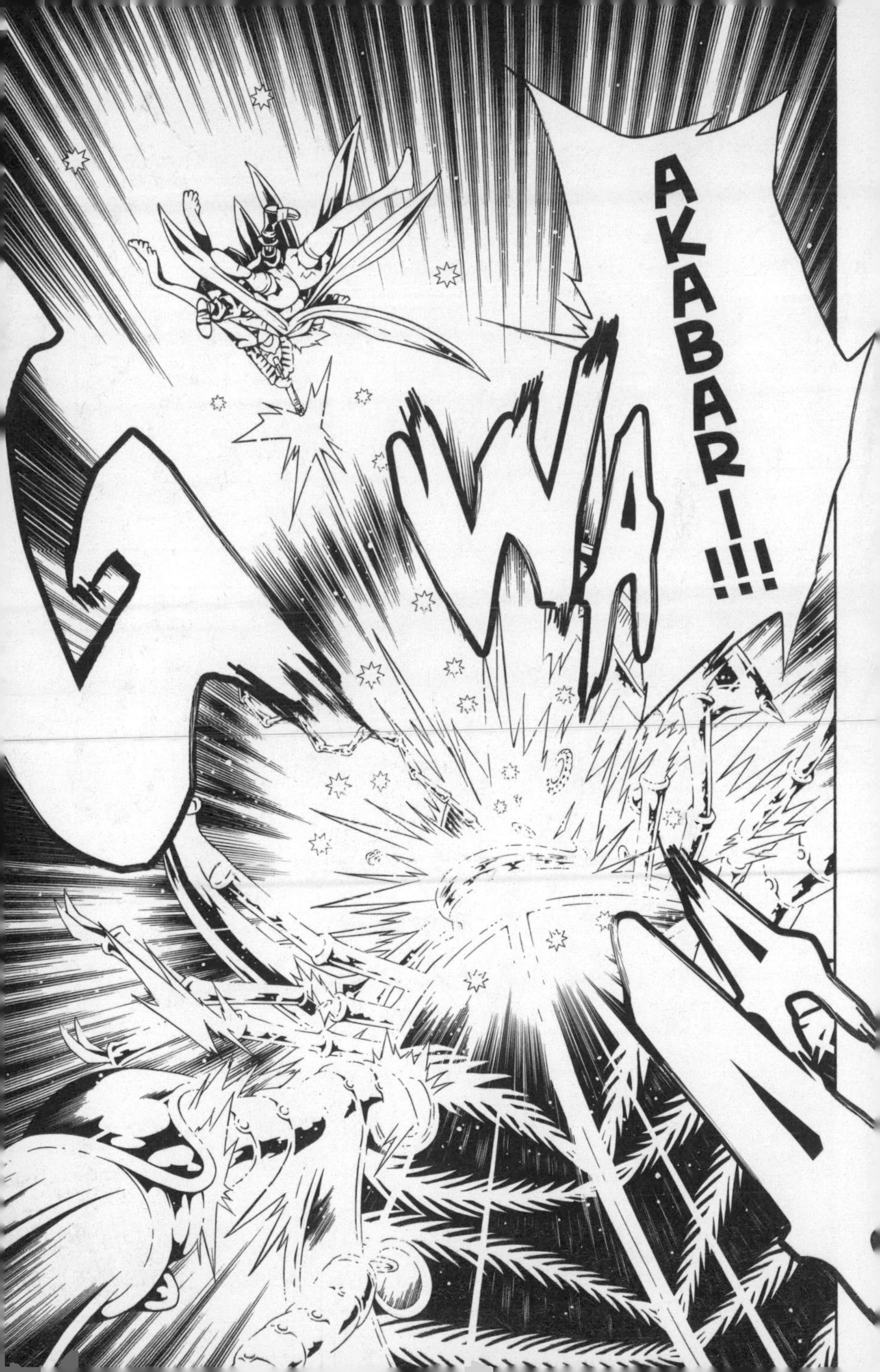
AKABARI!!!

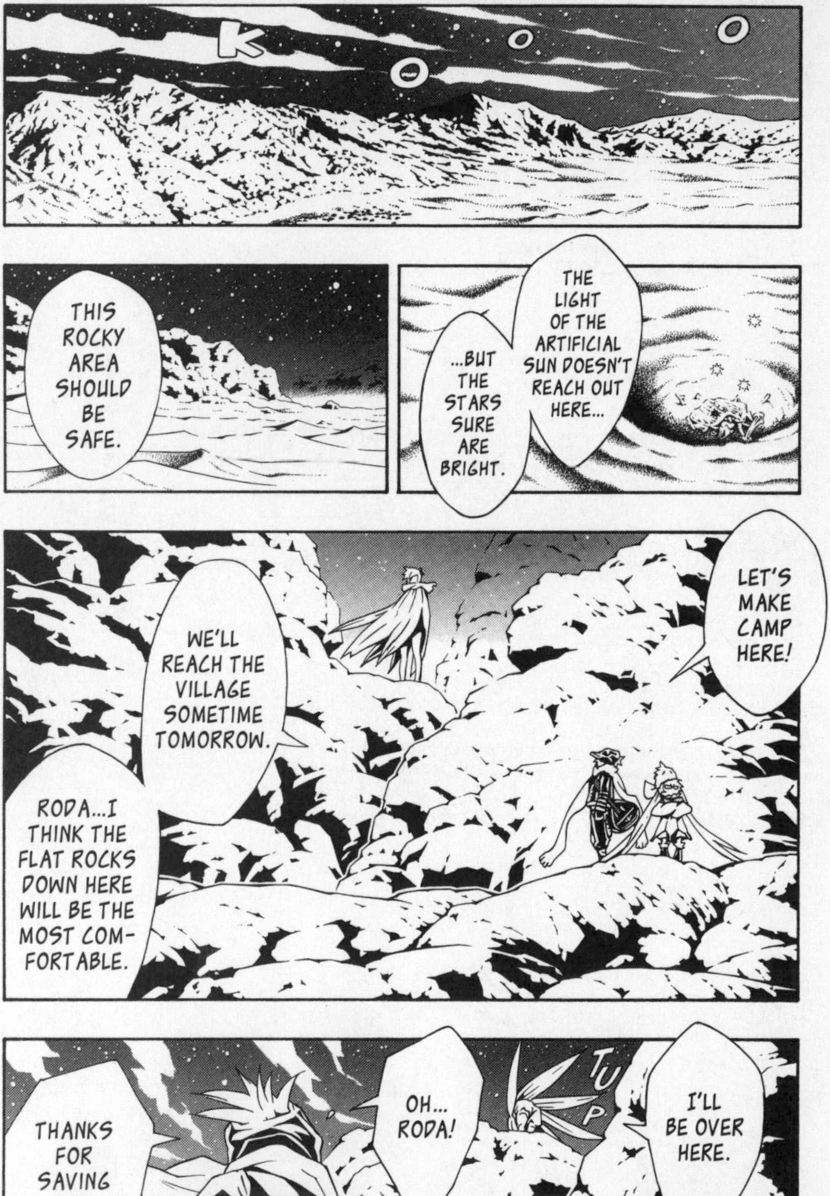
KOOO
THE LIGHT OF THE ARTIFICIAL SUN DOESN'T REACH OUT HERE...
...BUT THE STARS SURE ARE BRIGHT.
THIS ROCKY AREA SHOULD BE SAFE.
LET'S MAKE CAMP HERE!
WE'LL REACH THE VILLAGE SOMETIME TOMORROW.
RODA...I THINK THE FLAT ROCKS DOWN HERE WILL BE THE MOST COM-FORTABLE.
I'LL BE OVER HERE.
TUP
OH... RODA!
THANKS FOR SAVING ME TODAY!

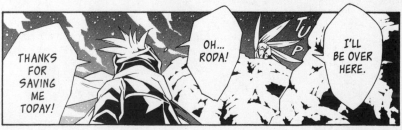

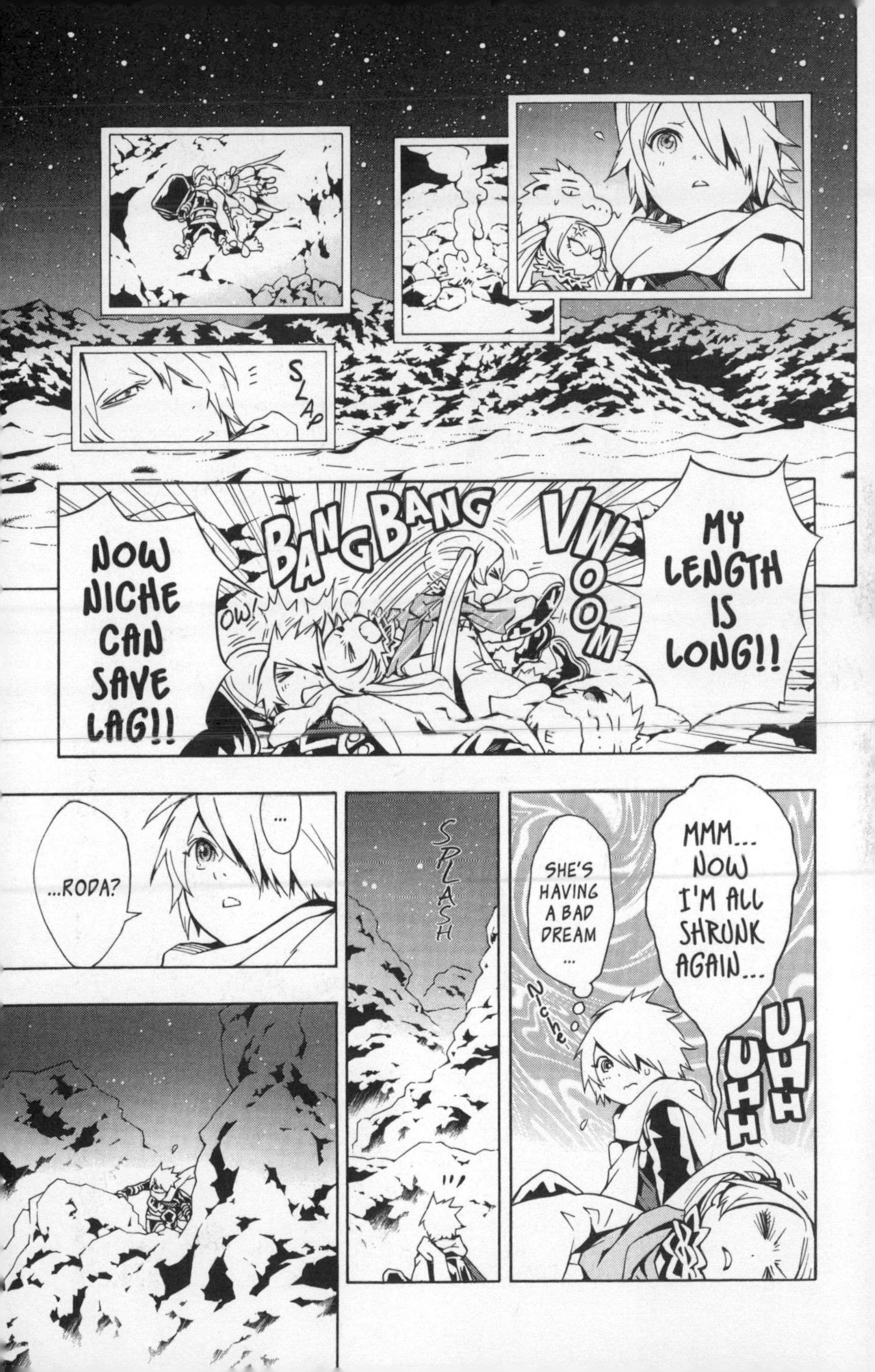
SLAP
MY LENGTH IS LONG!!
VWOOOM
BANG BANG
OW!
NOW NICHE CAN SAVE LAG!!
MMM... NOW I'M ALL SHRUNK AGAIN...
SHE'S HAVING A BAD DREAM ...
Niche
UHH UHH
SPLASH
...
...RODA?

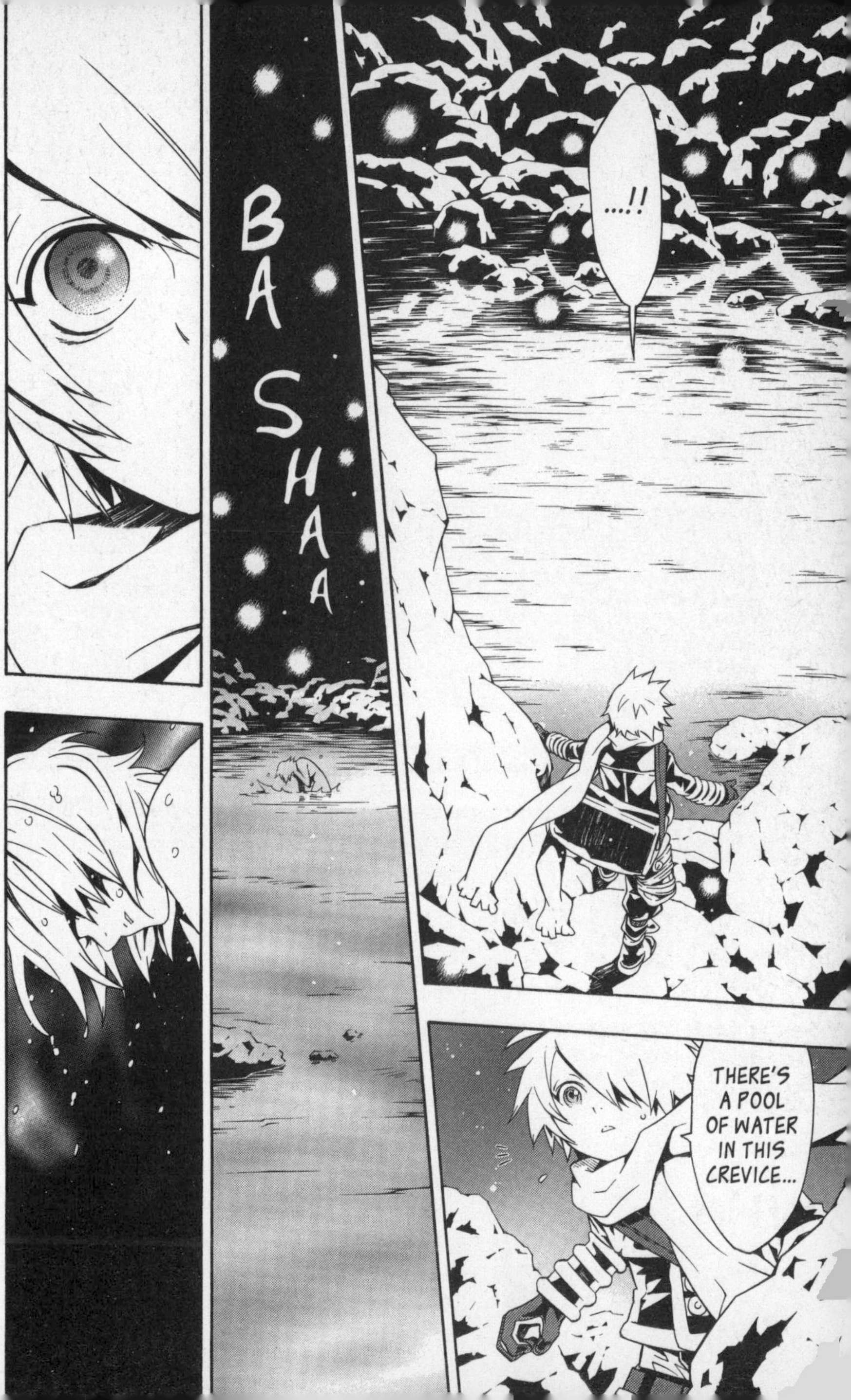
...!!
BA SHAA
THERE'S A POOL OF WATER IN THIS CREVICE...

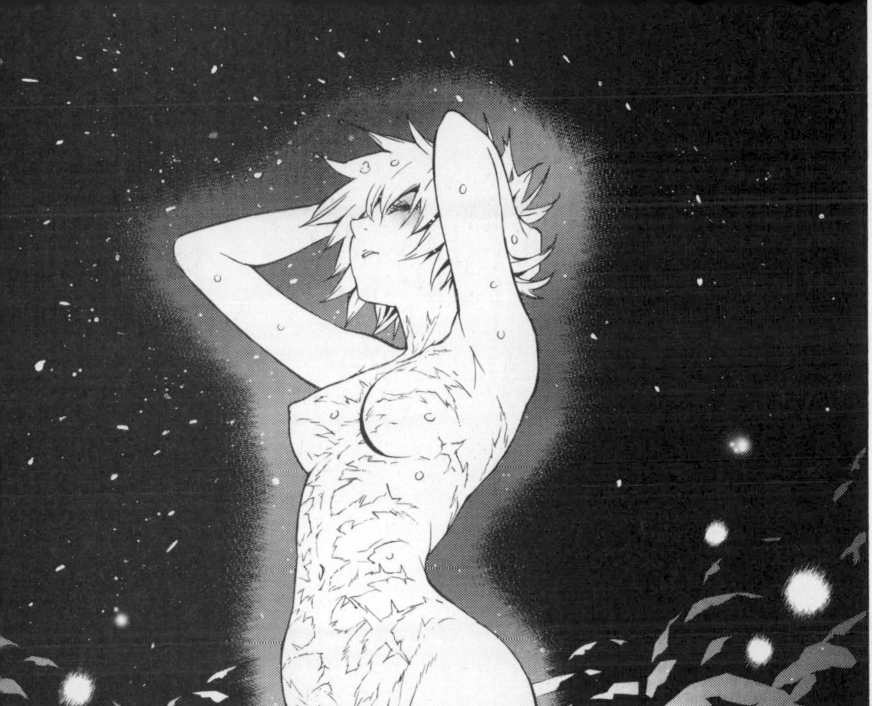

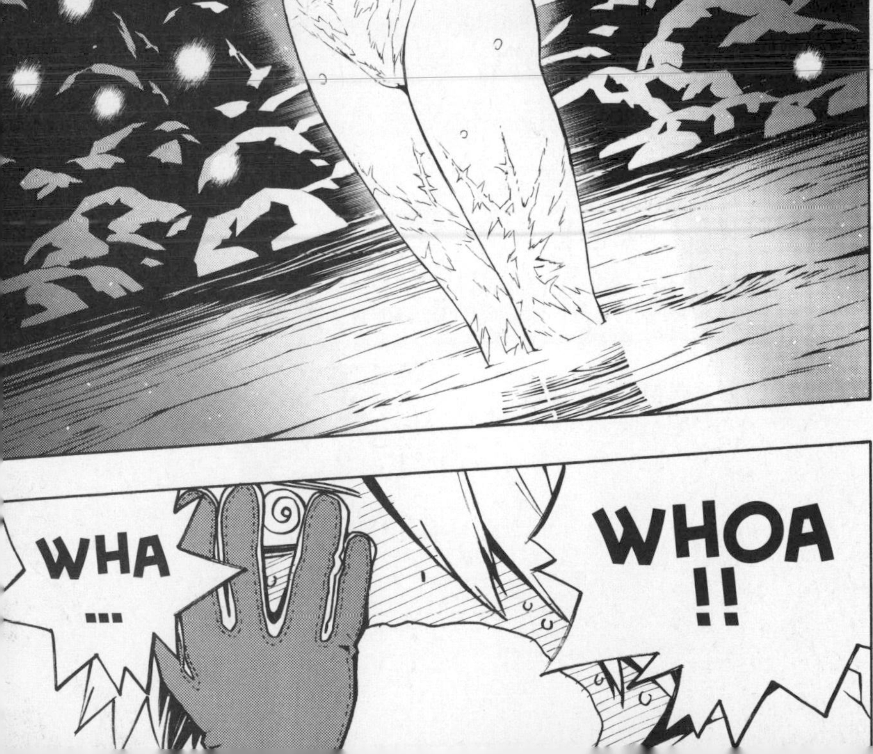
WHOA !!
WHA ...

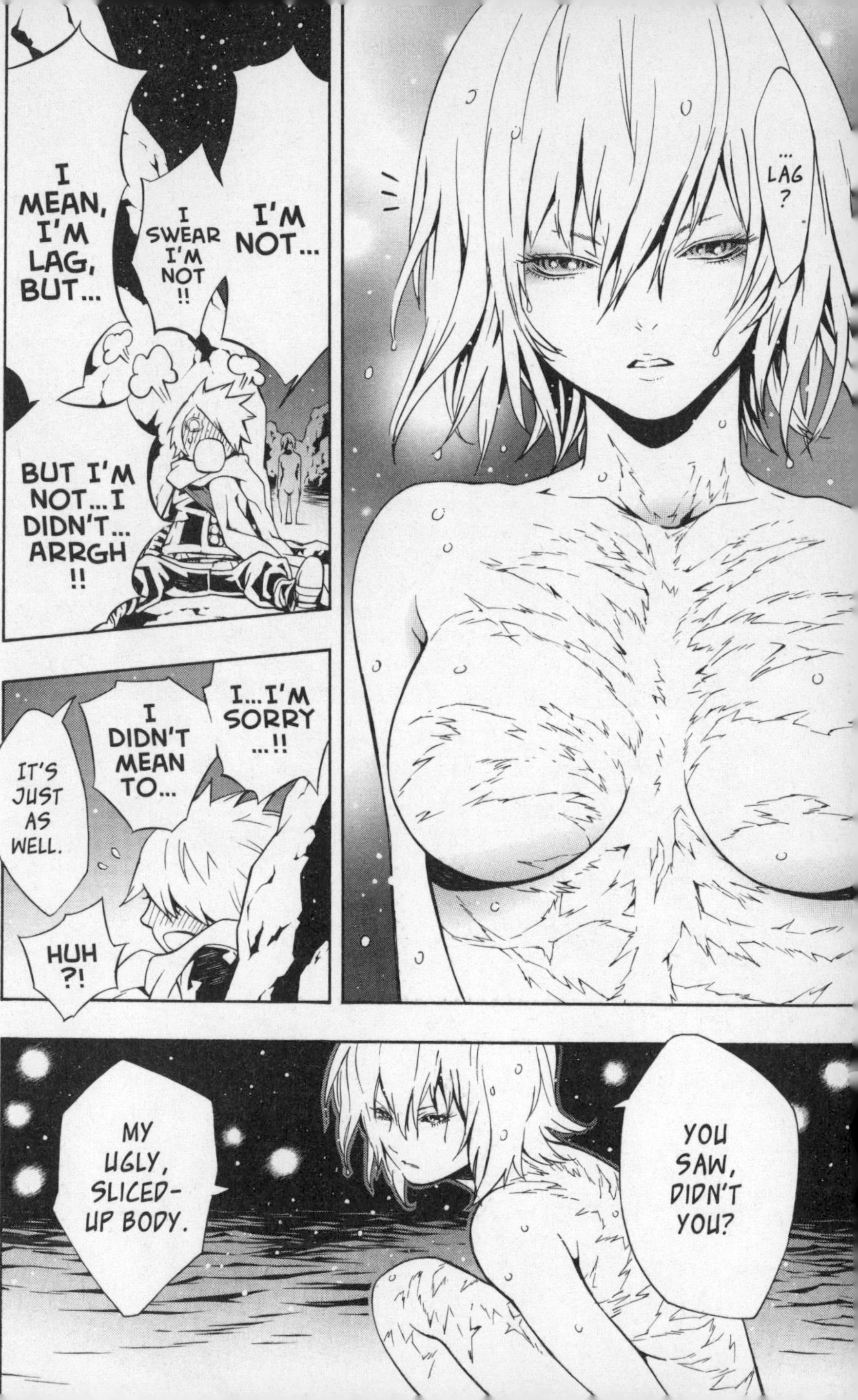
...LAG?
I'M NOT...
I SWEAR I'M NOT!!
I MEAN, I'M LAG, BUT...
BUT I'M NOT... I DIDN'T... ARRGH!!
I...I'M SORRY...!!
I DIDN'T MEAN TO...
IT'S JUST AS WELL.
HUH?!
YOU SAW, DIDN'T YOU?
MY UGLY, SLICED-UP BODY.

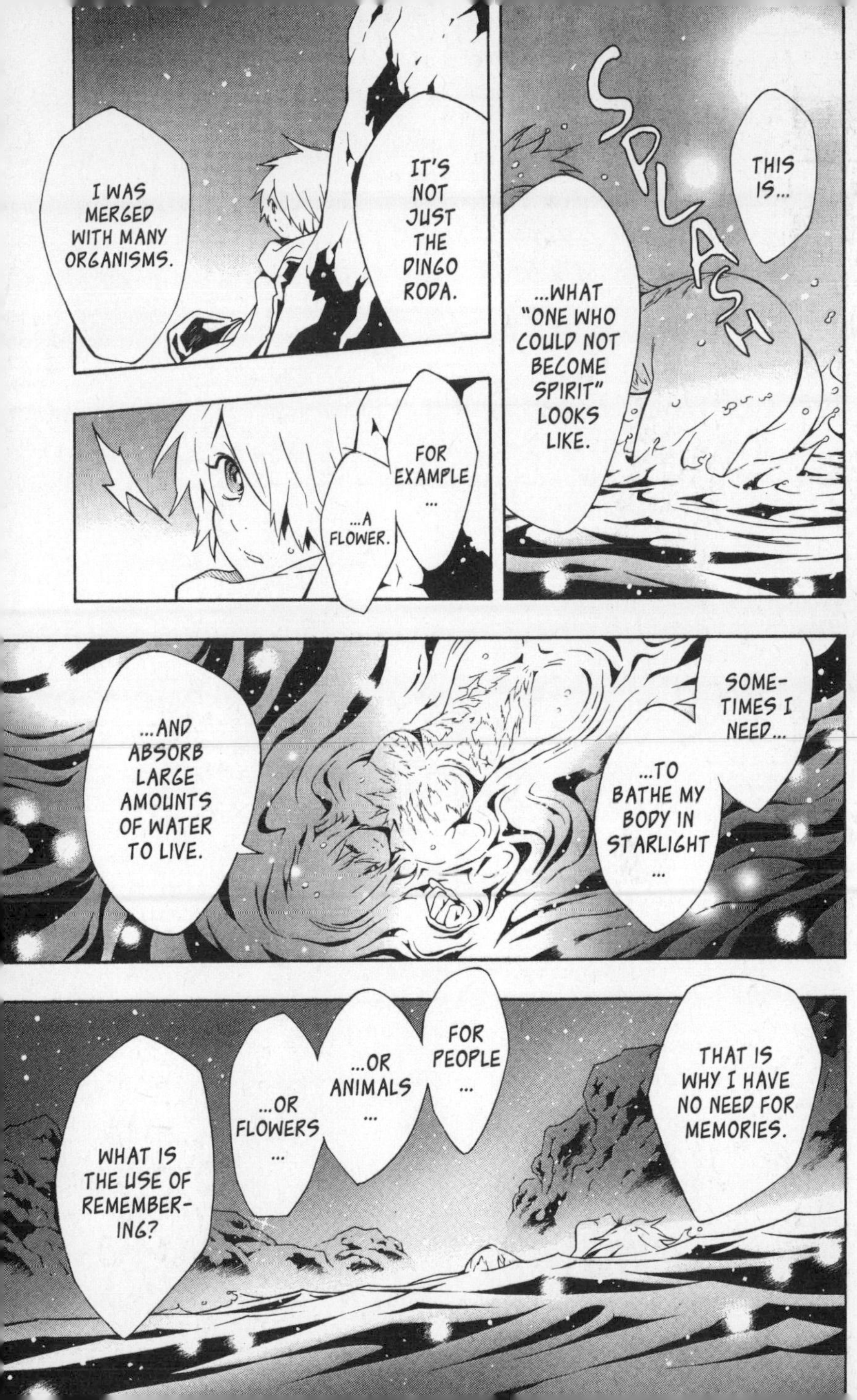
THIS IS...
SPLASH
...WHAT "ONE WHO COULD NOT BECOME SPIRIT" LOOKS LIKE.
IT'S NOT JUST THE DINGO RODA.
I WAS MERGED WITH MANY ORGANISMS.
FOR EXAMPLE...
...A FLOWER.
SOME-TIMES I NEED...
...TO BATHE MY BODY IN STARLIGHT...
...AND ABSORB LARGE AMOUNTS OF WATER TO LIVE.
THAT IS WHY I HAVE NO NEED FOR MEMORIES.
FOR PEOPLE...
...OR ANIMALS...
...OR FLOWERS...
WHAT IS THE USE OF REMEMBER-ING?

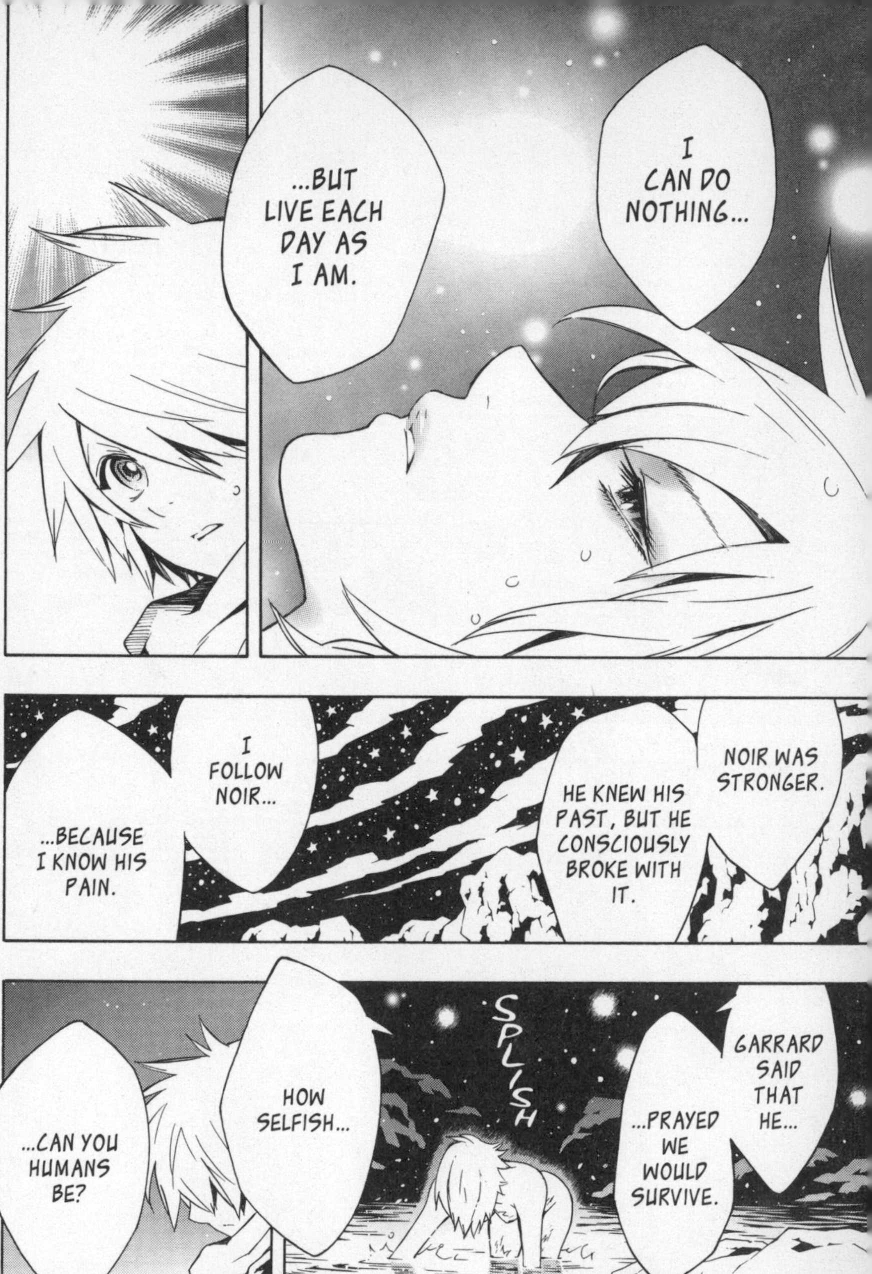
I CAN DO NOTHING...
...BUT LIVE EACH DAY AS I AM.
NOIR WAS STRONGER.
HE KNEW HIS PAST, BUT HE CONSCIOUSLY BROKE WITH IT.
I FOLLOW NOIR...
...BECAUSE I KNOW HIS PAIN.
GARRARD SAID THAT HE...
...PRAYED WE WOULD SURVIVE.
SPLISH
HOW SELFISH...
...CAN YOU HUMANS BE?

I'M SORRY!!

...I'M HAPPY...

...I...

I'M SORRY...

...BUT STILL...

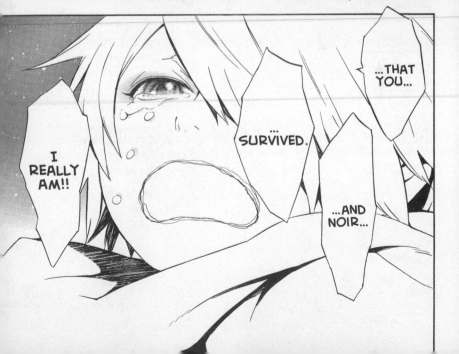

...THAT YOU...

...SURVIVED.

I REALLY AM!!

...AND NOIR...

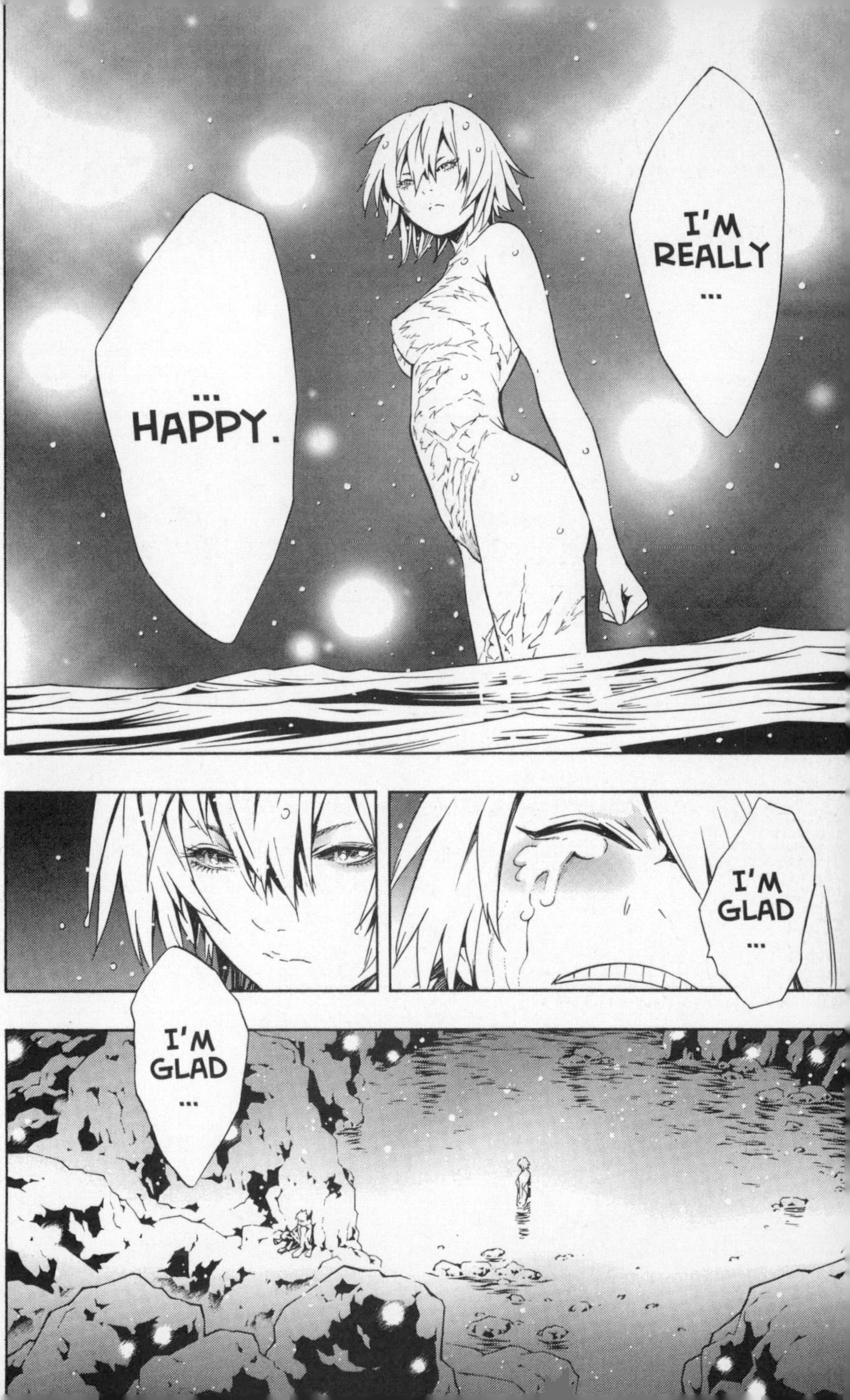
I'M REALLY ...
... HAPPY.
I'M GLAD ...
I'M GLAD ...

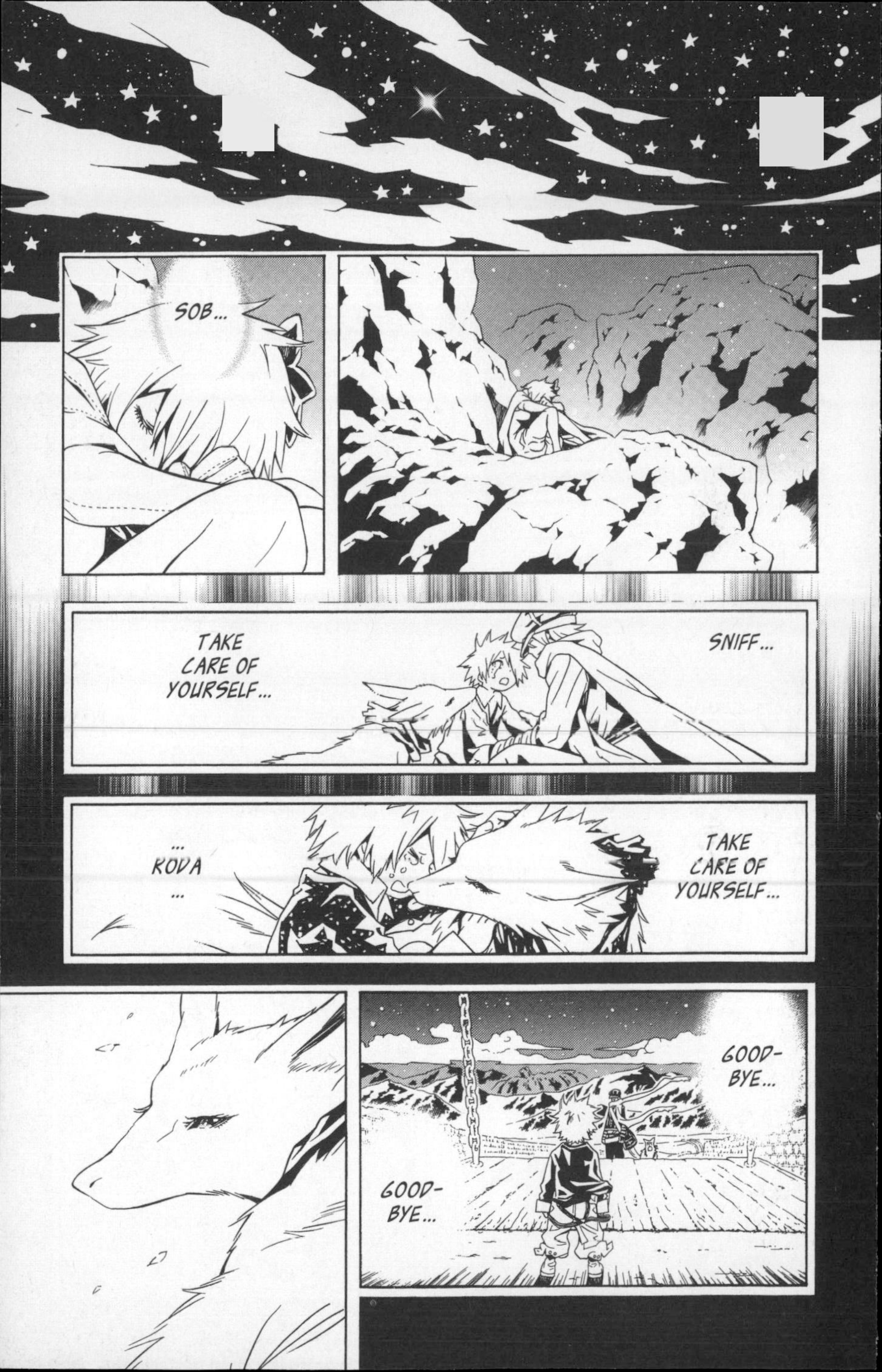
SOB...
SNIFF...
TAKE CARE OF YOURSELF...
TAKE CARE OF YOURSELF...
... RODA ...
GOOD-BYE...
GOOD-BYE...

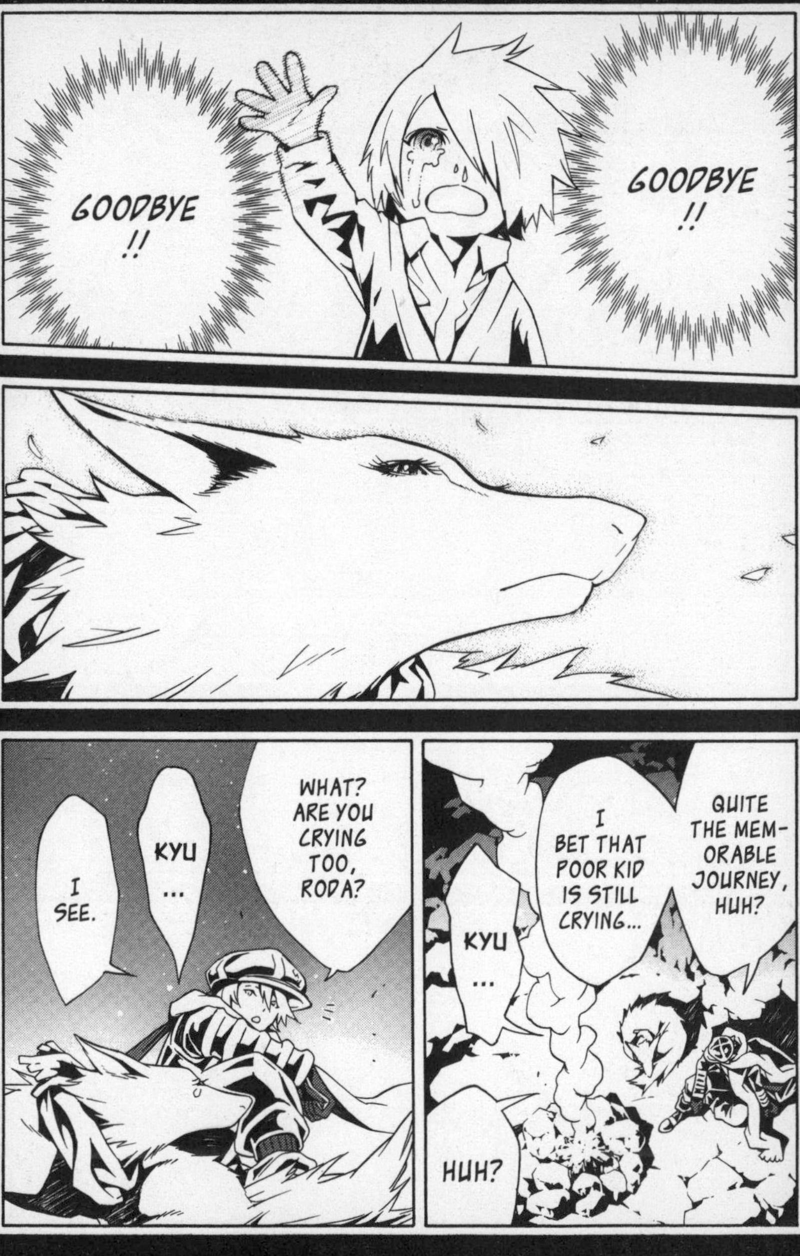
GOODBYE !!
GOODBYE !!
QUITE THE MEMORABLE JOURNEY, HUH?
I BET THAT POOR KID IS STILL CRYING...
KYU ...
HUH?
WHAT? ARE YOU CRYING TOO, RODA?
KYU ...
I SEE.

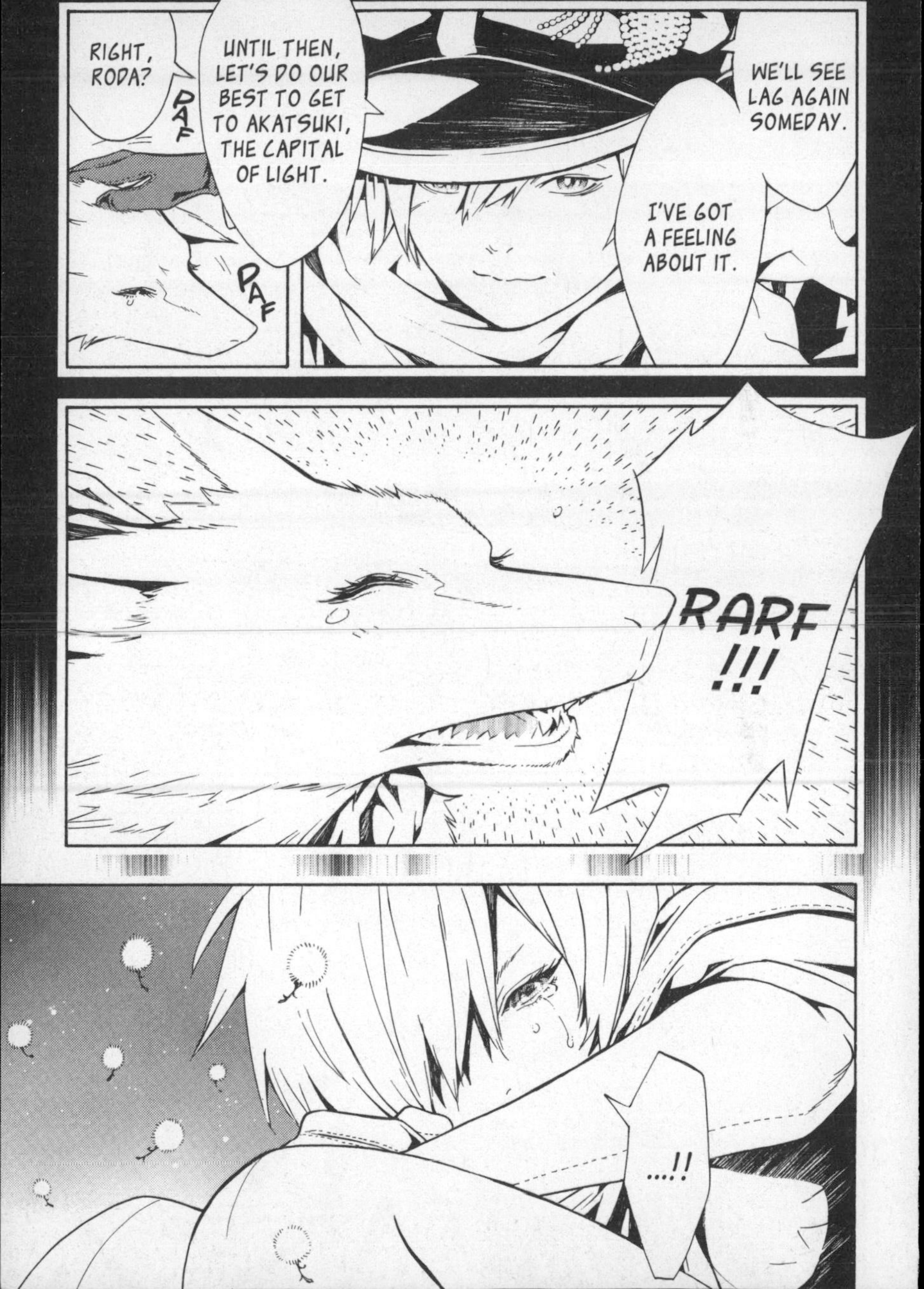
WE'LL SEE LAG AGAIN SOMEDAY.
I'VE GOT A FEELING ABOUT IT.
UNTIL THEN, LET'S DO OUR BEST TO GET TO AKATSUKI, THE CAPITAL OF LIGHT.
RIGHT, RODA?
PAF
PAF
RARF !!!
...!!

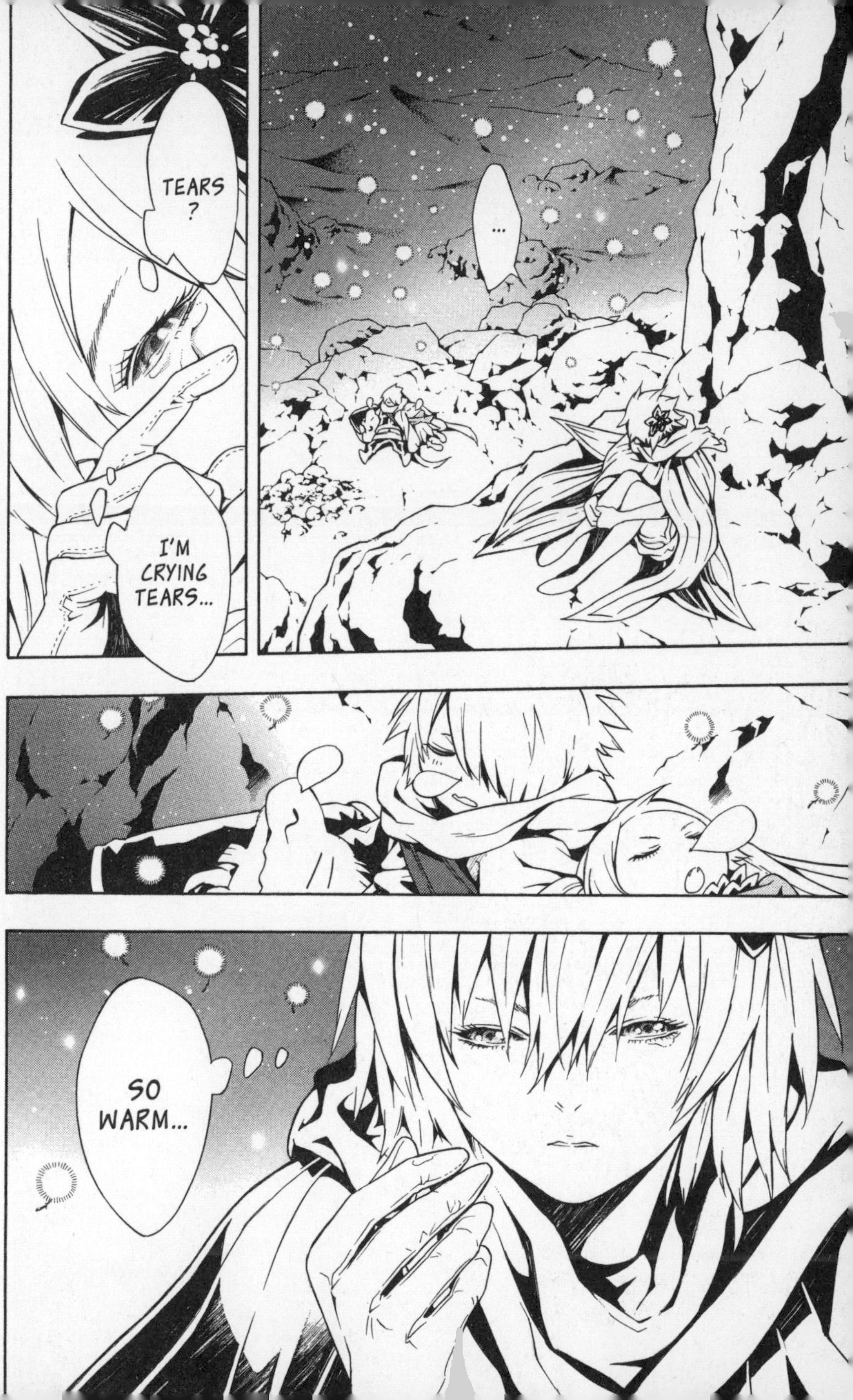
...
TEARS?
I'M CRYING TEARS...
SO WARM...

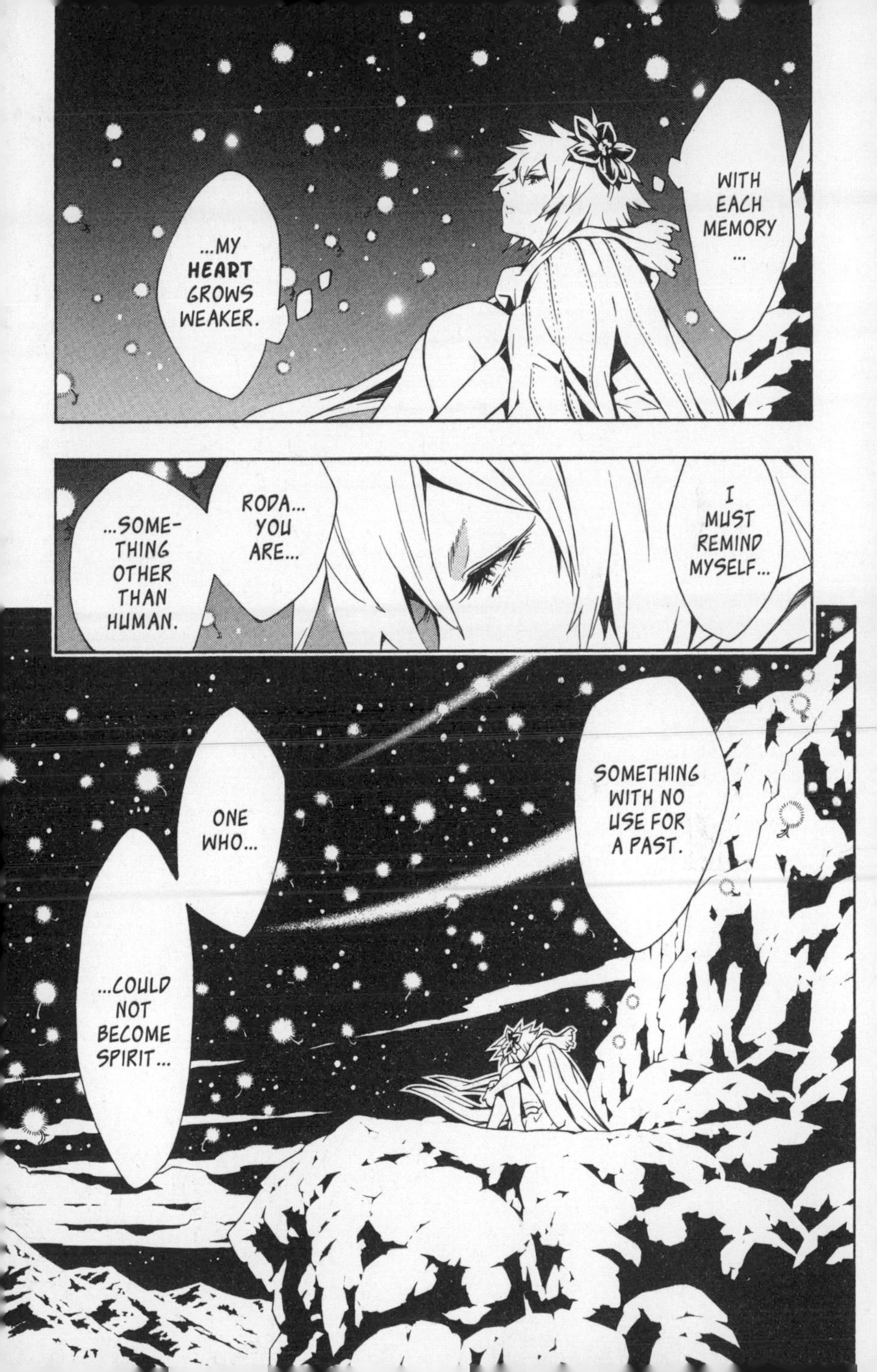
WITH EACH MEMORY ...
...MY **HEART** GROWS WEAKER.
I MUST REMIND MYSELF...
RODA... YOU ARE...
...SOME-THING OTHER THAN HUMAN.
SOMETHING WITH NO USE FOR A PAST.
ONE WHO...
...COULD NOT BECOME SPIRIT...

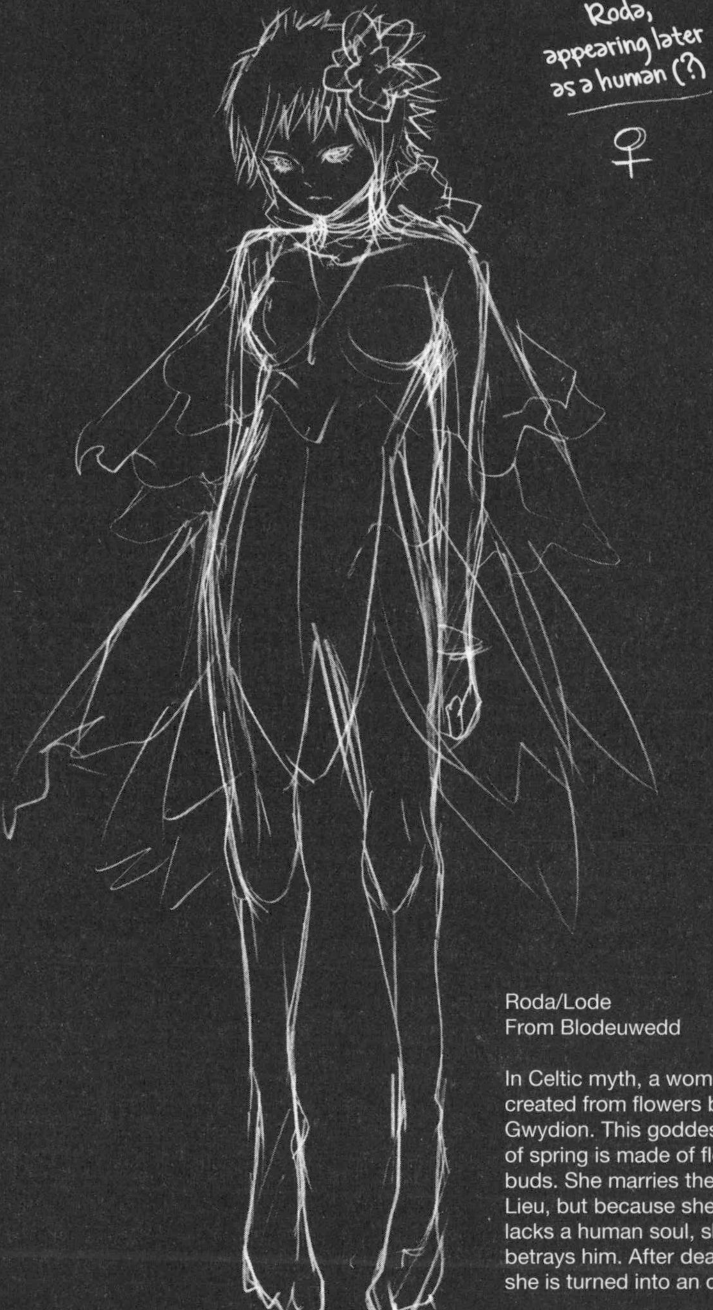
Roda, appearing later as a human (?)
♀

Roda/Lode
From Blodeuwedd

In Celtic myth, a woman created from flowers by Gwydion. This goddess of spring is made of flower buds. She marries the hero Lieu, but because she lacks a human soul, she betrays him. After death, she is turned into an owl.

Early rough sketch of Roda.

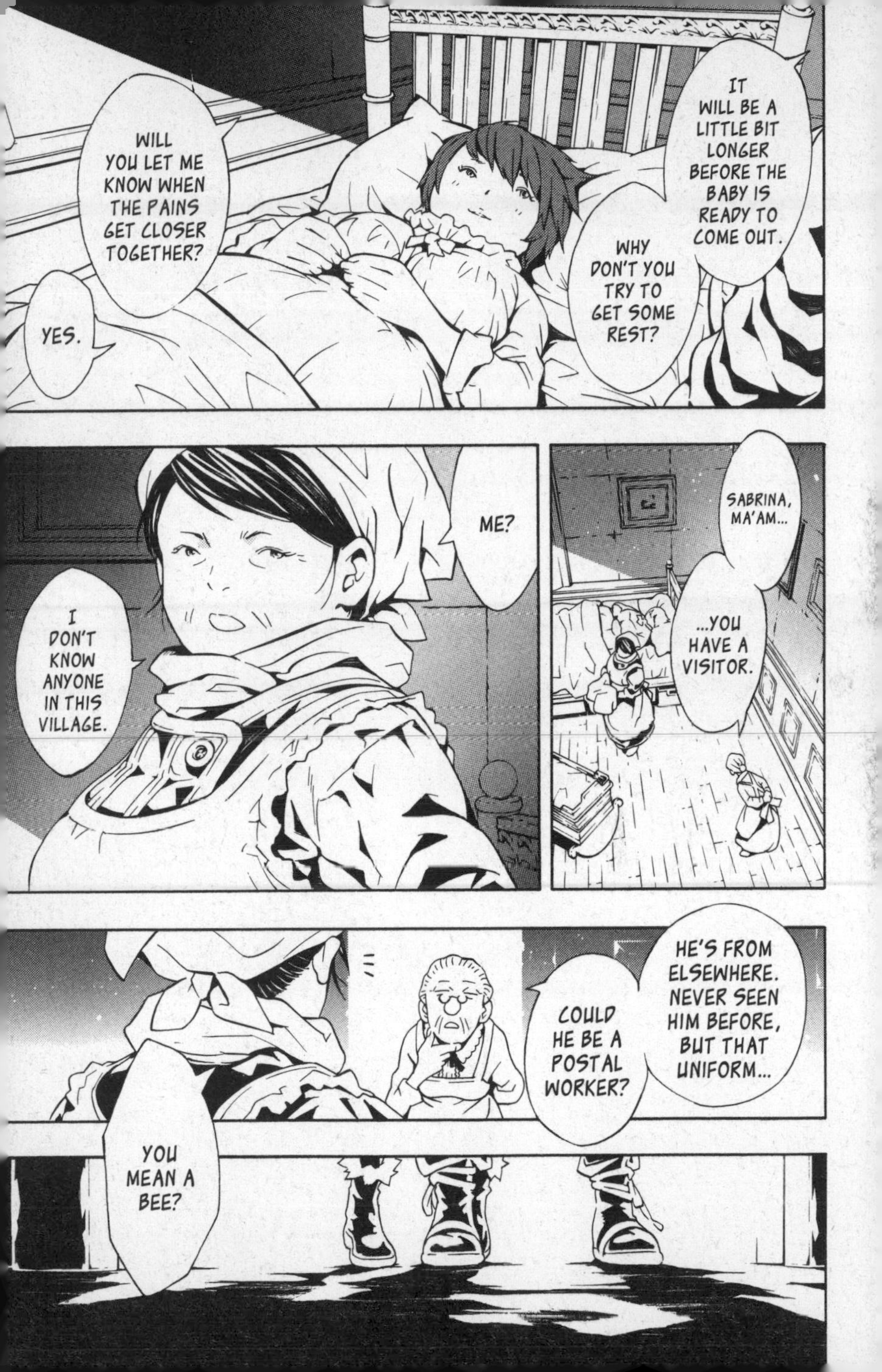
IT WILL BE A LITTLE BIT LONGER BEFORE THE BABY IS READY TO COME OUT.
WHY DON'T YOU TRY TO GET SOME REST?
WILL YOU LET ME KNOW WHEN THE PAINS GET CLOSER TOGETHER?
YES.
SABRINA, MA'AM...
...YOU HAVE A VISITOR.
ME?
I DON'T KNOW ANYONE IN THIS VILLAGE.
HE'S FROM ELSEWHERE. NEVER SEEN HIM BEFORE, BUT THAT UNIFORM...
COULD HE BE A POSTAL WORKER?
YOU MEAN A BEE?

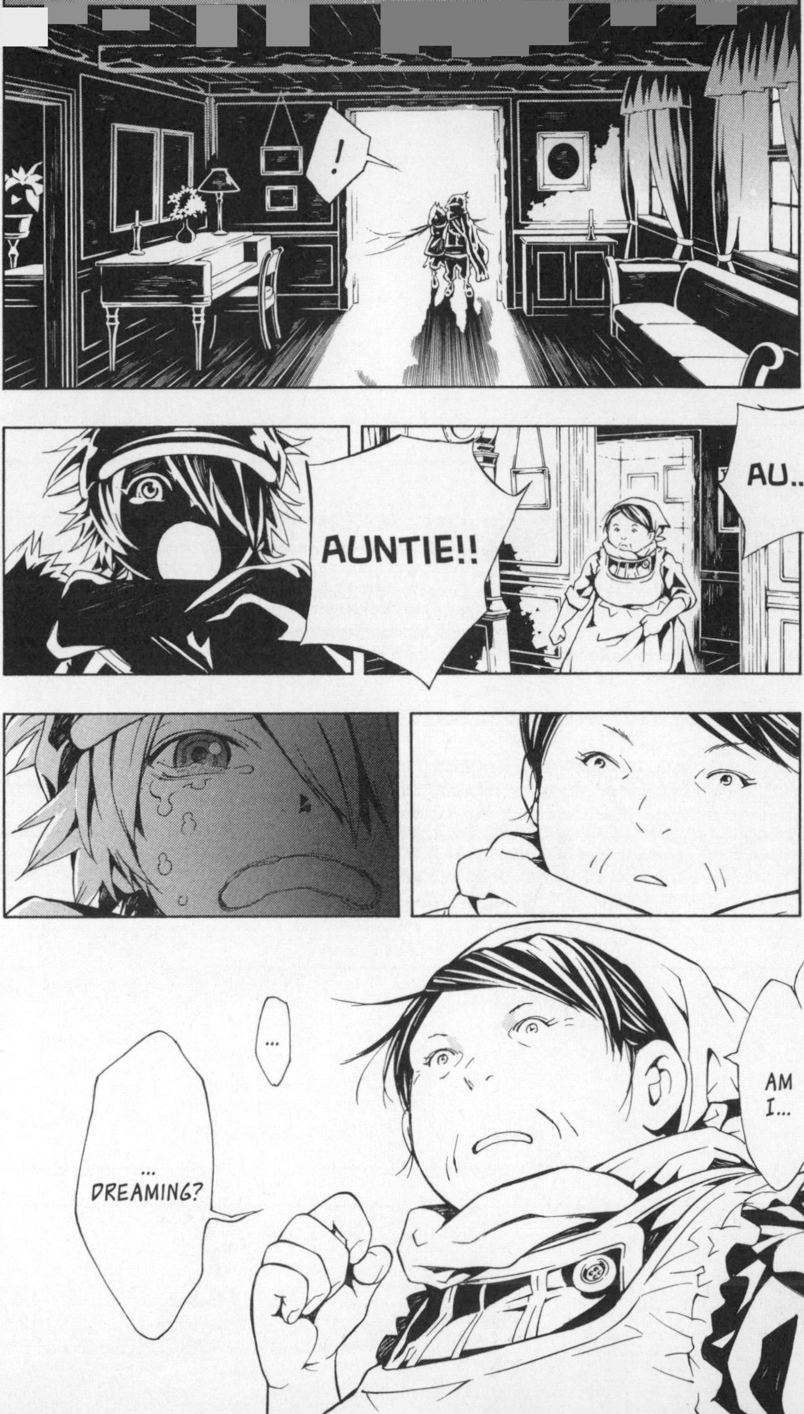
!
AU...
AUNTIE!!
...
AM I...
...
... DREAMING?

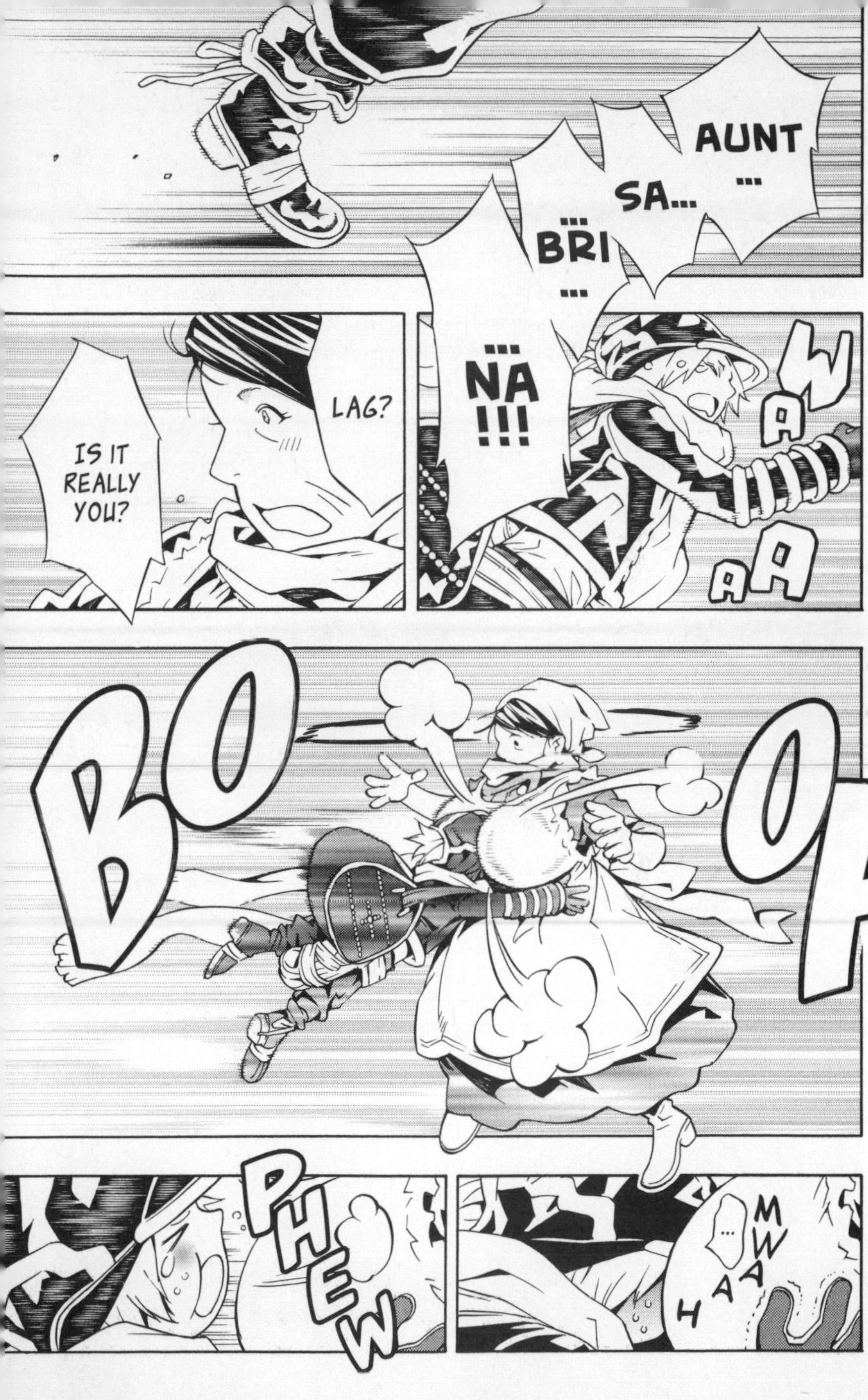
AUNT ...
SA...
... BRI ...
... NÄ !!!
WAAAA
LAG?
IS IT REALLY YOU?
BOOF
...
MWAAH
PHEW

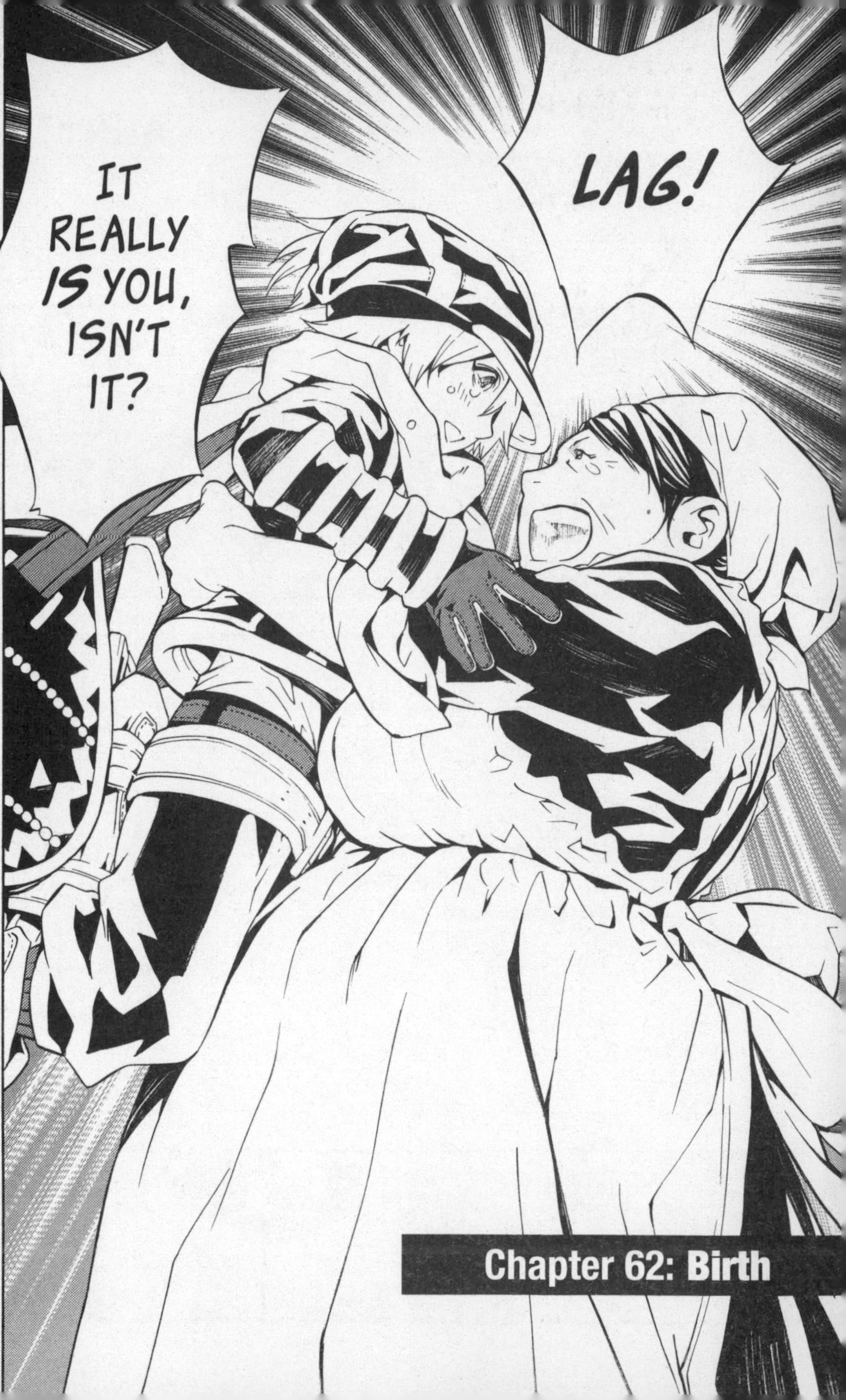
LAG!
IT REALLY *IS* YOU, ISN'T IT?

Chapter 62: Birth

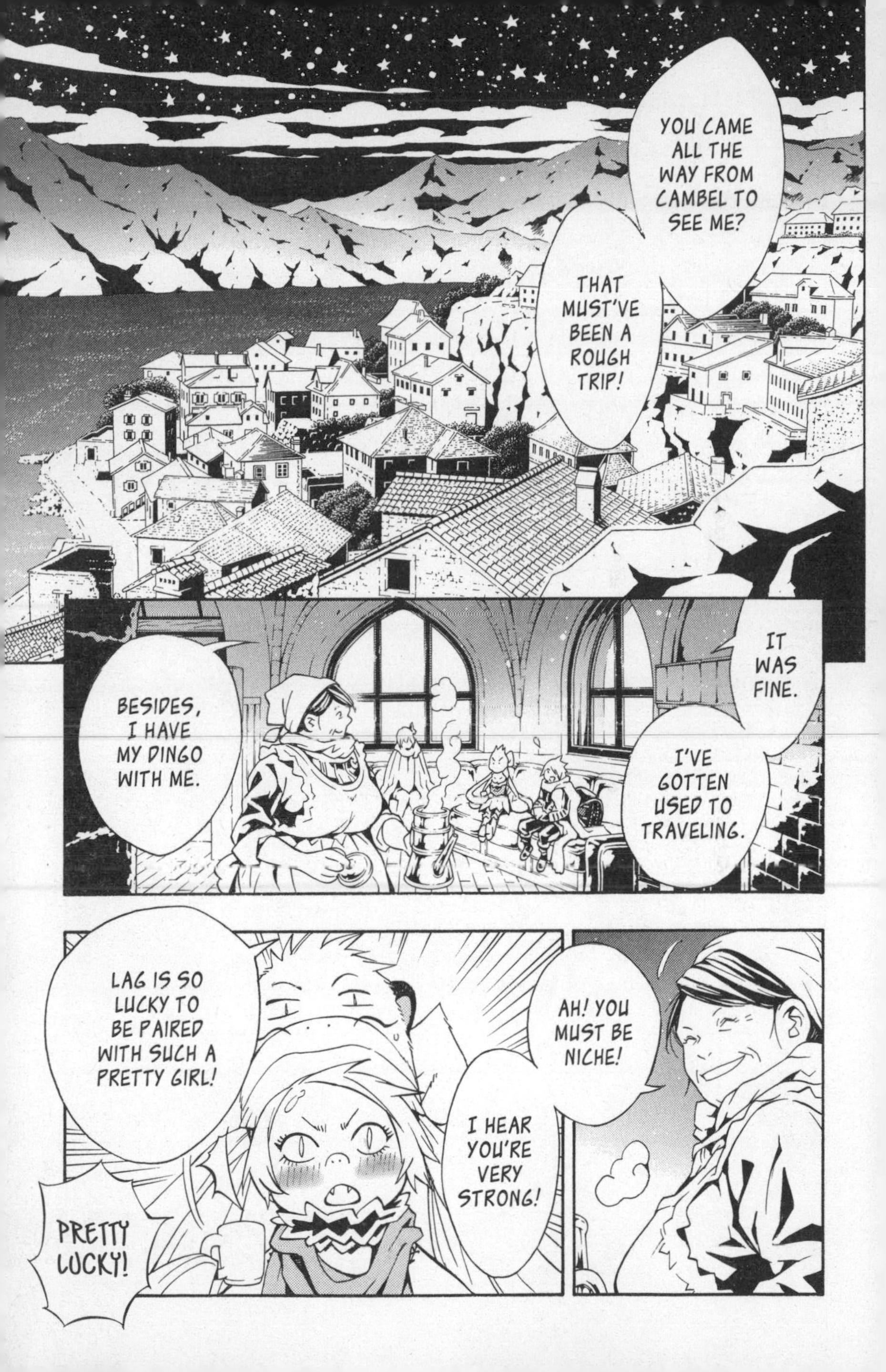
YOU CAME ALL THE WAY FROM CAMBEL TO SEE ME?
THAT MUST'VE BEEN A ROUGH TRIP!
IT WAS FINE.
I'VE GOTTEN USED TO TRAVELING.
BESIDES, I HAVE MY DINGO WITH ME.
AH! YOU MUST BE NICHE!
I HEAR YOU'RE VERY STRONG!
LAG IS SO LUCKY TO BE PAIRED WITH SUCH A PRETTY GIRL!
PRETTY LUCKY!

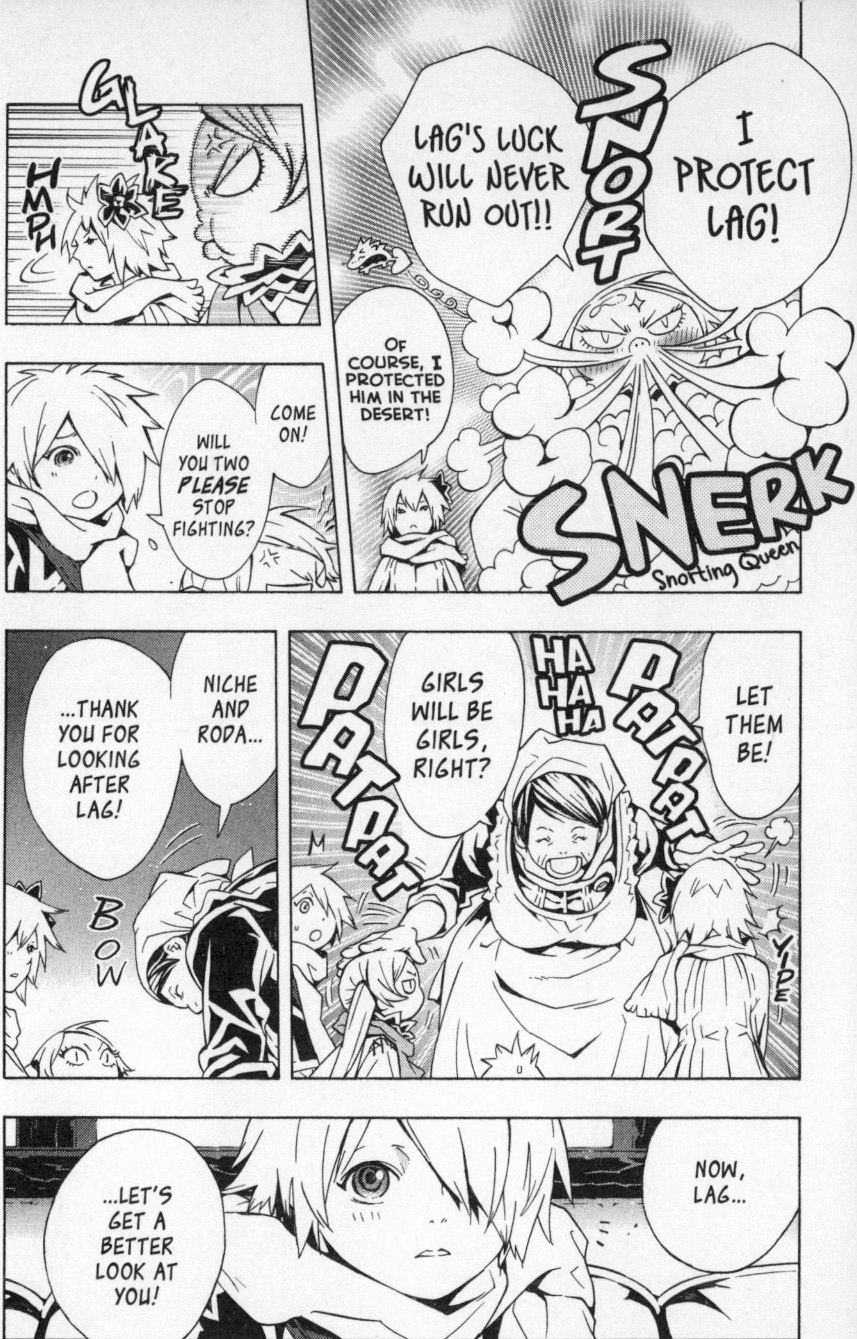
I PROTECT LAG!
SNORT
LAG'S LUCK WILL NEVER RUN OUT!!
OF COURSE, I PROTECTED HIM IN THE DESERT!
SNERK
Snotting Queen
GLAKE
HMPH
COME ON!
WILL YOU TWO PLEASE STOP FIGHTING?
LET THEM BE!
PATPAT
HA HA HA
GIRLS WILL BE GIRLS, RIGHT?
PATPAT
M
YIPE
NICHE AND RODA...
...THANK YOU FOR LOOKING AFTER LAG!
BOW
NOW, LAG...
...LET'S GET A BETTER LOOK AT YOU!

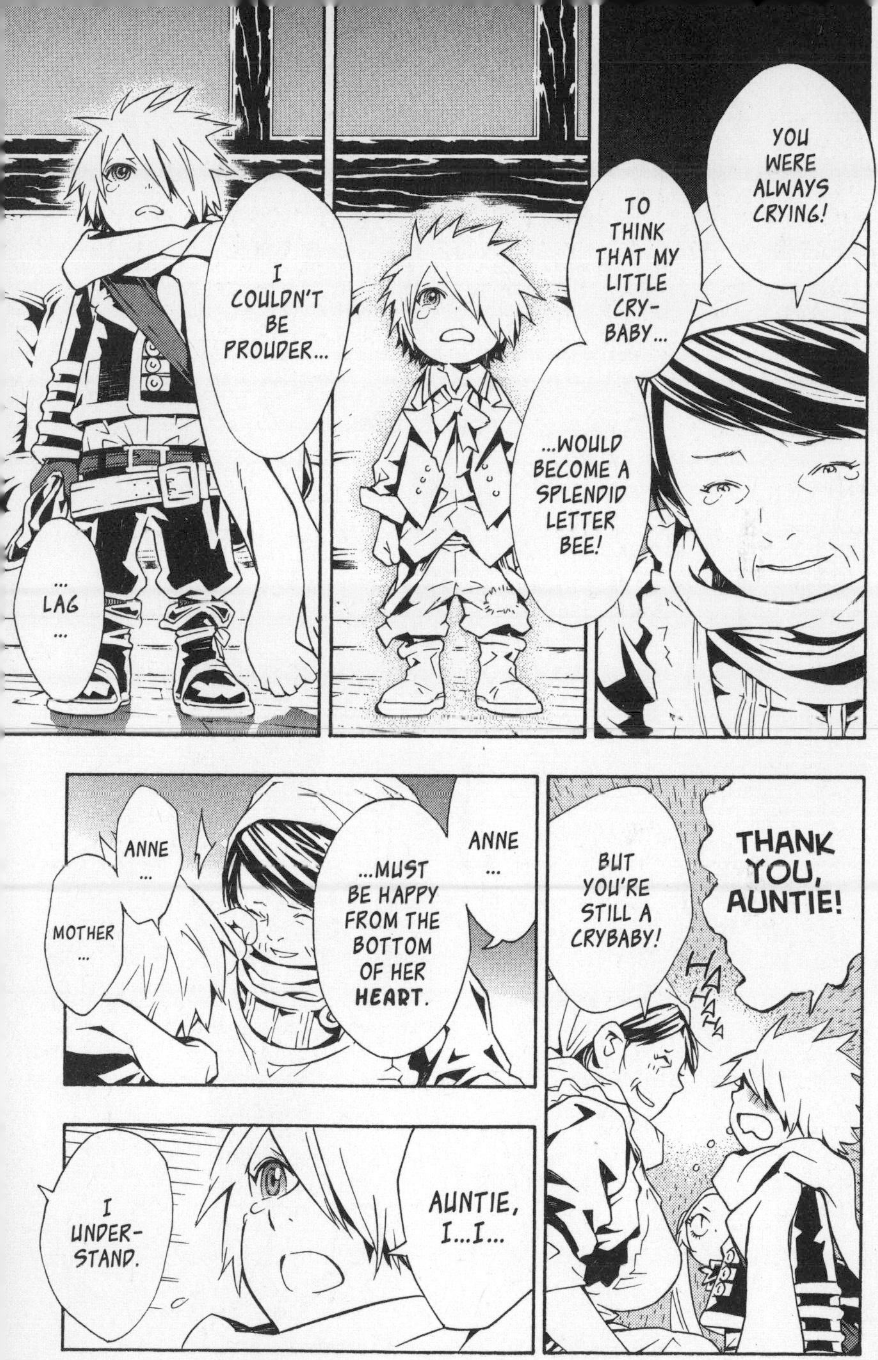
YOU WERE ALWAYS CRYING!
TO THINK THAT MY LITTLE CRY-BABY...
...WOULD BECOME A SPLENDID LETTER BEE!
I COULDN'T BE PROUDER...
...LAG...
THANK YOU, AUNTIE!
BUT YOU'RE STILL A CRYBABY!
HAHAHA
ANNE...
...MUST BE HAPPY FROM THE BOTTOM OF HER HEART.
ANNE...
MOTHER...
AUNTIE, I...I...
I UNDERSTAND.

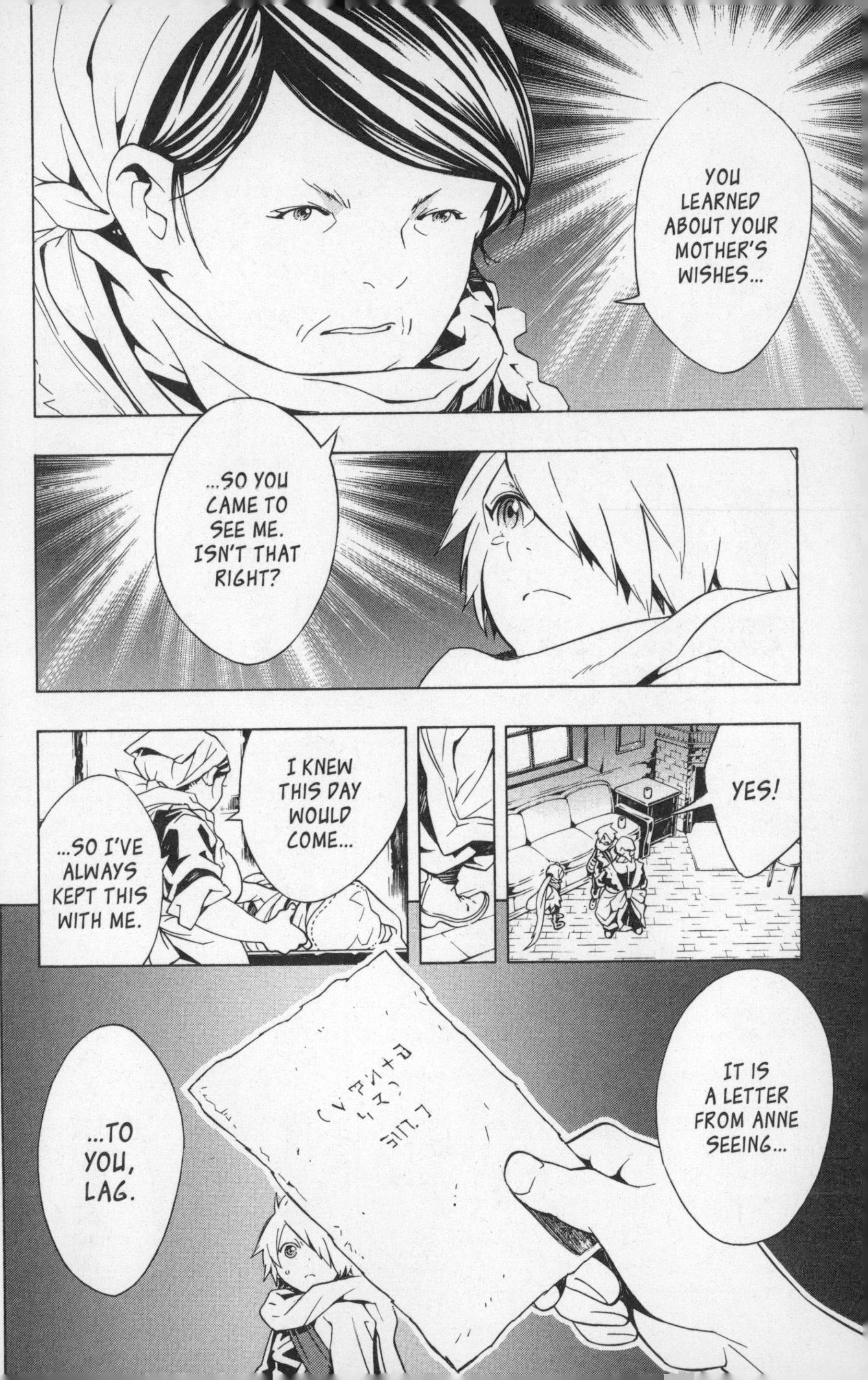
YOU LEARNED ABOUT YOUR MOTHER'S WISHES...
...SO YOU CAME TO SEE ME. ISN'T THAT RIGHT?
YES!
I KNEW THIS DAY WOULD COME...
...SO I'VE ALWAYS KEPT THIS WITH ME.
IT IS A LETTER FROM ANNE SEEING...
...TO YOU, LAG.

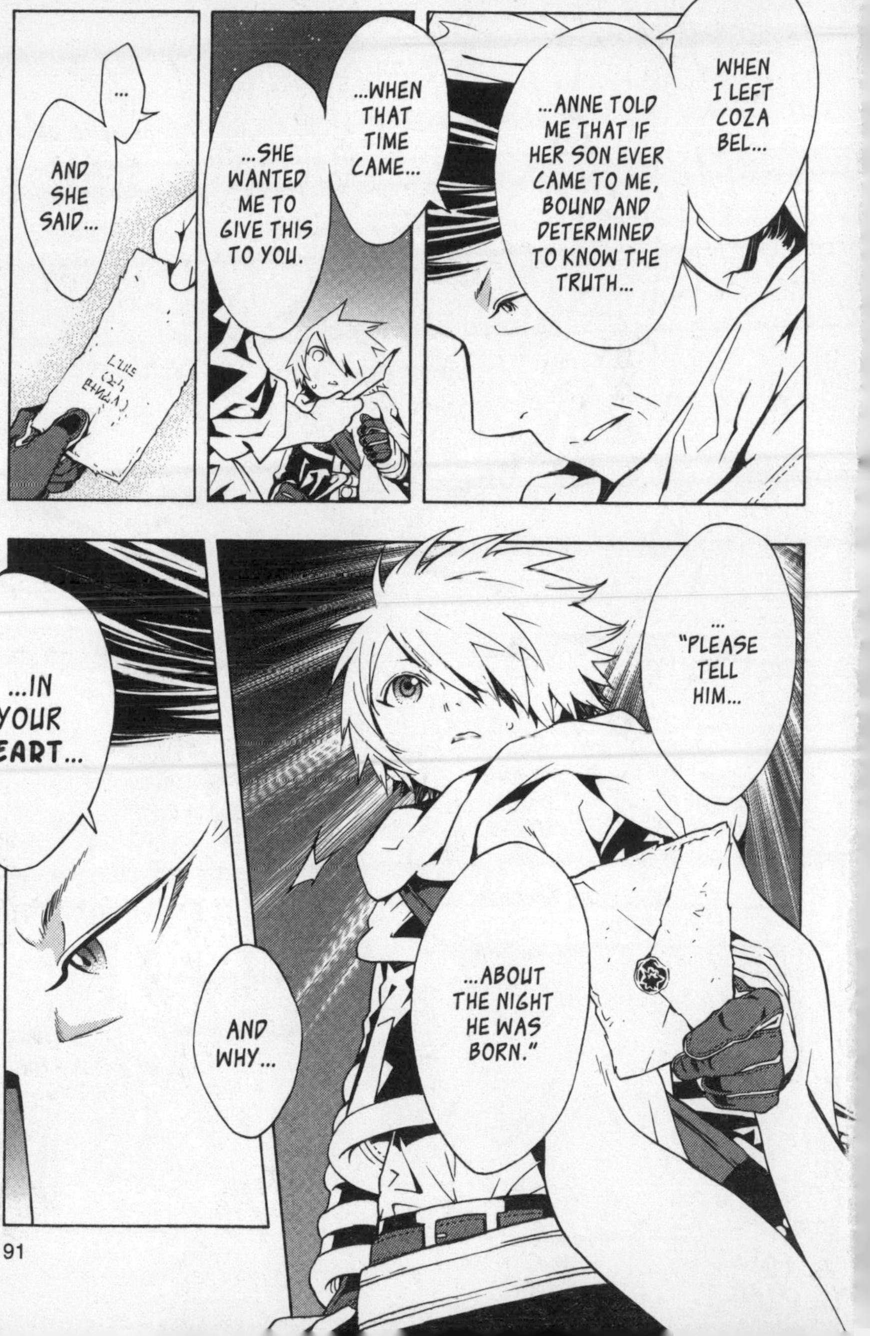
WHEN I LEFT COZA BEL...
...ANNE TOLD ME THAT IF HER SON EVER CAME TO ME, BOUND AND DETERMINED TO KNOW THE TRUTH...
...WHEN THAT TIME CAME...
...SHE WANTED ME TO GIVE THIS TO YOU.
...
AND SHE SAID...
... "PLEASE TELL HIM...
...ABOUT THE NIGHT HE WAS BORN."
AND WHY...
...IN YOUR HEART...

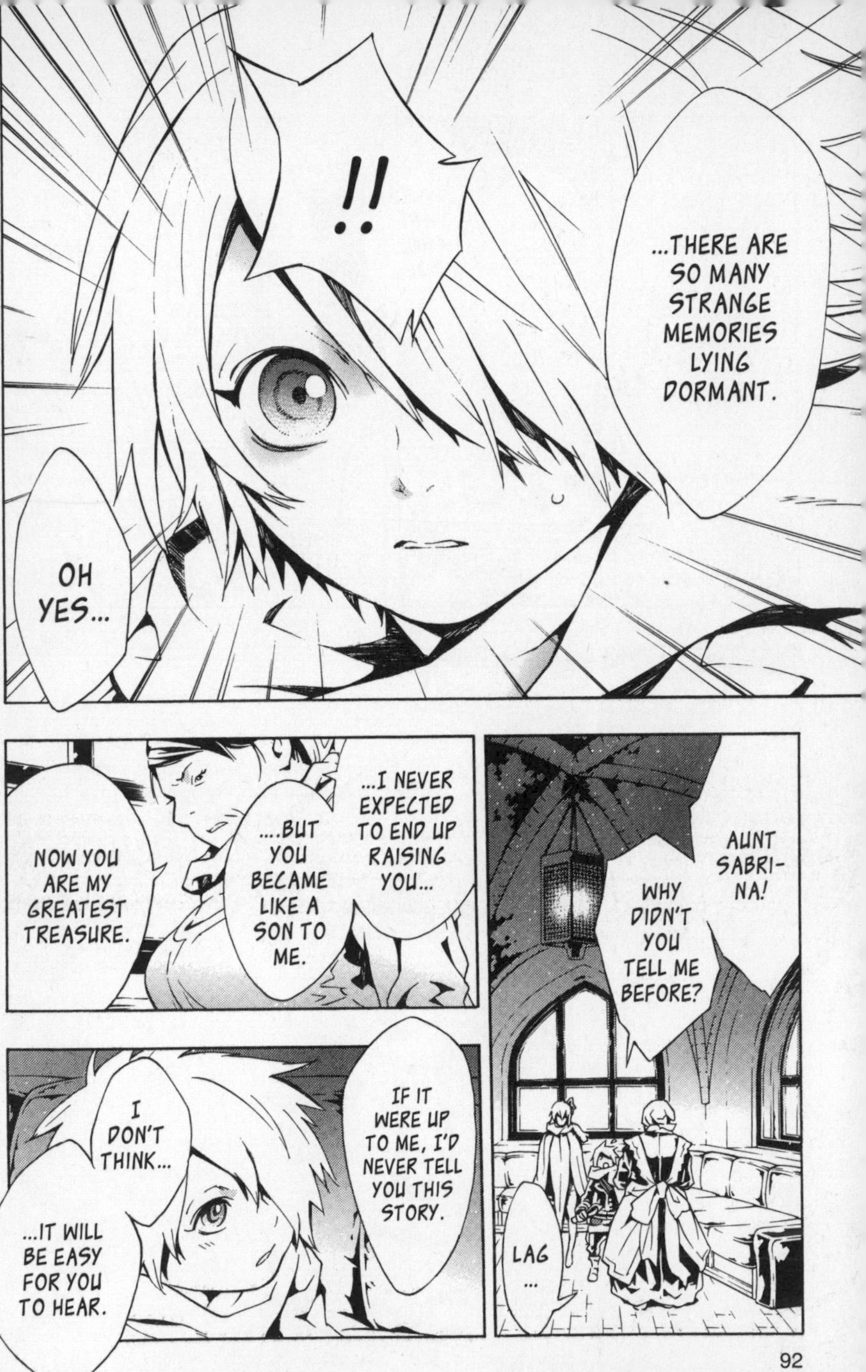
...THERE ARE SO MANY STRANGE MEMORIES LYING DORMANT.
!!
OH YES...
AUNT SABRI-NA!
WHY DIDN'T YOU TELL ME BEFORE?
LAG ...
...I NEVER EXPECTED TO END UP RAISING YOU...
....BUT YOU BECAME LIKE A SON TO ME.
NOW YOU ARE MY GREATEST TREASURE.
IF IT WERE UP TO ME, I'D NEVER TELL YOU THIS STORY.
I DON'T THINK...
...IT WILL BE EASY FOR YOU TO HEAR.

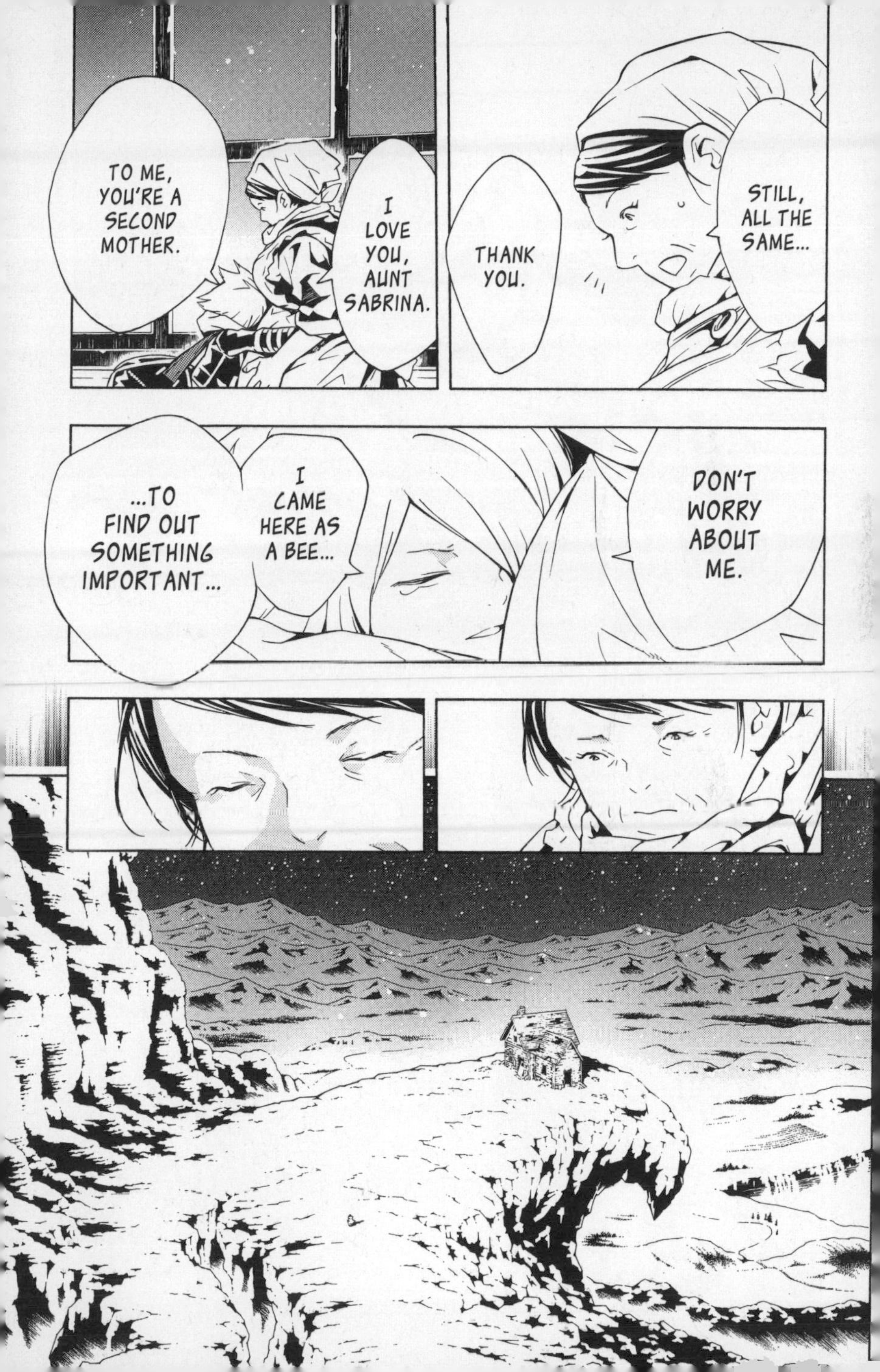
STILL, ALL THE SAME...
THANK YOU.
I LOVE YOU, AUNT SABRINA.
TO ME, YOU'RE A SECOND MOTHER.
DON'T WORRY ABOUT ME.
I CAME HERE AS A BEE...
...TO FIND OUT SOMETHING IMPORTANT...

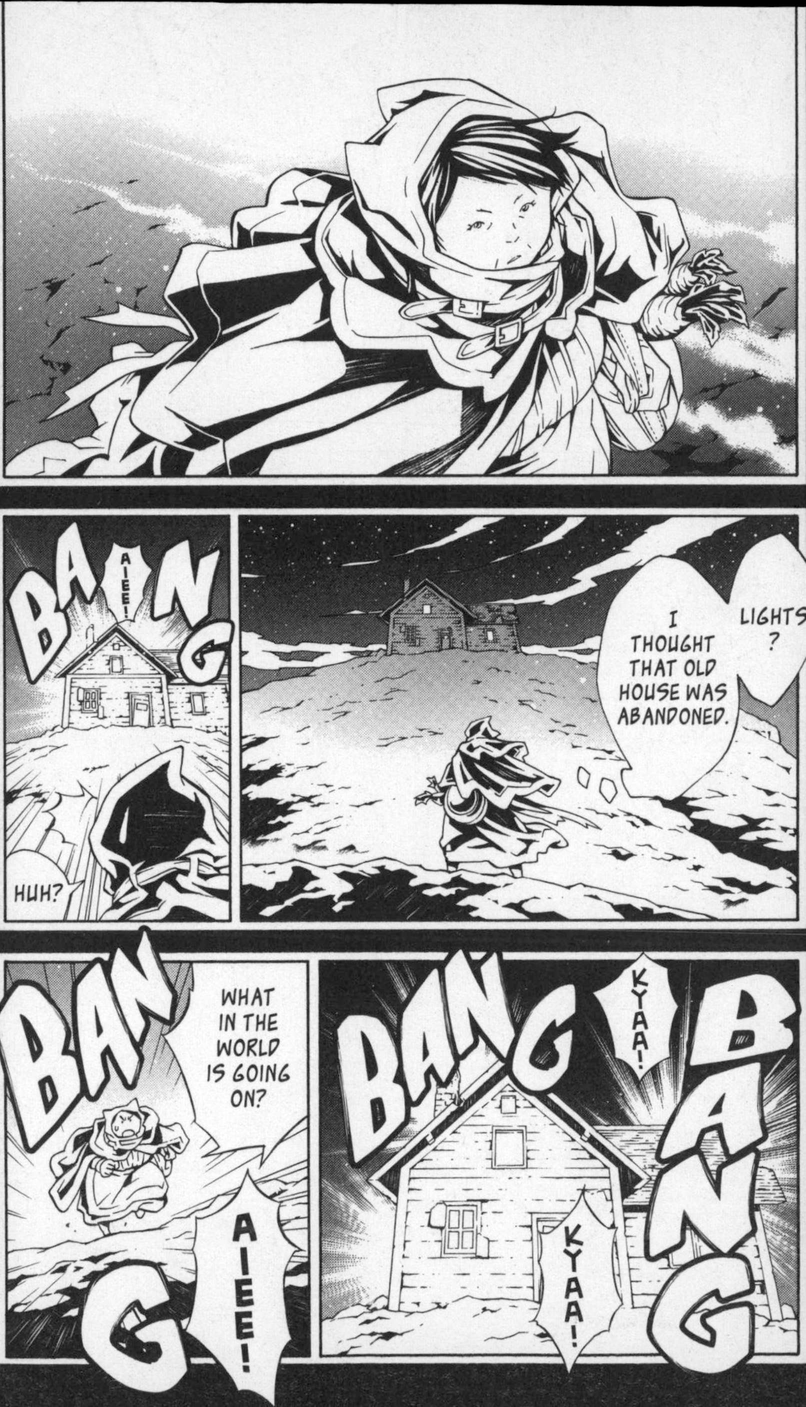

LIGHTS?
I THOUGHT THAT OLD HOUSE WAS ABANDONED.
BANG
AIEE!
HUH?
KYAA!
BANG
BANG
KYAA!
WHAT IN THE WORLD IS GOING ON?
BANG
AIEE!

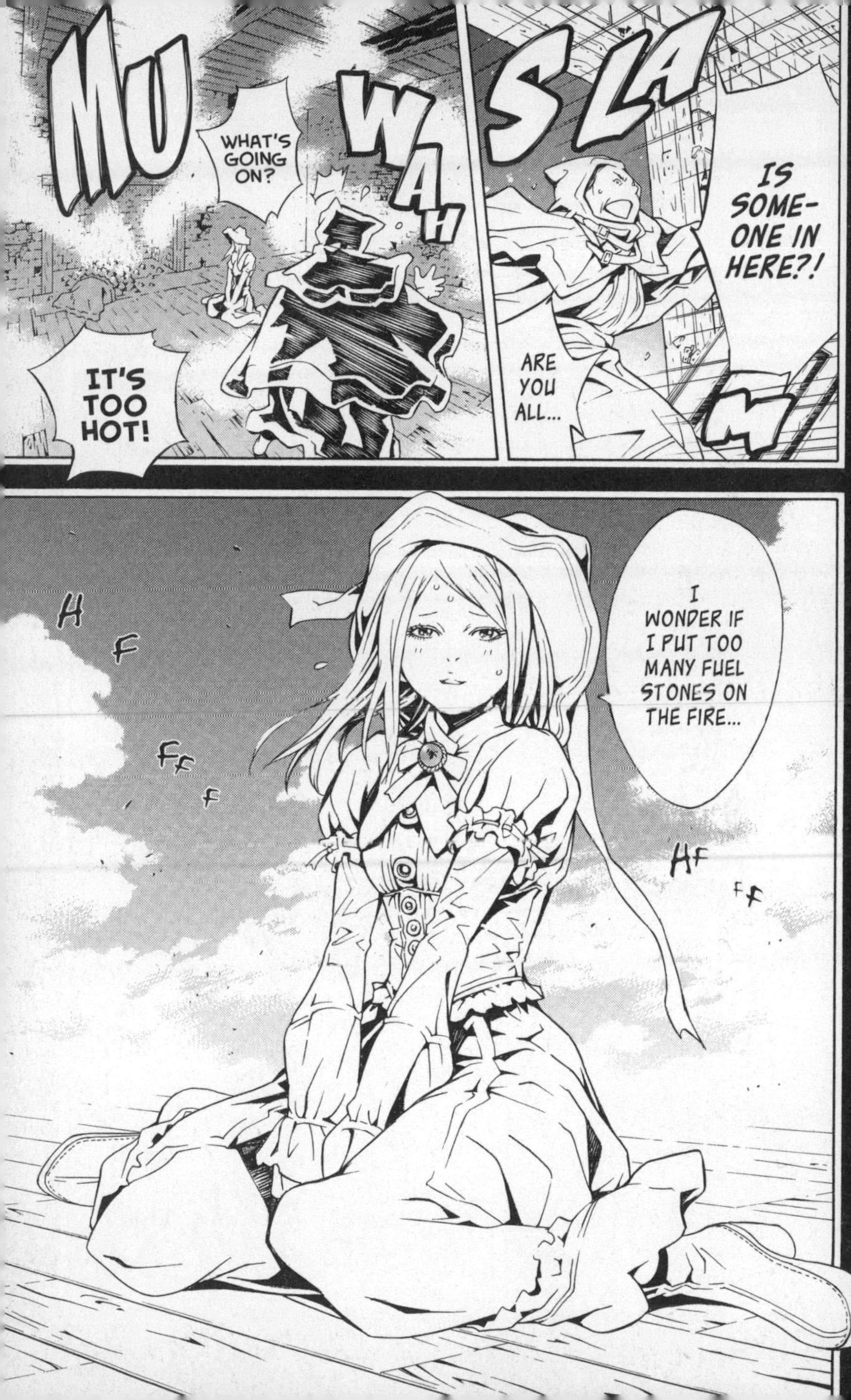
S LA
IS SOME-ONE IN HERE?!
ARE YOU ALL...
M
MU
WHAT'S GOING ON?
WAH
IT'S TOO HOT!
I WONDER IF I PUT TOO MANY FUEL STONES ON THE FIRE...
HF
FF
H
F
FF
F

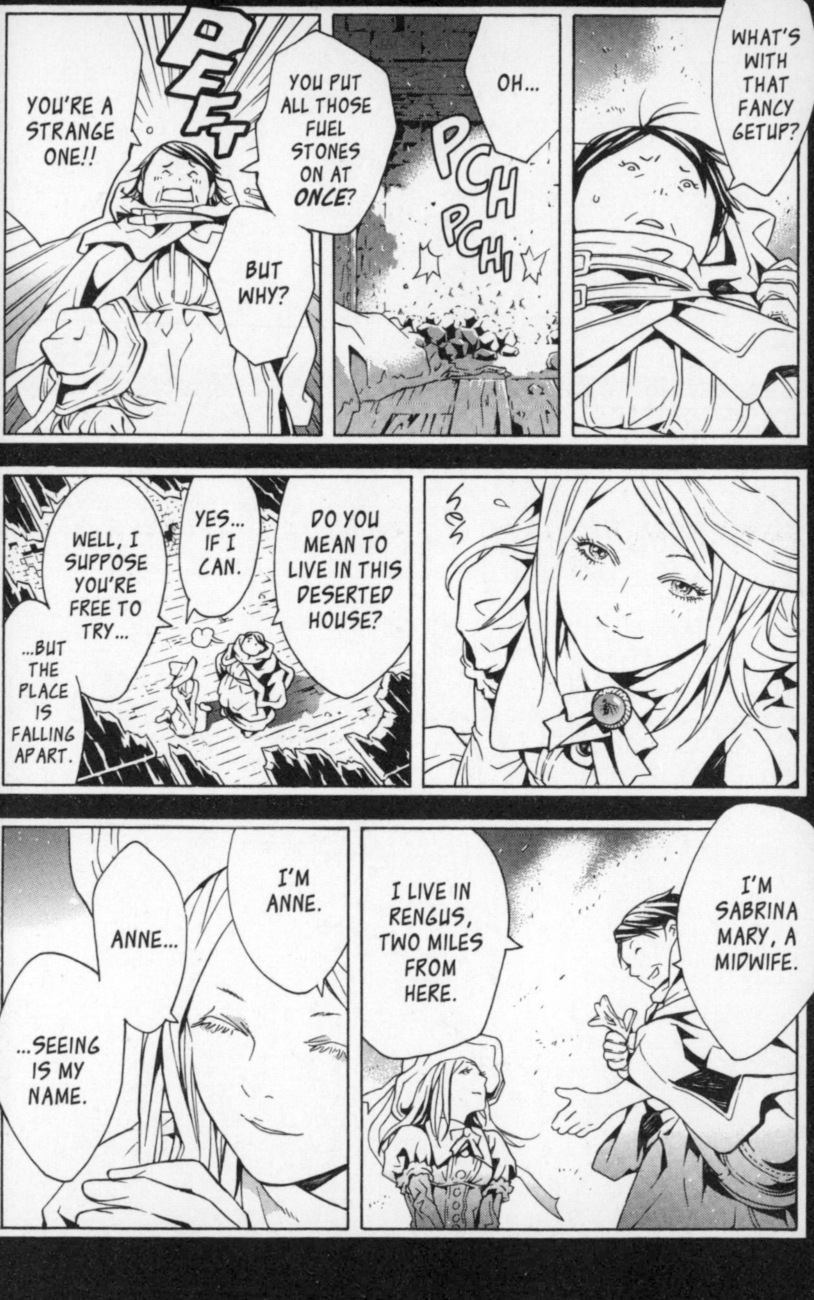
WHAT'S WITH THAT FANCY GETUP?
OH...
PCH
PCHI
YOU PUT ALL THOSE FUEL STONES ON AT ONCE?
BUT WHY?
PFFT
YOU'RE A STRANGE ONE!!
DO YOU MEAN TO LIVE IN THIS DESERTED HOUSE?
YES... IF I CAN.
WELL, I SUPPOSE YOU'RE FREE TO TRY...
...BUT THE PLACE IS FALLING APART.
I'M SABRINA MARY, A MIDWIFE.
I LIVE IN RENGUS, TWO MILES FROM HERE.
I'M ANNE.
ANNE...
...SEEING IS MY NAME.

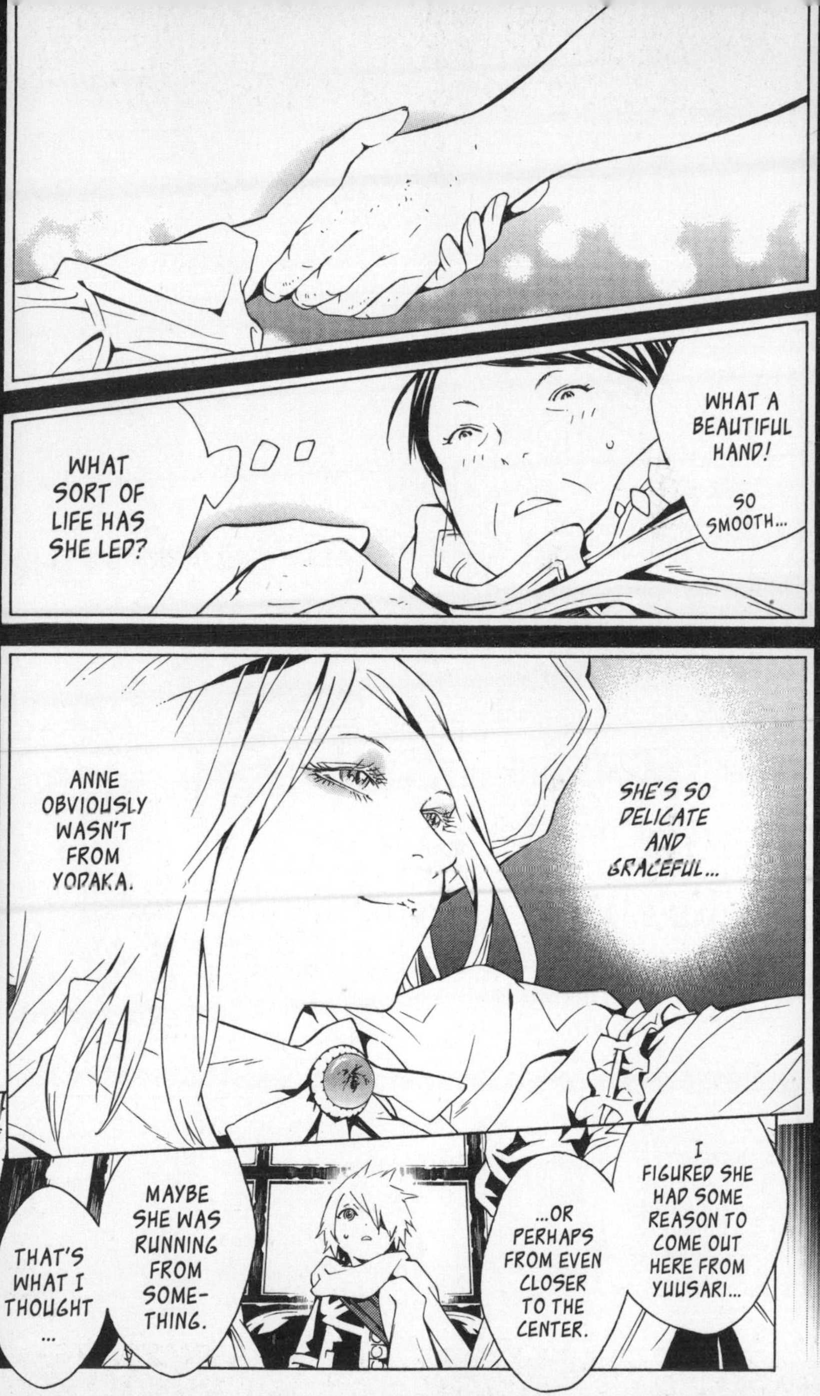
WHAT A BEAUTIFUL HAND!
SO SMOOTH...
WHAT SORT OF LIFE HAS SHE LED?
SHE'S SO DELICATE AND GRACEFUL...
ANNE OBVIOUSLY WASN'T FROM YODAKA.
I FIGURED SHE HAD SOME REASON TO COME OUT HERE FROM YUUSARI...
...OR PERHAPS FROM EVEN CLOSER TO THE CENTER.
MAYBE SHE WAS RUNNING FROM SOME-THING.
THAT'S WHAT I THOUGHT ...

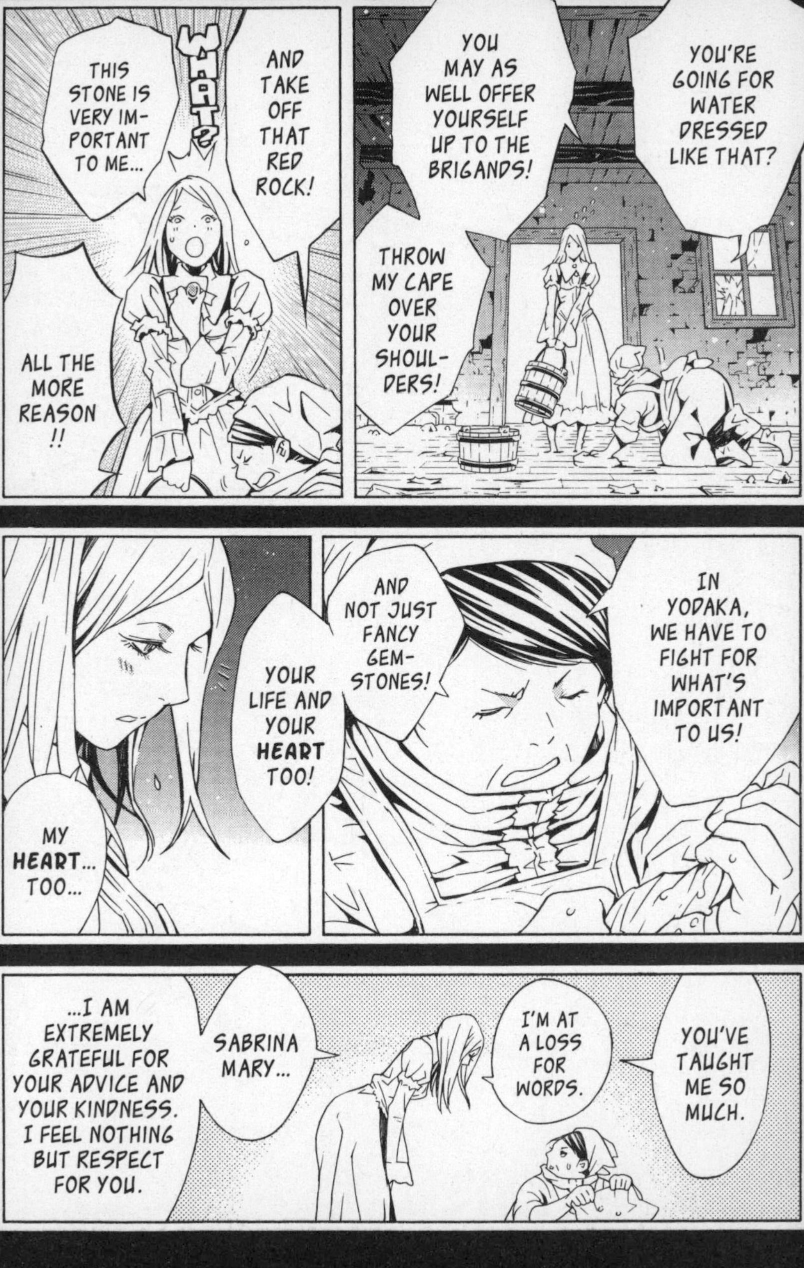
YOU'RE GOING FOR WATER DRESSED LIKE THAT?
YOU MAY AS WELL OFFER YOURSELF UP TO THE BRIGANDS!
THROW MY CAPE OVER YOUR SHOULDERS!
AND TAKE OFF THAT RED ROCK!
WHAT?
THIS STONE IS VERY IMPORTANT TO ME...
ALL THE MORE REASON !!
IN YODAKA, WE HAVE TO FIGHT FOR WHAT'S IMPORTANT TO US!
AND NOT JUST FANCY GEMSTONES!
YOUR LIFE AND YOUR **HEART** TOO!
MY **HEART**... TOO...
YOU'VE TAUGHT ME SO MUCH.
I'M AT A LOSS FOR WORDS.
SABRINA MARY...
...I AM EXTREMELY GRATEFUL FOR YOUR ADVICE AND YOUR KINDNESS. I FEEL NOTHING BUT RESPECT FOR YOU.

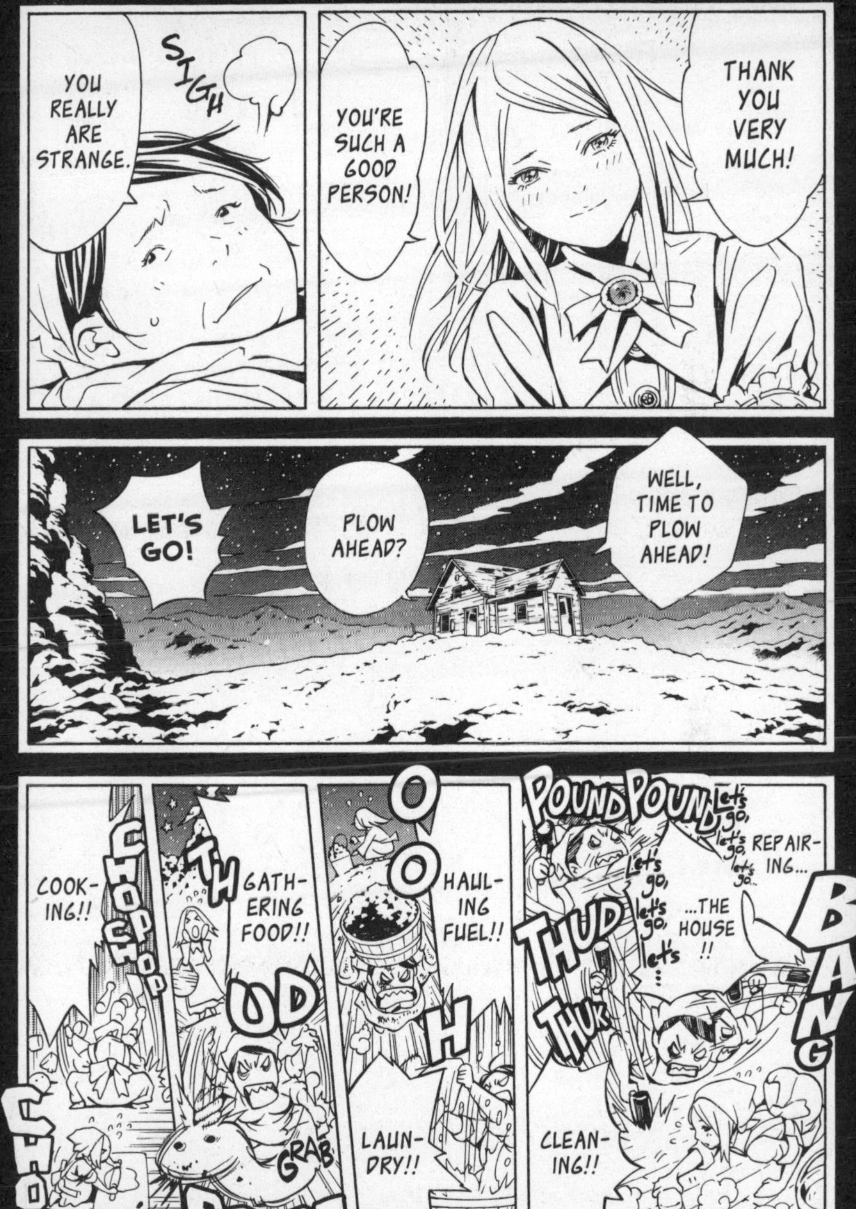
THANK YOU VERY MUCH!
YOU'RE SUCH A GOOD PERSON!
SIGH
YOU REALLY ARE STRANGE.
WELL, TIME TO PLOW AHEAD!
PLOW AHEAD?
LET'S GO!
POUND POUND
Let's go, let's go, let's go..
REPAIR-ING...
Let's go, let's go, let's...
...THE HOUSE!!
BANG
THUD
THUK
CLEAN-ING!!
OO
HAUL-ING FUEL!!
H
LAUN-DRY!!
TH
GATH-ERING FOOD!!
UD
GRAB
SPLAT
COOK-ING!!
CHOP CHOP CHOP
CHOP

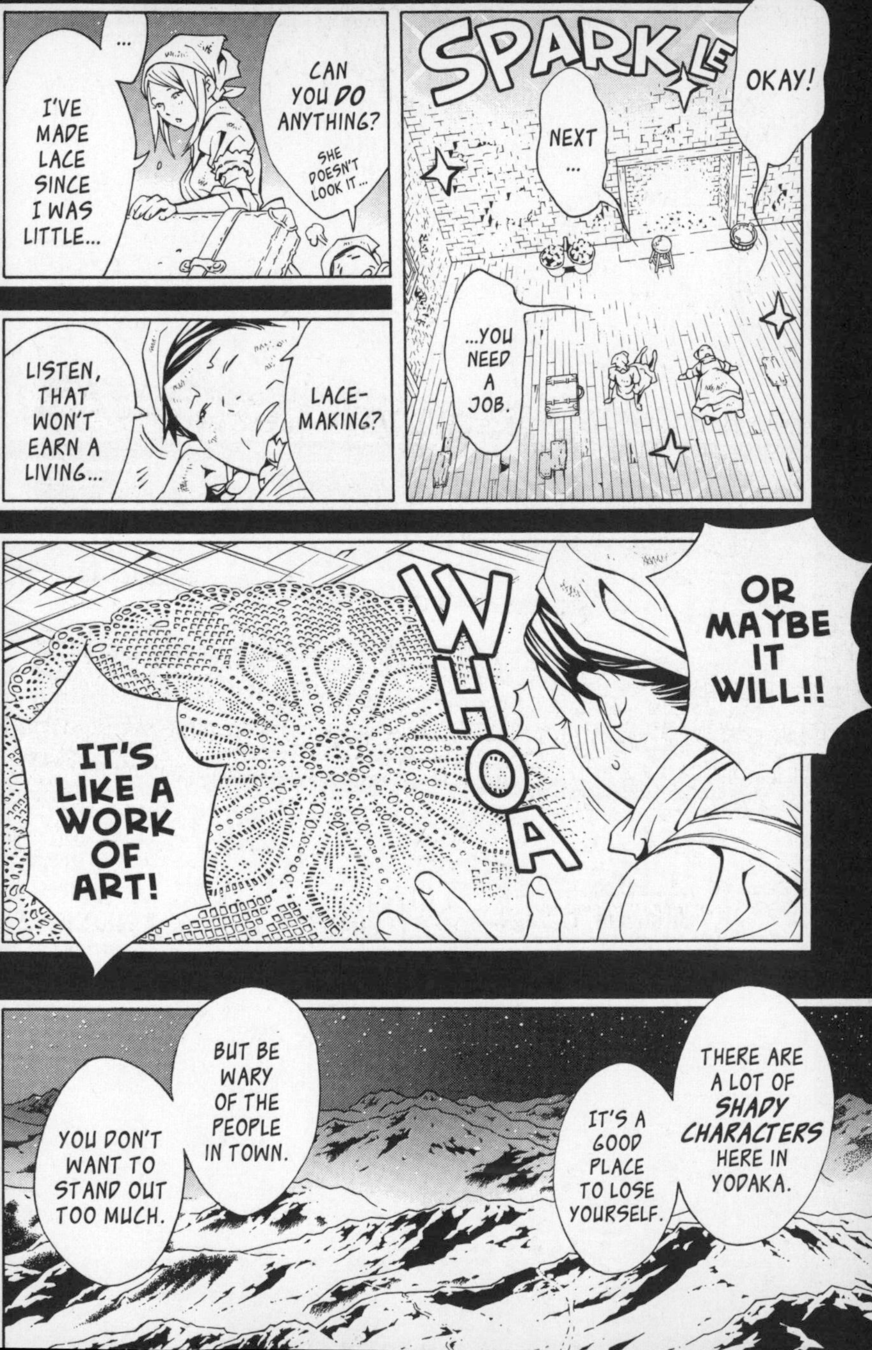
SPARKLE
OKAY!
NEXT...
...YOU NEED A JOB.
CAN YOU DO ANYTHING?
SHE DOESN'T LOOK IT...
...
I'VE MADE LACE SINCE I WAS LITTLE...
LACE-MAKING?
LISTEN, THAT WON'T EARN A LIVING...
OR MAYBE IT WILL!!
WHOA
IT'S LIKE A WORK OF ART!
THERE ARE A LOT OF SHADY CHARACTERS HERE IN YODAKA.
IT'S A GOOD PLACE TO LOSE YOURSELF.
BUT BE WARY OF THE PEOPLE IN TOWN.
YOU DON'T WANT TO STAND OUT TOO MUCH.

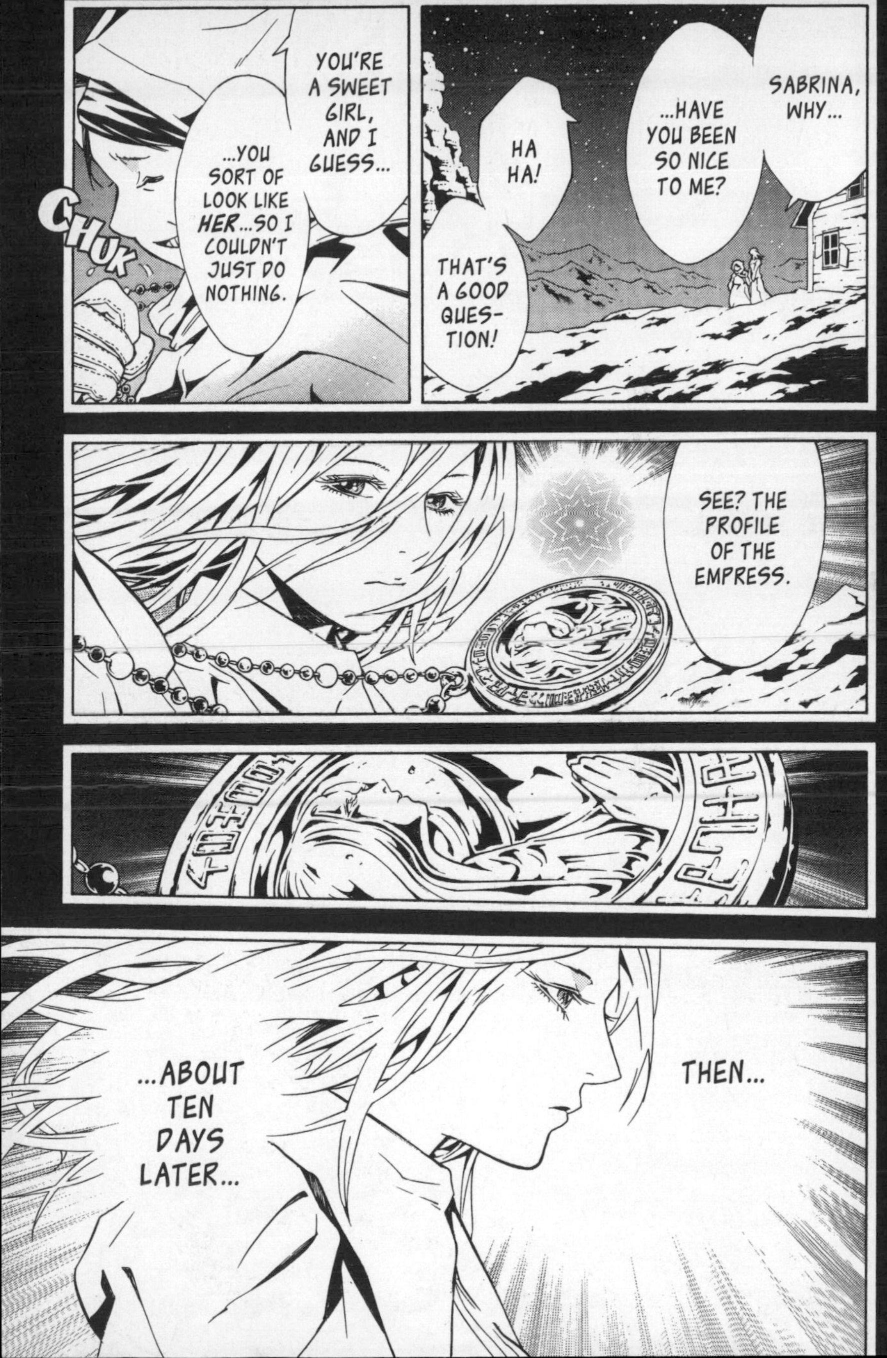
SABRINA, WHY...
...HAVE YOU BEEN SO NICE TO ME?
HA HA!
THAT'S A GOOD QUESTION!
YOU'RE A SWEET GIRL, AND I GUESS...
...YOU SORT OF LOOK LIKE HER...SO I COULDN'T JUST DO NOTHING.
CHUK
SEE? THE PROFILE OF THE EMPRESS.
THEN...
...ABOUT TEN DAYS LATER...

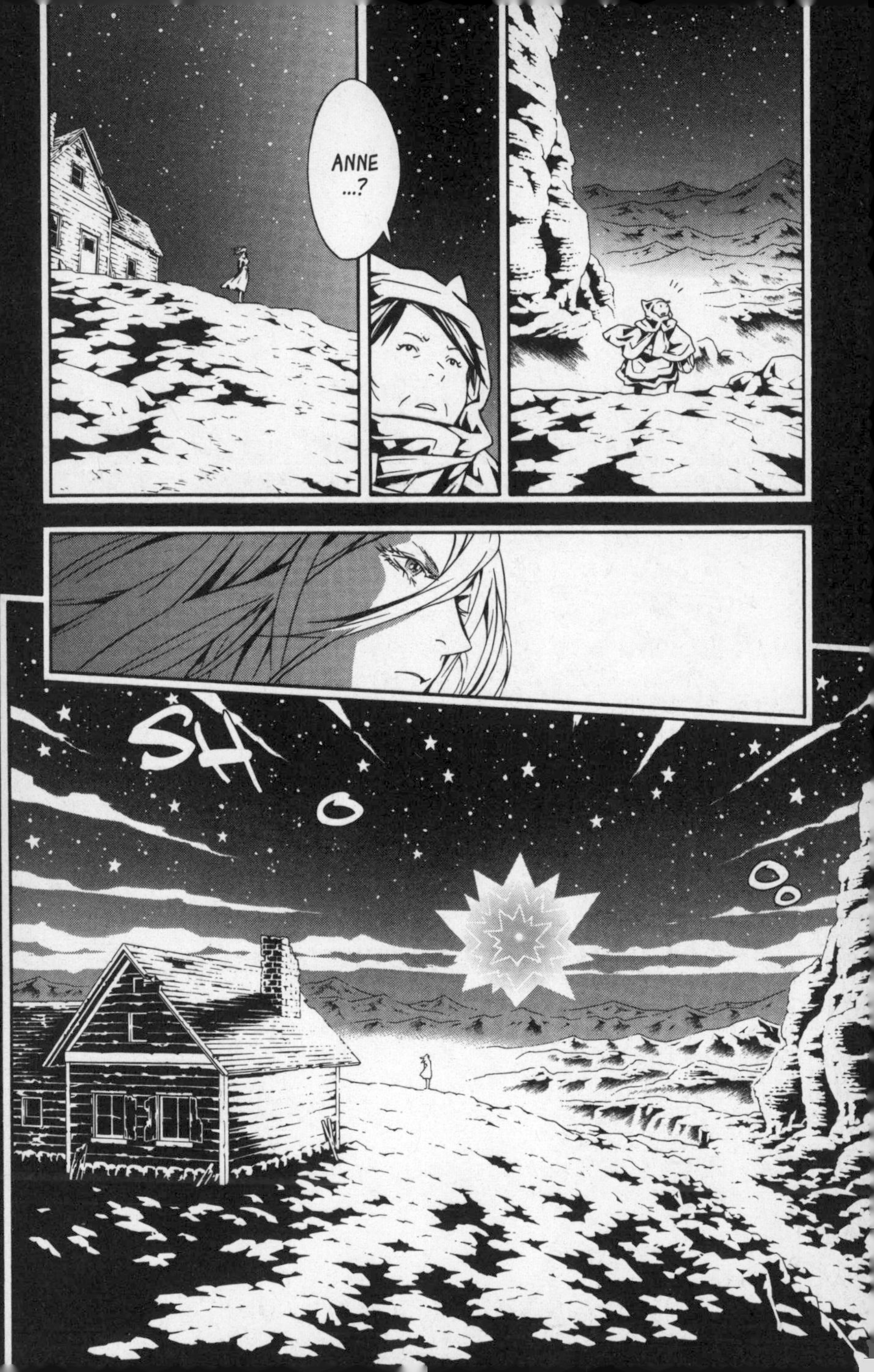

ANNE ...?
SHOO

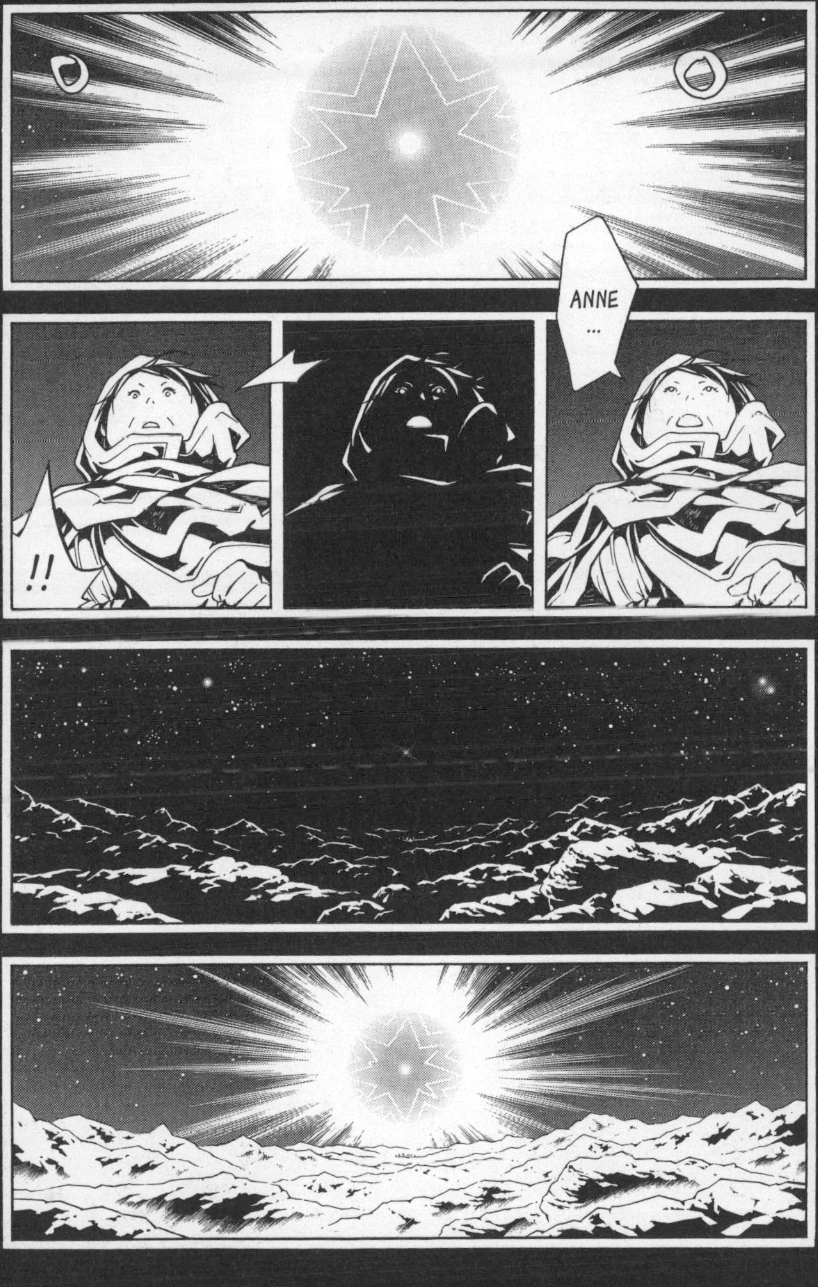
ANNE ...
!!

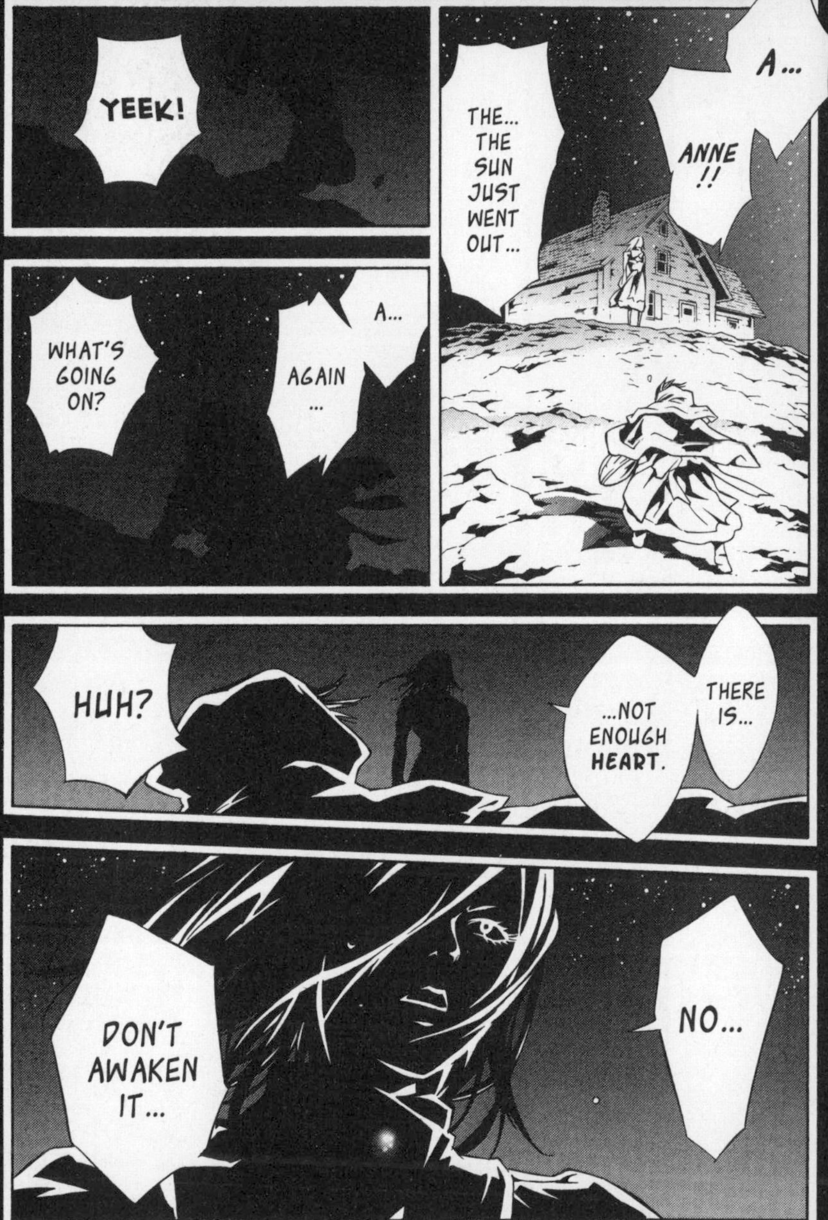
A...
ANNE !!
THE... THE SUN JUST WENT OUT...
YEEK!
A... AGAIN ...
WHAT'S GOING ON?
THERE IS...
...NOT ENOUGH HEART.
HUH?
NO...
DON'T AWAKEN IT...

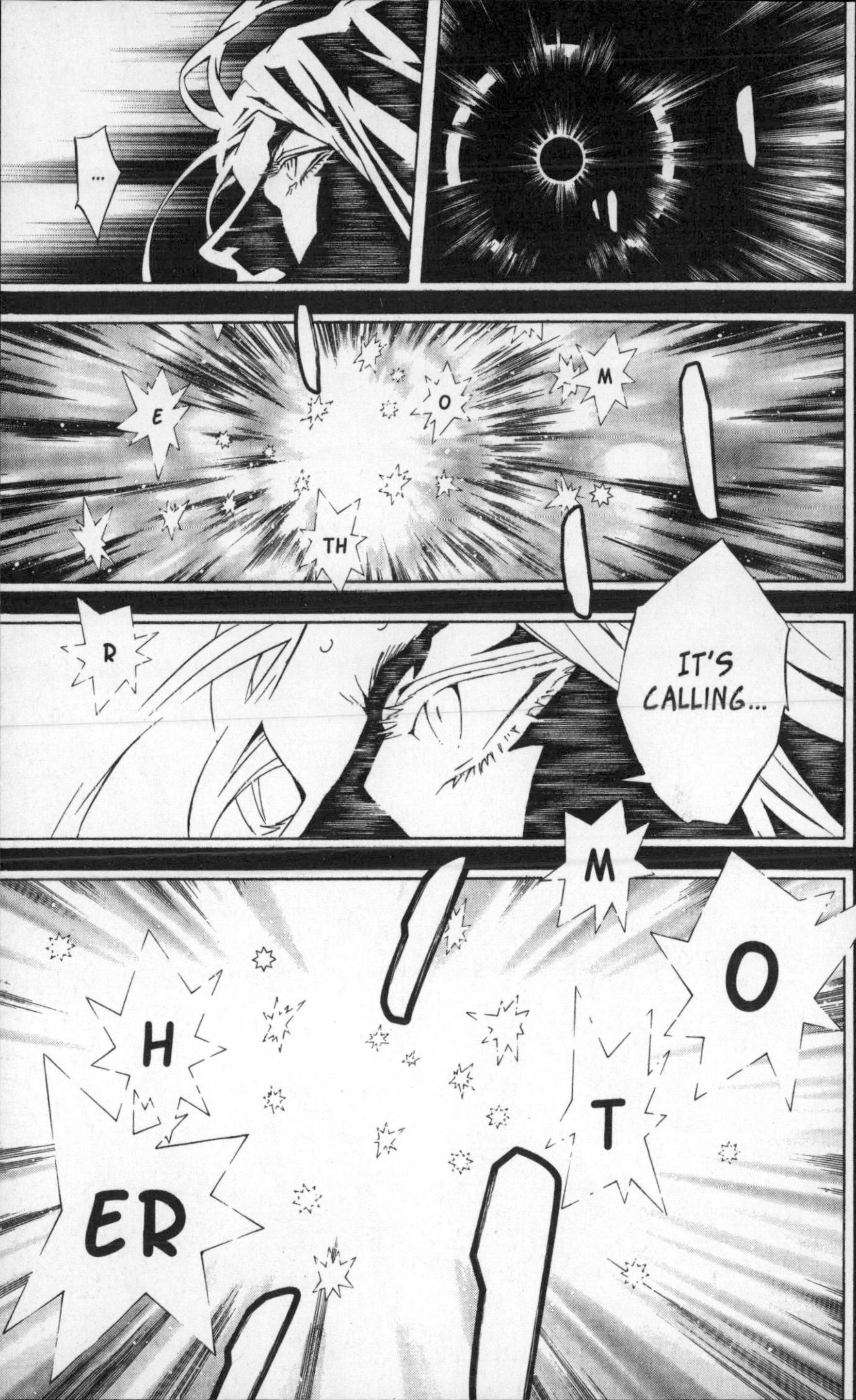
...
M
O
TH
E
IT'S CALLING...
R
M
O
T
H
ER

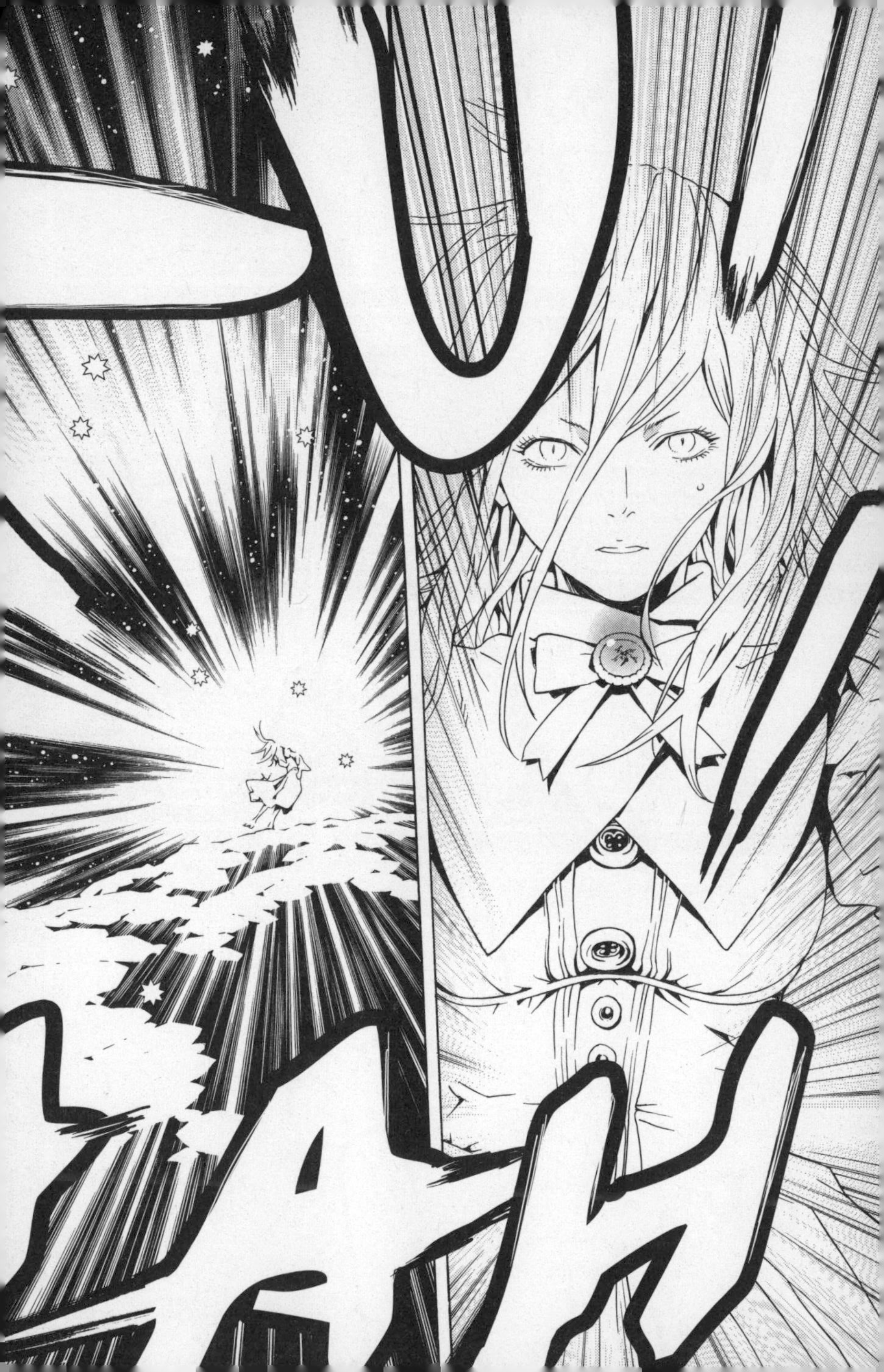

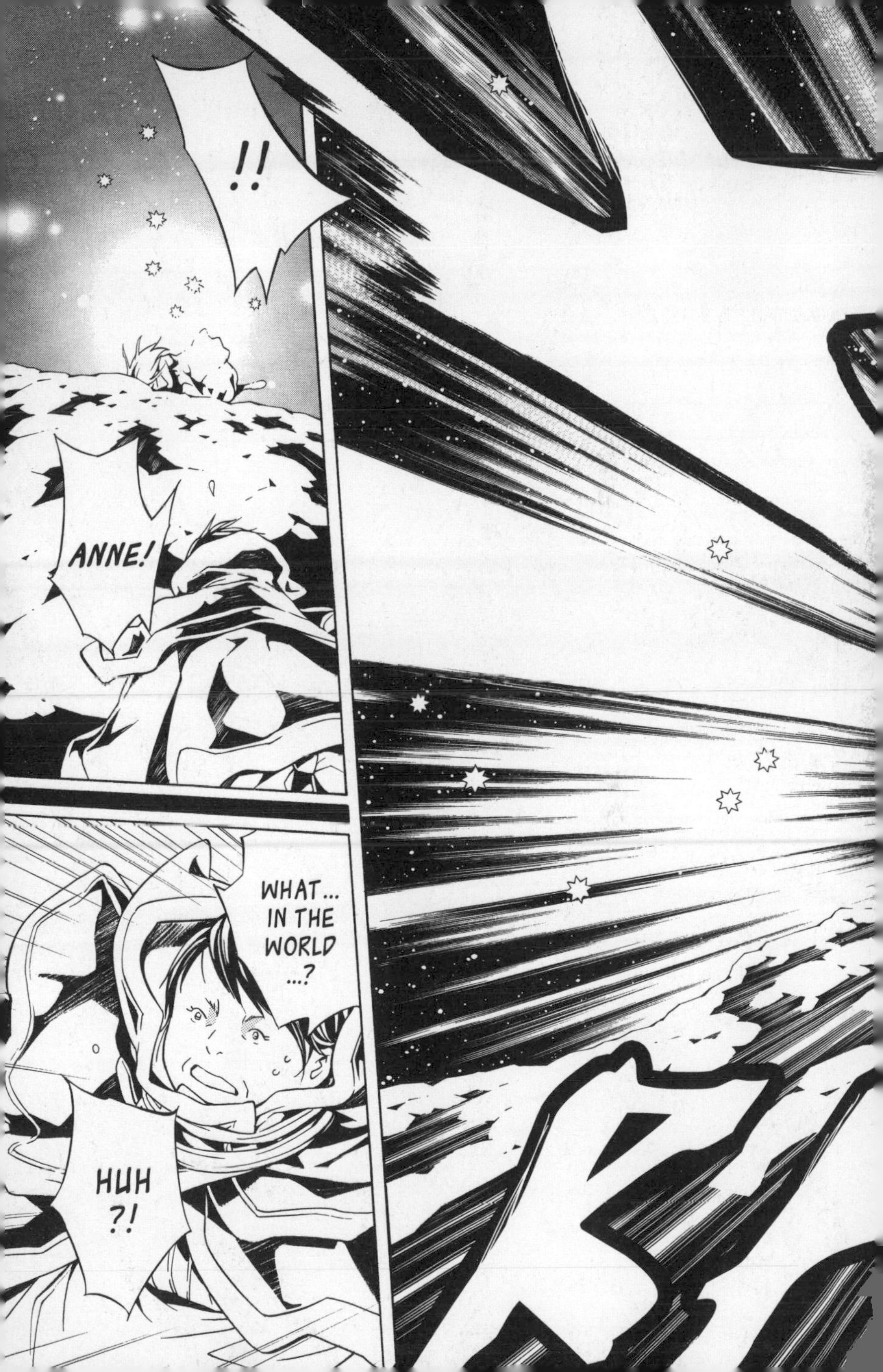
!!
ANNE!
WHAT... IN THE WORLD ...?
HUH ?!

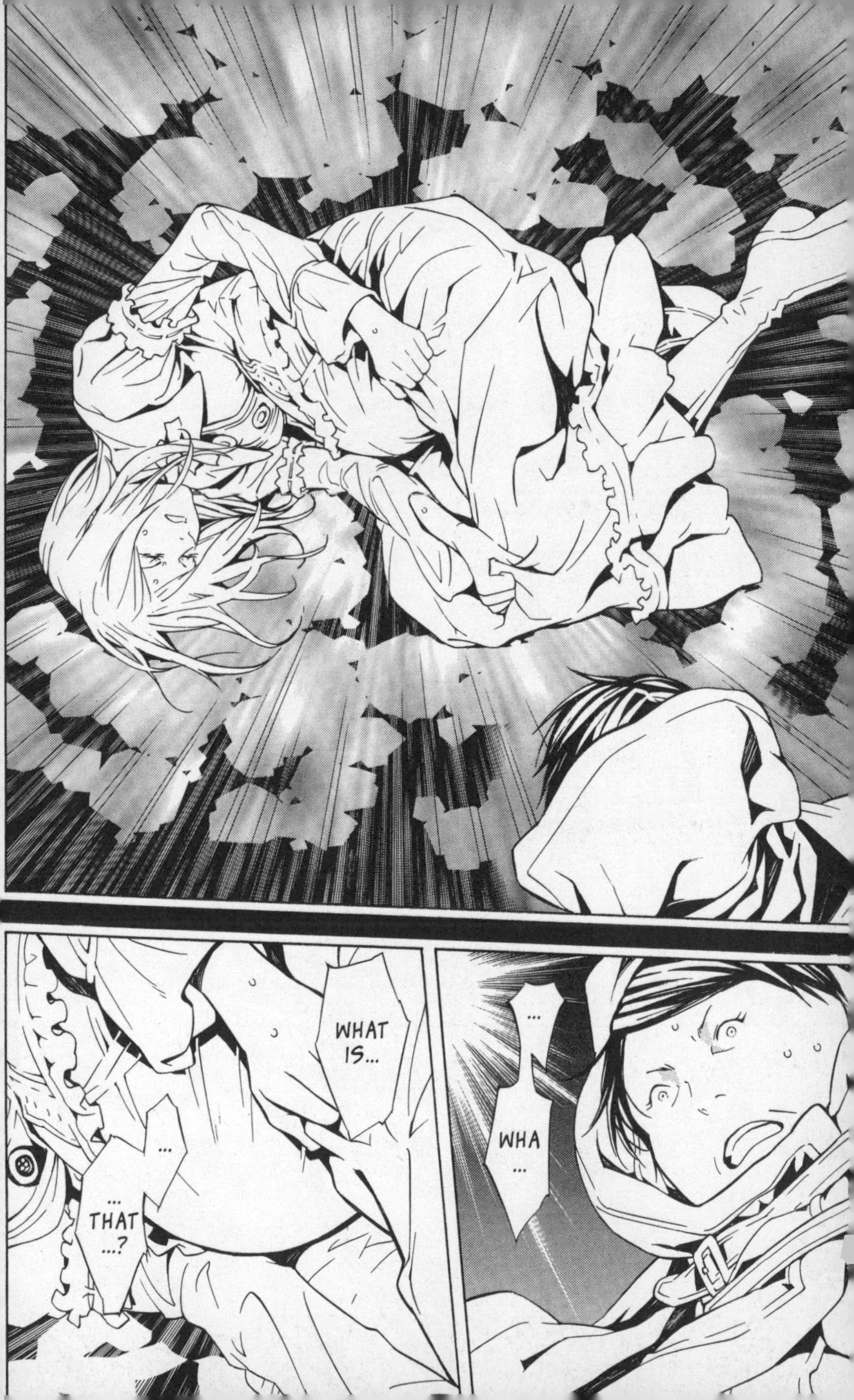
... WHA ...
WHAT IS...
... ... THAT ...?

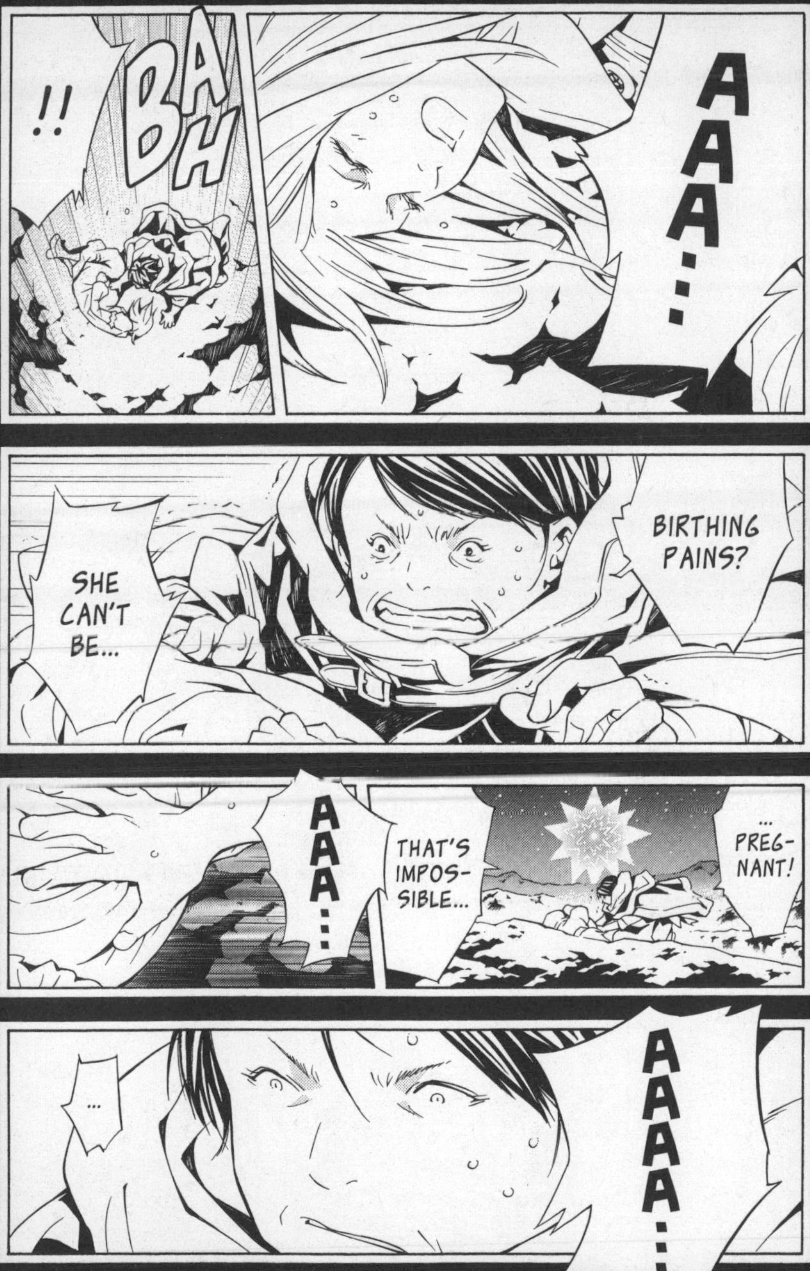
AAA...
BAH
!!
BIRTHING PAINS?
SHE CAN'T BE...
... PREG-NANT!
THAT'S IMPOS-SIBLE...
AAA...
AAAA...
...

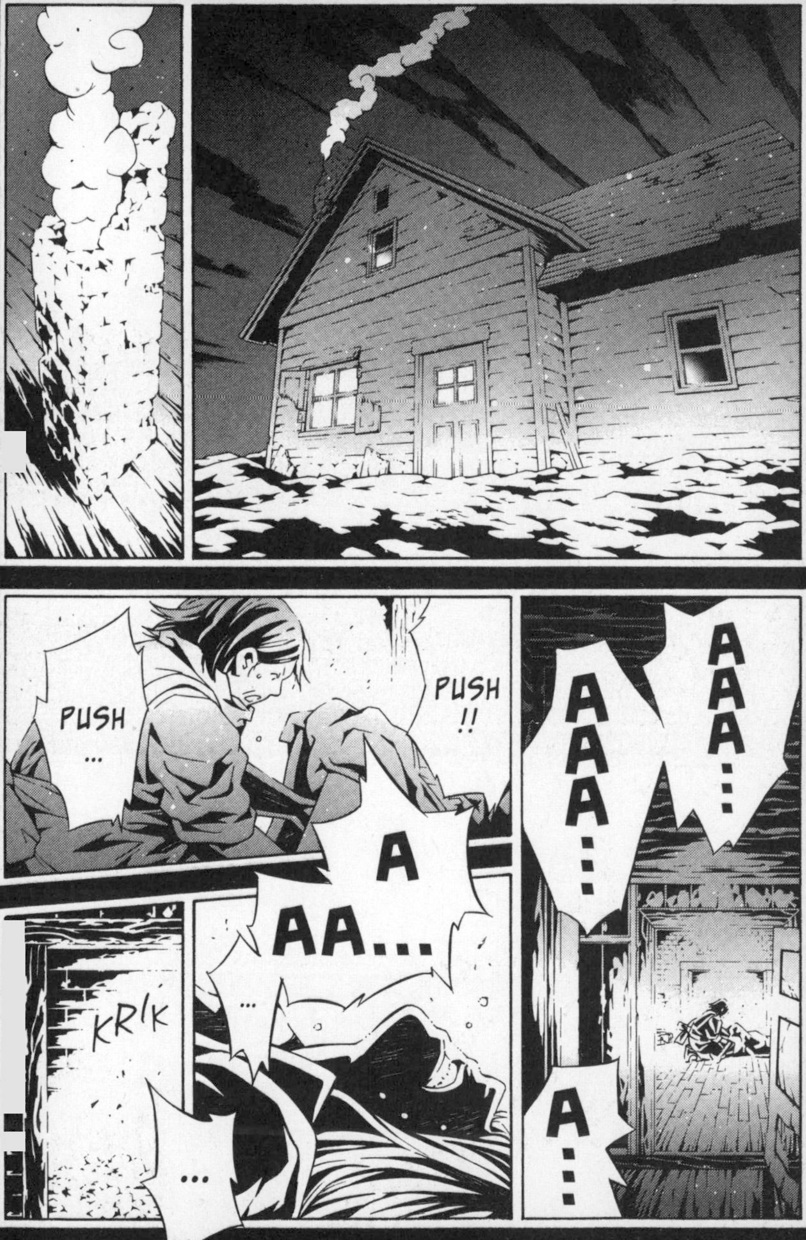
AAA...
AAA...
A...
PUSH!!
PUSH...
A
AA...
...
KRIK
...

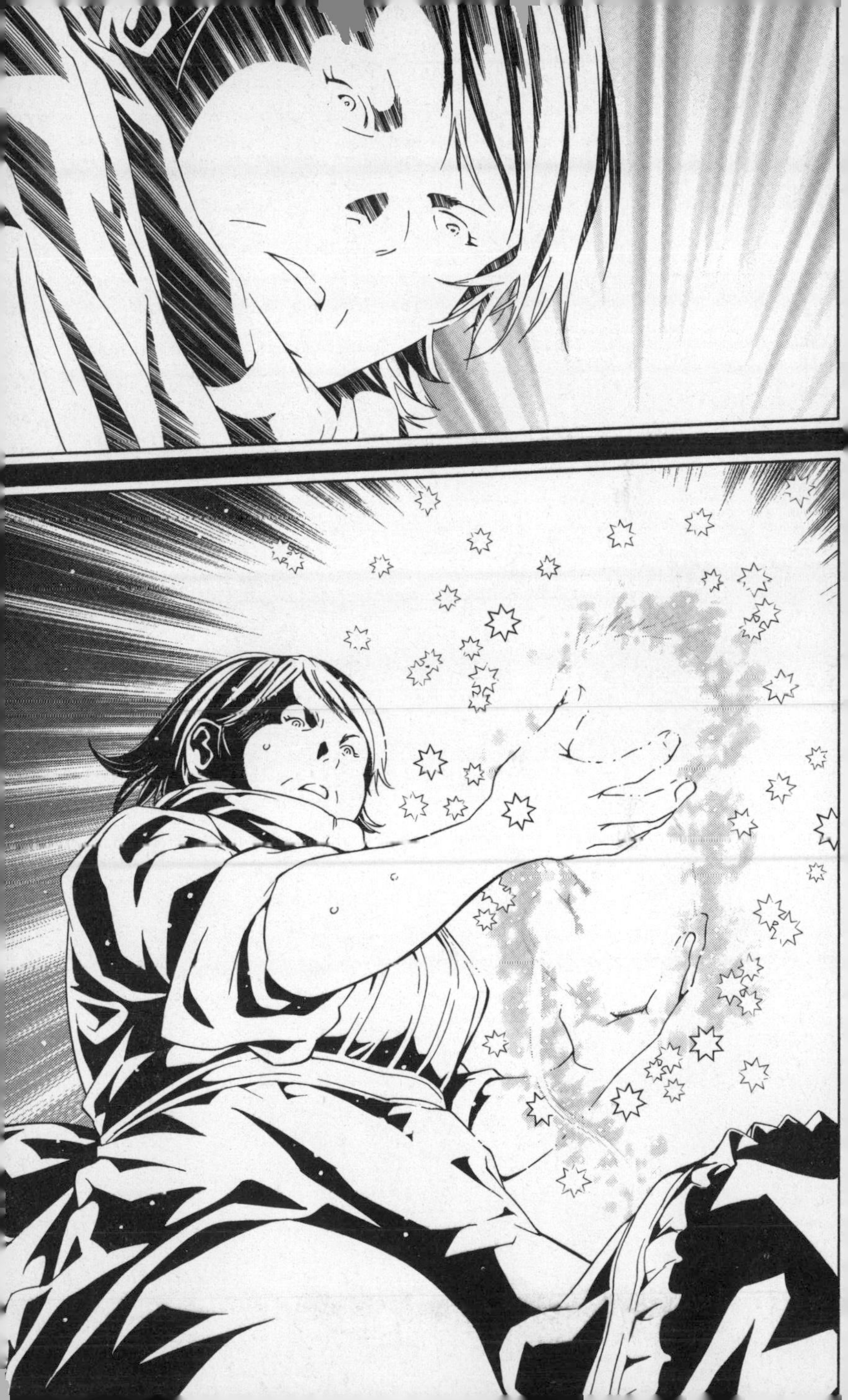

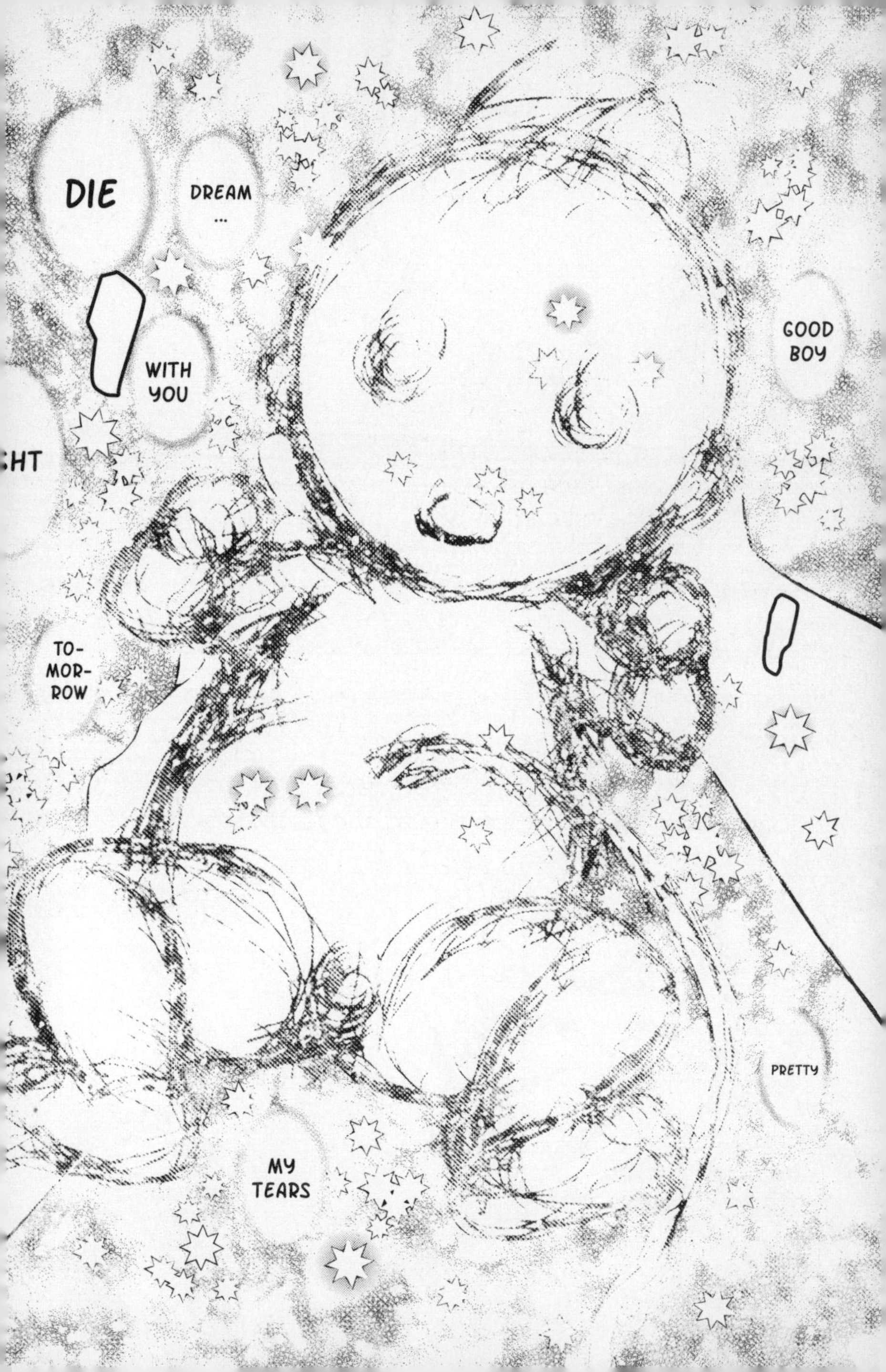
GOOD BOY
PRETTY
DREAM ...
DIE
WITH YOU
HT
TO-MOR-ROW
MY TEARS

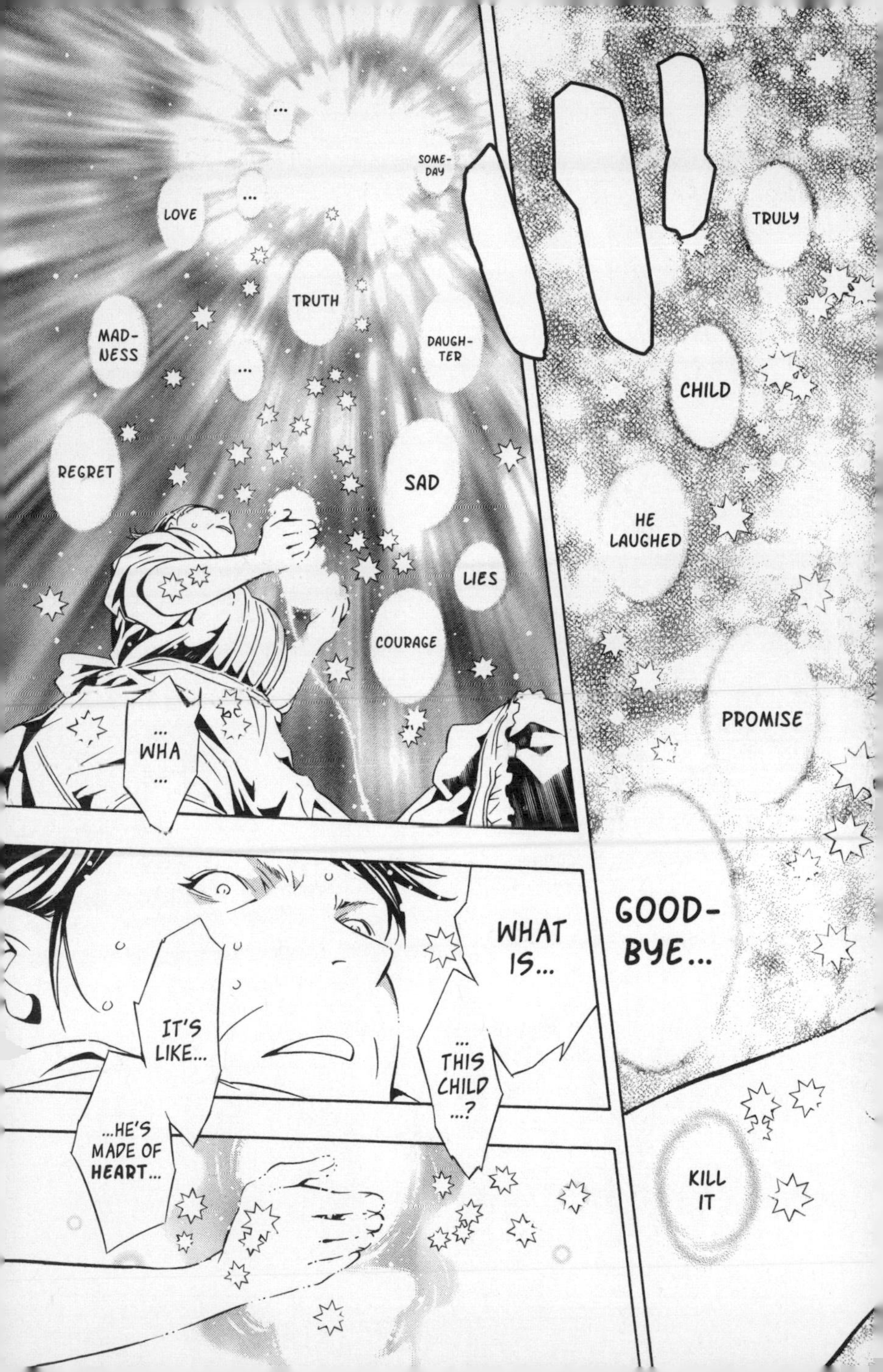
TRULY
CHILD
HE LAUGHED
PROMISE
GOOD-BYE...
KILL IT
SOME-DAY
...
LOVE
...
TRUTH
DAUGHTER
MADNESS
...
REGRET
SAD
LIES
COURAGE
...WHA...
WHAT IS...
...THIS CHILD...?
IT'S LIKE...
...HE'S MADE OF HEART...

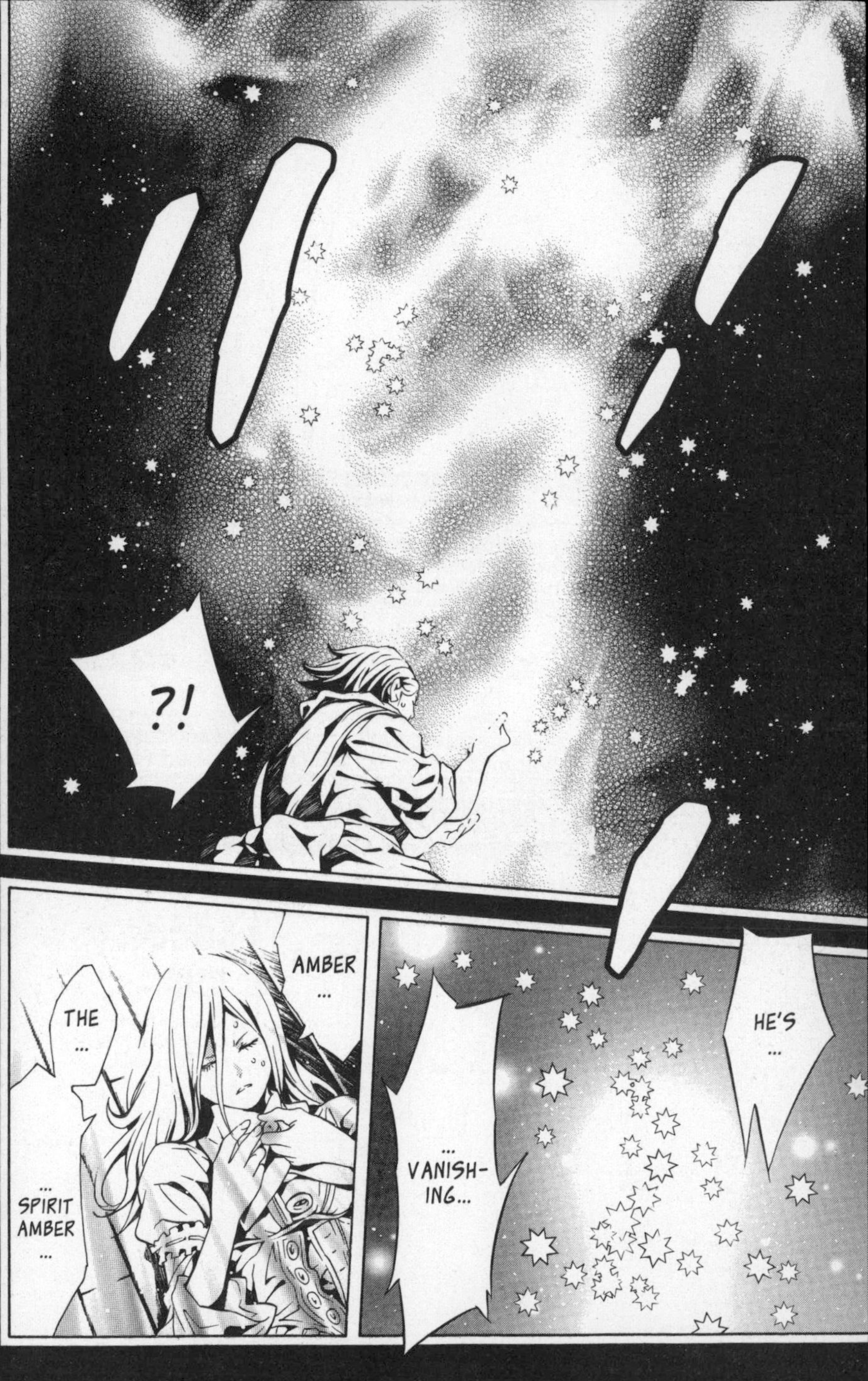
?!
HE'S ...
... VANISH-ING...
AMBER ...
THE ...
... SPIRIT AMBER ...

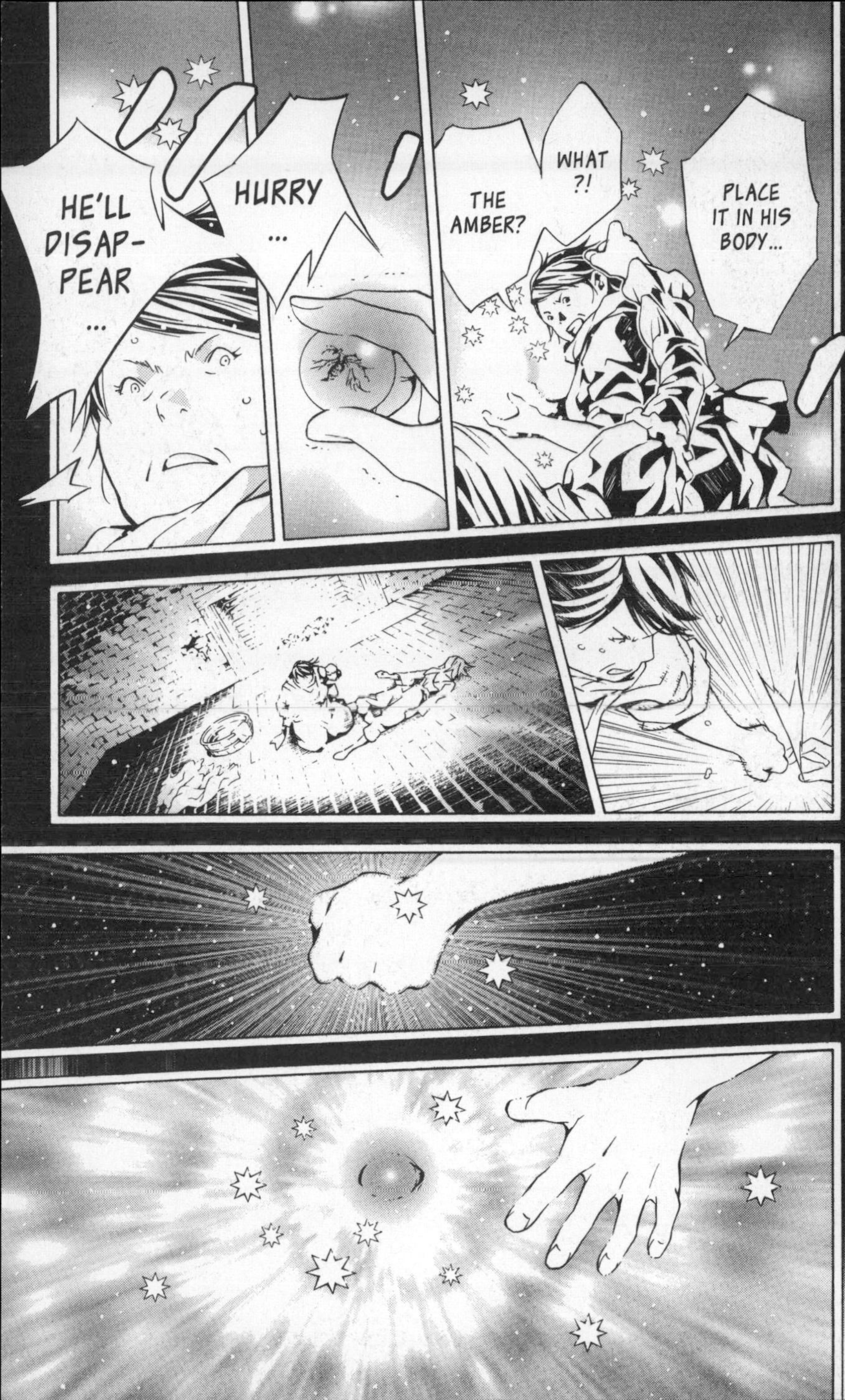
PLACE IT IN HIS BODY...
WHAT ?!
THE AMBER?
HURRY ...
HE'LL DISAP-PEAR ...

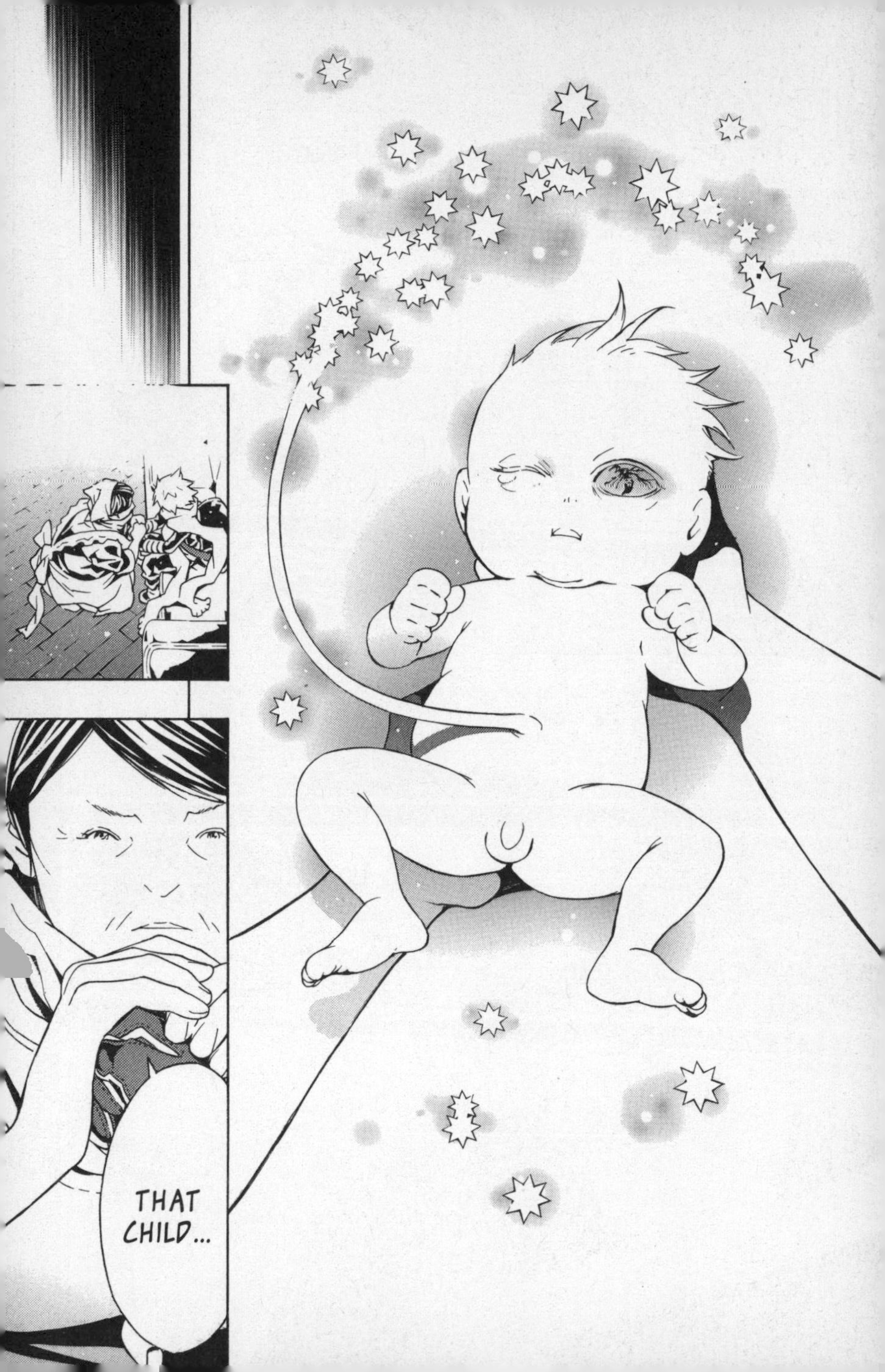
THAT CHILD...

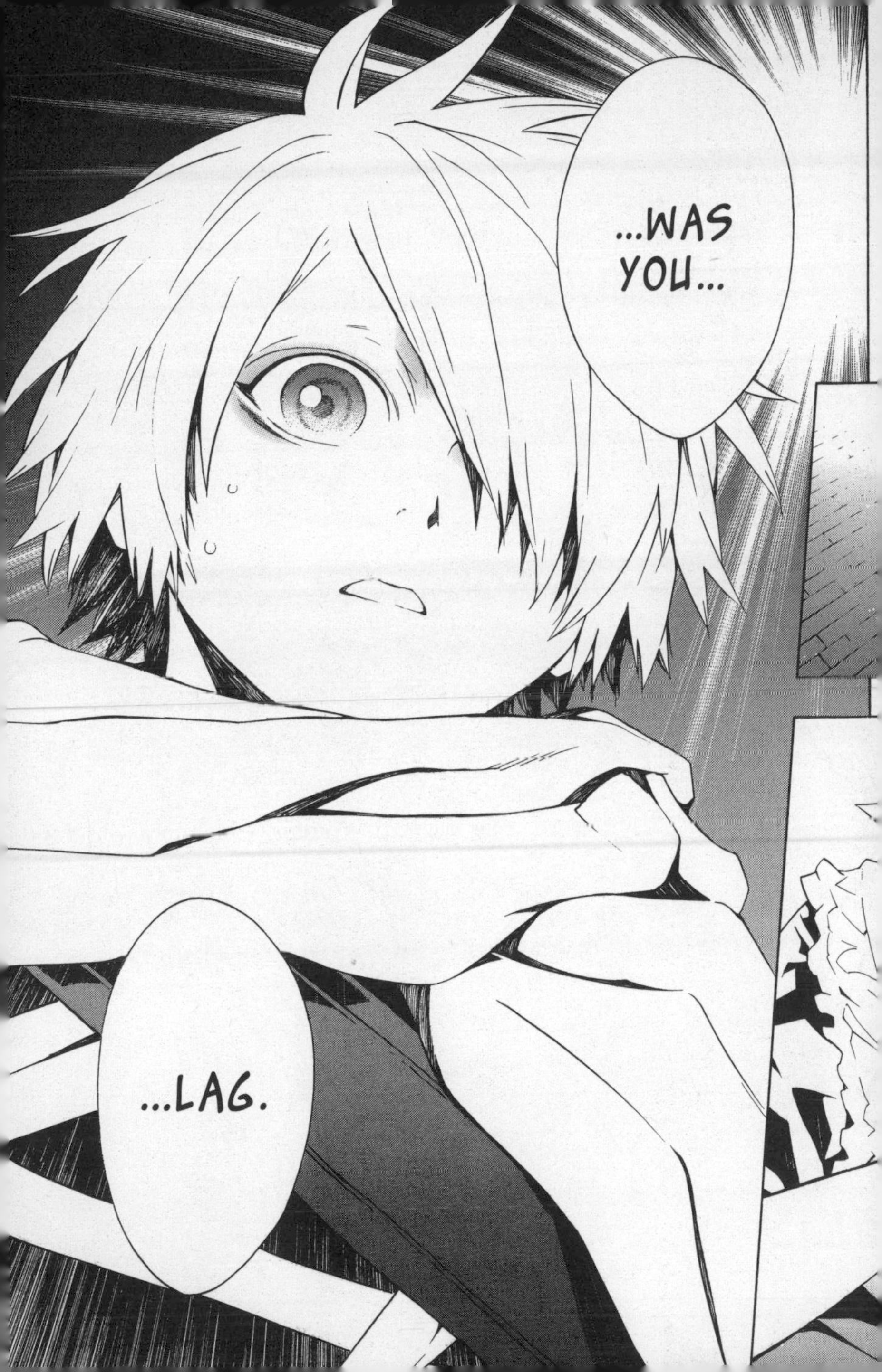
...WAS YOU...
...LAG.

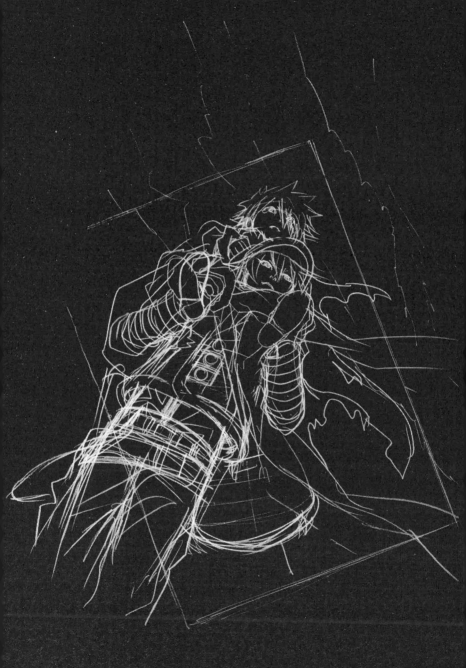

Rough draft for a *Mirai Bunko* cover.

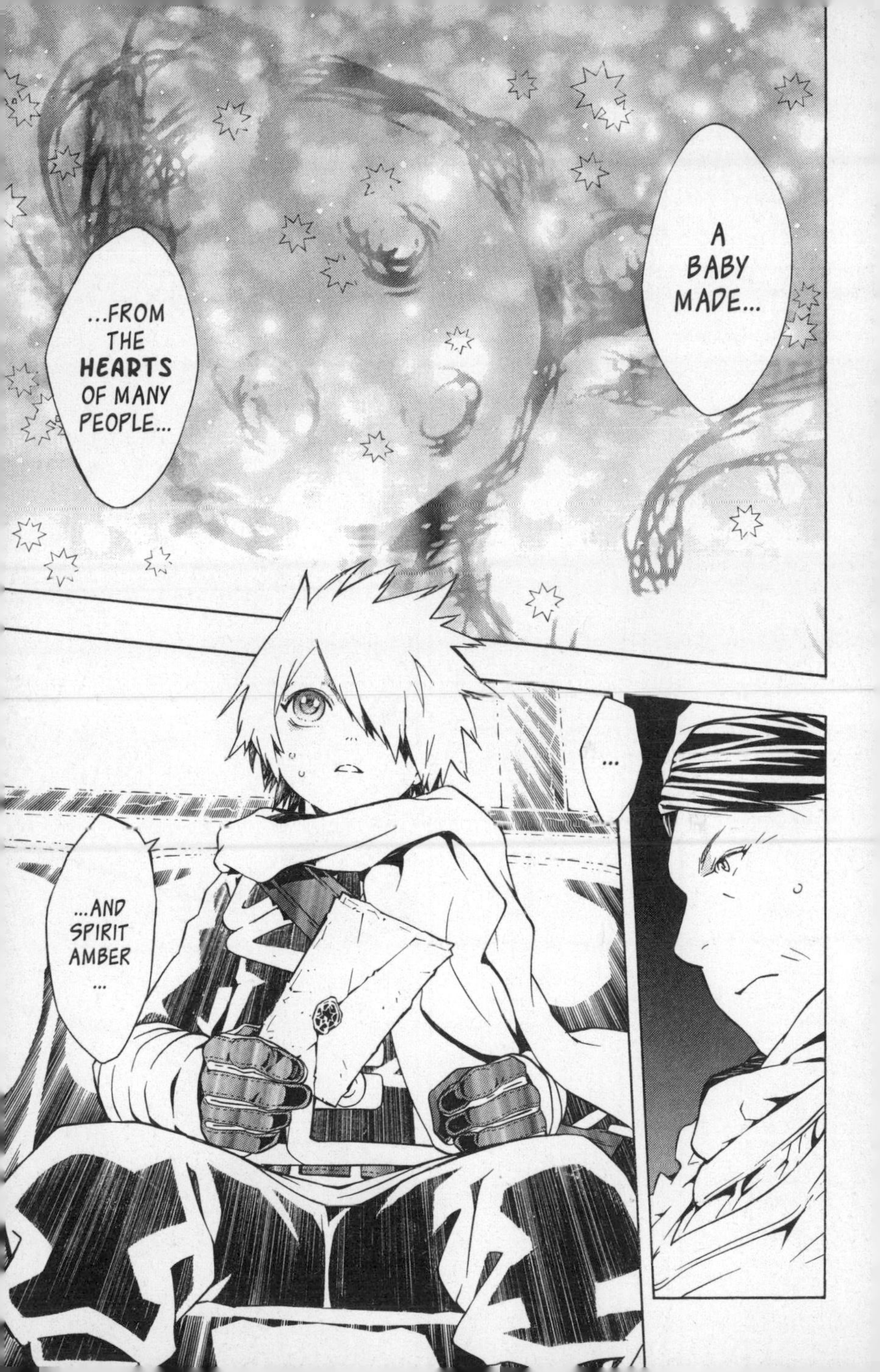
A BABY MADE...
...FROM THE **HEARTS** OF MANY PEOPLE...
...
...AND SPIRIT AMBER ...

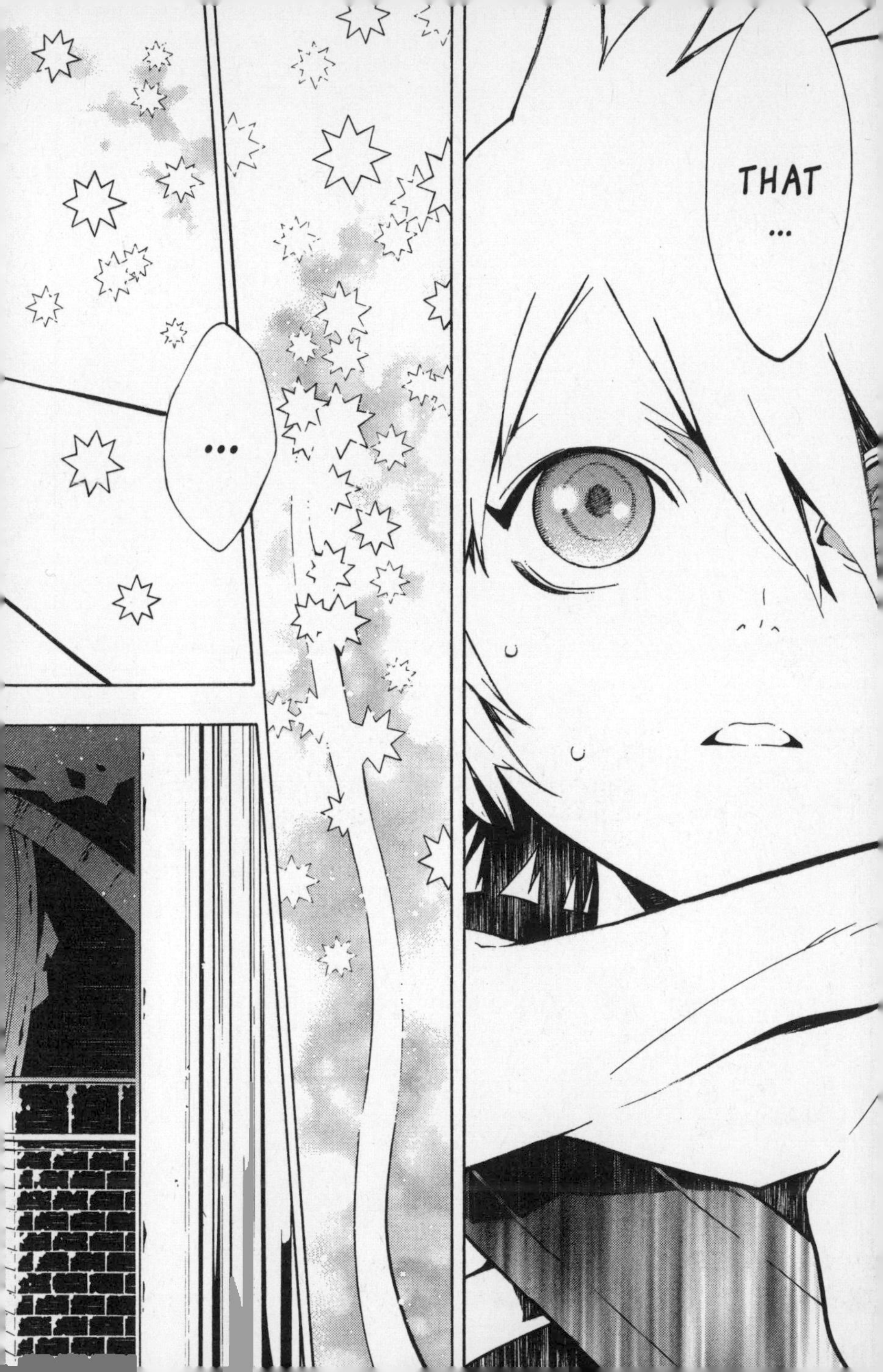
THAT
...
...

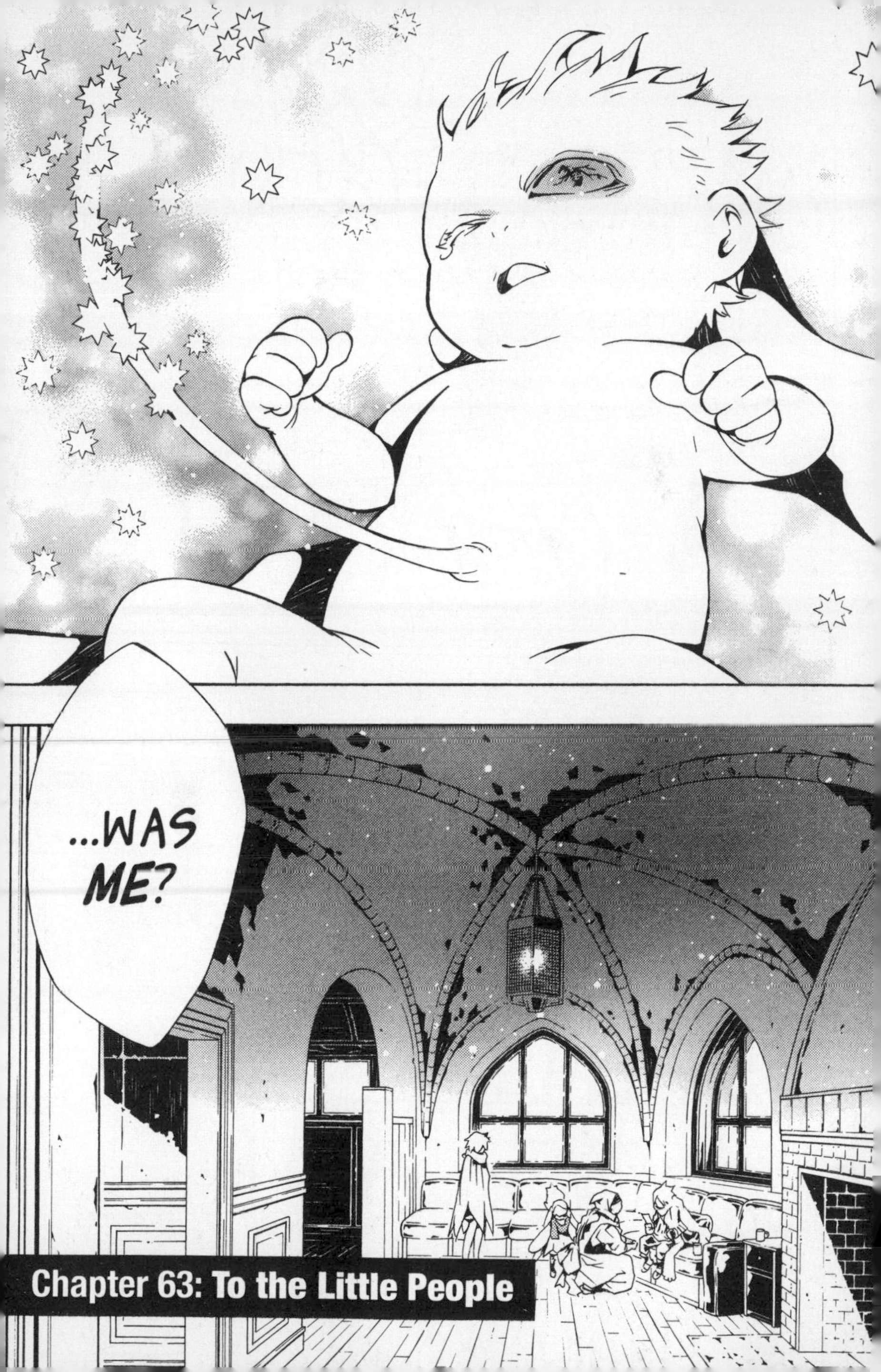
...WAS ME?
Chapter 63: To the Little People

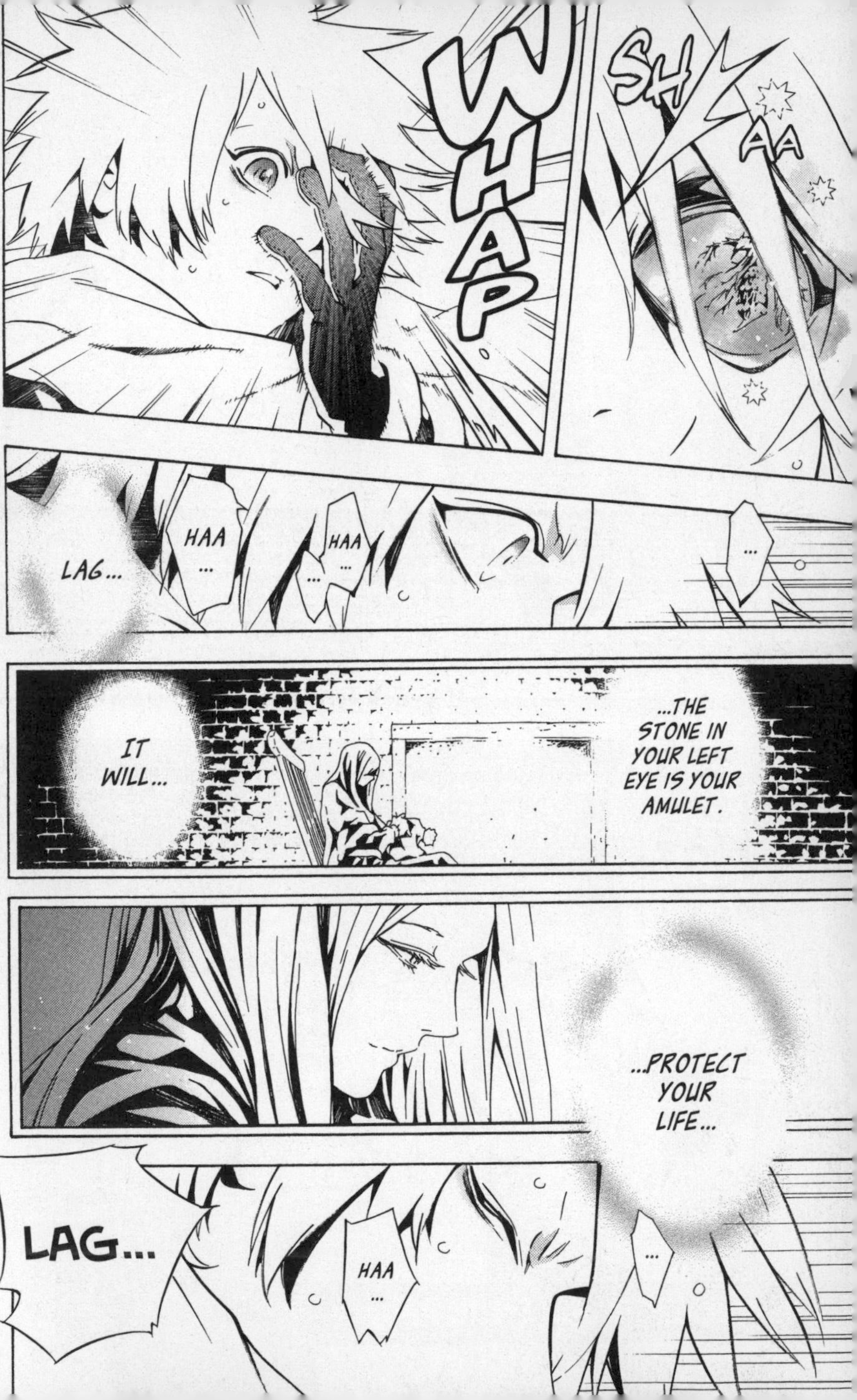
SHAA
WHAP
...
HAA ...
...
HAA ...
LAG...
...THE STONE IN YOUR LEFT EYE IS YOUR AMULET.
IT WILL...
...PROTECT YOUR LIFE...
...
HAA ...
LAG...

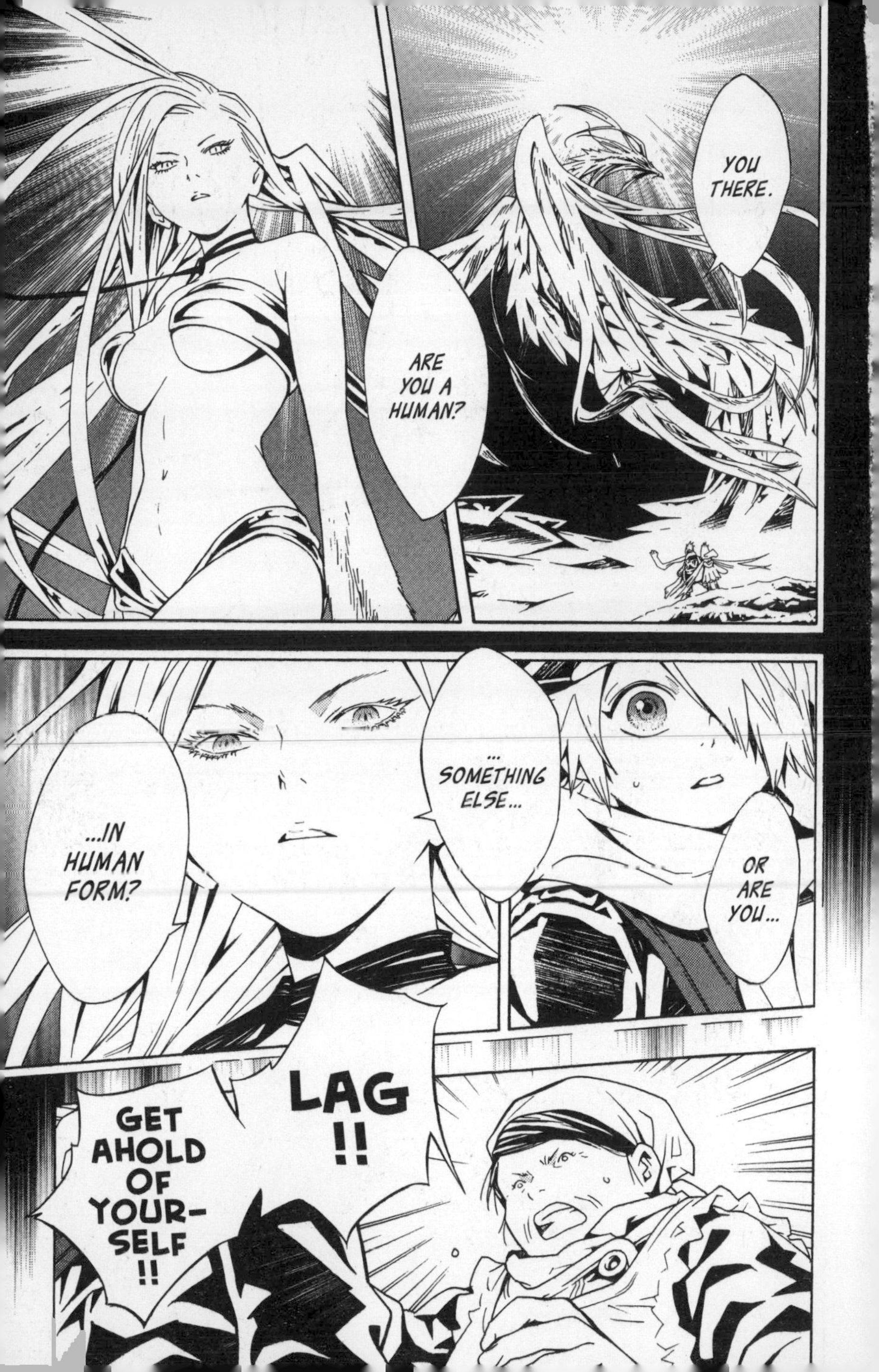
YOU THERE.
ARE YOU A HUMAN?
OR ARE YOU...
... SOMETHING ELSE...
...IN HUMAN FORM?
LAG !!
GET AHOLD OF YOUR-SELF !!

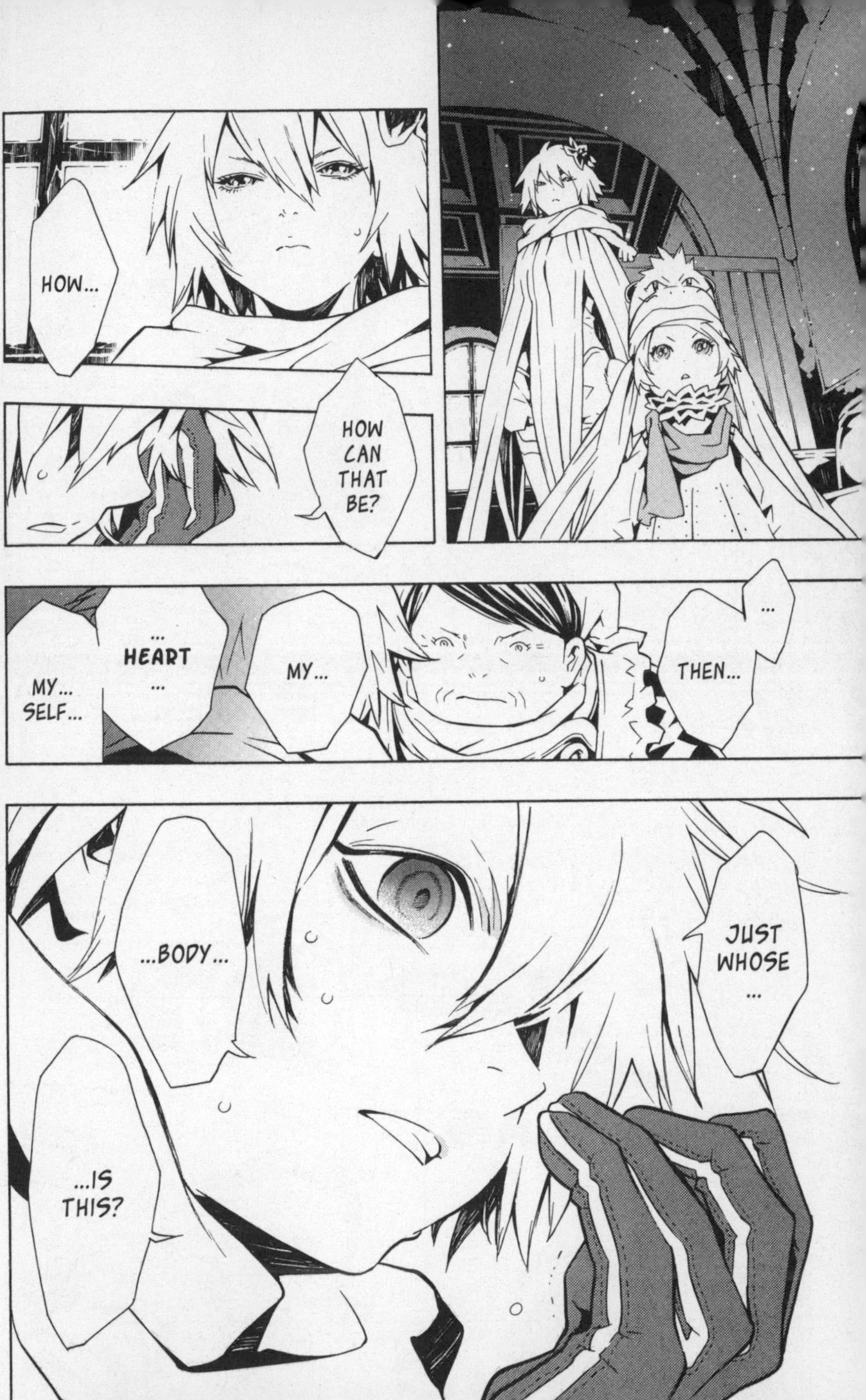
HOW...
HOW CAN THAT BE?
... THEN...
MY...
... HEART ...
MY... SELF...
JUST WHOSE ...
...BODY...
...IS THIS?

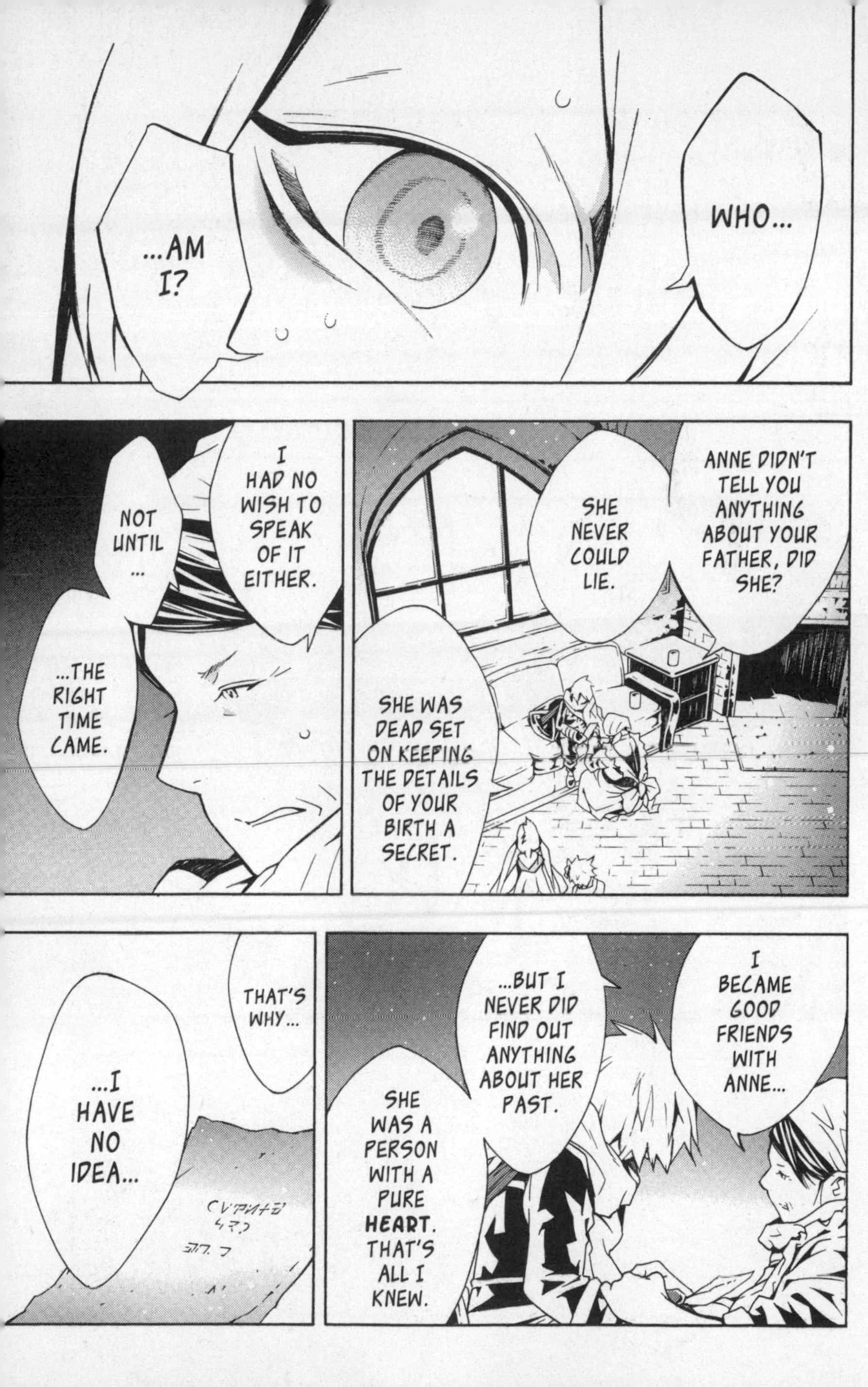
WHO...
...AM I?
ANNE DIDN'T TELL YOU ANYTHING ABOUT YOUR FATHER, DID SHE?
SHE NEVER COULD LIE.
SHE WAS DEAD SET ON KEEPING THE DETAILS OF YOUR BIRTH A SECRET.
I HAD NO WISH TO SPEAK OF IT EITHER.
NOT UNTIL ...
...THE RIGHT TIME CAME.
I BECAME GOOD FRIENDS WITH ANNE...
...BUT I NEVER DID FIND OUT ANYTHING ABOUT HER PAST.
SHE WAS A PERSON WITH A PURE **HEART**. THAT'S ALL I KNEW.
THAT'S WHY...
...I HAVE NO IDEA...

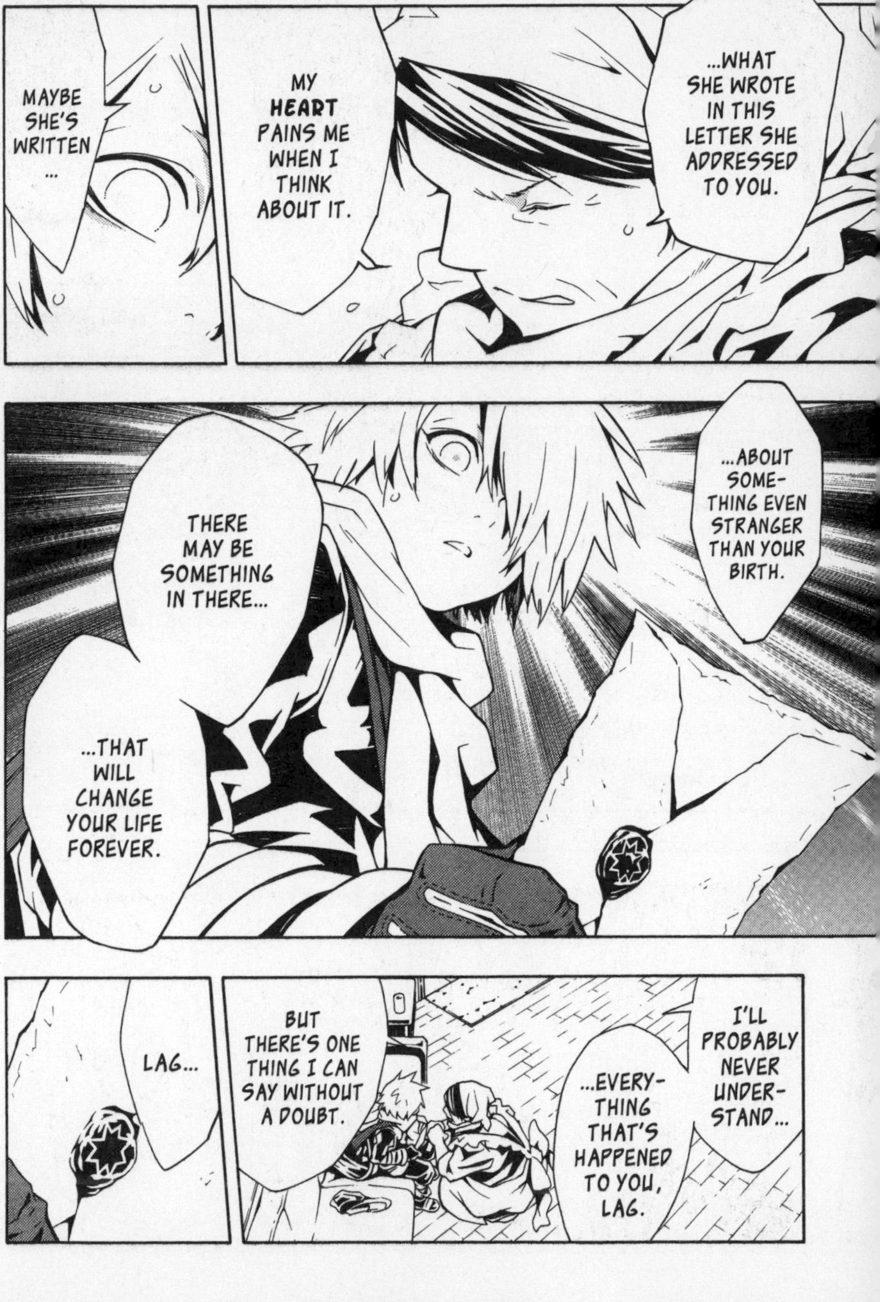
...WHAT SHE WROTE IN THIS LETTER SHE ADDRESSED TO YOU.
MY **HEART** PAINS ME WHEN I THINK ABOUT IT.
MAYBE SHE'S WRITTEN ...
...ABOUT SOME-THING EVEN STRANGER THAN YOUR BIRTH.
THERE MAY BE SOMETHING IN THERE...
...THAT WILL CHANGE YOUR LIFE FOREVER.
I'LL PROBABLY NEVER UNDER-STAND...
...EVERY-THING THAT'S HAPPENED TO YOU, LAG.
BUT THERE'S ONE THING I CAN SAY WITHOUT A DOUBT.
LAG...

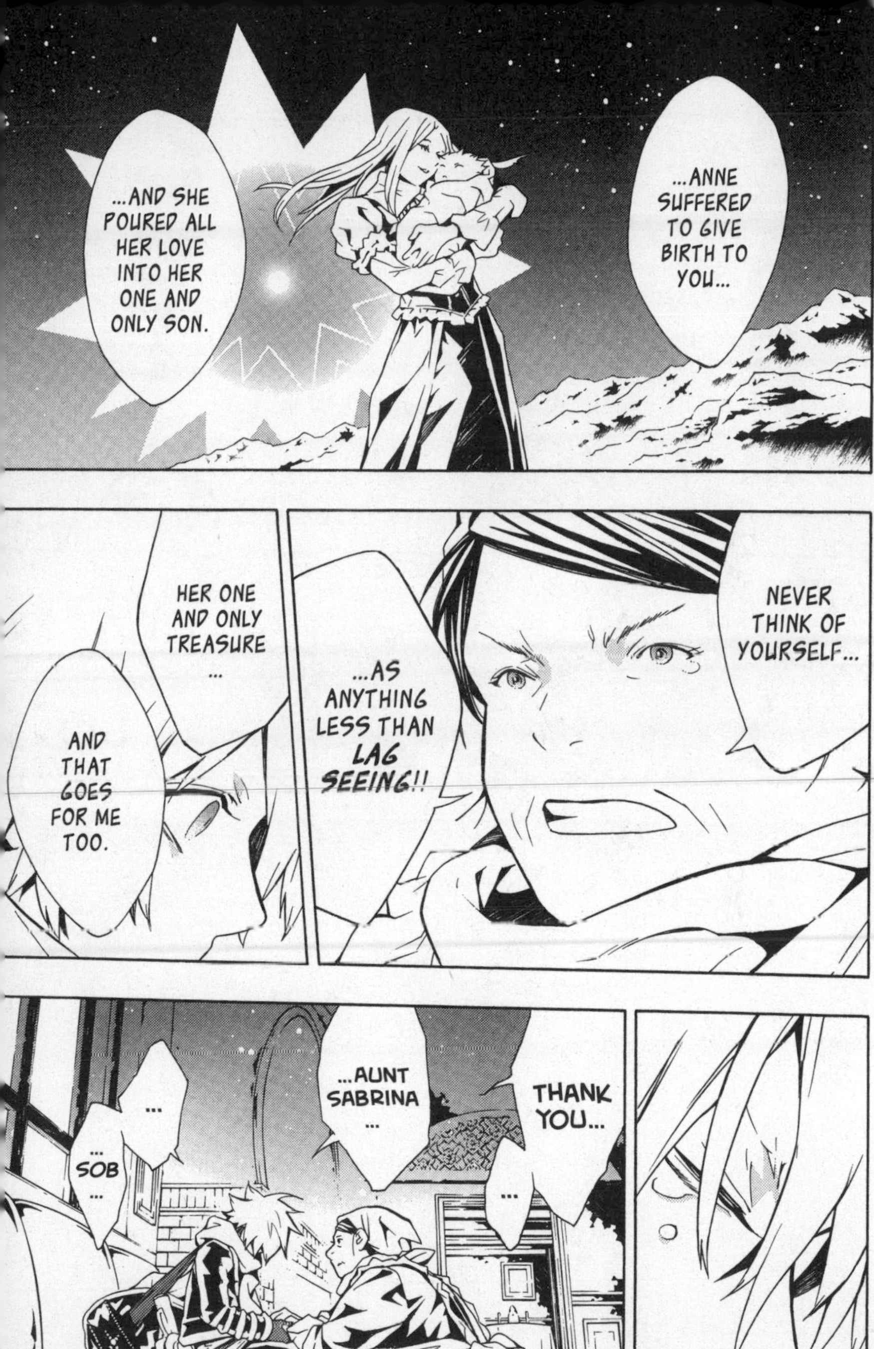
...ANNE SUFFERED TO GIVE BIRTH TO YOU...
...AND SHE POURED ALL HER LOVE INTO HER ONE AND ONLY SON.
NEVER THINK OF YOURSELF...
...AS ANYTHING LESS THAN *LAG SEEING*!!
HER ONE AND ONLY TREASURE ...
AND THAT GOES FOR ME TOO.
THANK YOU...
...
...AUNT SABRINA ...
...
... SOB ...

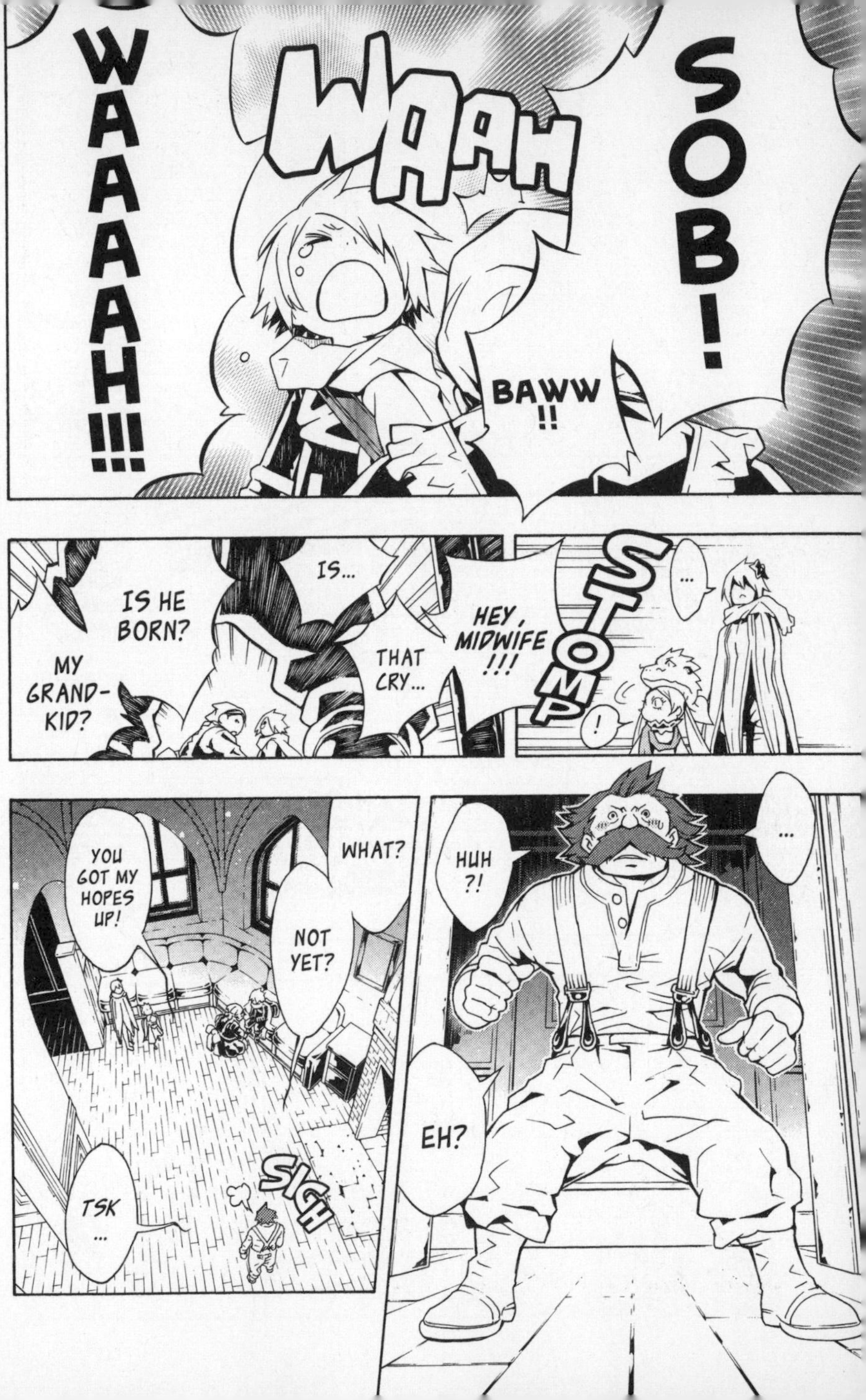
SOB!
WAAH
WAAAAAH!!!
BAWW !!
...
STOMP
!
HEY, MIDWIFE!!!
THAT CRY...
IS...
IS HE BORN?
MY GRAND-KID?
...
HUH ?!
EH?
WHAT?
NOT YET?
YOU GOT MY HOPES UP!
SIGH
TSK ...

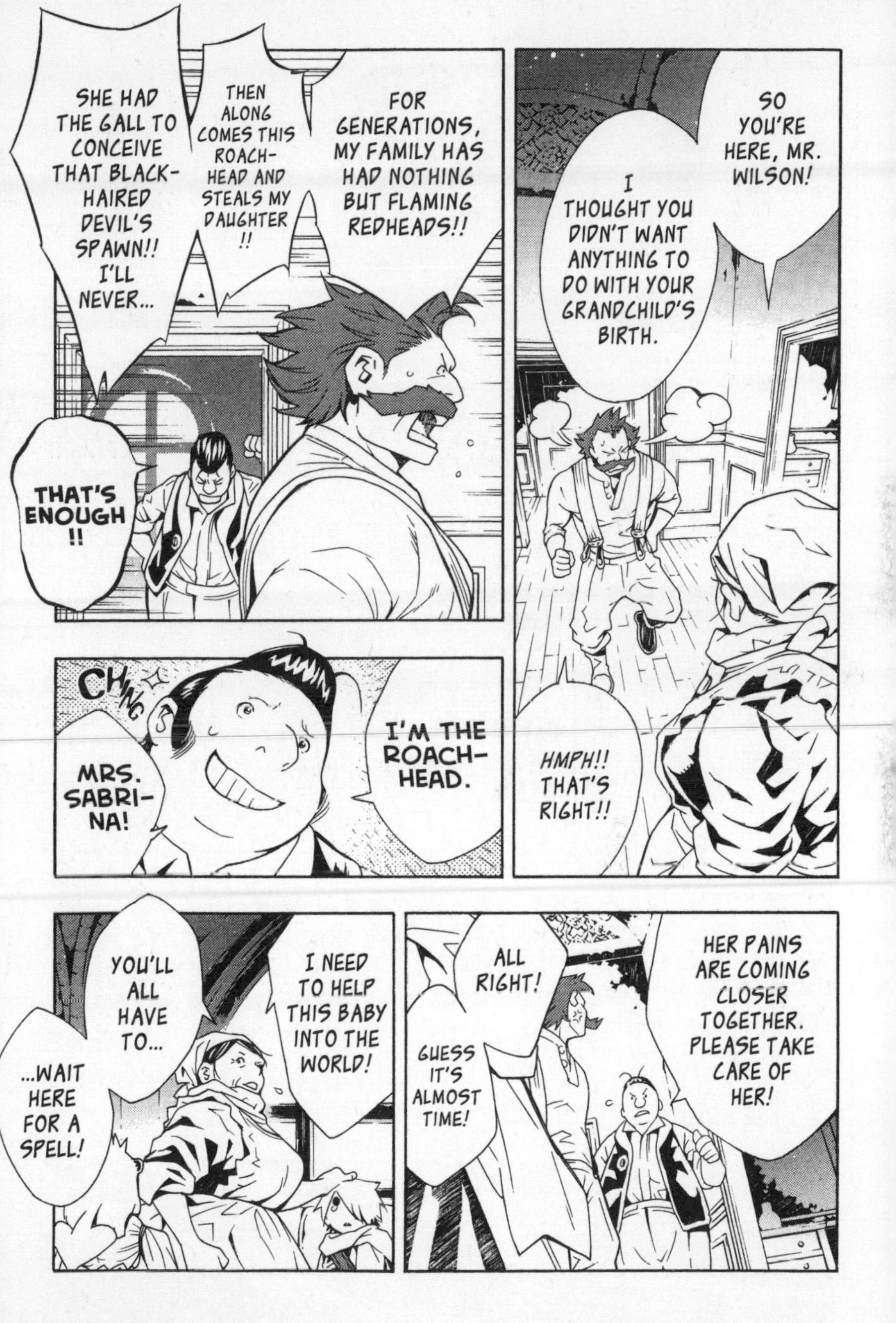
SO YOU'RE HERE, MR. WILSON!
I THOUGHT YOU DIDN'T WANT ANYTHING TO DO WITH YOUR GRANDCHILD'S BIRTH.
HMPH!! THAT'S RIGHT!!
FOR GENERATIONS, MY FAMILY HAS HAD NOTHING BUT FLAMING REDHEADS!!
THEN ALONG COMES THIS ROACH-HEAD AND STEALS MY DAUGHTER!!
SHE HAD THE GALL TO CONCEIVE THAT BLACK-HAIRED DEVIL'S SPAWN!! I'LL NEVER...
THAT'S ENOUGH!!
I'M THE ROACH-HEAD.
CHING
MRS. SABRI-NA!
HER PAINS ARE COMING CLOSER TOGETHER. PLEASE TAKE CARE OF HER!
ALL RIGHT!
GUESS IT'S ALMOST TIME!
I NEED TO HELP THIS BABY INTO THE WORLD!
YOU'LL ALL HAVE TO...
...WAIT HERE FOR A SPELL!

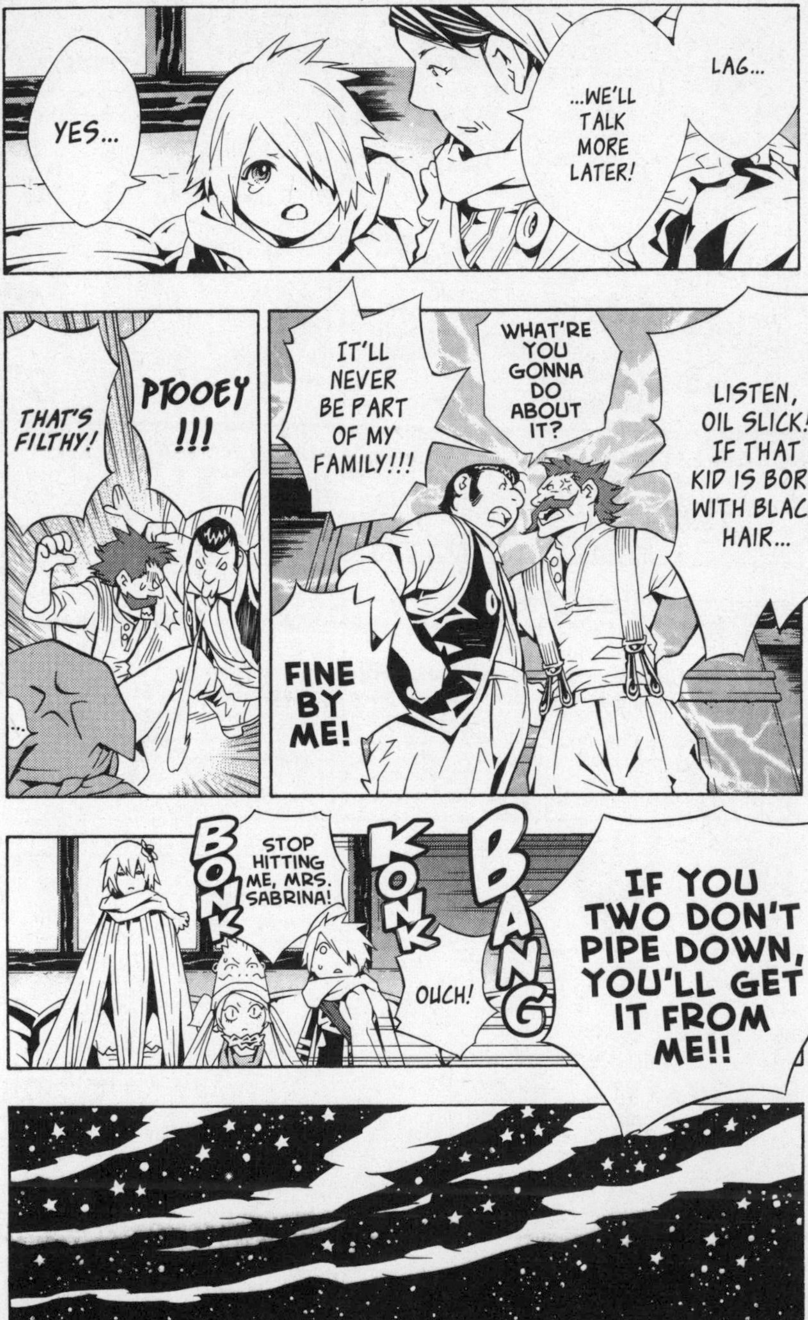
LAG...
...WE'LL TALK MORE LATER!
YES...
LISTEN, OIL SLICK! IF THAT KID IS BORN WITH BLACK HAIR...
WHAT'RE YOU GONNA DO ABOUT IT?
IT'LL NEVER BE PART OF MY FAMILY!!!
FINE BY ME!
PTOOEY!!!
THAT'S FILTHY!
...
IF YOU TWO DON'T PIPE DOWN, YOU'LL GET IT FROM ME!!
BANG
KONK
OUCH!
STOP HITTING ME, MRS. SABRINA!
BONK

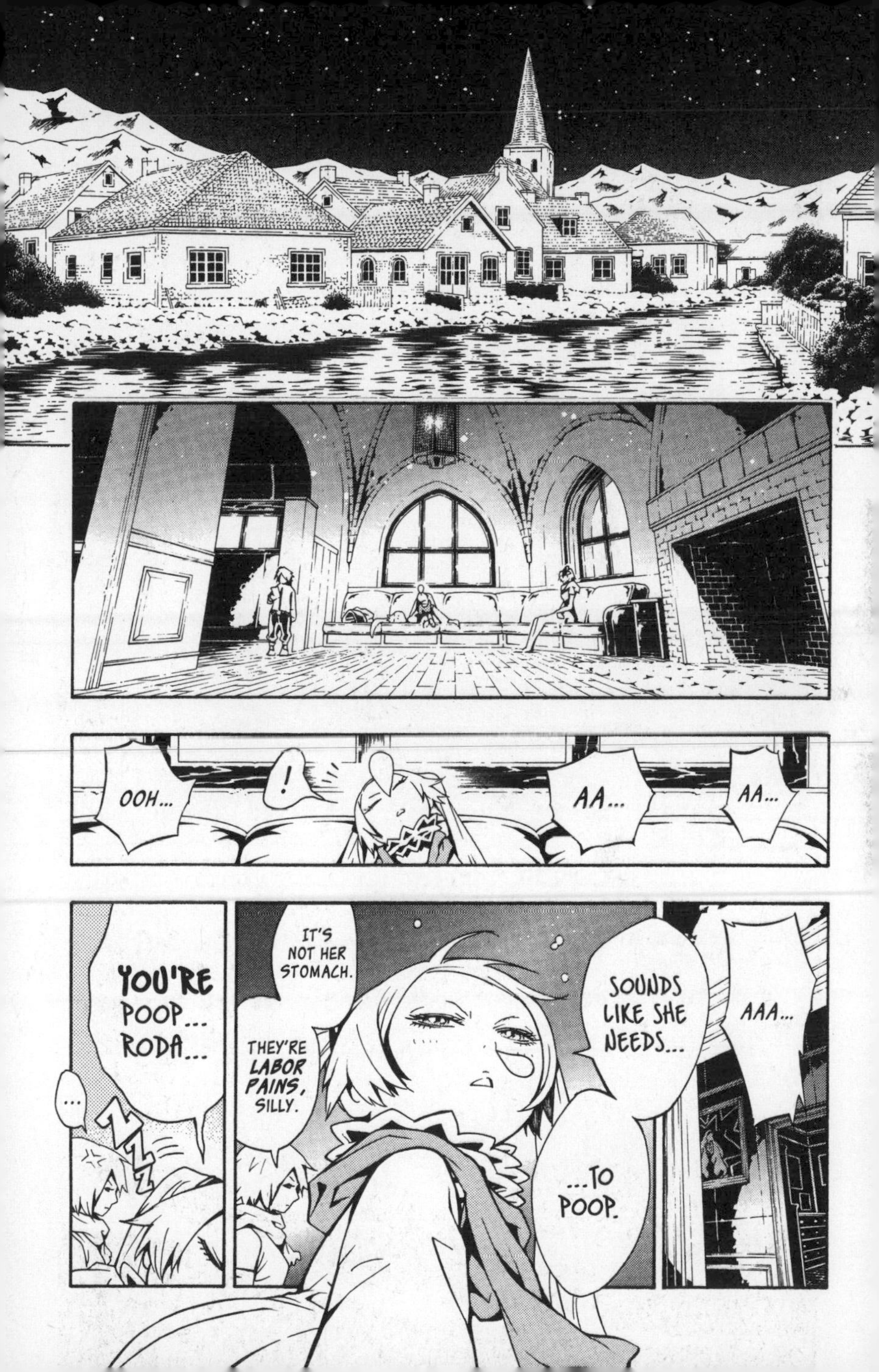
AA...
AA...
!
OOH...
AAA...
SOUNDS LIKE SHE NEEDS...
...TO POOP.
IT'S NOT HER STOMACH.
THEY'RE LABOR PAINS, SILLY.
YOU'RE POOP... RODA...
...
ZZZ

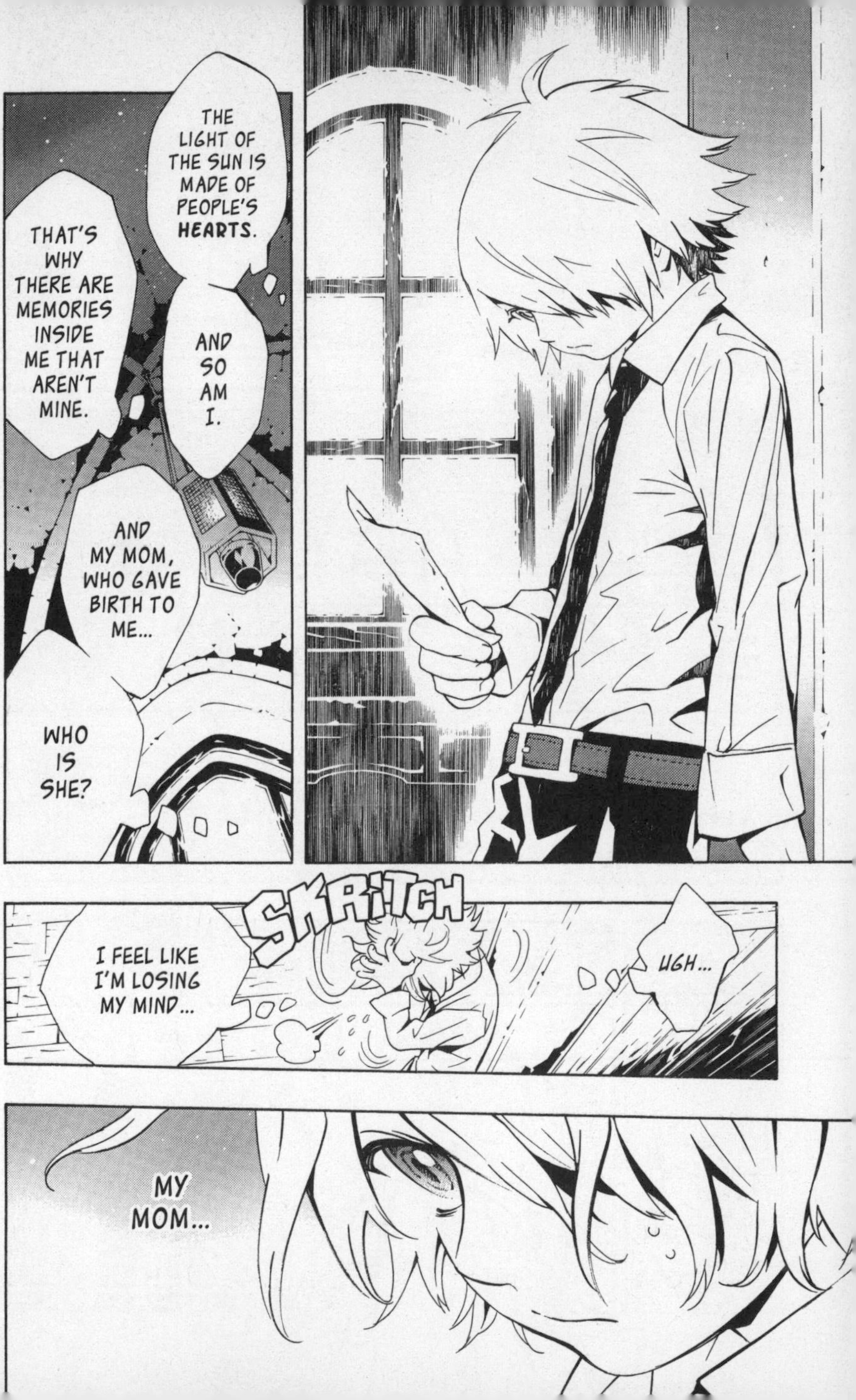
THE LIGHT OF THE SUN IS MADE OF PEOPLE'S HEARTS.
AND SO AM I.
THAT'S WHY THERE ARE MEMORIES INSIDE ME THAT AREN'T MINE.
AND MY MOM, WHO GAVE BIRTH TO ME...
WHO IS SHE?
UGH...
SKRITCH
I FEEL LIKE I'M LOSING MY MIND...
MY MOM...

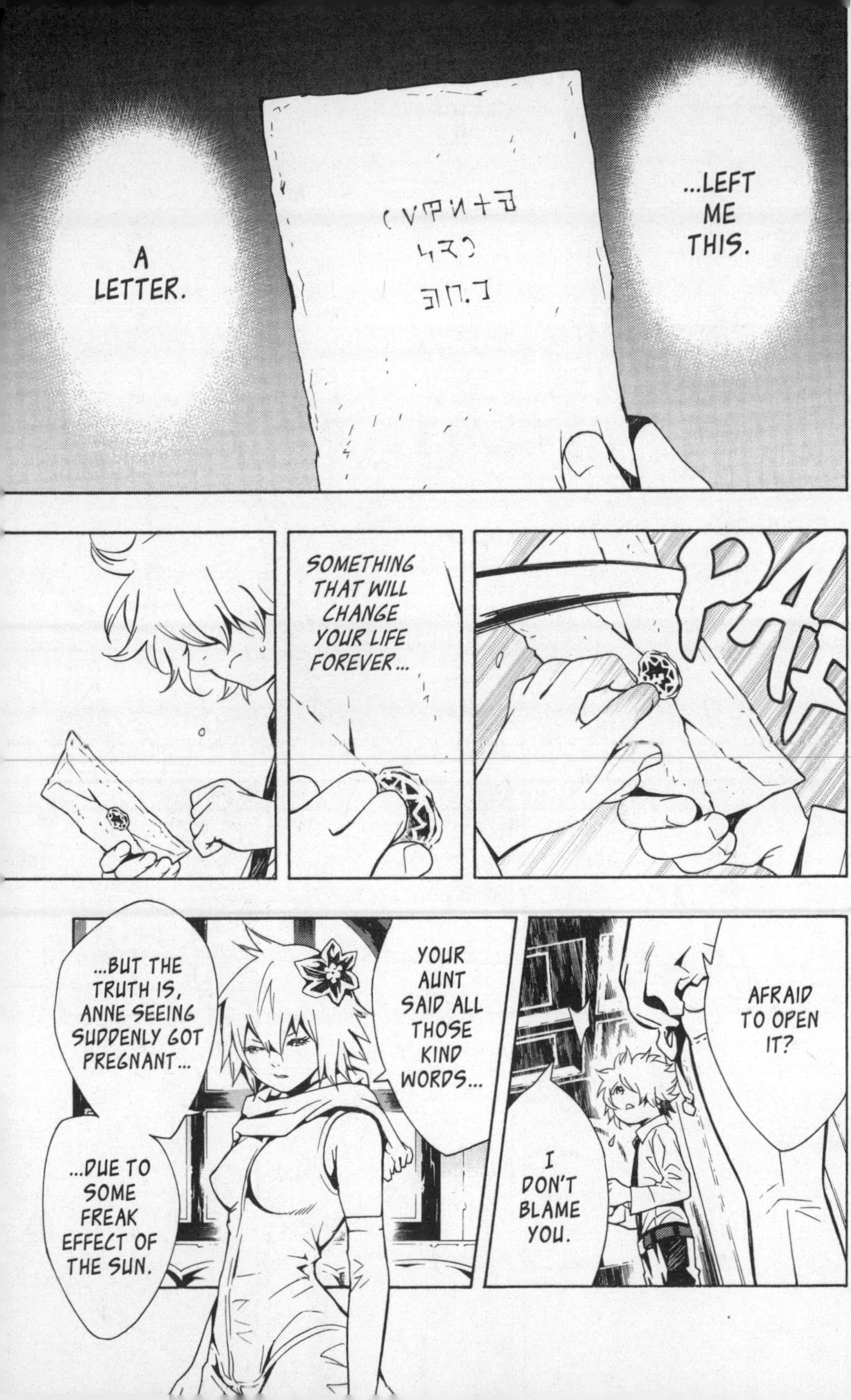
...LEFT ME THIS.
A LETTER.
PA
SOMETHING THAT WILL CHANGE YOUR LIFE FOREVER...
AFRAID TO OPEN IT?
I DON'T BLAME YOU.
YOUR AUNT SAID ALL THOSE KIND WORDS...
...BUT THE TRUTH IS, ANNE SEEING SUDDENLY GOT PREGNANT...
...DUE TO SOME FREAK EFFECT OF THE SUN.

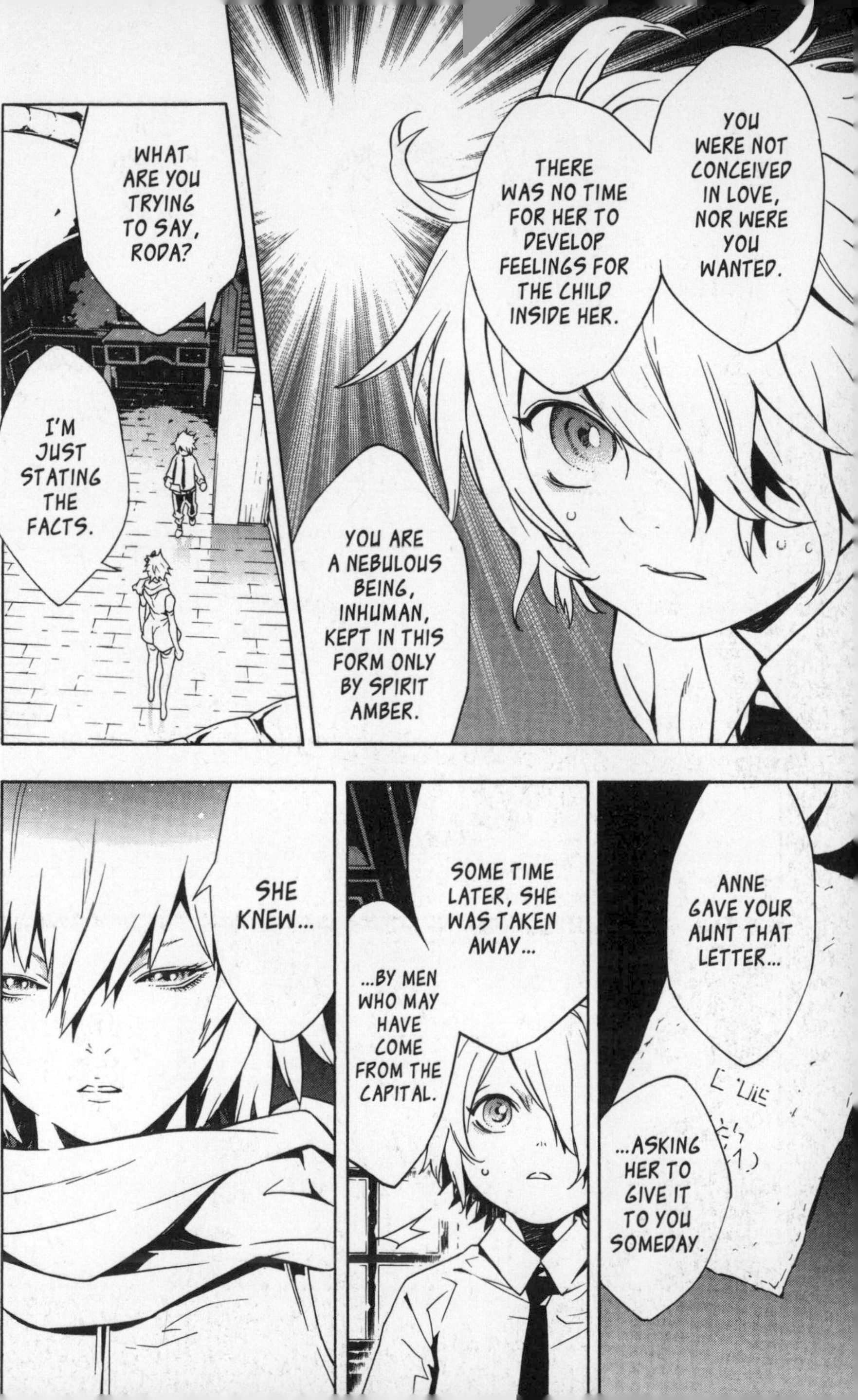
YOU WERE NOT CONCEIVED IN LOVE, NOR WERE YOU WANTED.
THERE WAS NO TIME FOR HER TO DEVELOP FEELINGS FOR THE CHILD INSIDE HER.
YOU ARE A NEBULOUS BEING, INHUMAN, KEPT IN THIS FORM ONLY BY SPIRIT AMBER.
WHAT ARE YOU TRYING TO SAY, RODA?
I'M JUST STATING THE FACTS.
ANNE GAVE YOUR AUNT THAT LETTER...
...ASKING HER TO GIVE IT TO YOU SOMEDAY.
SOME TIME LATER, SHE WAS TAKEN AWAY...
...BY MEN WHO MAY HAVE COME FROM THE CAPITAL.
SHE KNEW...

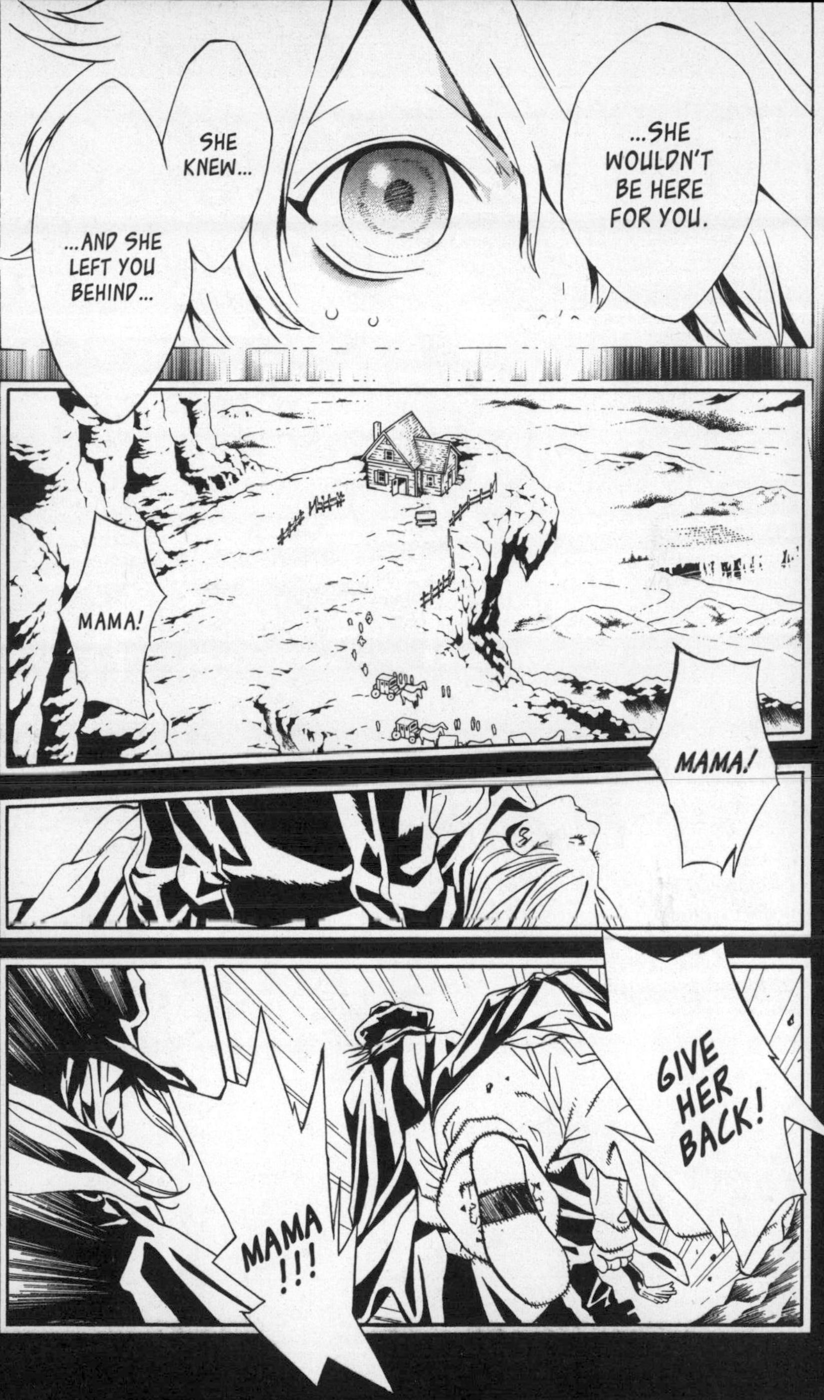
...SHE WOULDN'T BE HERE FOR YOU.
SHE KNEW...
...AND SHE LEFT YOU BEHIND...
MAMA!
MAMA!
GIVE HER BACK!
MAMA !!!

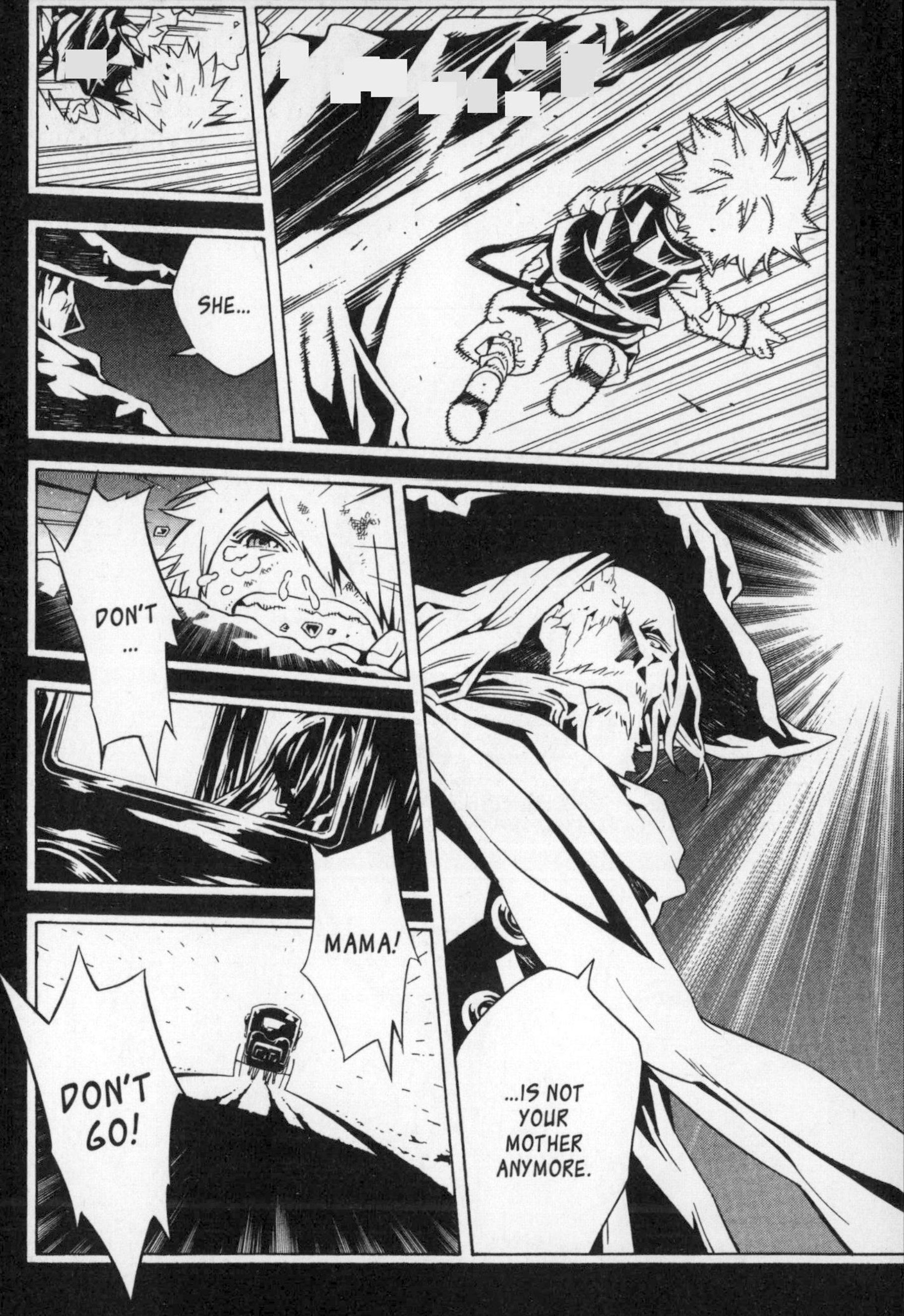
SHE...
...IS NOT YOUR MOTHER ANYMORE.
DON'T ...
MAMA!
DON'T GO!

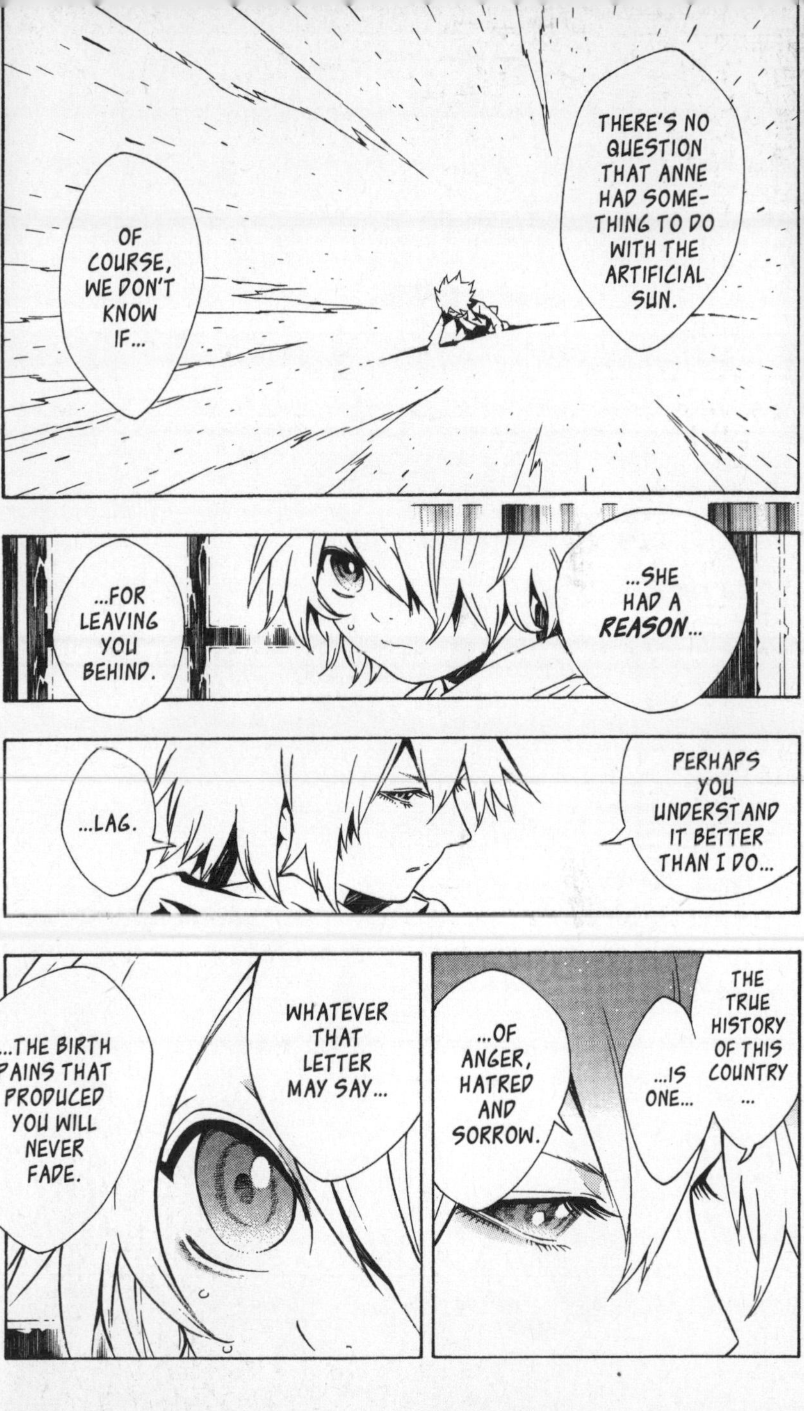
THERE'S NO QUESTION THAT ANNE HAD SOME-THING TO DO WITH THE ARTIFICIAL SUN.
OF COURSE, WE DON'T KNOW IF...
...SHE HAD A *REASON*...
...FOR LEAVING YOU BEHIND.
PERHAPS YOU UNDERSTAND IT BETTER THAN I DO...
...LAG.
THE TRUE HISTORY OF THIS COUNTRY ...
...IS ONE...
...OF ANGER, HATRED AND SORROW.
WHATEVER THAT LETTER MAY SAY...
...THE BIRTH PAINS THAT PRODUCED YOU WILL NEVER FADE.

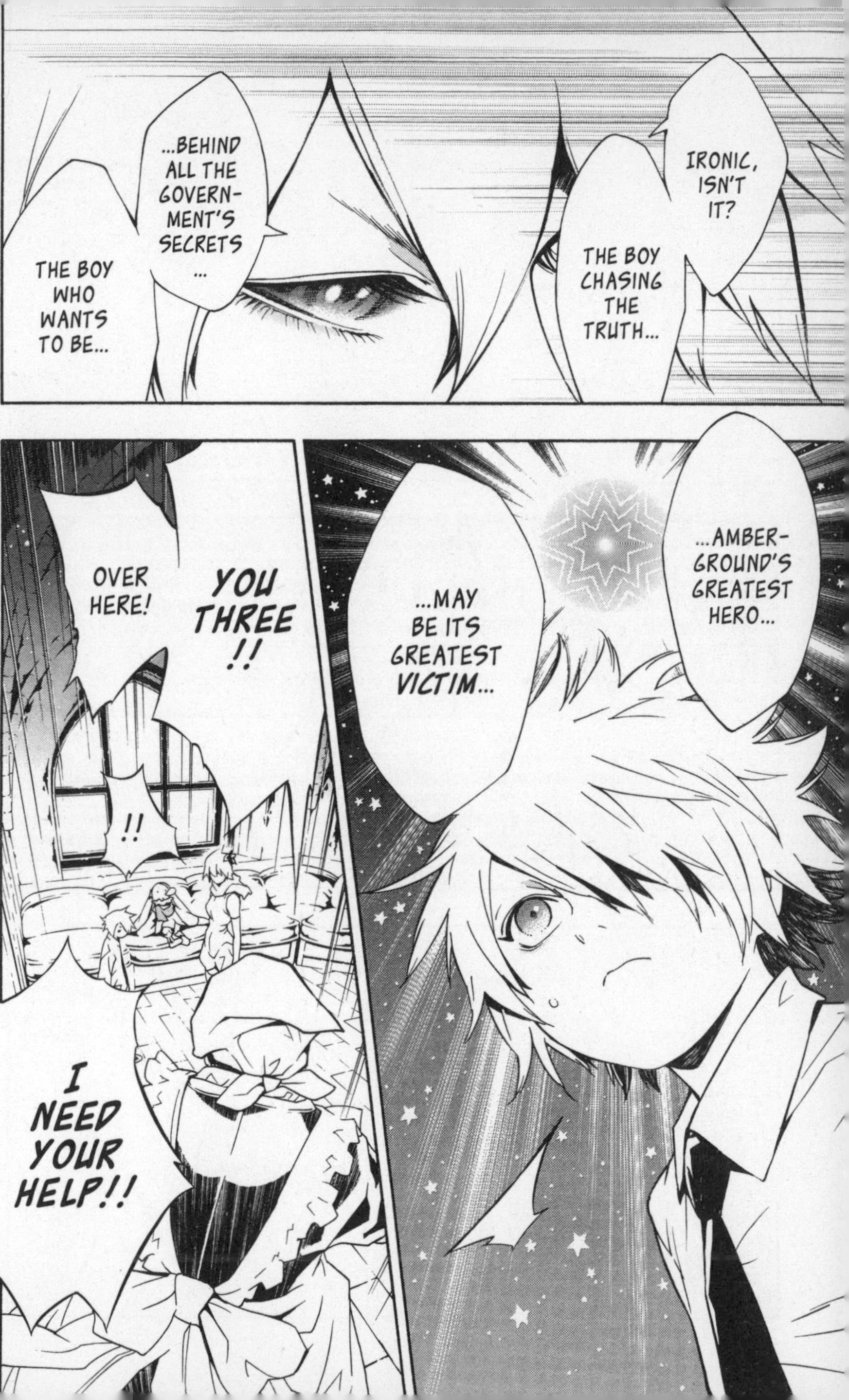
IRONIC, ISN'T IT?
THE BOY CHASING THE TRUTH...
...BEHIND ALL THE GOVERN-MENT'S SECRETS...
THE BOY WHO WANTS TO BE...
...AMBER-GROUND'S GREATEST HERO...
...MAY BE ITS GREATEST VICTIM...
YOU THREE!!
OVER HERE!
!!
I NEED YOUR HELP!!

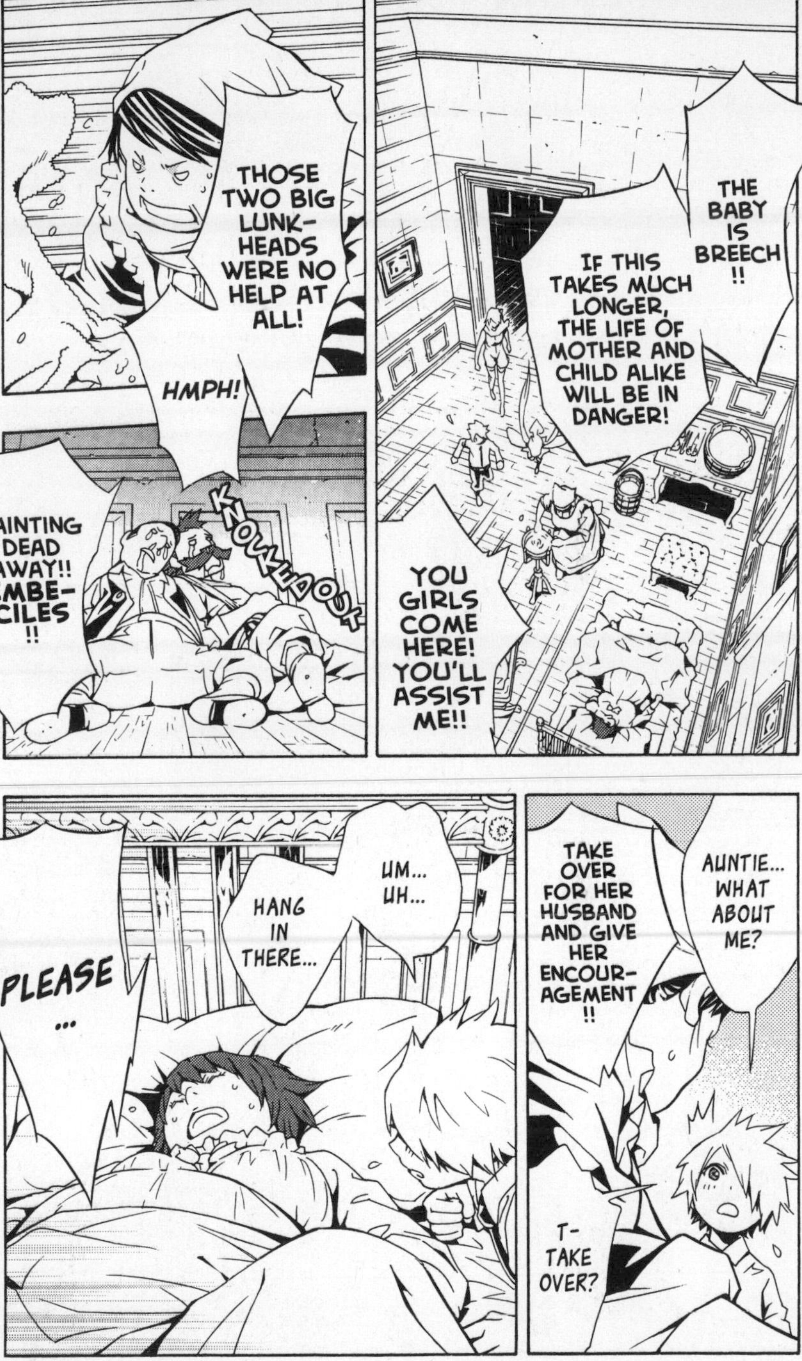
THE BABY IS BREECH!!
IF THIS TAKES MUCH LONGER, THE LIFE OF MOTHER AND CHILD ALIKE WILL BE IN DANGER!
YOU GIRLS COME HERE! YOU'LL ASSIST ME!!
THOSE TWO BIG LUNKHEADS WERE NO HELP AT ALL!
HMPH!
KNOCKED OUT
FAINTING DEAD AWAY!! IMBECILES!!
AUNTIE... WHAT ABOUT ME?
TAKE OVER FOR HER HUSBAND AND GIVE HER ENCOURAGEMENT!!
T-TAKE OVER?
UM... UH...
HANG IN THERE...
PLEASE...

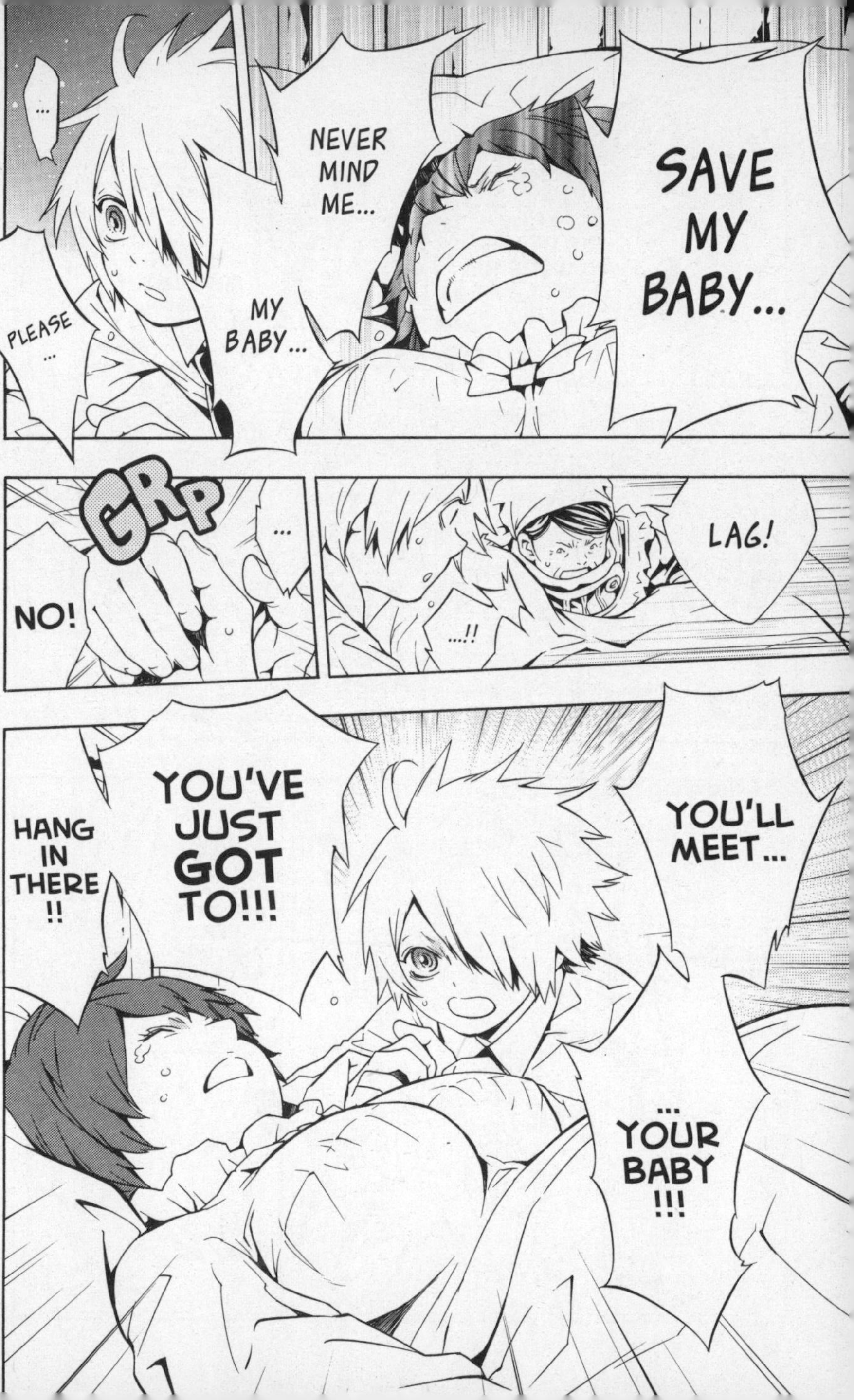
SAVE MY BABY...
NEVER MIND ME...
...
MY BABY...
PLEASE ...
LAG!
...!!
GRP
...
NO!
YOU'LL MEET...
... YOUR BABY !!!
YOU'VE JUST GOT TO!!!
HANG IN THERE !!

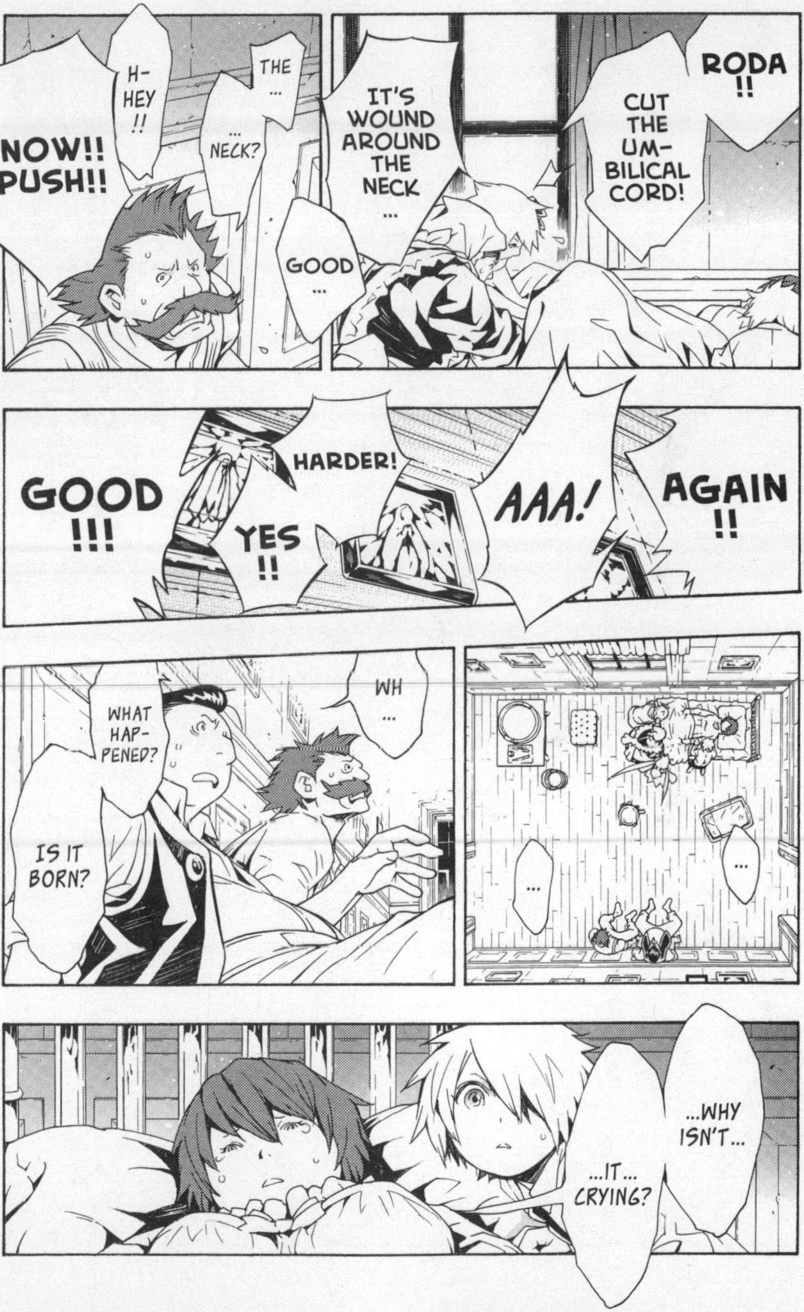
RODA!!
CUT THE UM-BILICAL CORD!
IT'S WOUND AROUND THE NECK ...
GOOD ...
THE ...
... NECK?
H-HEY!!
NOW!! PUSH!!
AGAIN!!
AAA!
YES!!
HARDER!
GOOD!!!
...
...
WH ...
WHAT HAP-PENED?
IS IT BORN?
...WHY ISN'T...
...IT... CRYING?

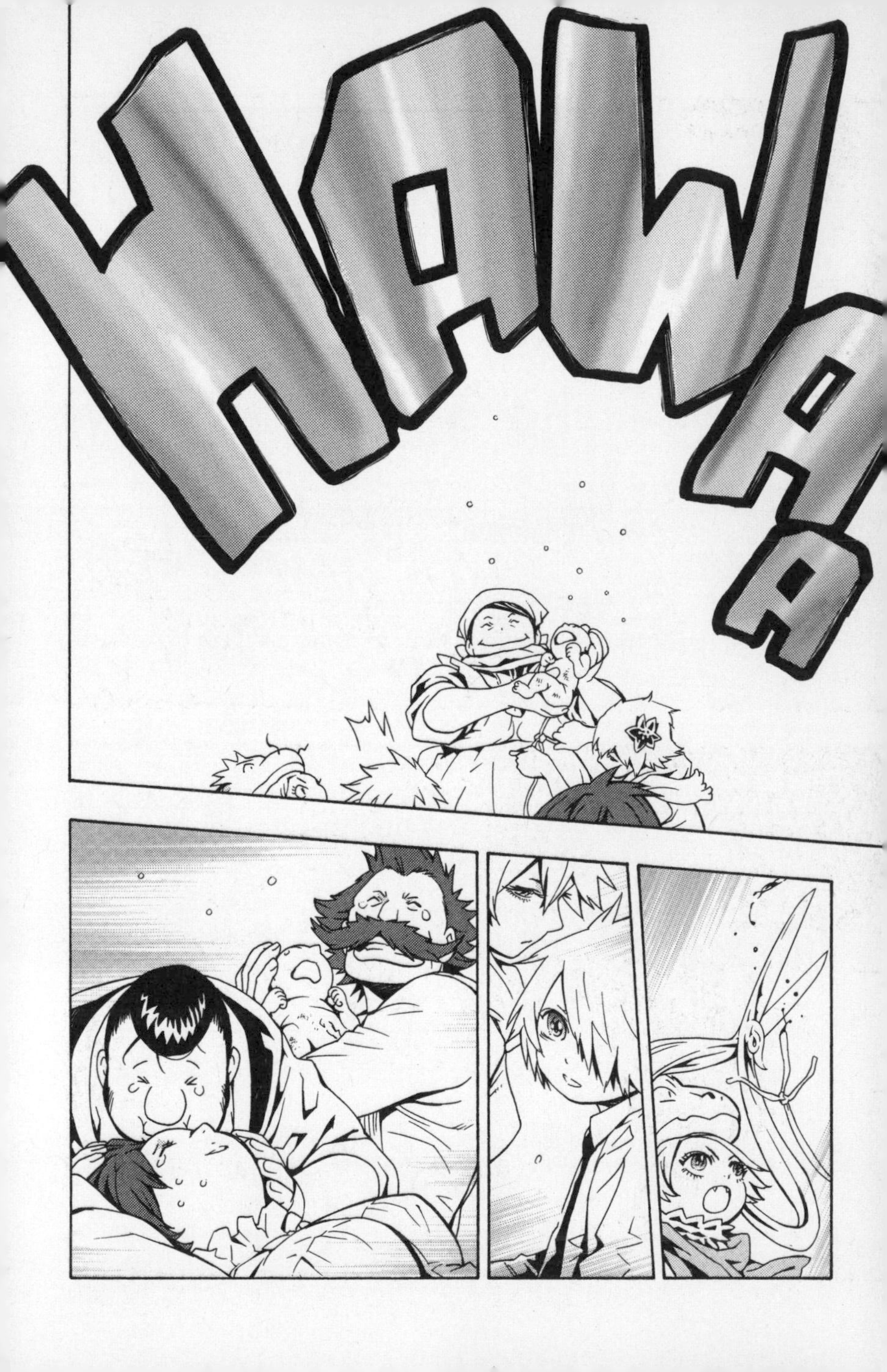
HAWAA

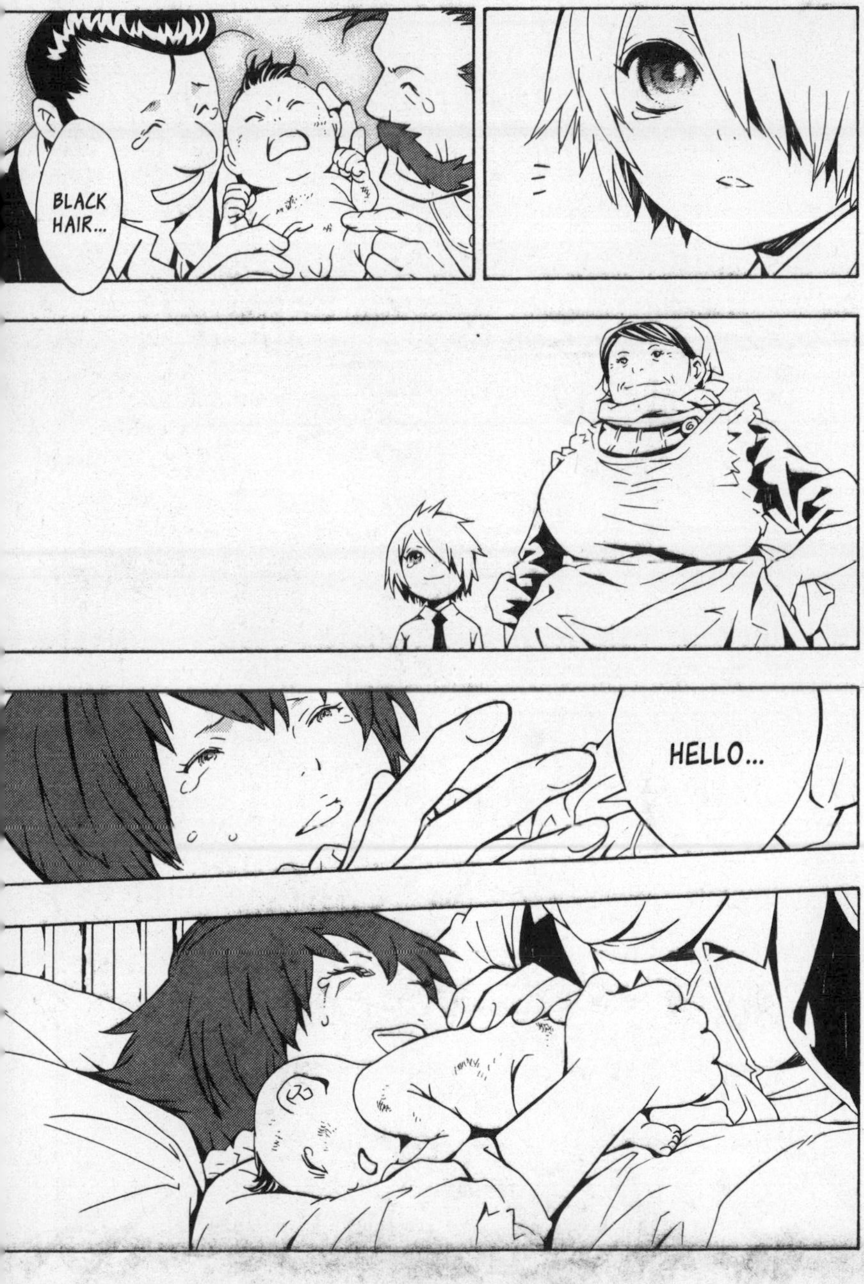
BLACK HAIR...
HELLO...

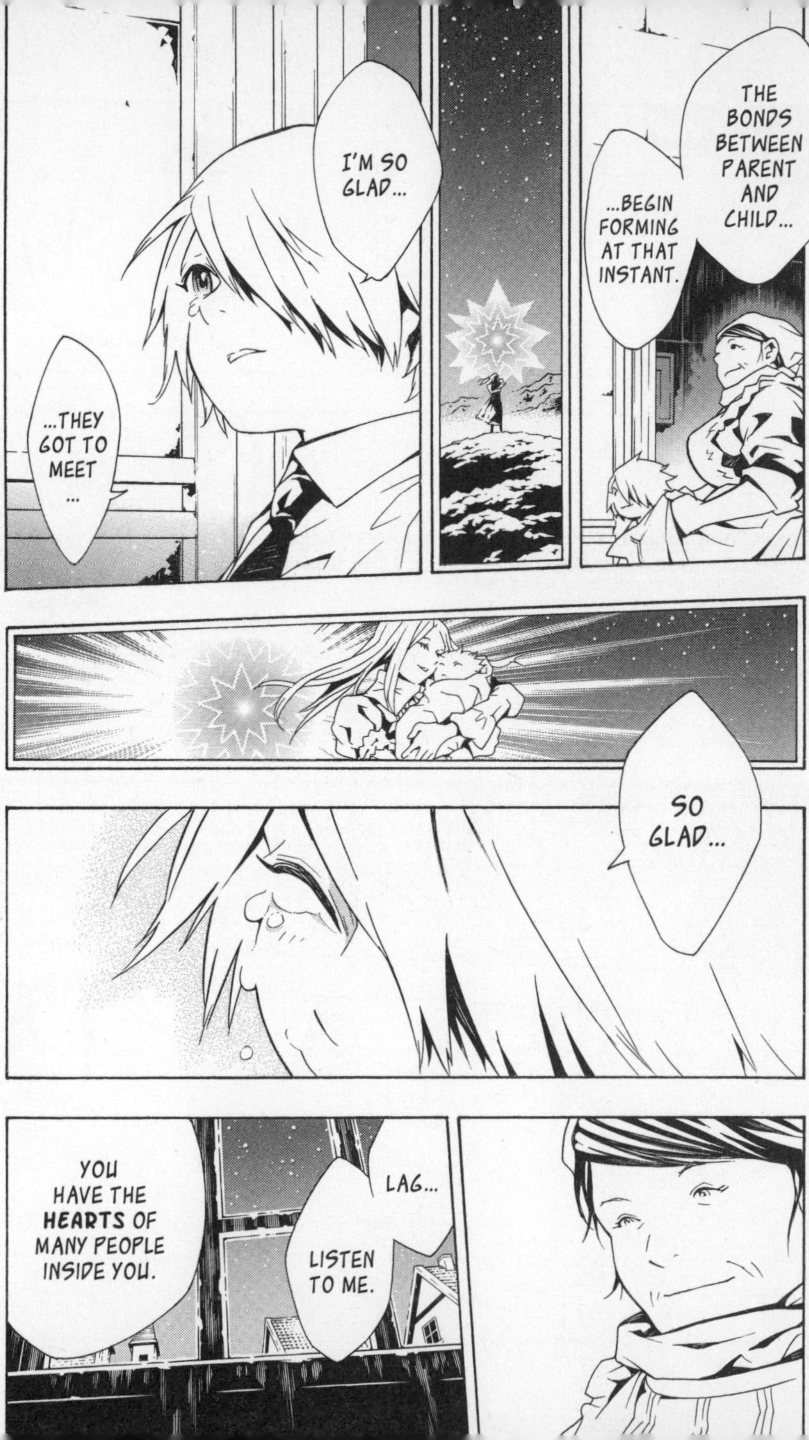
THE BONDS BETWEEN PARENT AND CHILD...
...BEGIN FORMING AT THAT INSTANT.
I'M SO GLAD...
...THEY GOT TO MEET ...
SO GLAD...
LAG...
LISTEN TO ME.
YOU HAVE THE **HEARTS** OF MANY PEOPLE INSIDE YOU.

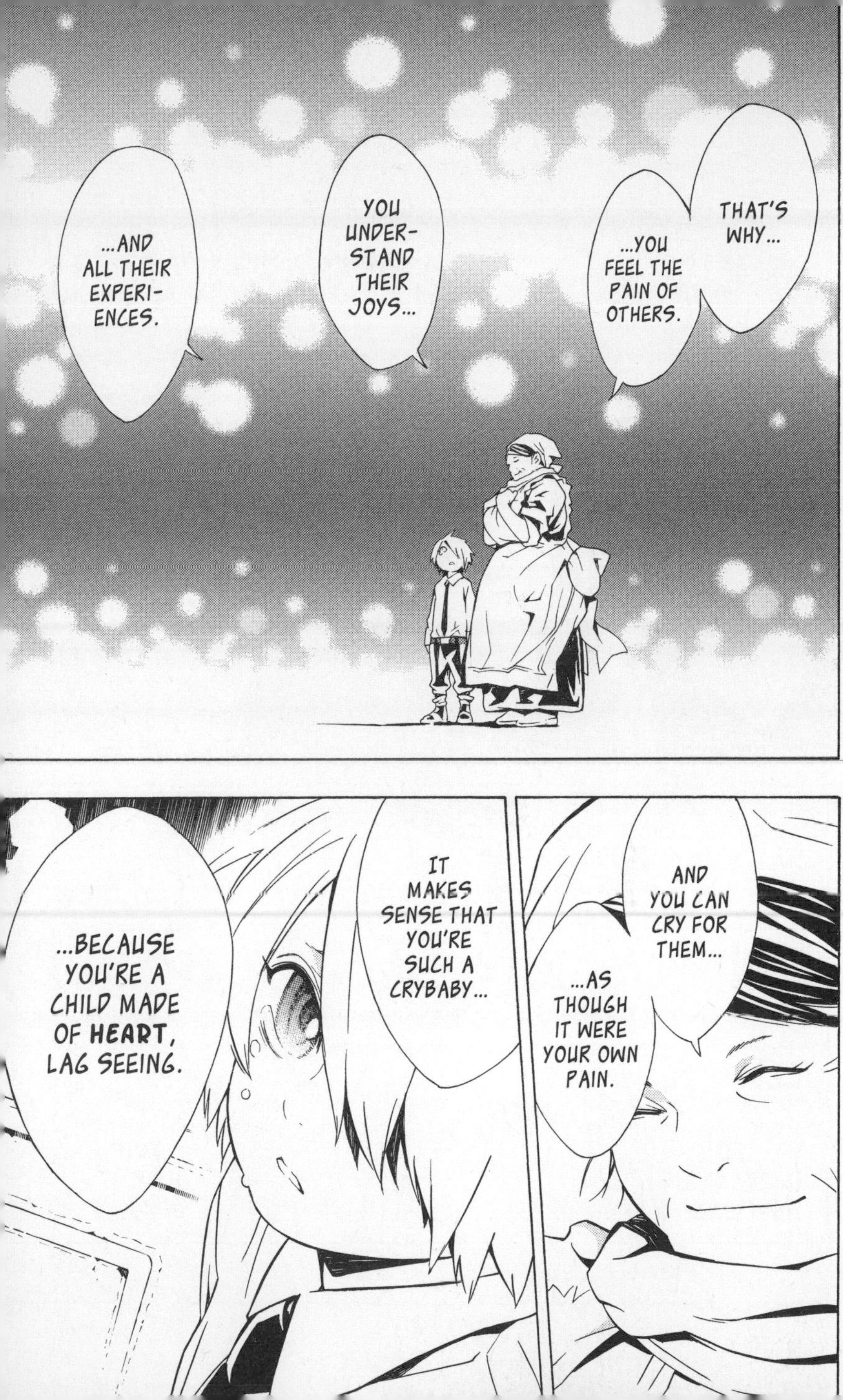
THAT'S WHY...
...YOU FEEL THE PAIN OF OTHERS.
YOU UNDER-STAND THEIR JOYS...
...AND ALL THEIR EXPERI-ENCES.
AND YOU CAN CRY FOR THEM...
...AS THOUGH IT WERE YOUR OWN PAIN.
IT MAKES SENSE THAT YOU'RE SUCH A CRYBABY...
...BECAUSE YOU'RE A CHILD MADE OF **HEART**, LAG SEEING.

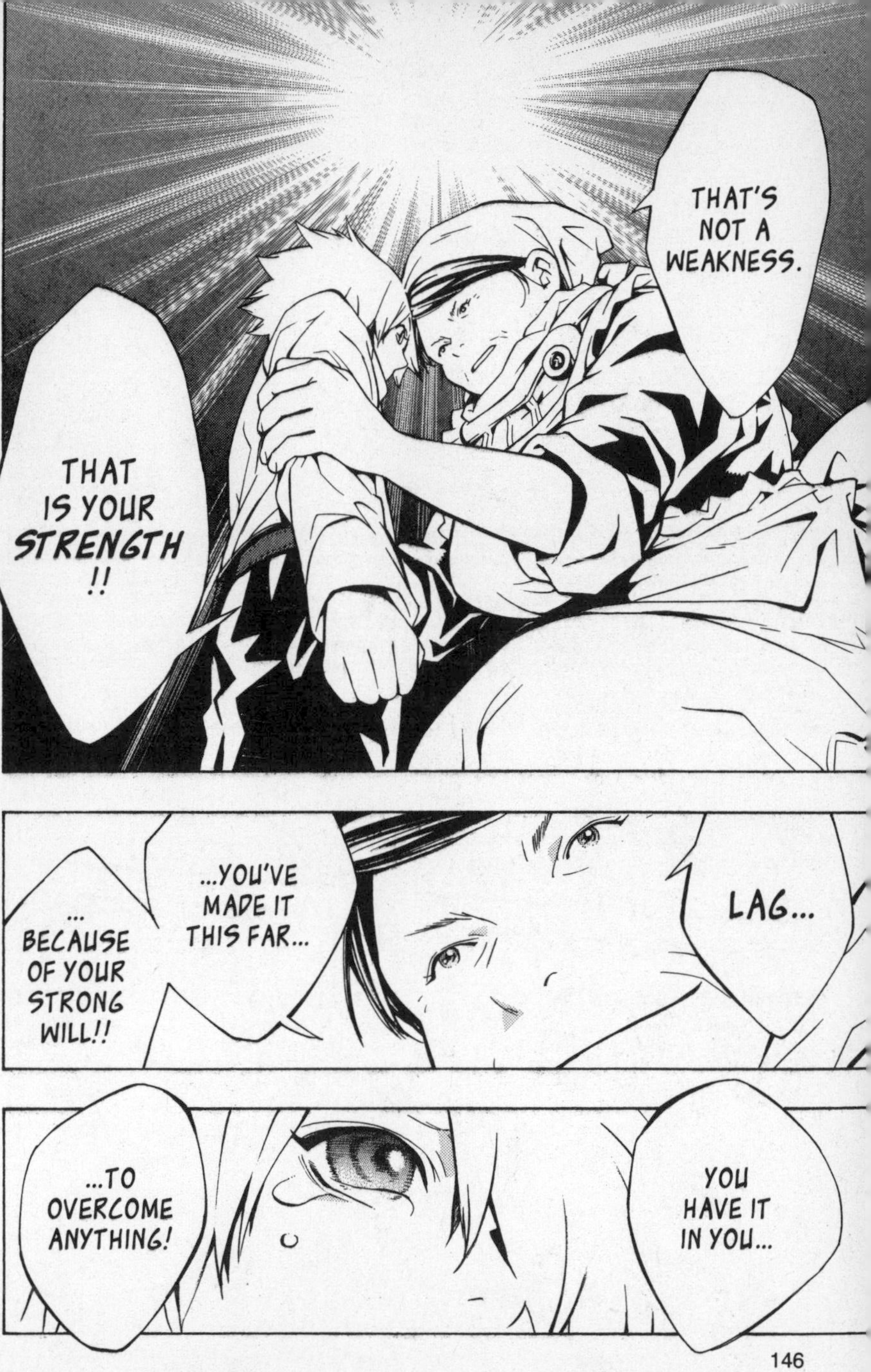
THAT'S NOT A WEAKNESS.
THAT IS YOUR *STRENGTH* !!
LAG...
...YOU'VE MADE IT THIS FAR...
... BECAUSE OF YOUR STRONG WILL!!
YOU HAVE IT IN YOU...
...TO OVERCOME ANYTHING!

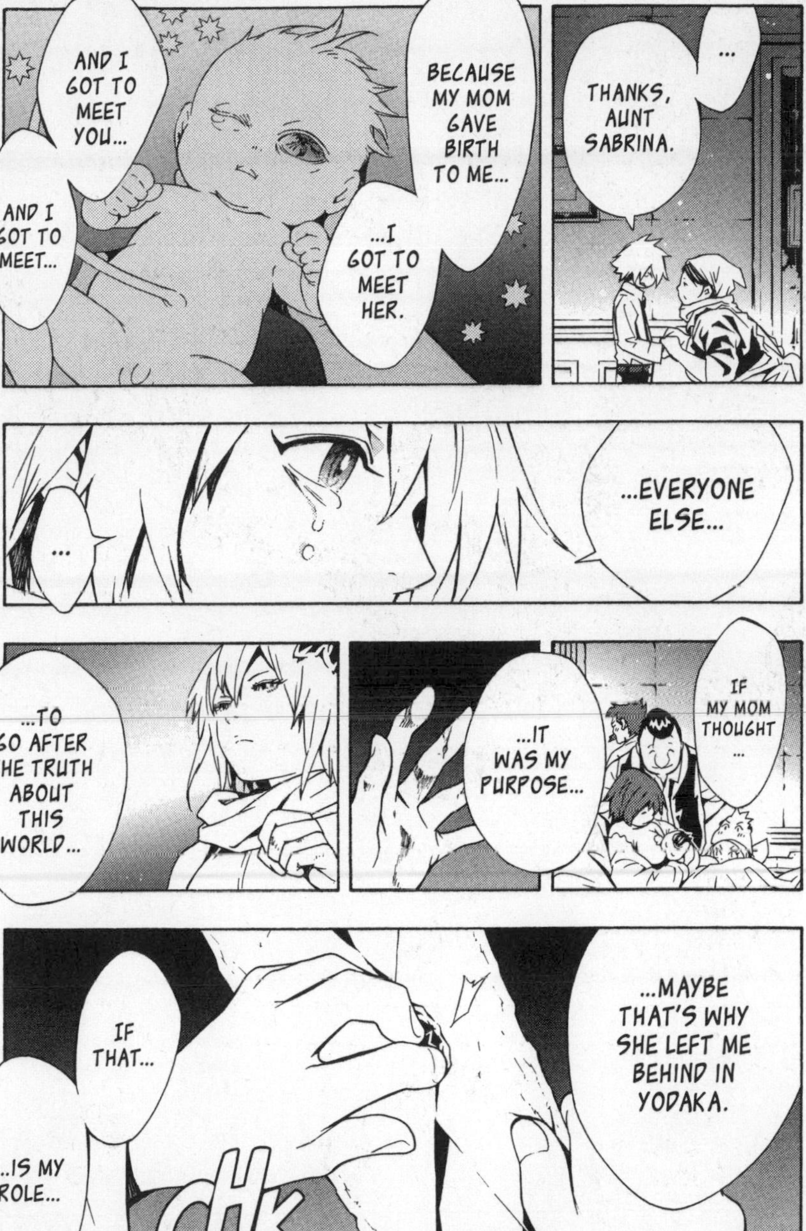
...
THANKS, AUNT SABRINA.
BECAUSE MY MOM GAVE BIRTH TO ME...
...I GOT TO MEET HER.
AND I GOT TO MEET YOU...
AND I GOT TO MEET...
...EVERYONE ELSE...
...
IF MY MOM THOUGHT ...
...IT WAS MY PURPOSE...
...TO GO AFTER THE TRUTH ABOUT THIS WORLD...
...MAYBE THAT'S WHY SHE LEFT ME BEHIND IN YODAKA.
IF THAT...
...IS MY ROLE...
CHK

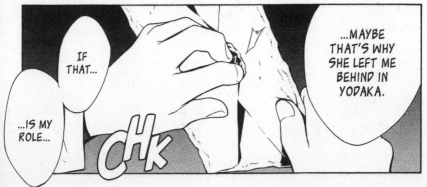

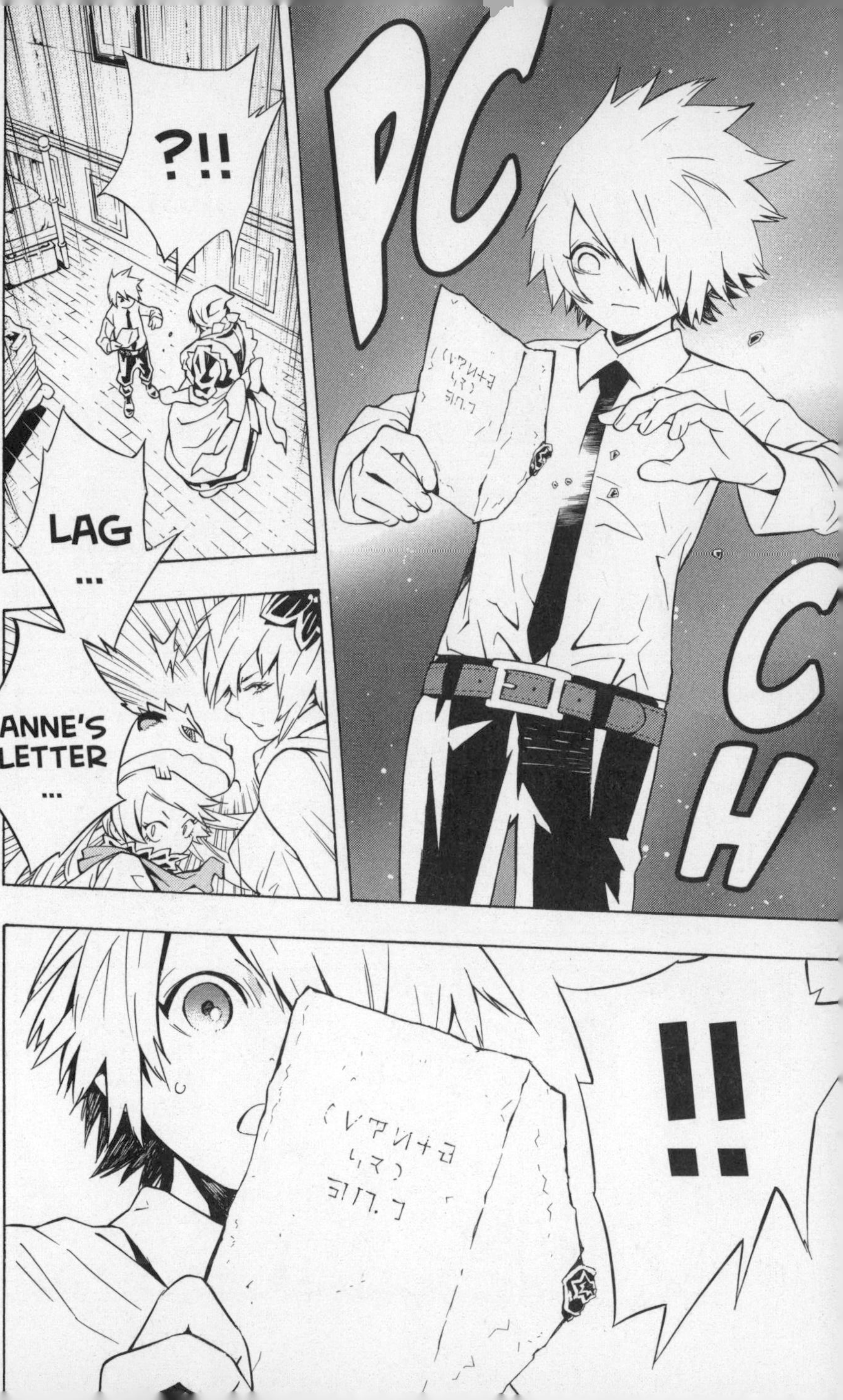
PC
CH
?!!
LAG ...
ANNE'S LETTER ...
!!

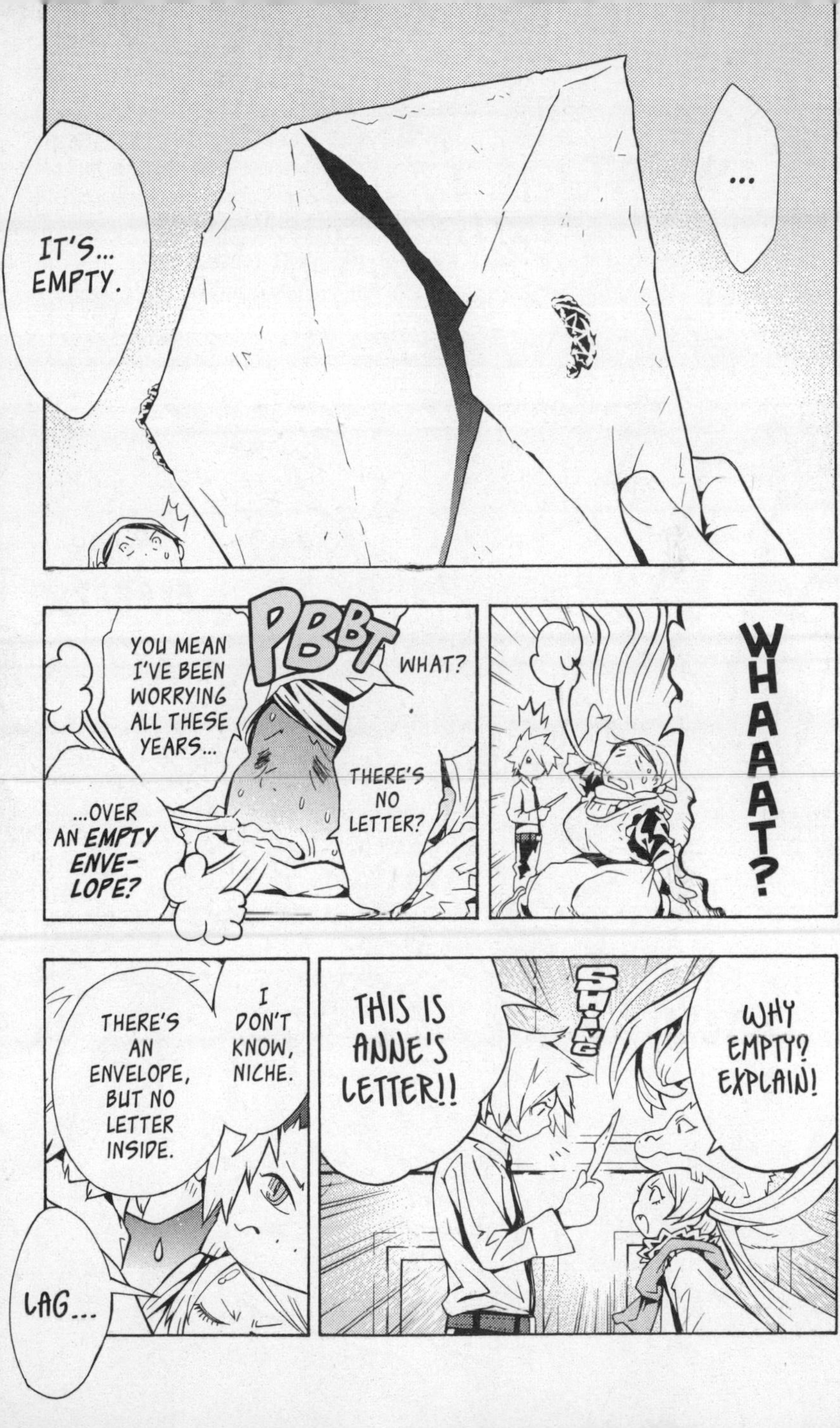
...
IT'S... EMPTY.
WHAAAAT?
PBBT
WHAT?
THERE'S NO LETTER?
YOU MEAN I'VE BEEN WORRYING ALL THESE YEARS...
...OVER AN *EMPTY ENVELOPE?*
WHY EMPTY? EXPLAIN!
SHING
THIS IS ANNE'S LETTER!!
I DON'T KNOW, NICHE.
THERE'S AN ENVELOPE, BUT NO LETTER INSIDE.
LAG...

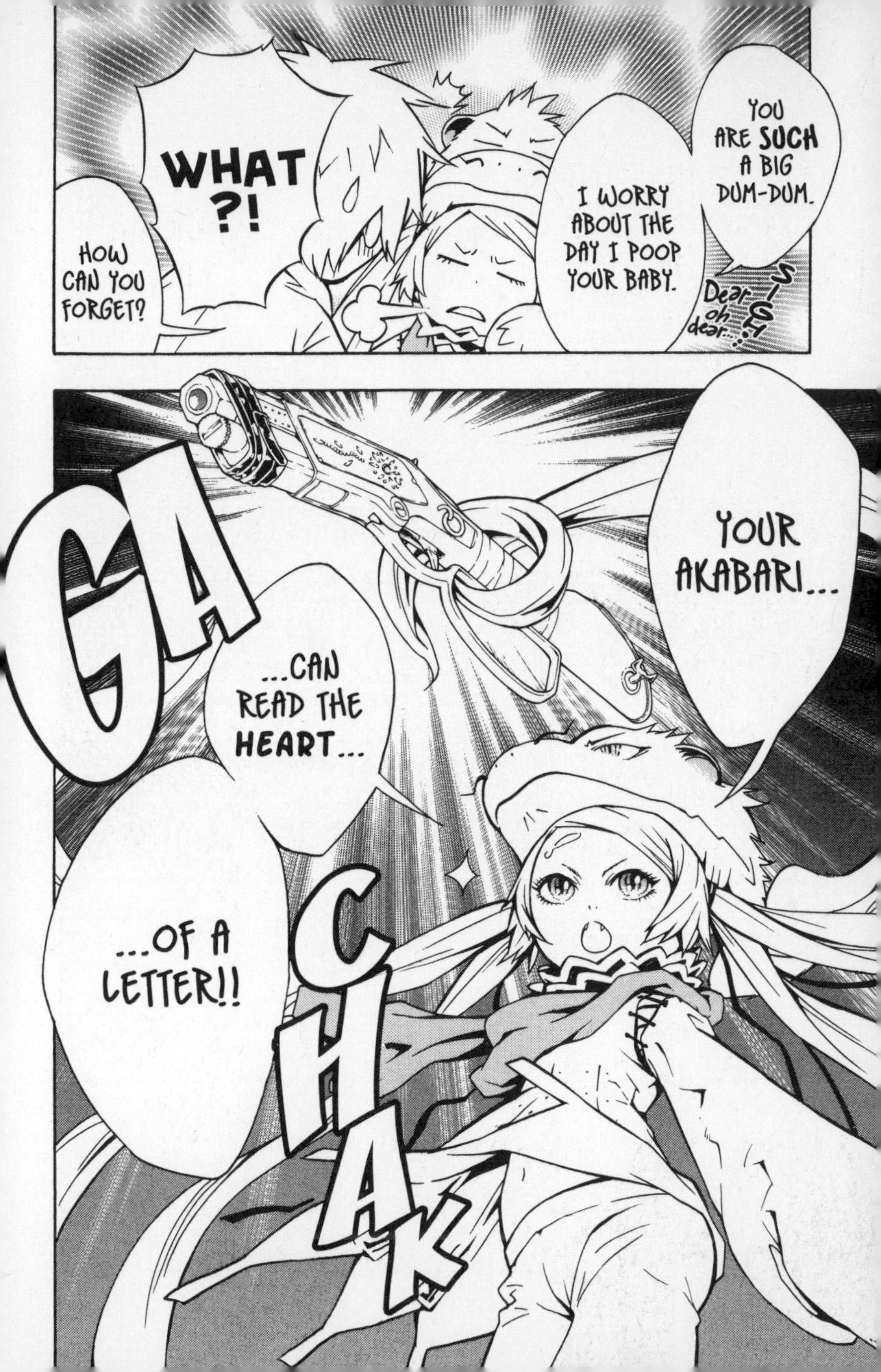
YOU ARE **SUCH** A BIG DUM-DUM.
SIGH
Dear oh dear...!
I WORRY ABOUT THE DAY I POOP YOUR BABY.
WHAT?!
HOW CAN YOU FORGET?
YOUR AKABARI...
...CAN READ THE **HEART**...
...OF A LETTER!!
GA
CHAK

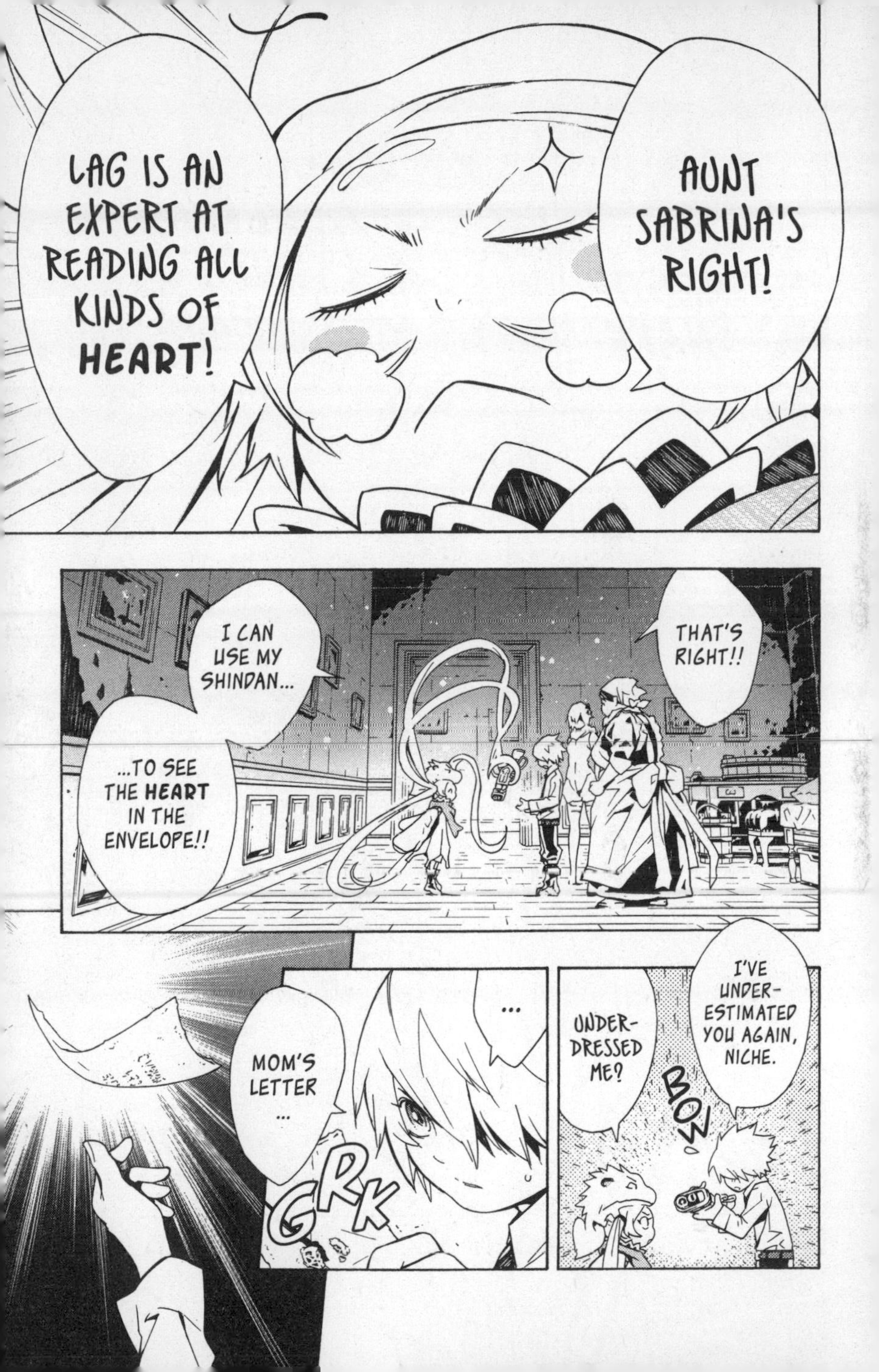
AUNT SABRINA'S RIGHT!
LAG IS AN EXPERT AT READING ALL KINDS OF HEART!
THAT'S RIGHT!!
I CAN USE MY SHINDAN...
...TO SEE THE HEART IN THE ENVELOPE!!
I'VE UNDER-ESTIMATED YOU AGAIN, NICHE.
BOW
UNDER-DRESSED ME?
...
MOM'S LETTER ...
GRK

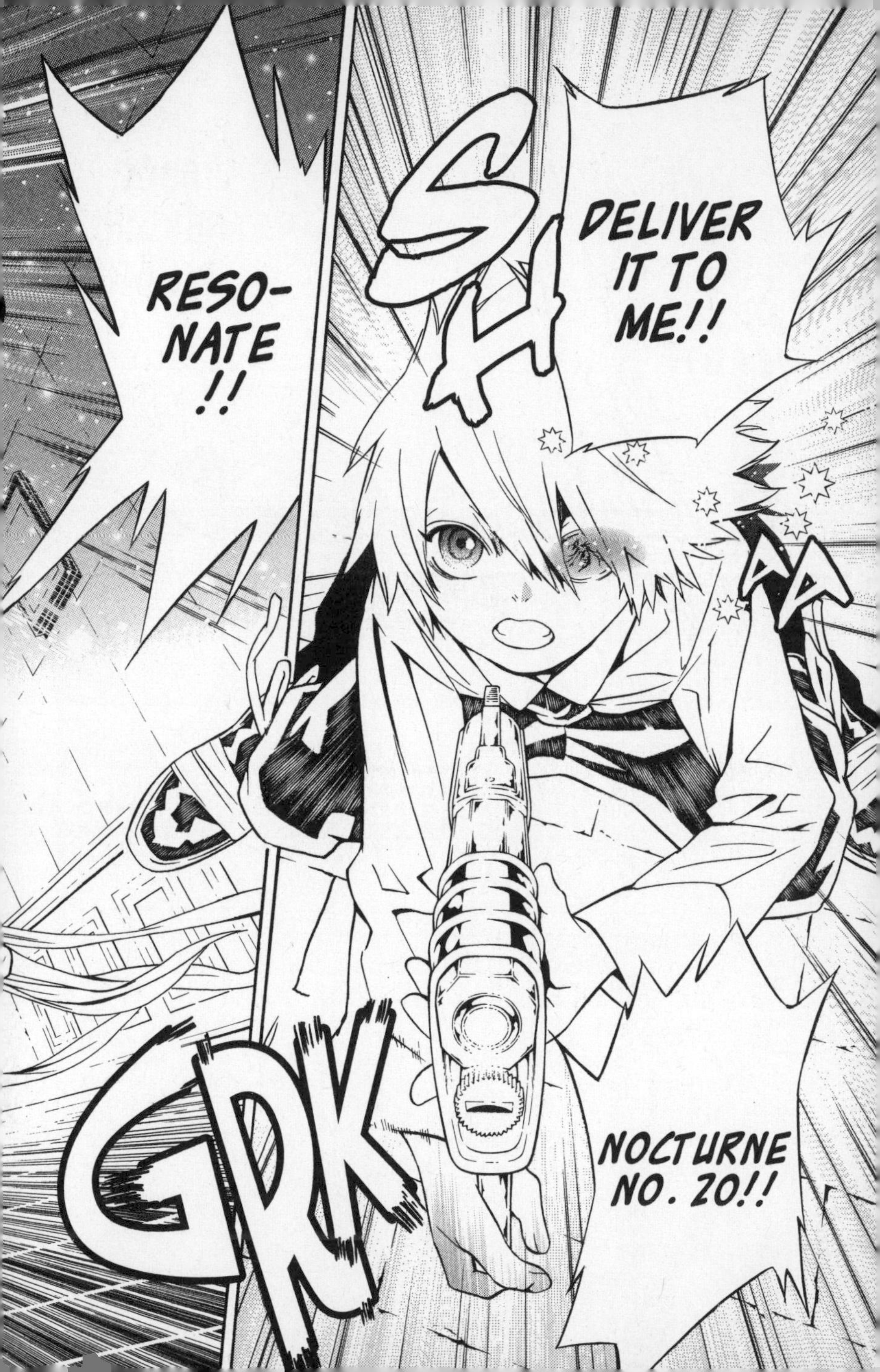
DELIVER IT TO ME!!
SH
RESO-NATE!!
NOCTURNE NO. 20!!
GRK

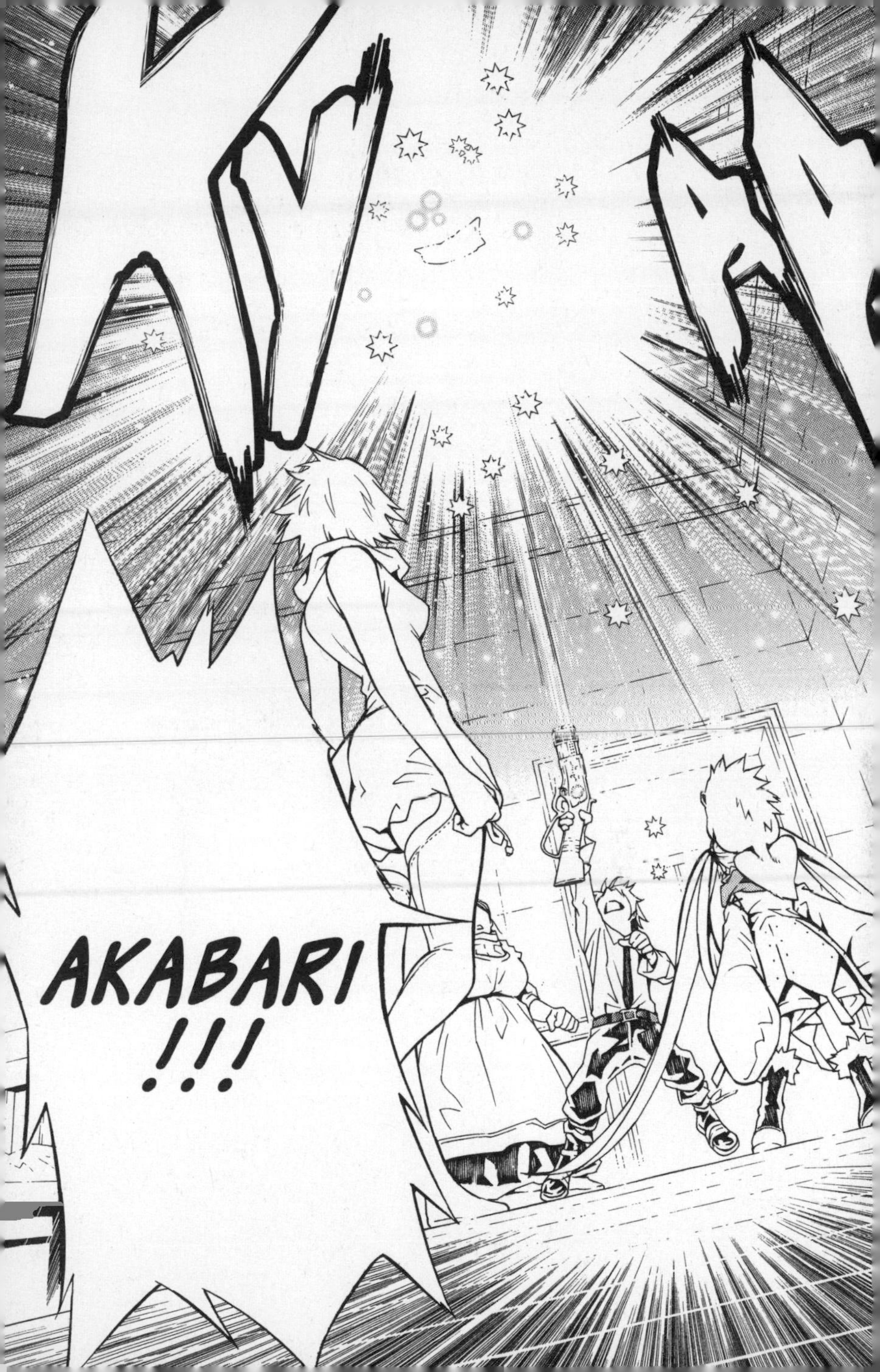
AKABARI
!!!

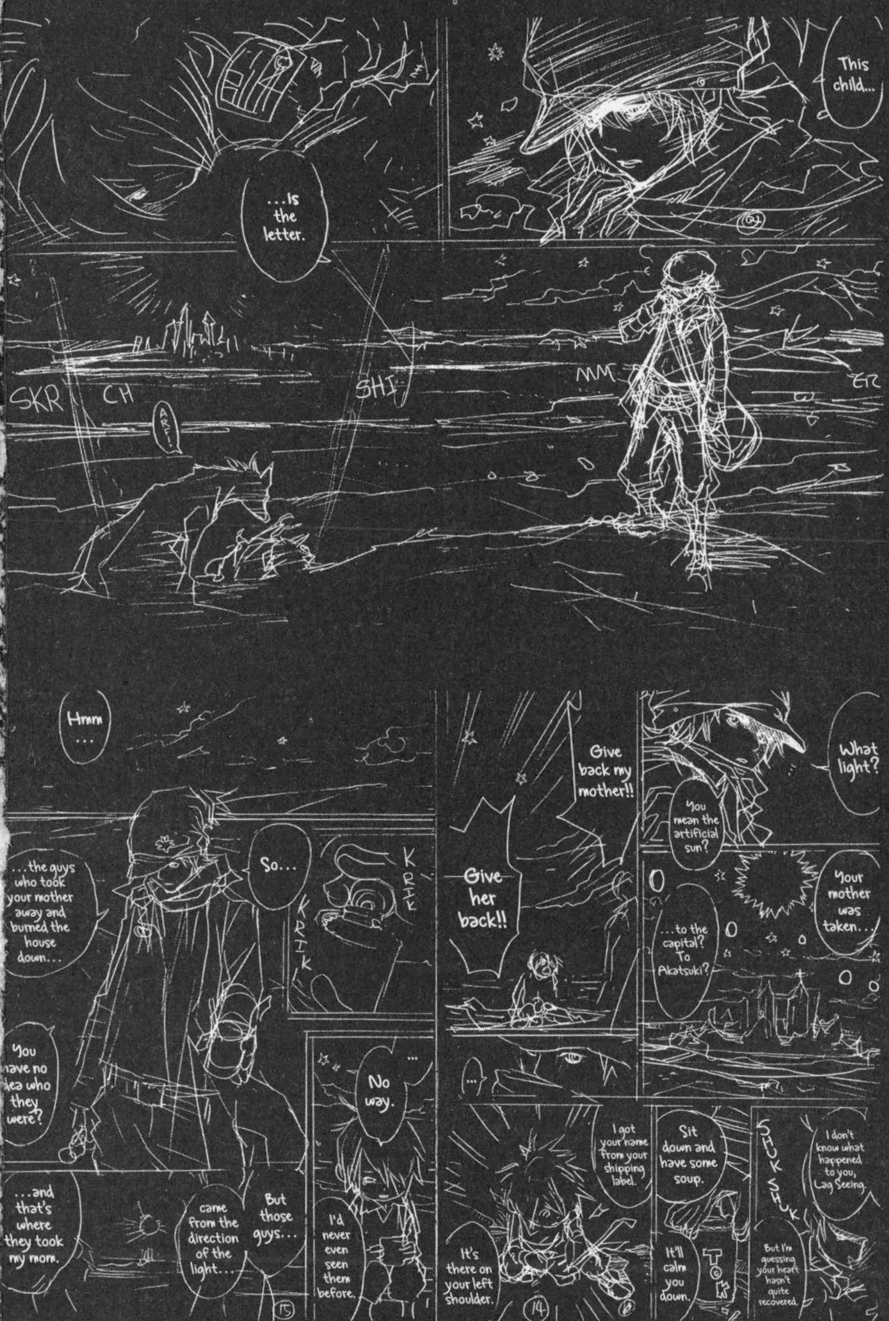
This child...
...is the letter.
SKR CH
ARF!
SHI MM ER
What light?
You mean the artificial sun?
Give back my mother!!
Give her back!!
Your mother was taken...
...to the capital? To Akatsuki?
...
I don't know what happened to you, Lag Seeing.
But I'm guessing your heart hasn't quite recovered.
SHUK SHUK
Sit down and have some soup.
TOK
It'll calm you down.
I got your name from your shipping label.
It's there on your left shoulder.
14
Hmm...
KRIK KRIK
So...
...the guys who took your mother away and burned the house down...
You have no idea who they were?
...
No way.
I'd never even seen them before.
But those guys...
came from the direction of the light...
...and that's where they took my mom.
15

Rough sketches for Chapter 1.

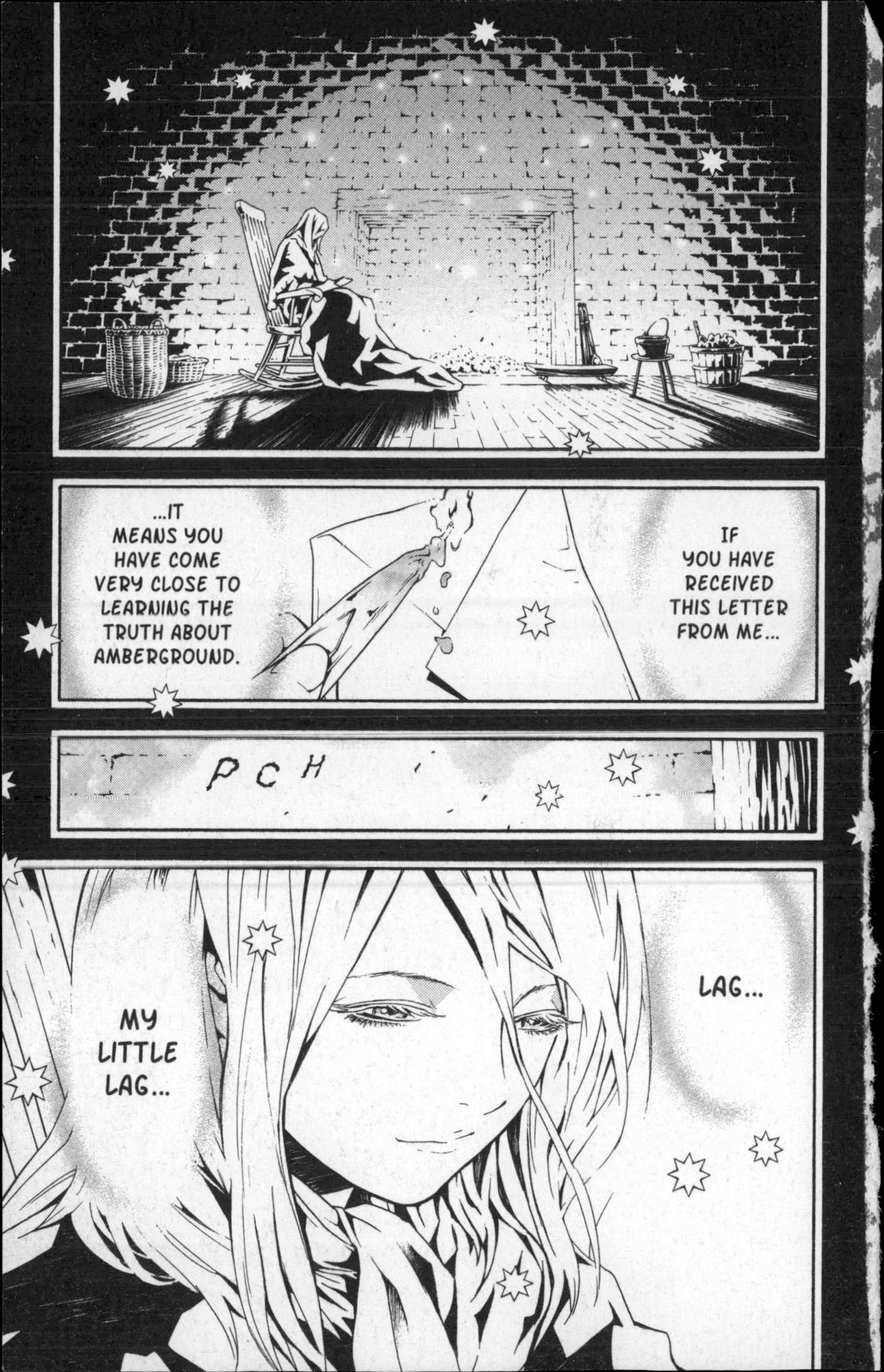
IF YOU HAVE RECEIVED THIS LETTER FROM ME...
...IT MEANS YOU HAVE COME VERY CLOSE TO LEARNING THE TRUTH ABOUT AMBERGROUND.
PCH
LAG...
MY LITTLE LAG...

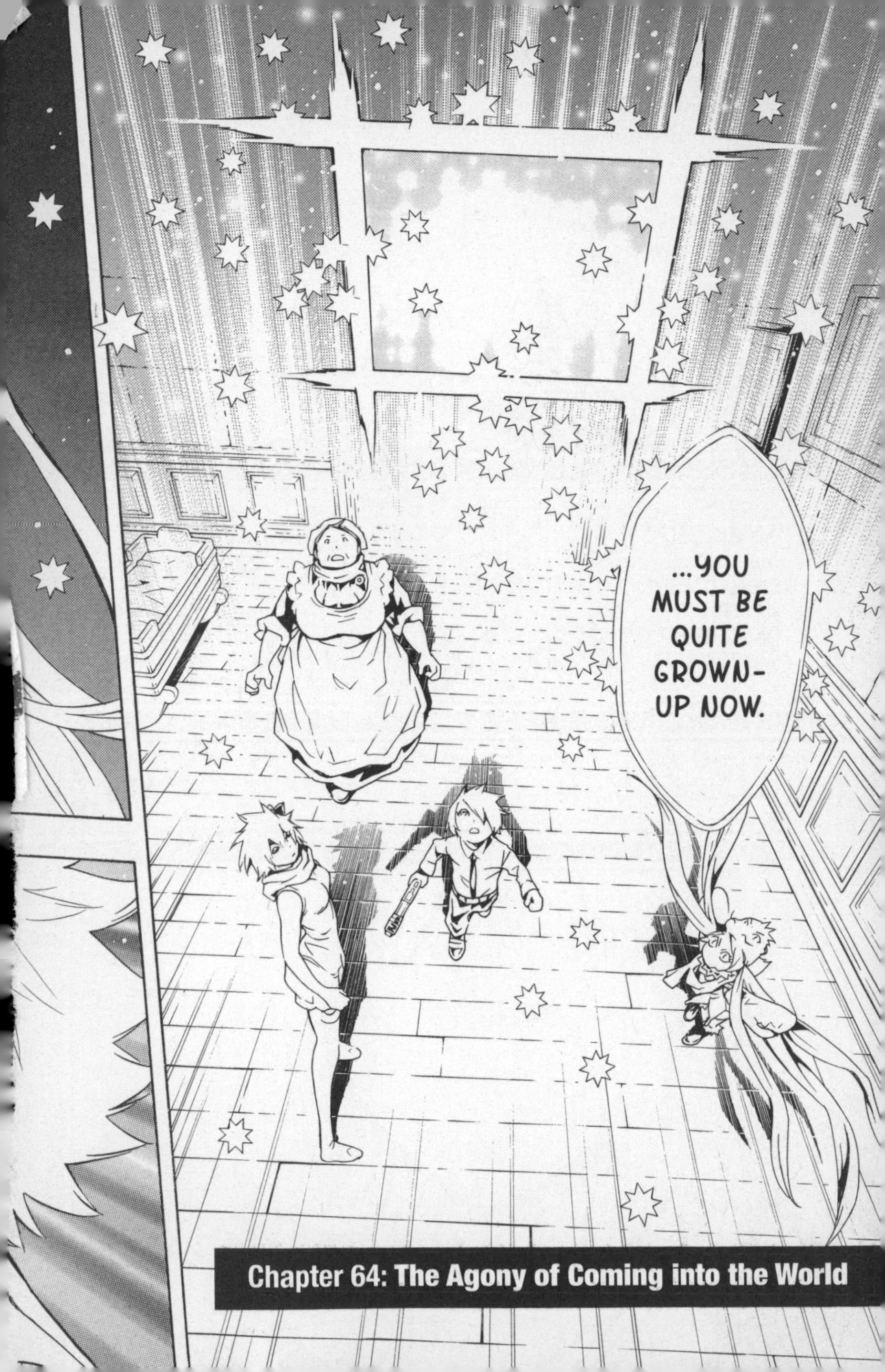
...YOU MUST BE QUITE GROWN-UP NOW.
Chapter 64: The Agony of Coming into the World

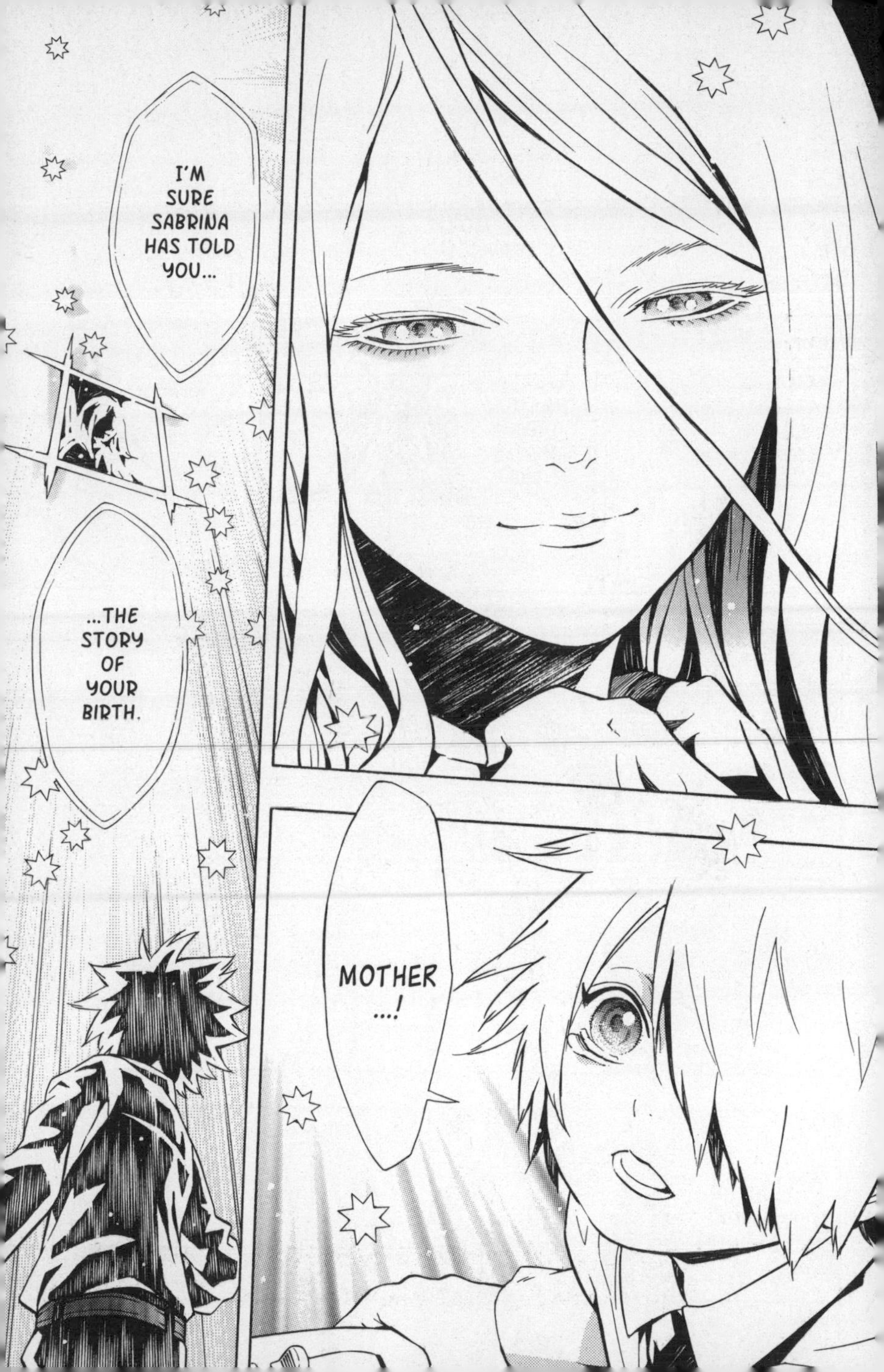
MOTHER ...!
I'M SURE SABRINA HAS TOLD YOU...
...THE STORY OF YOUR BIRTH.

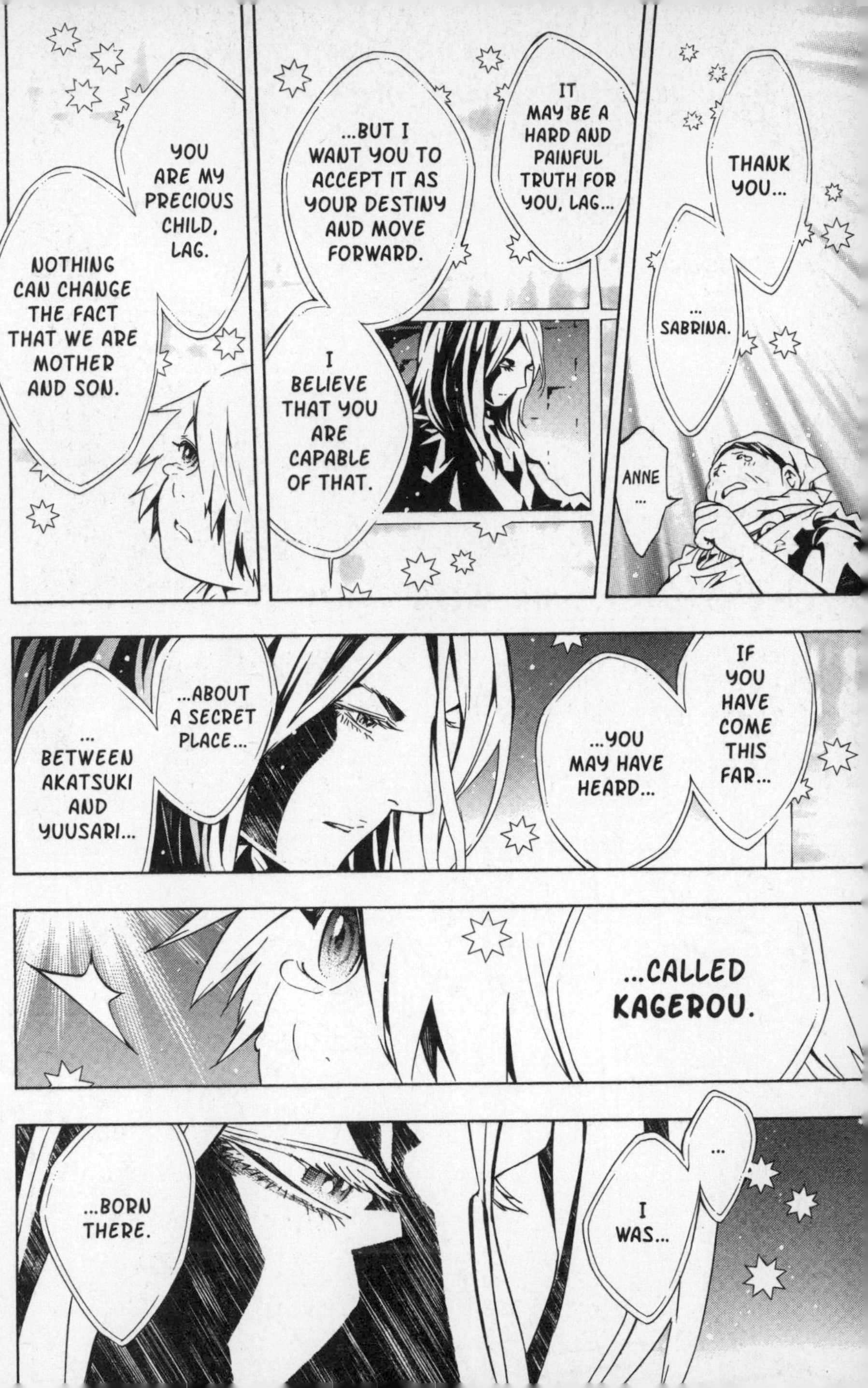
THANK YOU...
... SABRINA.
ANNE ...
IT MAY BE A HARD AND PAINFUL TRUTH FOR YOU, LAG...
...BUT I WANT YOU TO ACCEPT IT AS YOUR DESTINY AND MOVE FORWARD.
I BELIEVE THAT YOU ARE CAPABLE OF THAT.
YOU ARE MY PRECIOUS CHILD, LAG.
NOTHING CAN CHANGE THE FACT THAT WE ARE MOTHER AND SON.
IF YOU HAVE COME THIS FAR...
...YOU MAY HAVE HEARD...
...ABOUT A SECRET PLACE...
... BETWEEN AKATSUKI AND YUUSARI...
...CALLED KAGEROU.
... I WAS...
...BORN THERE.

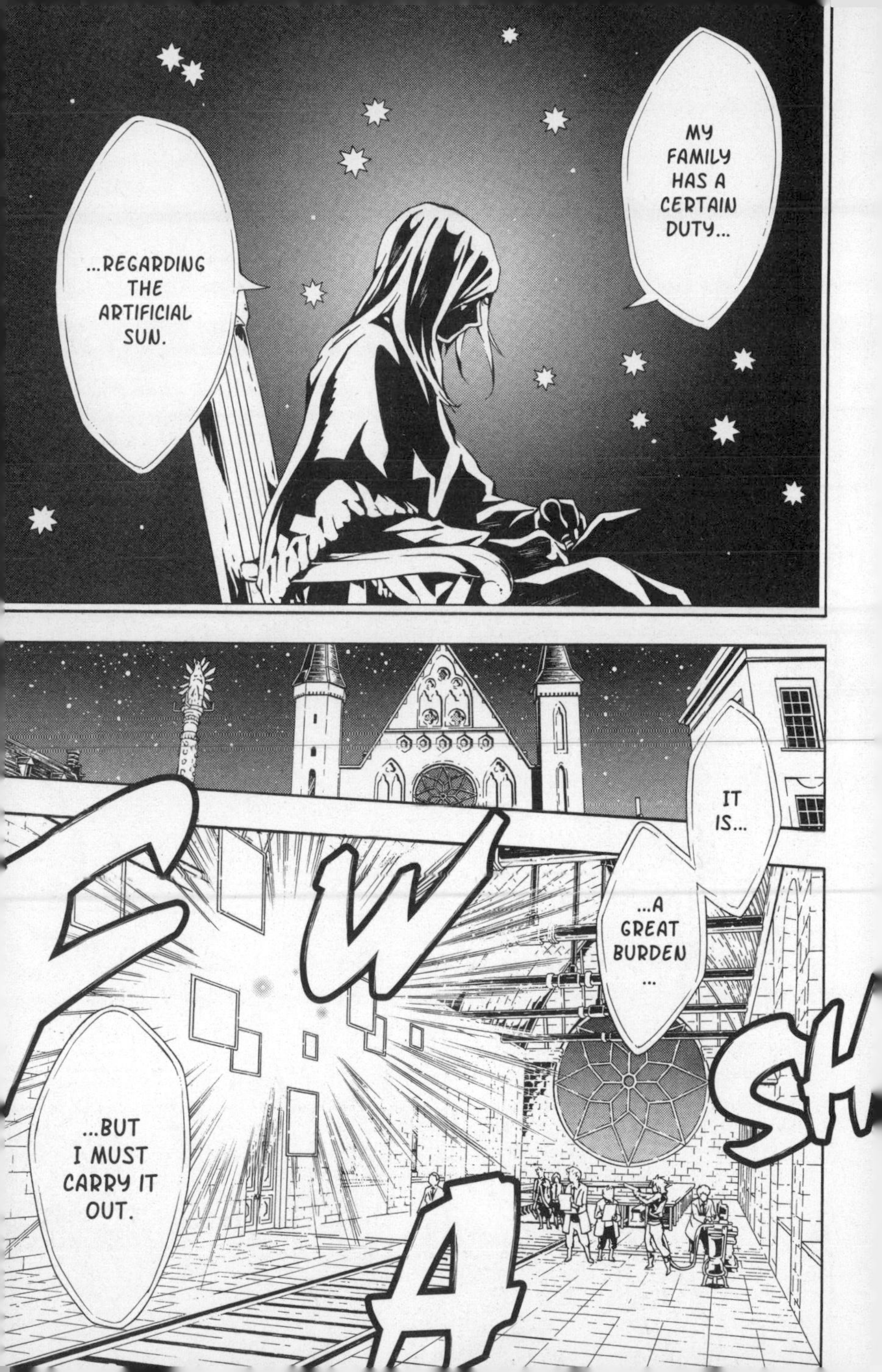
MY FAMILY HAS A CERTAIN DUTY...
...REGARDING THE ARTIFICIAL SUN.
IT IS...
...A GREAT BURDEN ...
...BUT I MUST CARRY IT OUT.

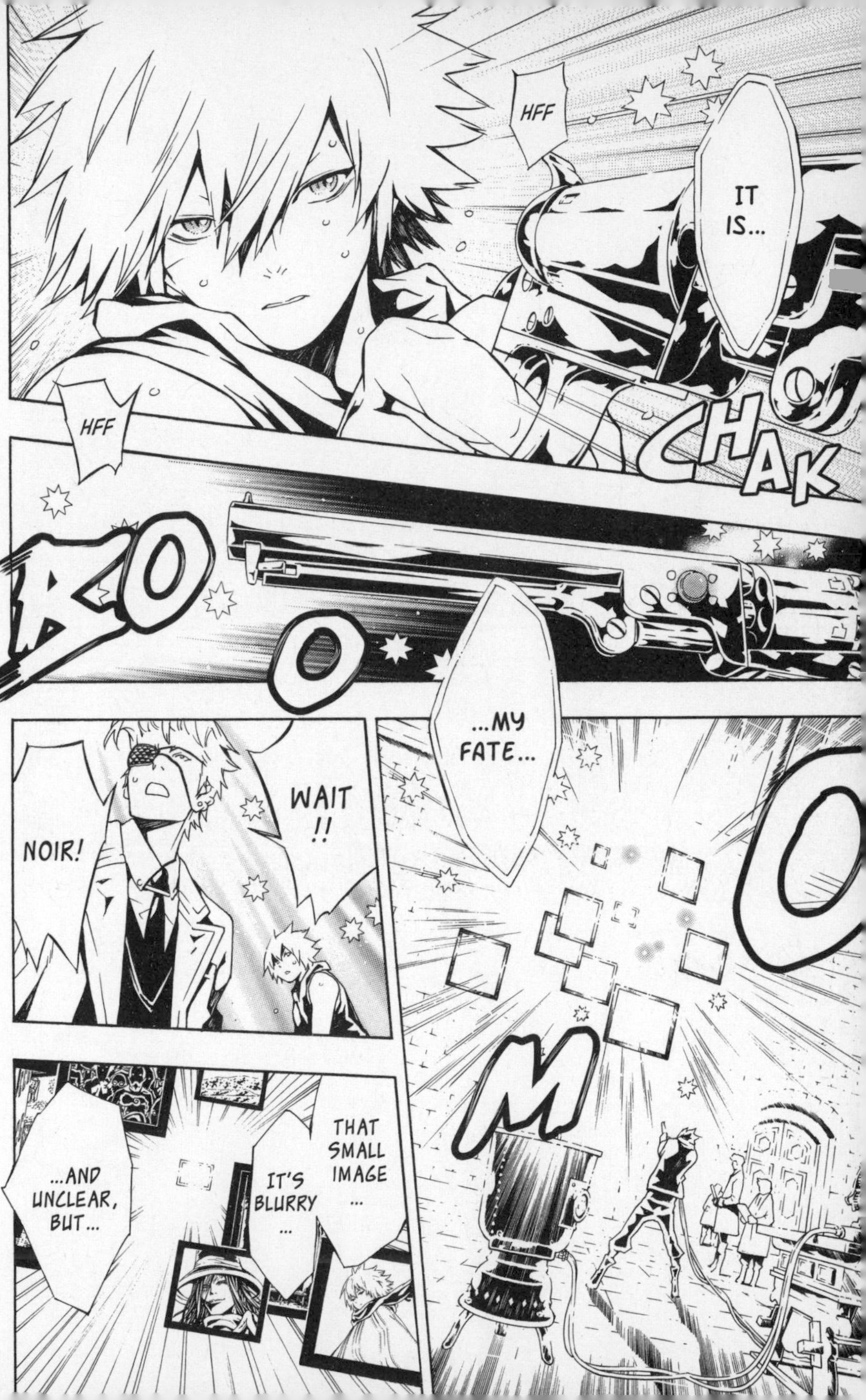
HFF
IT IS...
CHAK
HFF
BOOOM
...MY FATE...
WAIT !!
NOIR!
THAT SMALL IMAGE ...
IT'S BLURRY ...
...AND UNCLEAR, BUT...

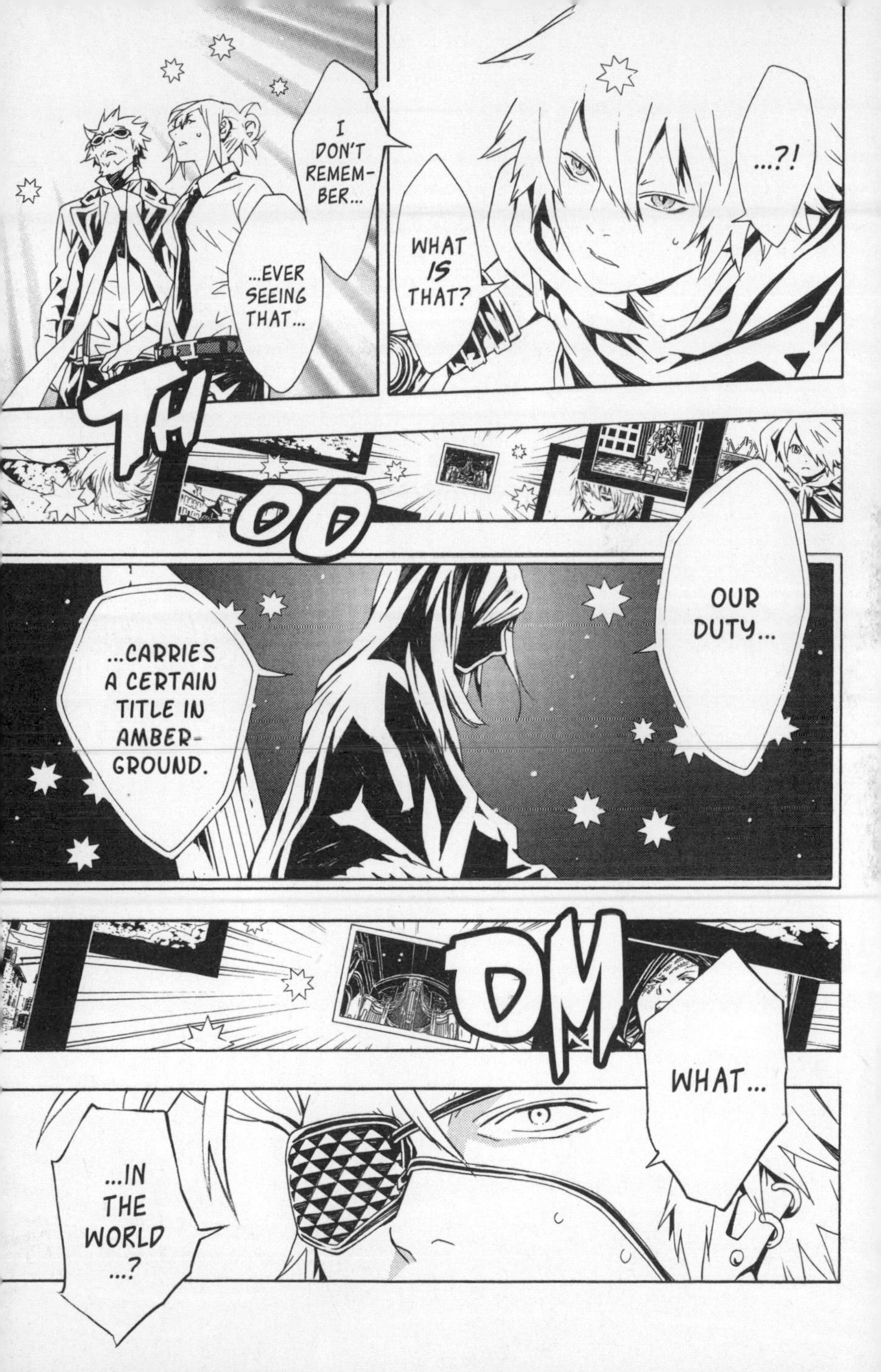
...?!
WHAT IS THAT?
I DON'T REMEMBER...
...EVER SEEING THAT...
TH
OD
OUR DUTY...
...CARRIES A CERTAIN TITLE IN AMBERGROUND.
DM
WHAT...
...IN THE WORLD ...?

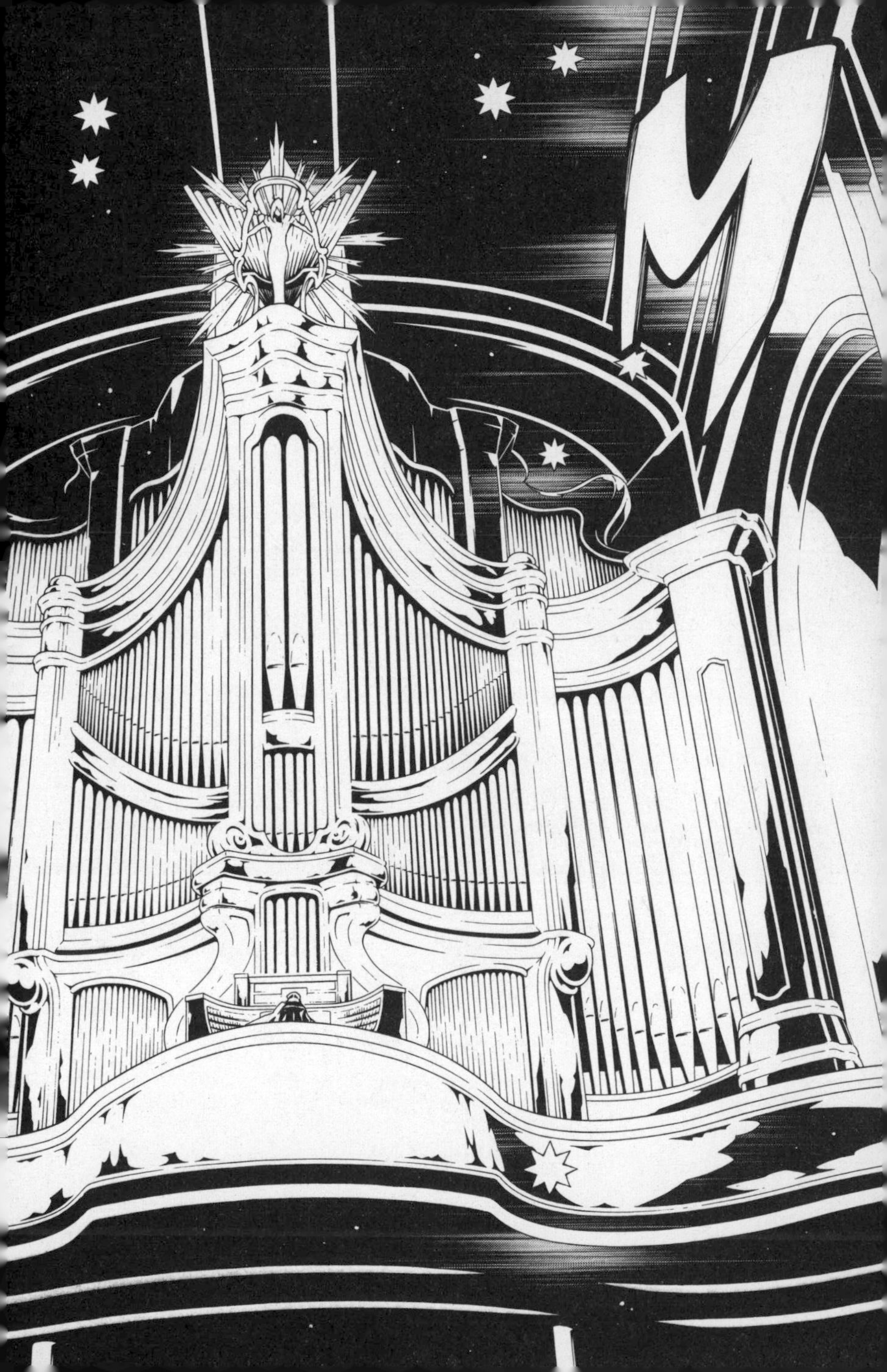

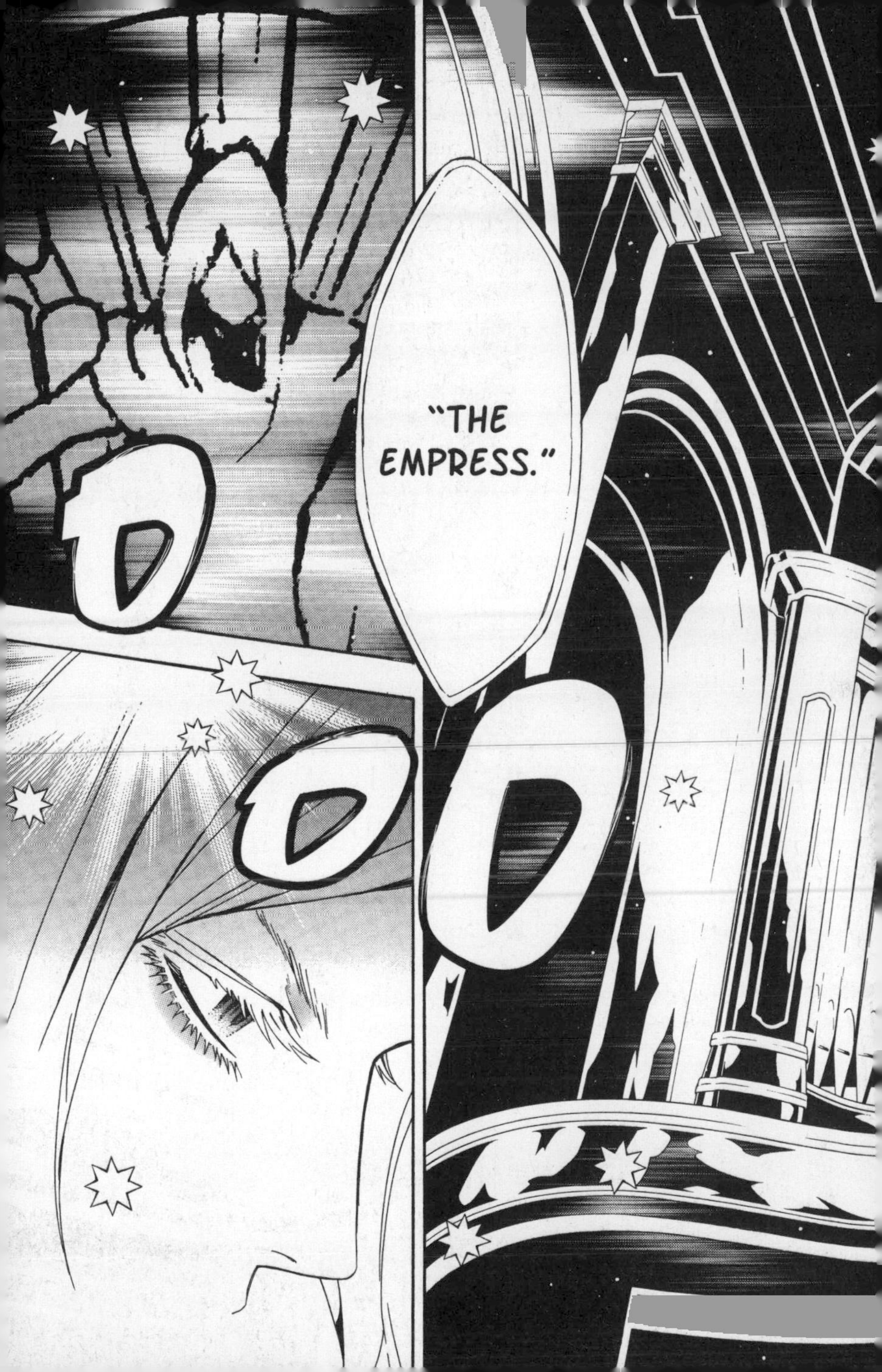
"THE EMPRESS."
D
D
D

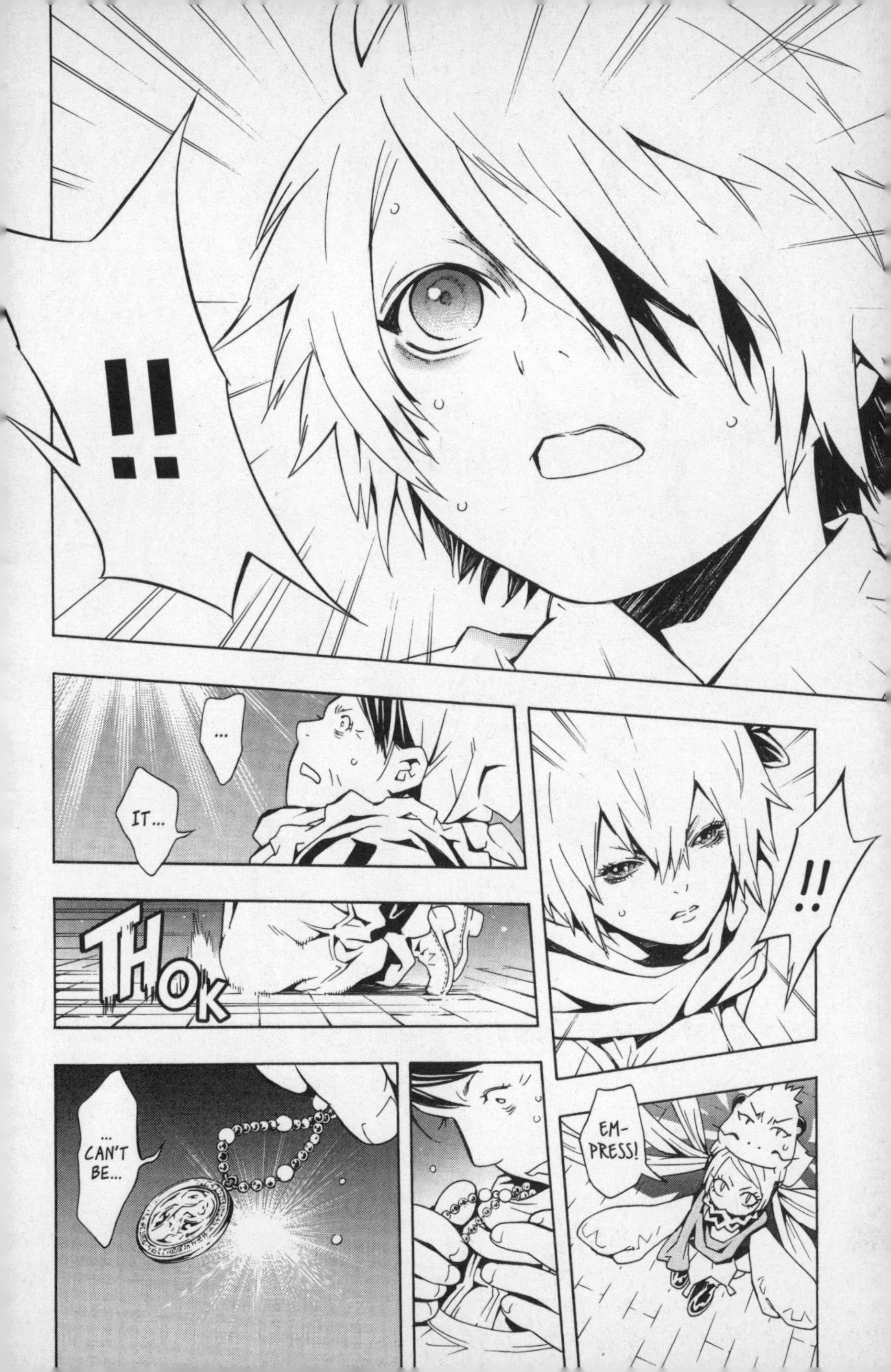
!!
!!
...
IT...
THOK
EM-PRESS!
... CAN'T BE...

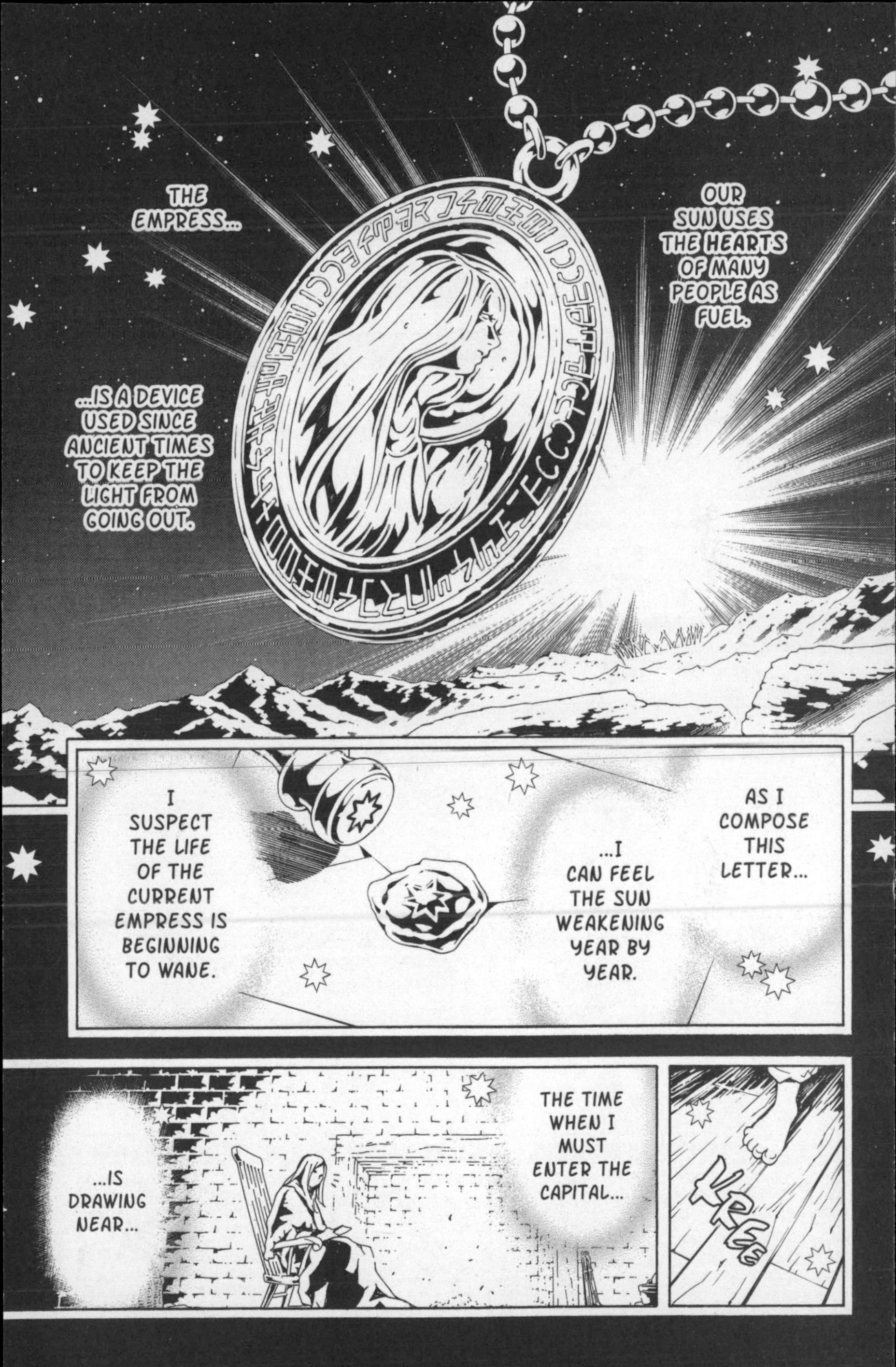
OUR SUN USES THE HEARTS OF MANY PEOPLE AS FUEL.
THE EMPRESS...
...IS A DEVICE USED SINCE ANCIENT TIMES TO KEEP THE LIGHT FROM GOING OUT.
AS I COMPOSE THIS LETTER...
...I CAN FEEL THE SUN WEAKENING YEAR BY YEAR.
I SUSPECT THE LIFE OF THE CURRENT EMPRESS IS BEGINNING TO WANE.
KREE
THE TIME WHEN I MUST ENTER THE CAPITAL...
...IS DRAWING NEAR...

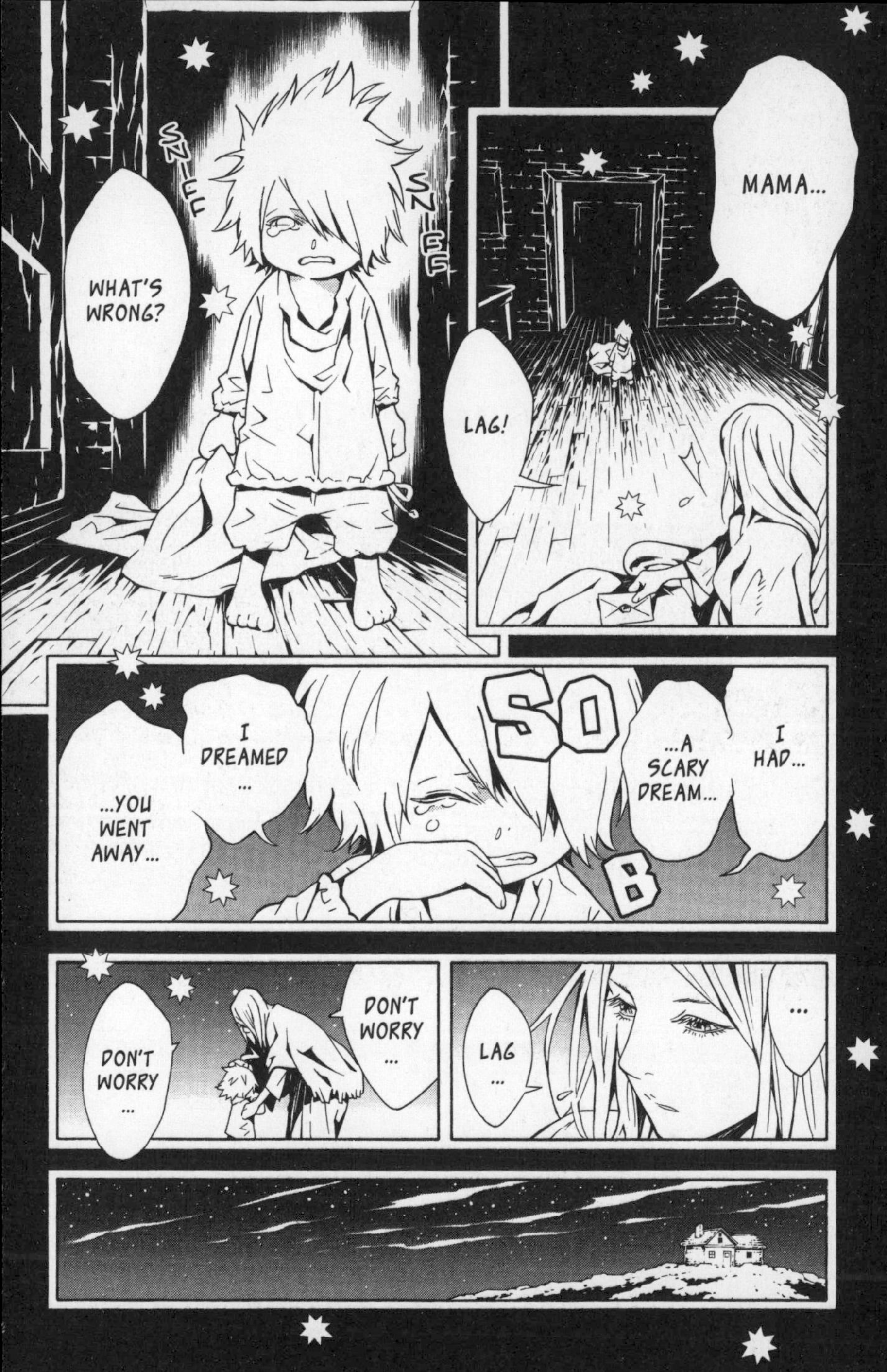
MAMA...
LAG!
SNIFF
SNIFF
WHAT'S WRONG?
I HAD...
...A SCARY DREAM...
SOB
I DREAMED ...
...YOU WENT AWAY...
...
LAG ...
DON'T WORRY ...
DON'T WORRY ...

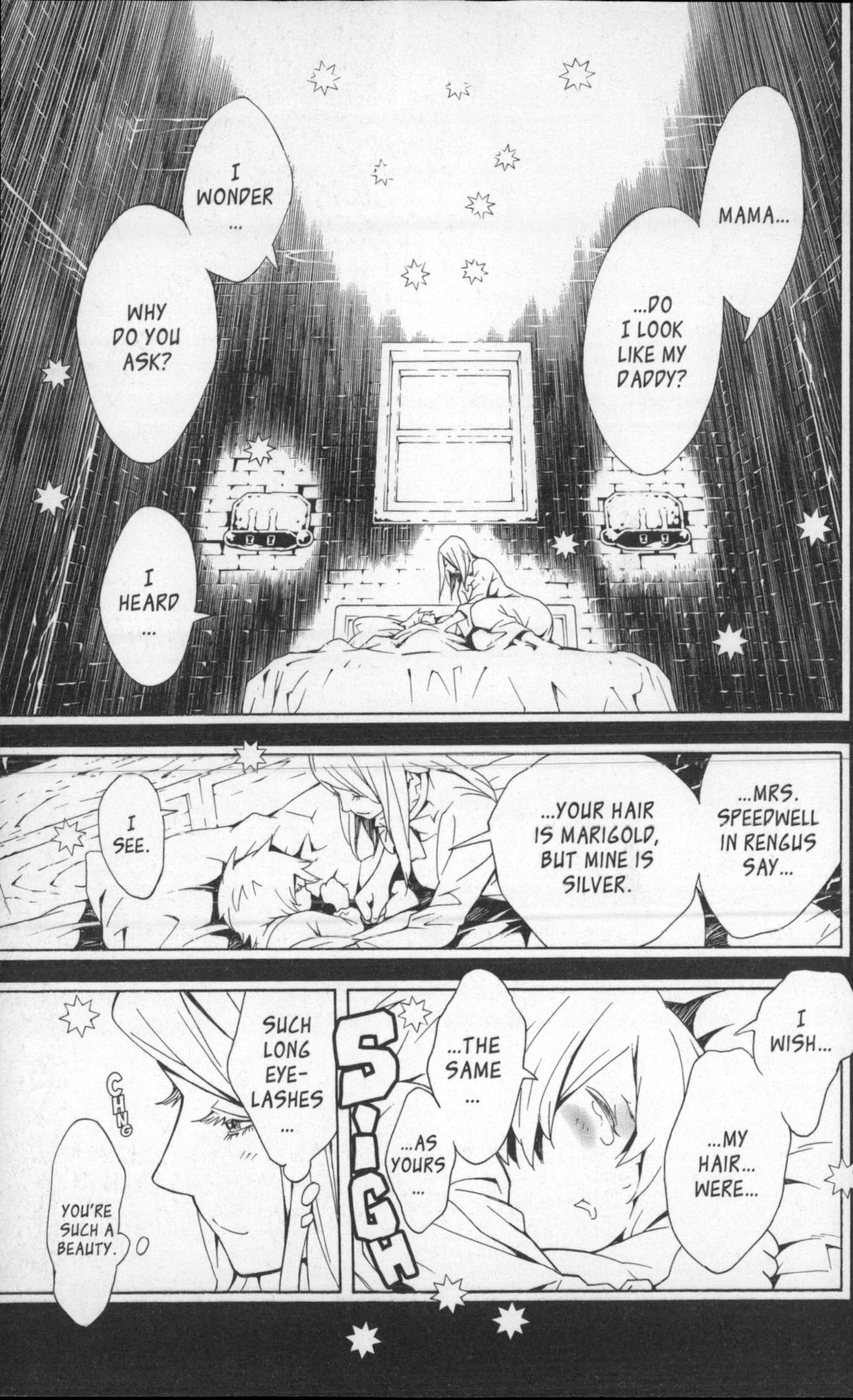
MAMA...
...DO I LOOK LIKE MY DADDY?
I WONDER ...
WHY DO YOU ASK?
I HEARD ...
...MRS. SPEEDWELL IN RENGUS SAY...
...YOUR HAIR IS MARIGOLD, BUT MINE IS SILVER.
I SEE.
I WISH...
...MY HAIR... WERE...
...THE SAME ...
...AS YOURS ...
SIGH
SUCH LONG EYE-LASHES ...
YOU'RE SUCH A BEAUTY.

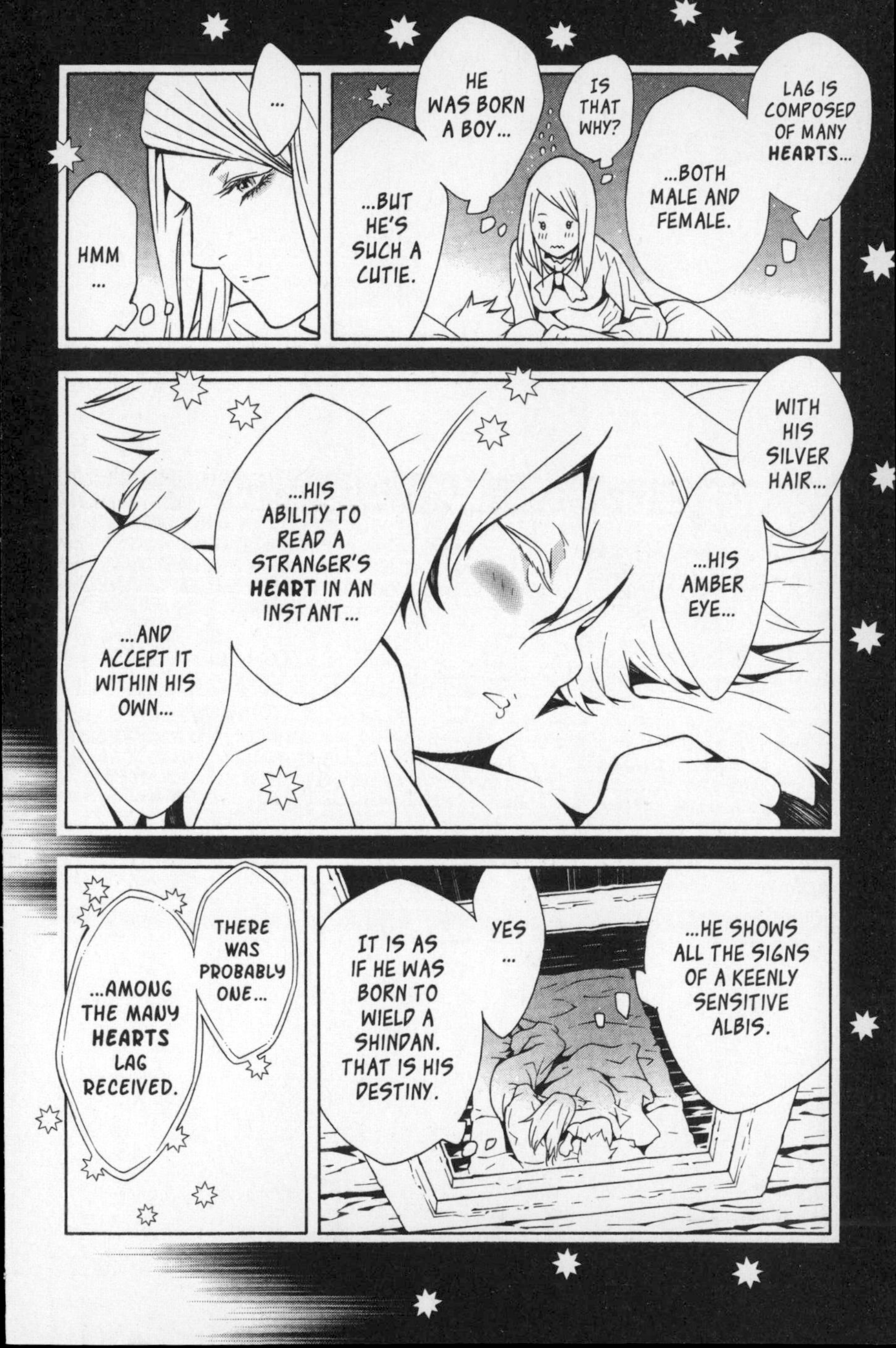
LAG IS COMPOSED OF MANY **HEARTS**...
...BOTH MALE AND FEMALE.
IS THAT WHY?
HE WAS BORN A BOY...
...BUT HE'S SUCH A CUTIE.
...
HMM ...
WITH HIS SILVER HAIR...
...HIS AMBER EYE...
...HIS ABILITY TO READ A STRANGER'S **HEART** IN AN INSTANT...
...AND ACCEPT IT WITHIN HIS OWN...
...HE SHOWS ALL THE SIGNS OF A KEENLY SENSITIVE ALBIS.
YES ...
IT IS AS IF HE WAS BORN TO WIELD A SHINDAN. THAT IS HIS DESTINY.
THERE WAS PROBABLY ONE...
...AMONG THE MANY **HEARTS** LAG RECEIVED.

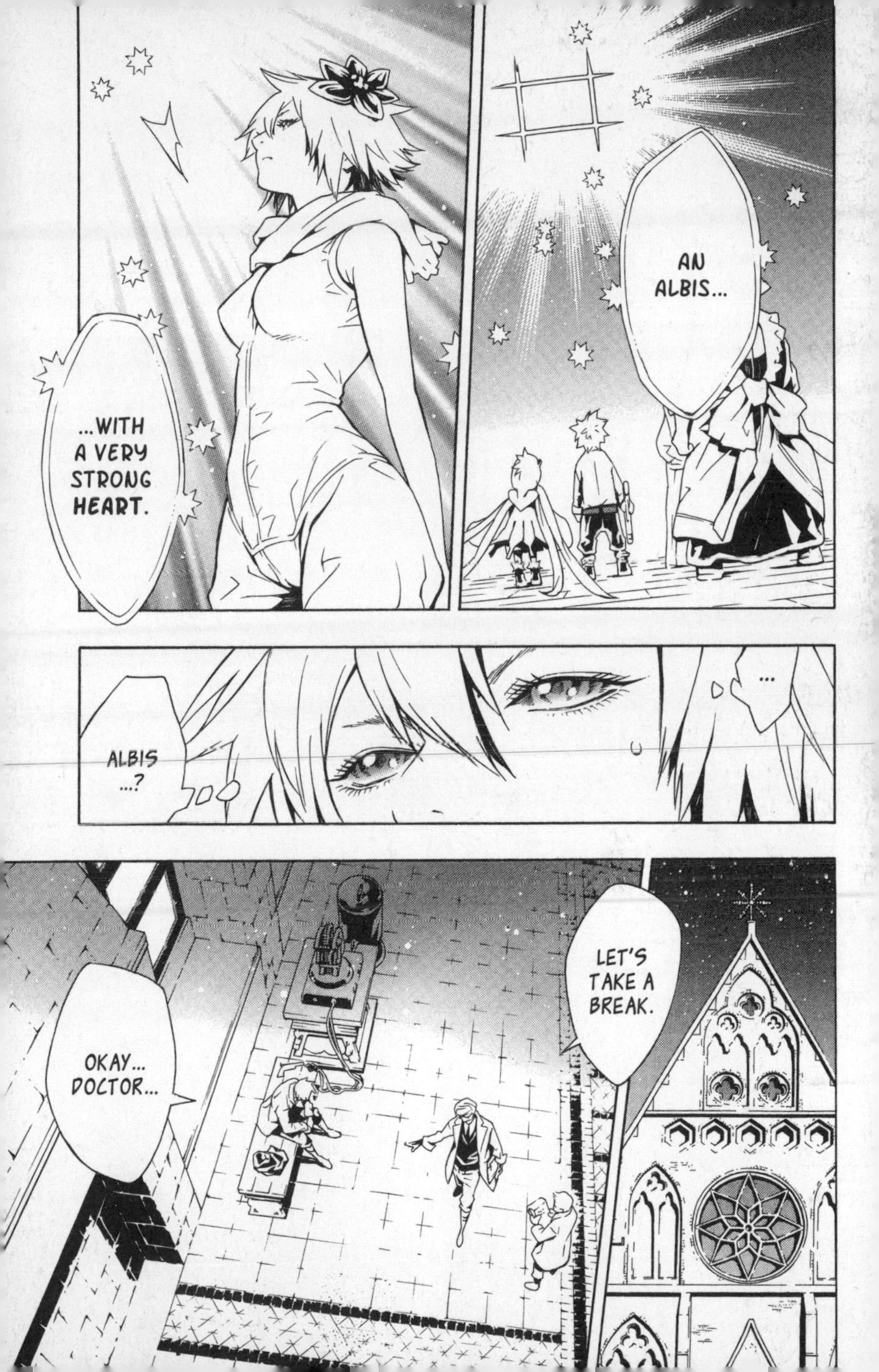
AN ALBIS...
...WITH A VERY STRONG HEART.
...
ALBIS ...?
LET'S TAKE A BREAK.
OKAY... DOCTOR...

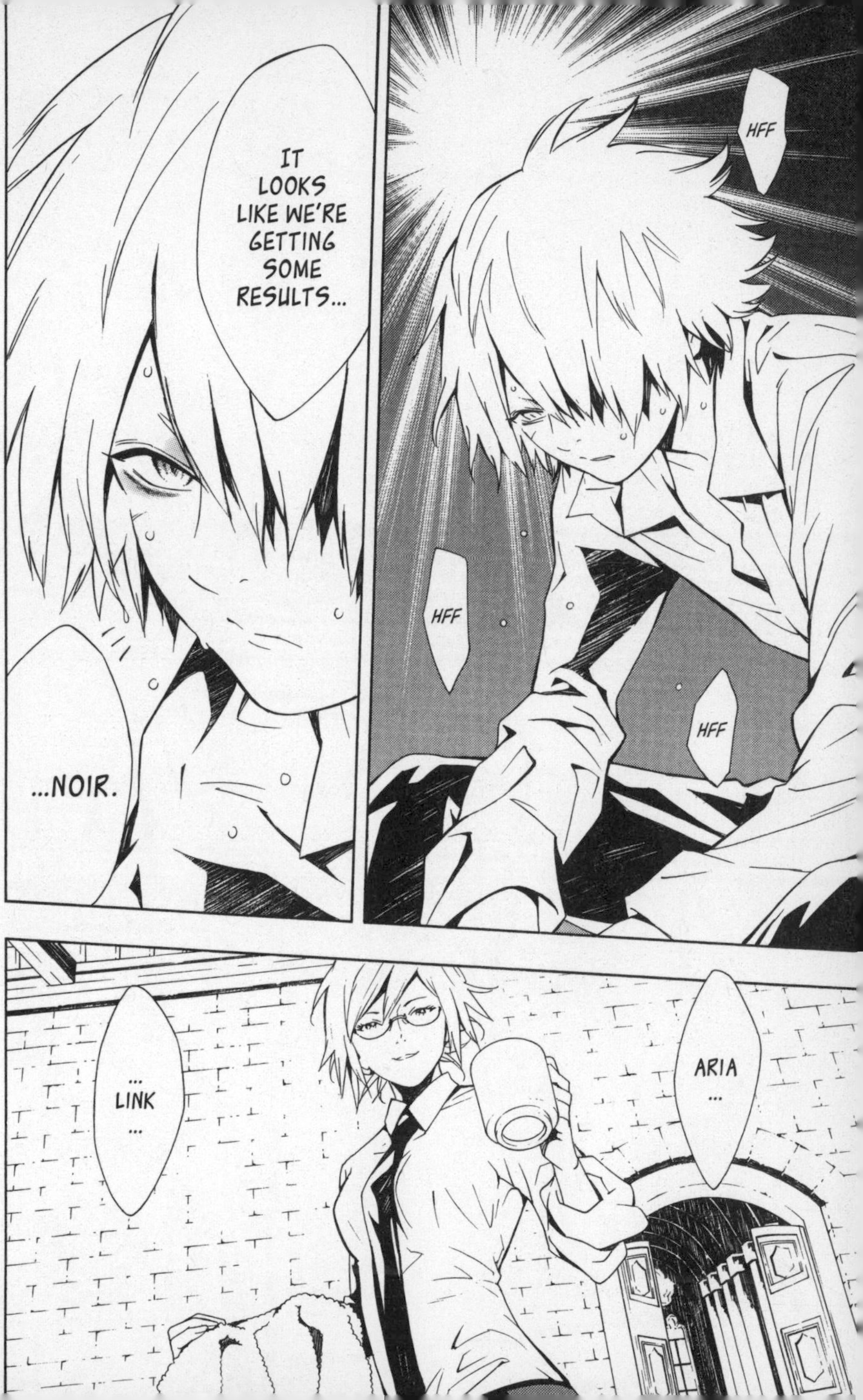
HFF
HFF
HFF
IT LOOKS LIKE WE'RE GETTING SOME RESULTS...
...NOIR.
ARIA ...
... LINK ...

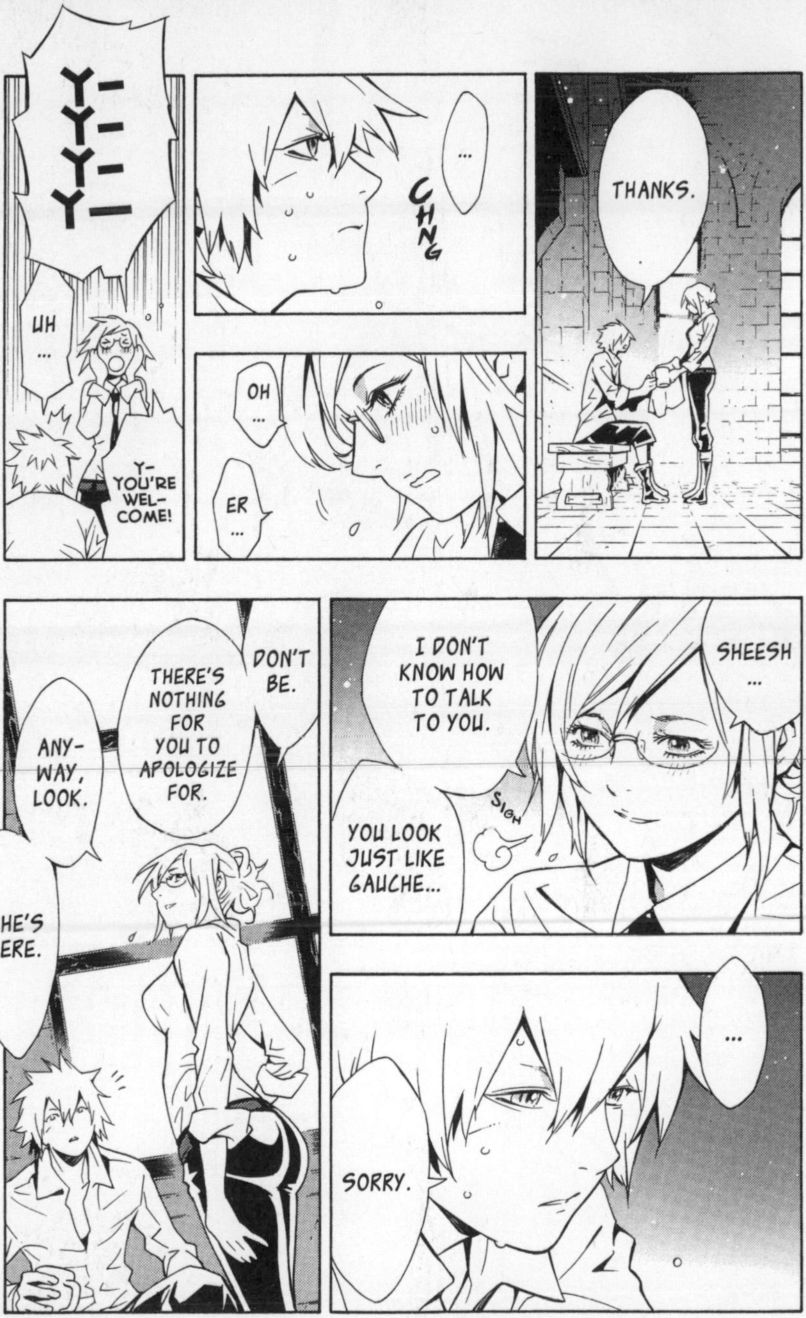
THANKS.
...
CHNG
OH ...
ER ...
Y- Y- Y- Y-
UH ...
Y- YOU'RE WEL-COME!
SHEESH ...
I DON'T KNOW HOW TO TALK TO YOU.
SIGH
YOU LOOK JUST LIKE GAUCHE...
...
SORRY.
DON'T BE.
THERE'S NOTHING FOR YOU TO APOLOGIZE FOR.
ANY-WAY, LOOK.
SHE'S HERE.

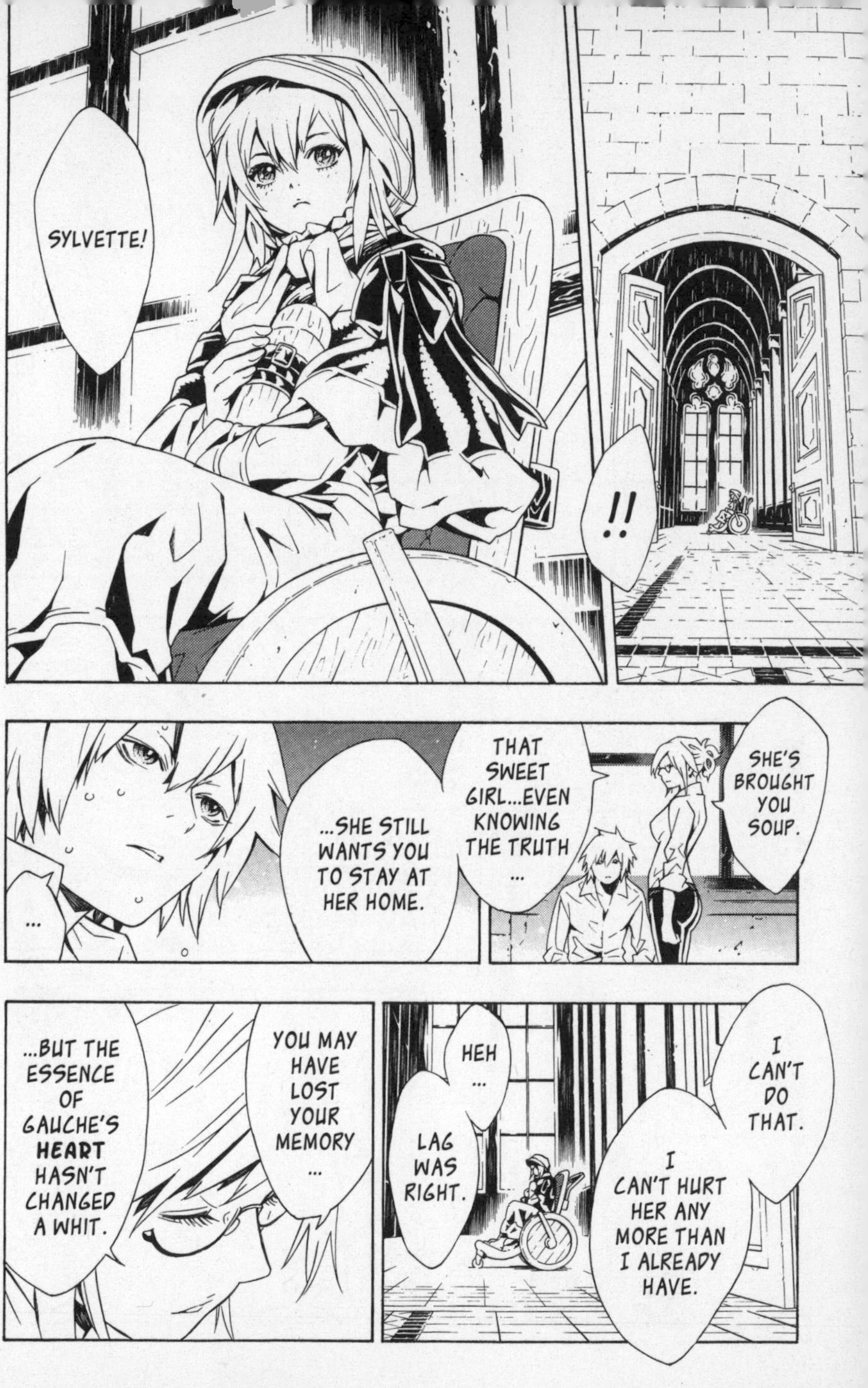
!!
SYLVETTE!
SHE'S BROUGHT YOU SOUP.
THAT SWEET GIRL...EVEN KNOWING THE TRUTH...
...SHE STILL WANTS YOU TO STAY AT HER HOME.
...
I CAN'T DO THAT.
I CAN'T HURT HER ANY MORE THAN I ALREADY HAVE.
HEH...
LAG WAS RIGHT.
YOU MAY HAVE LOST YOUR MEMORY...
...BUT THE ESSENCE OF GAUCHE'S HEART HASN'T CHANGED A WHIT.

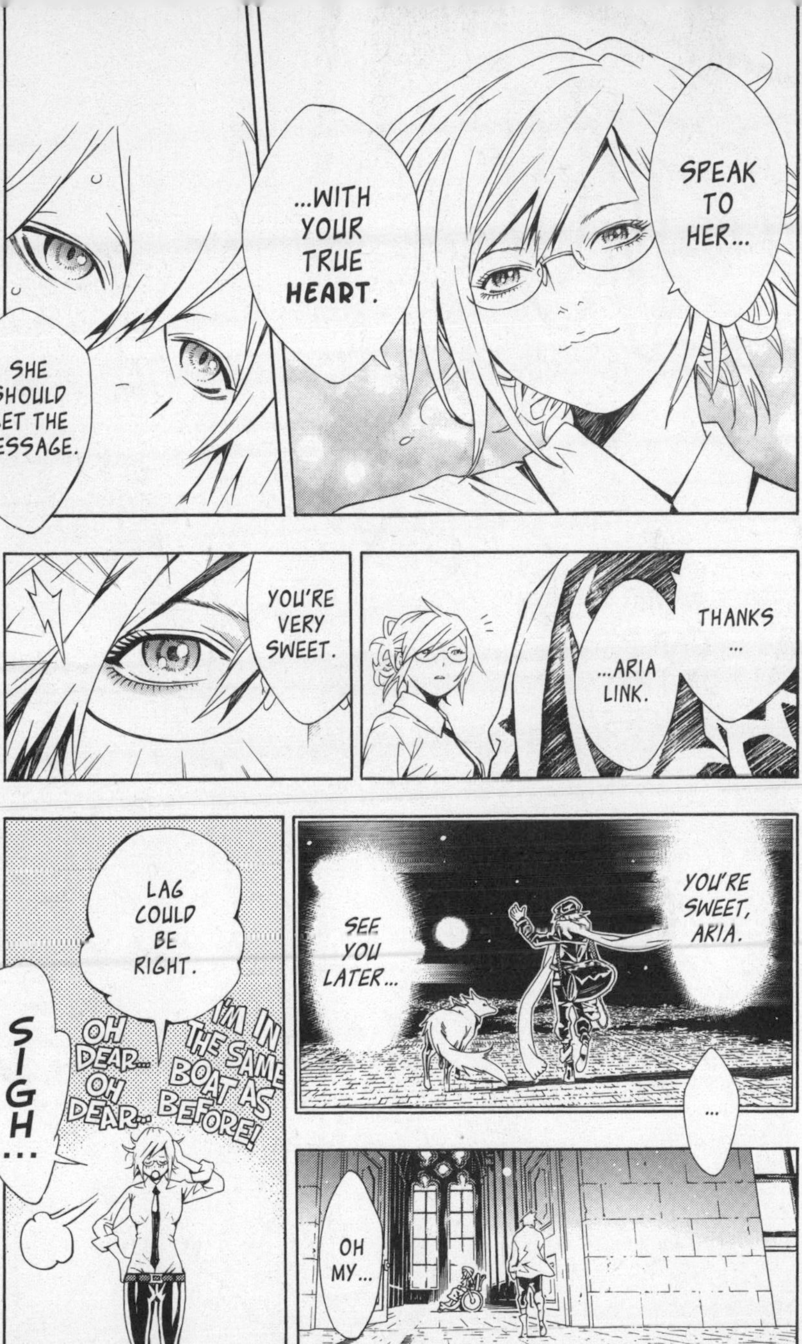
SPEAK TO HER...
...WITH YOUR TRUE HEART.
SHE SHOULD GET THE MESSAGE.
THANKS ...
...ARIA LINK.
YOU'RE VERY SWEET.
YOU'RE SWEET, ARIA.
SEE YOU LATER...
...
OH MY...
LAG COULD BE RIGHT.
I'M IN THE SAME BOAT AS BEFORE!
OH DEAR... OH DEAR...
SIGH...

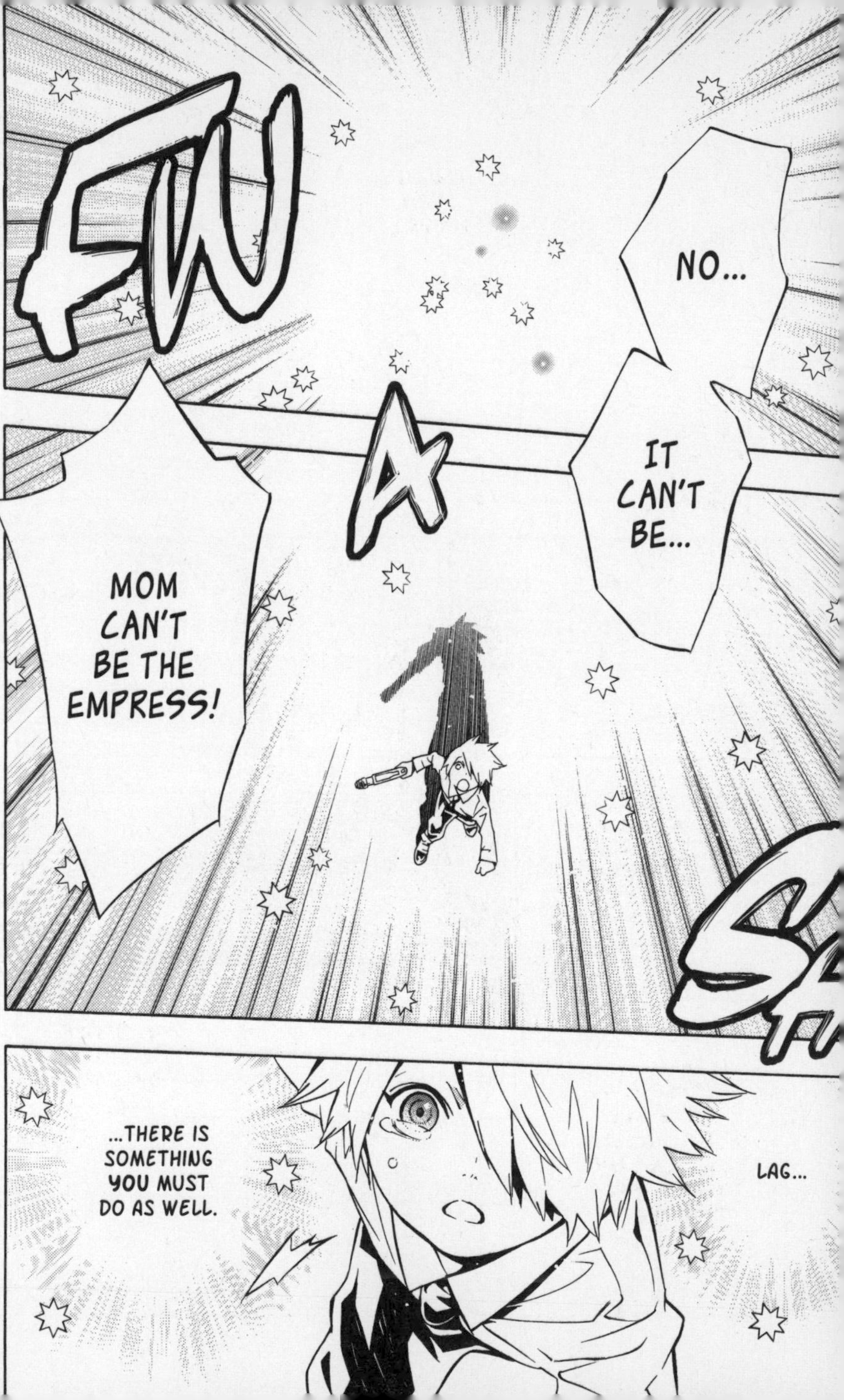
NO...
FWA
IT CAN'T BE...
MOM CAN'T BE THE EMPRESS!
LAG...
...THERE IS SOMETHING YOU MUST DO AS WELL.

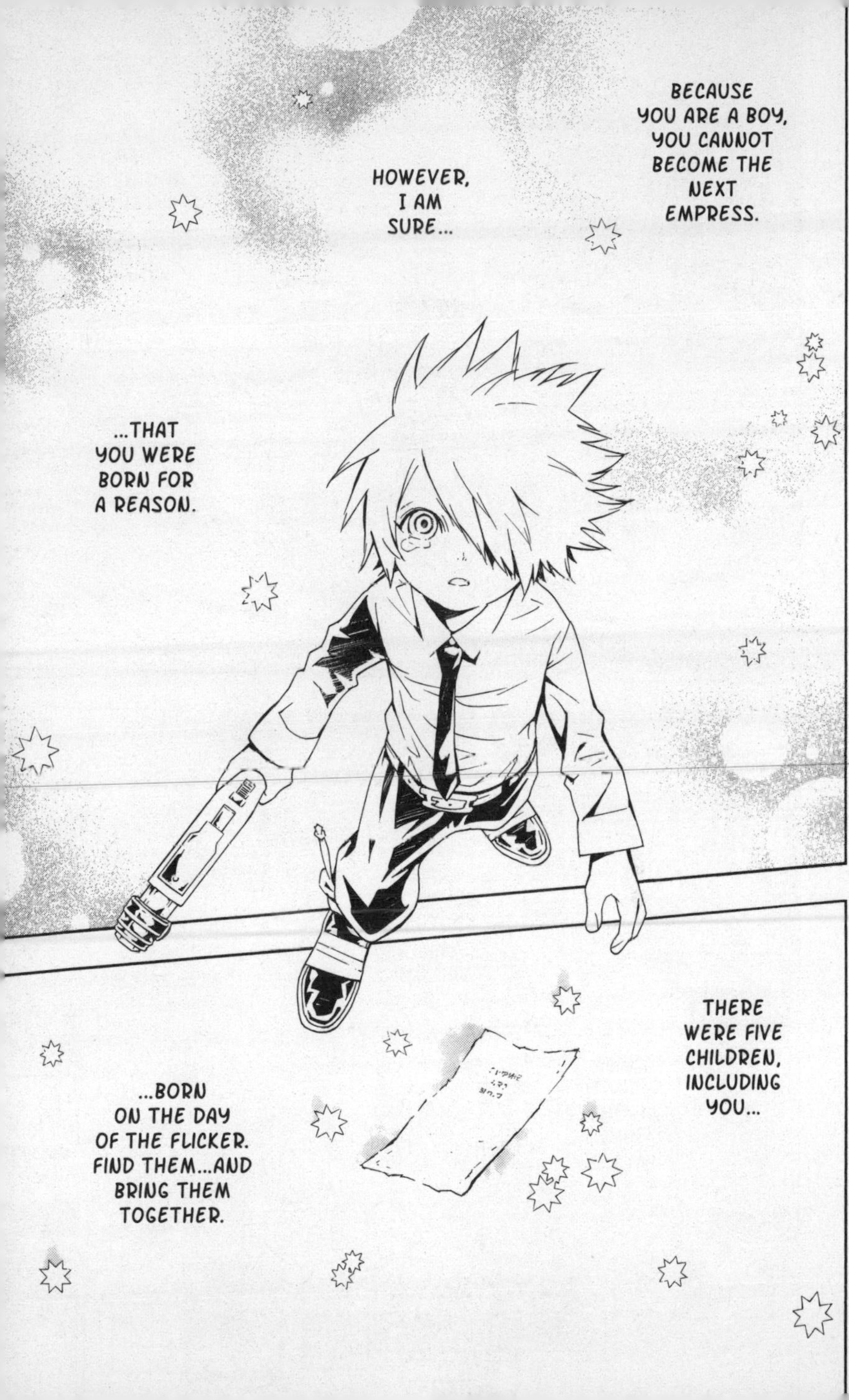
BECAUSE YOU ARE A BOY, YOU CANNOT BECOME THE NEXT EMPRESS.
HOWEVER, I AM SURE...
...THAT YOU WERE BORN FOR A REASON.
THERE WERE FIVE CHILDREN, INCLUDING YOU...
...BORN ON THE DAY OF THE FLICKER. FIND THEM...AND BRING THEM TOGETHER.

EACH OF THOSE CHILDREN WAS BORN INTO THIS WORLD WITH A FRAGMENT OF THE **HEART** OF THE SUN.

IF YOU CAN GATHER CRUCIAL MEMORIES...

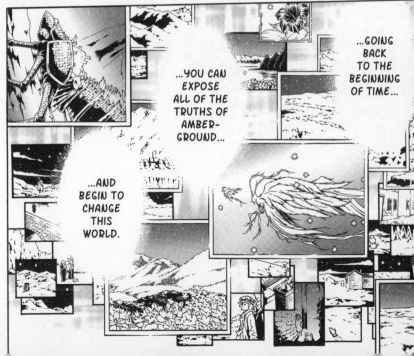

...GOING BACK TO THE BEGINNING OF TIME...

...YOU CAN EXPOSE ALL OF THE TRUTHS OF AMBER-GROUND...

...AND BEGIN TO CHANGE THIS WORLD.

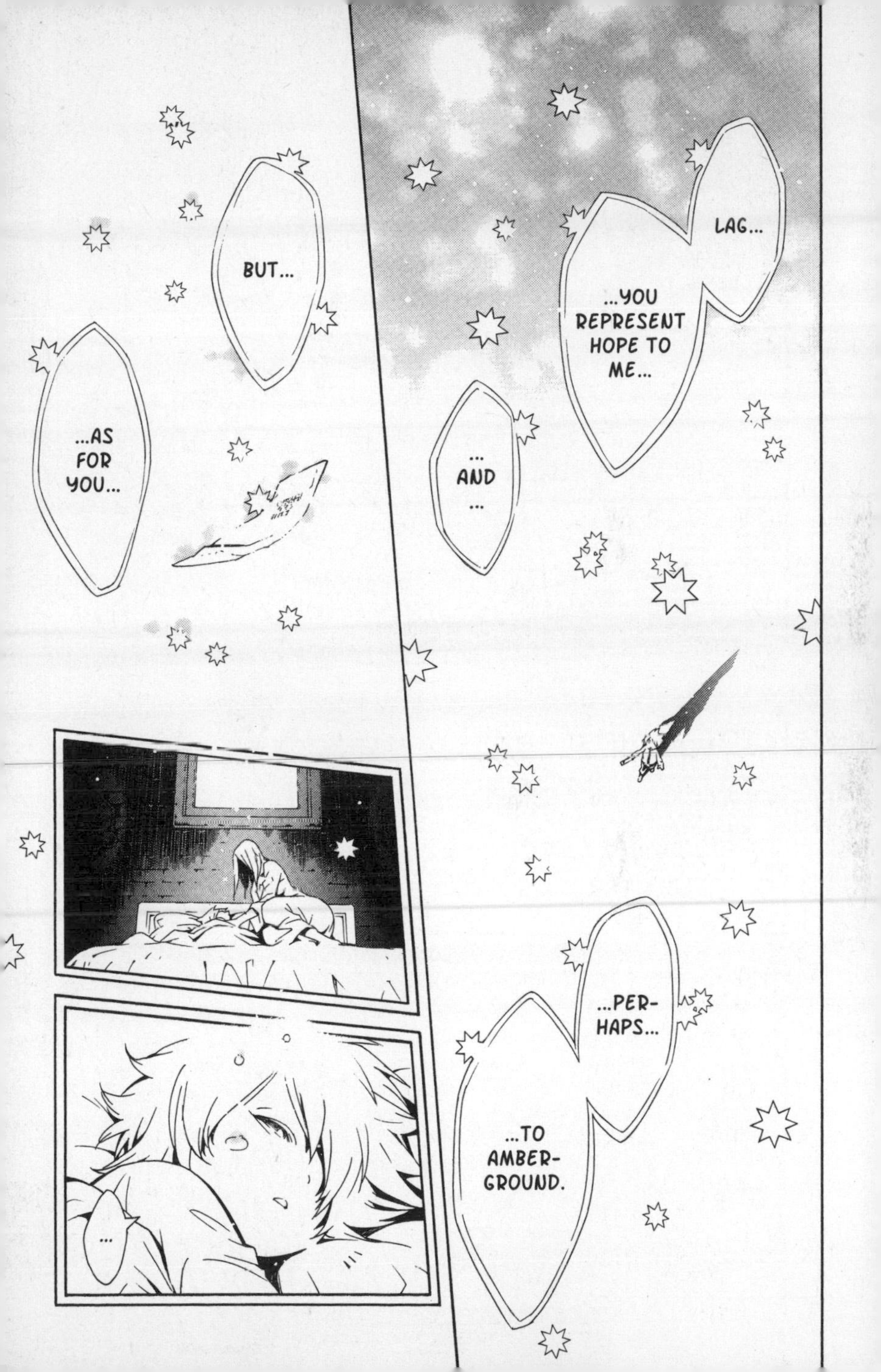
LAG...
...YOU REPRESENT HOPE TO ME...
... AND ...
...PER-HAPS...
...TO AMBER-GROUND.
BUT...
...AS FOR YOU...
...

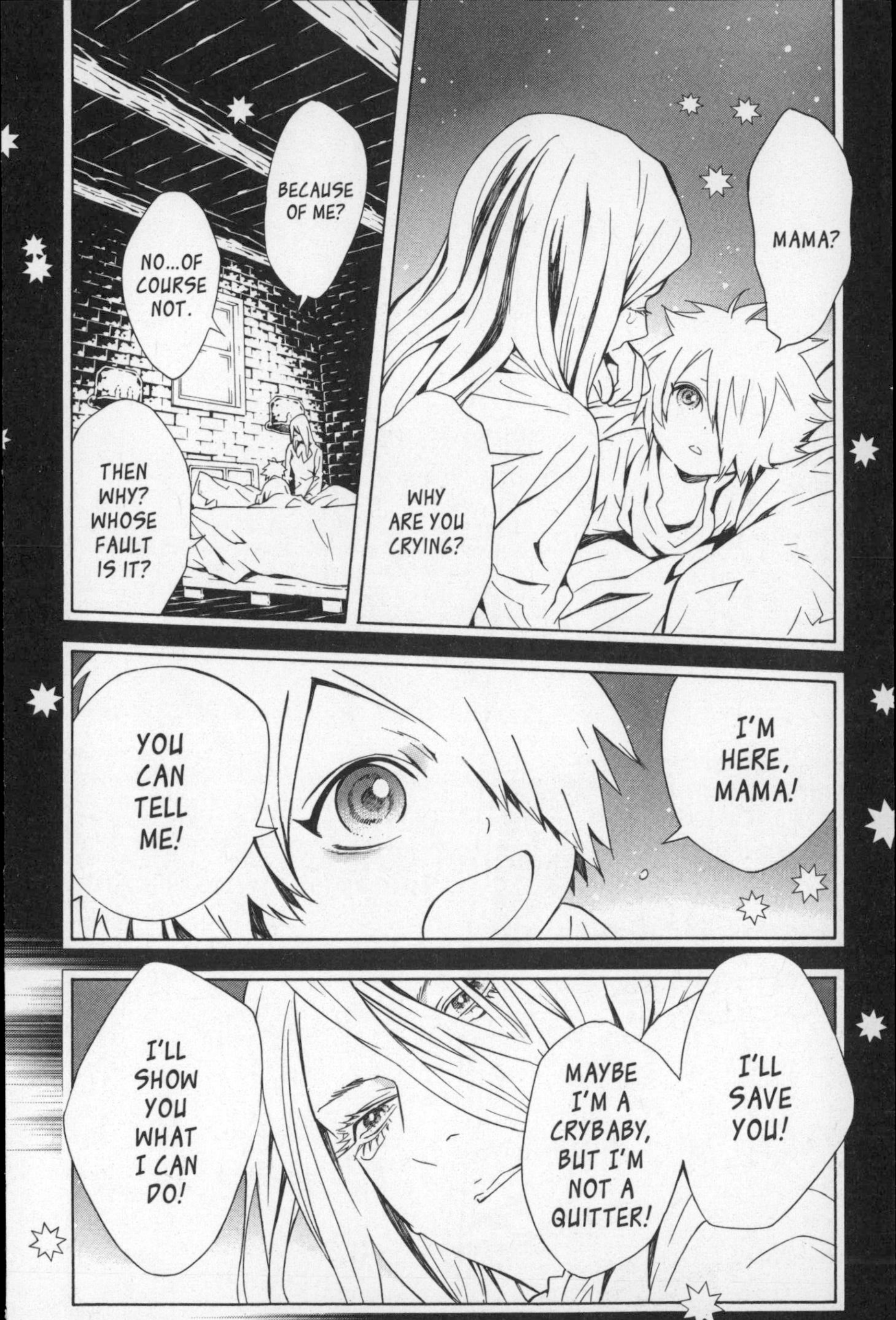
MAMA?
WHY ARE YOU CRYING?
BECAUSE OF ME?
NO...OF COURSE NOT.
THEN WHY? WHOSE FAULT IS IT?
I'M HERE, MAMA!
YOU CAN TELL ME!
I'LL SAVE YOU!
MAYBE I'M A CRYBABY, BUT I'M NOT A QUITTER!
I'LL SHOW YOU WHAT I CAN DO!

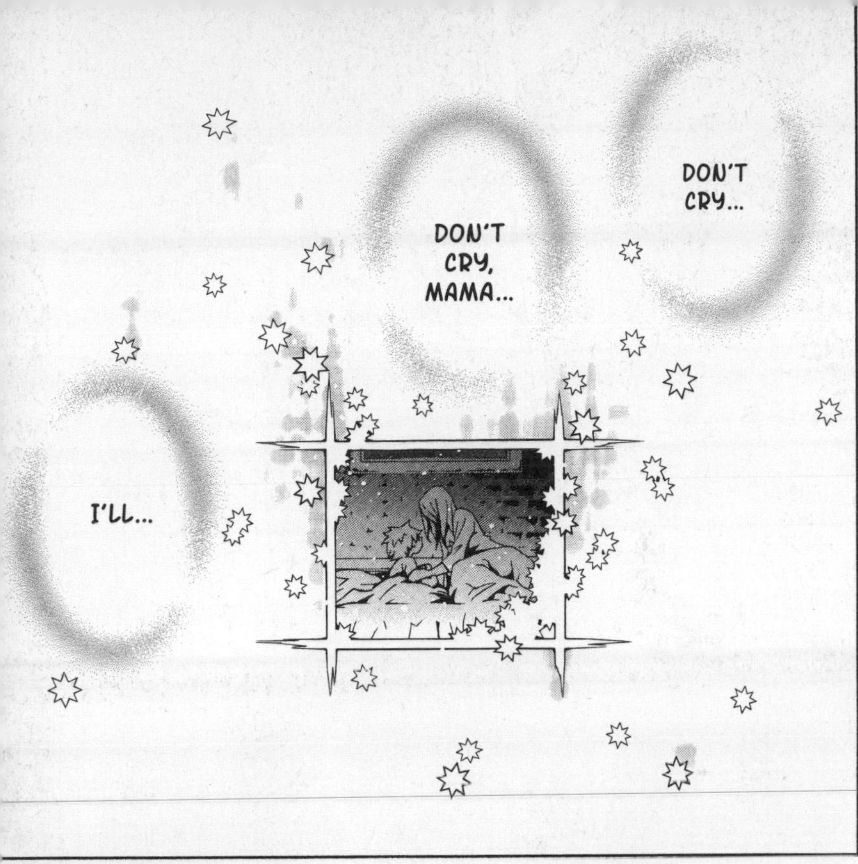
DON'T CRY...
DON'T CRY, MAMA...
I'LL...

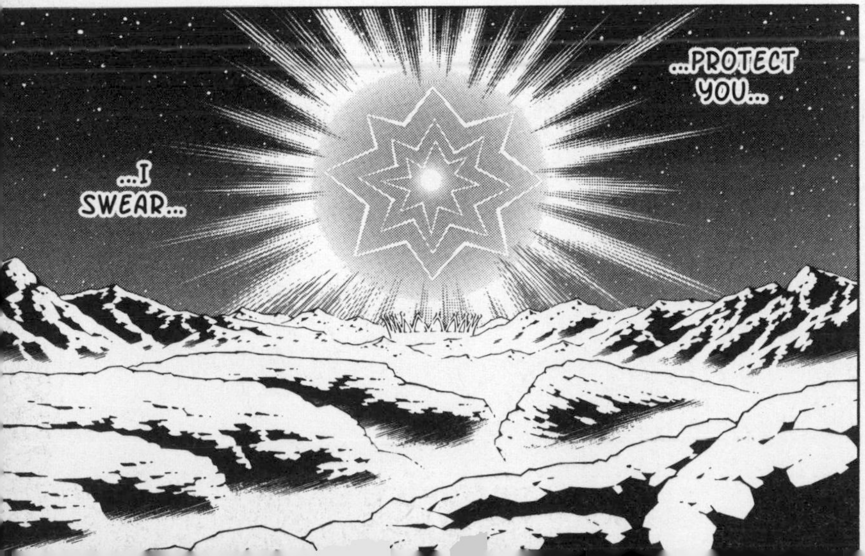
...PROTECT YOU...
...I SWEAR...

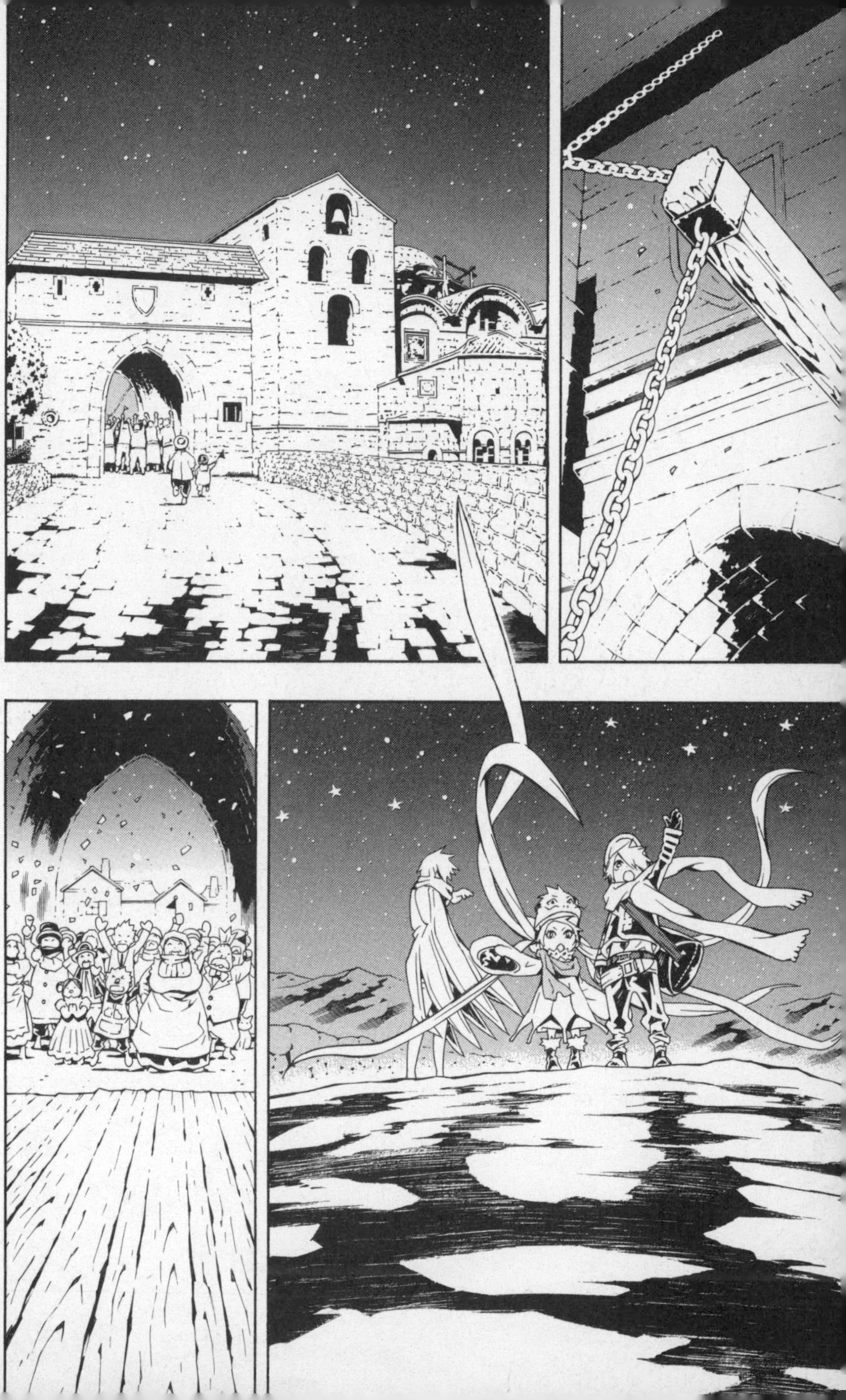

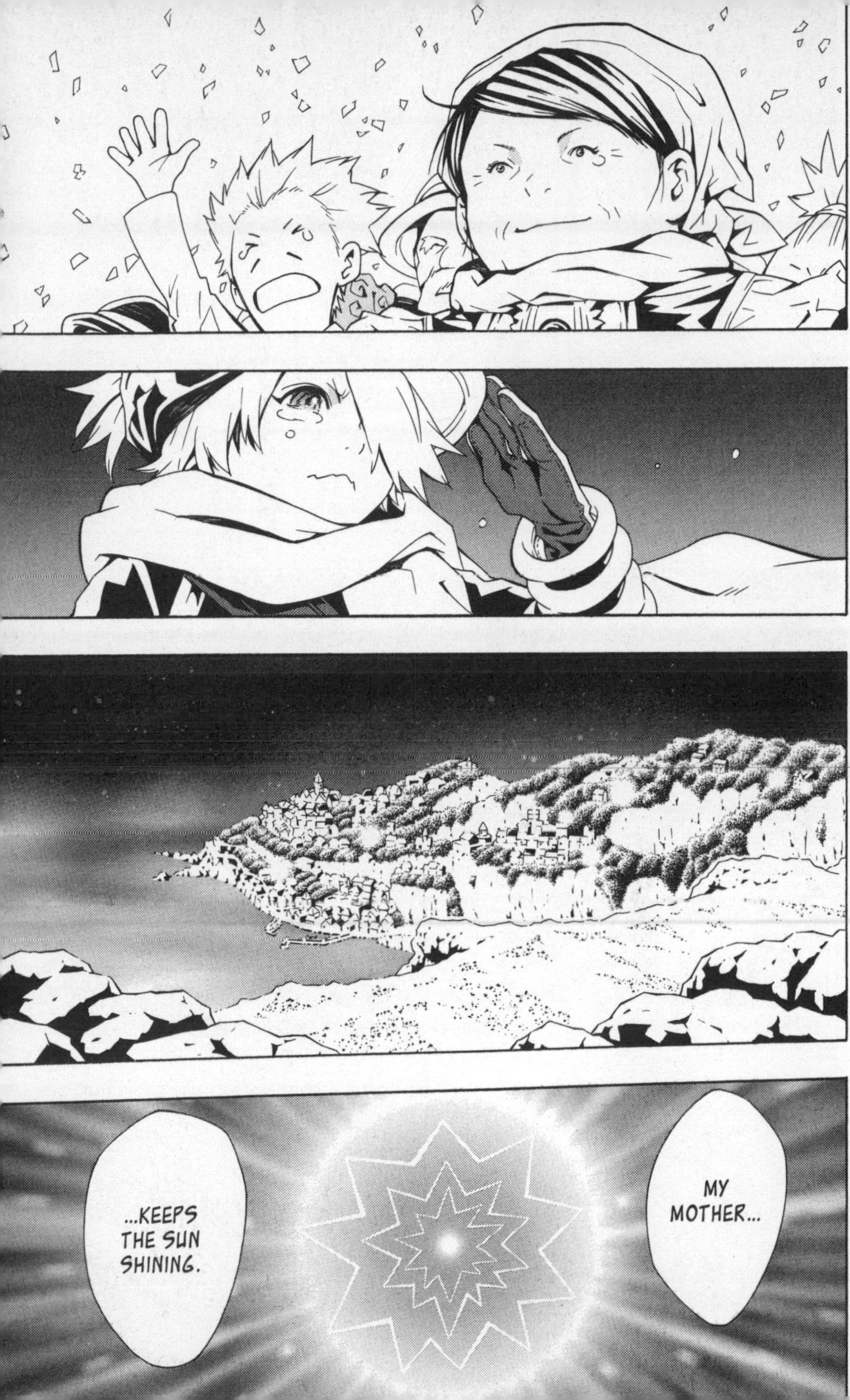
MY MOTHER...
...KEEPS THE SUN SHINING.

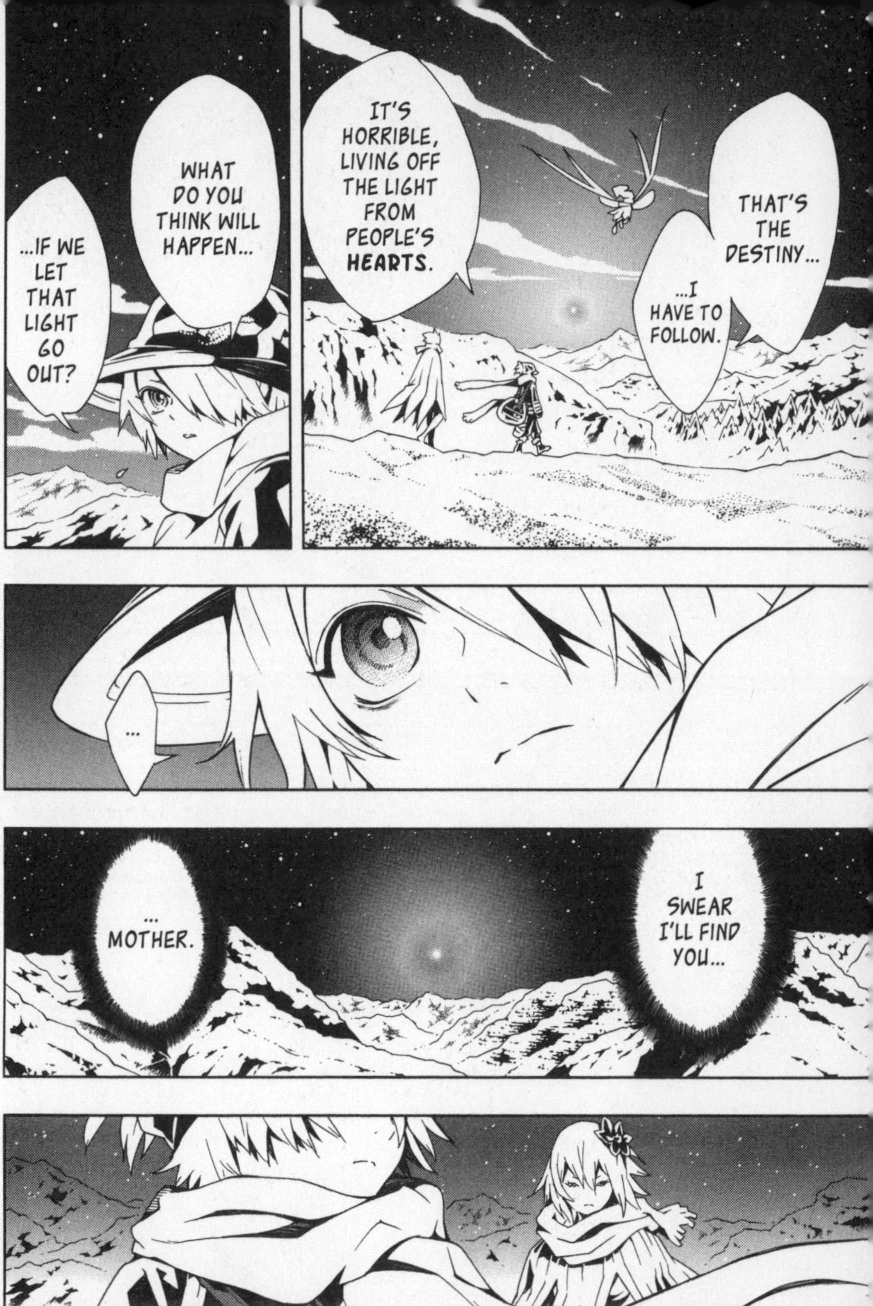
IT'S HORRIBLE, LIVING OFF THE LIGHT FROM PEOPLE'S **HEARTS.**
THAT'S THE DESTINY...
...I HAVE TO FOLLOW.
WHAT DO YOU THINK WILL HAPPEN...
...IF WE LET THAT LIGHT GO OUT?
...
I SWEAR I'LL FIND YOU...
...MOTHER.

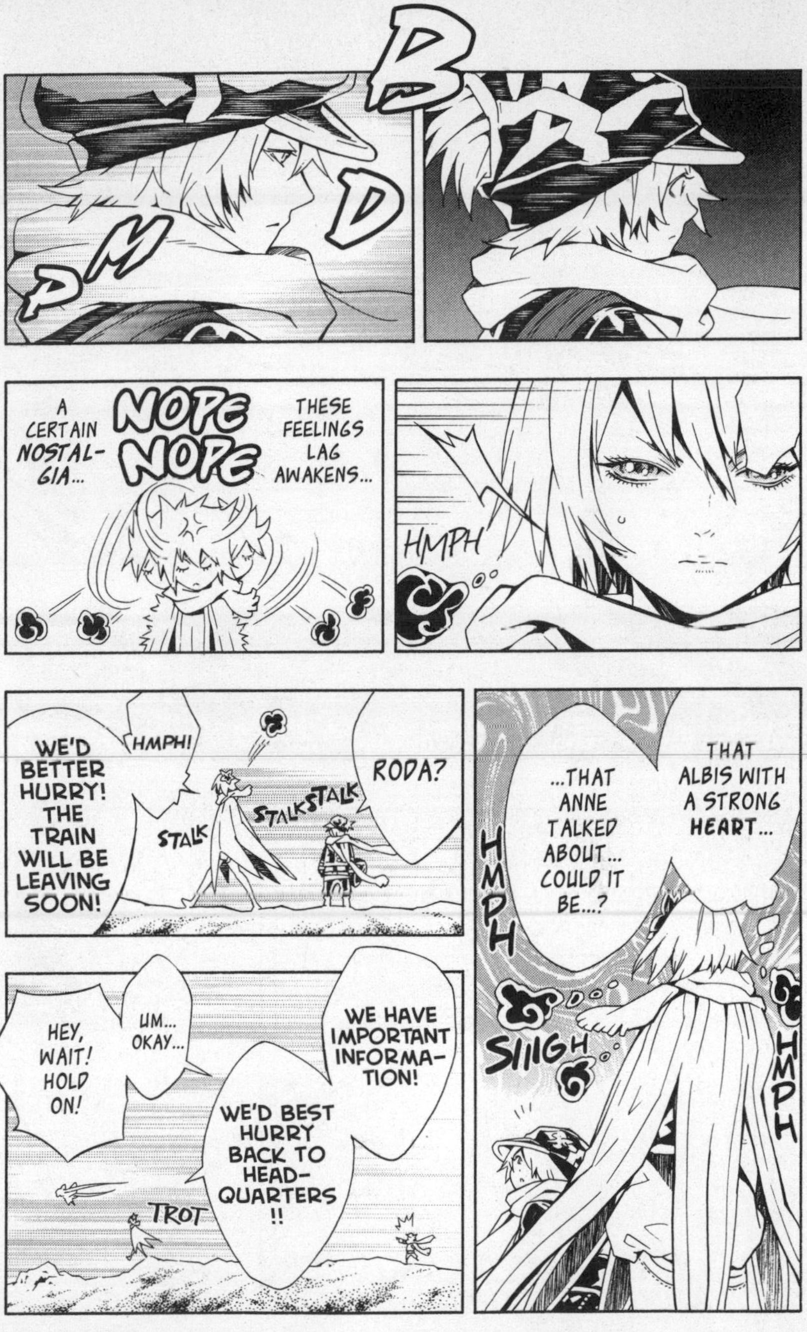
B
D
M
P
HMPH
THESE FEELINGS LAG AWAKENS...
NOPE NOPE
A CERTAIN NOSTALGIA...
THAT ALBIS WITH A STRONG HEART...
...THAT ANNE TALKED ABOUT... COULD IT BE...?
HMPH
HMPH
SIIGH
RODA?
STALKSTALK
HMPH!
STALK
WE'D BETTER HURRY! THE TRAIN WILL BE LEAVING SOON!
WE HAVE IMPORTANT INFORMATION!
WE'D BEST HURRY BACK TO HEADQUARTERS!!
UM... OKAY...
HEY, WAIT! HOLD ON!
TROT

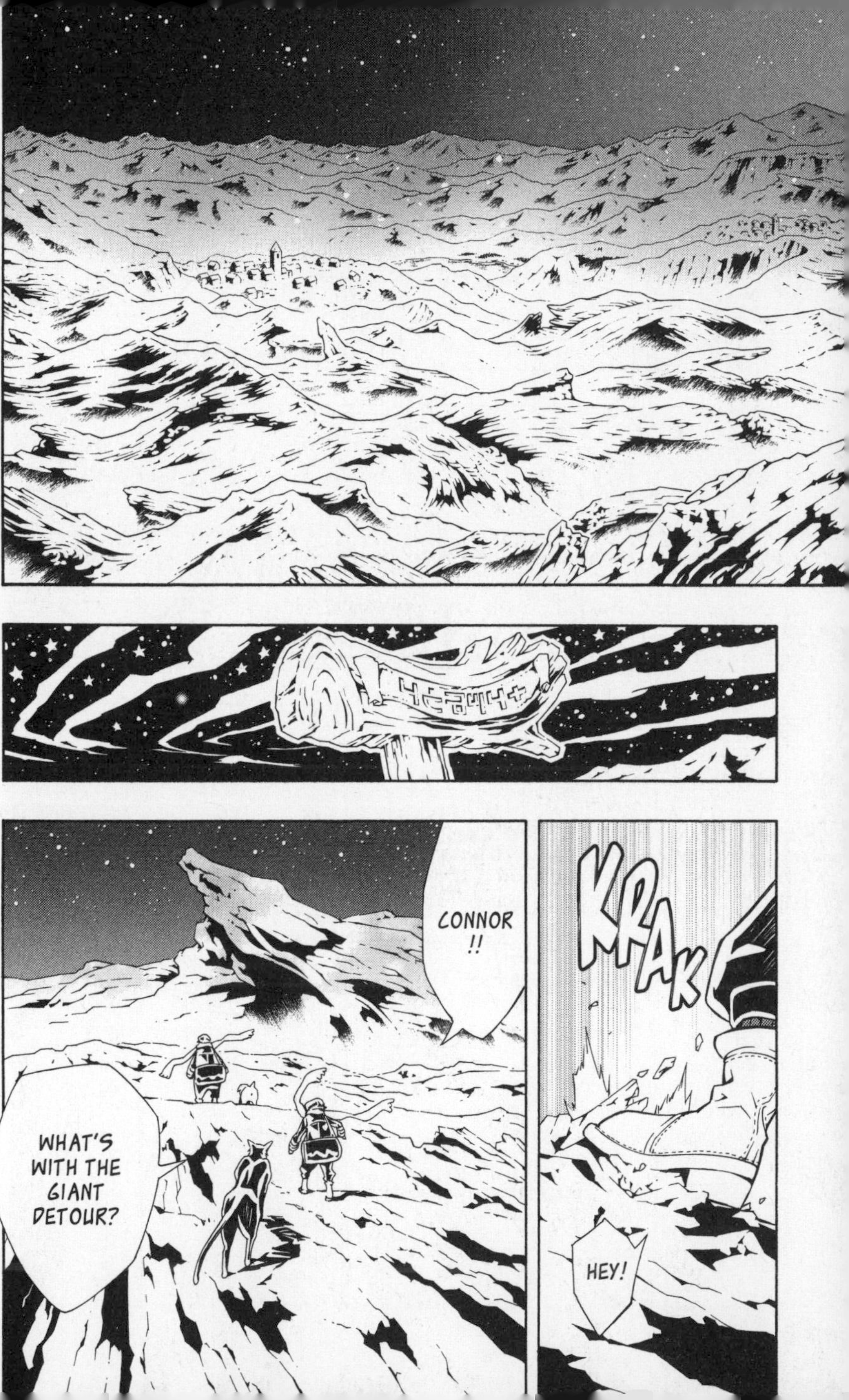
KRAK
HEY!
CONNOR !!
WHAT'S WITH THE GIANT DETOUR?

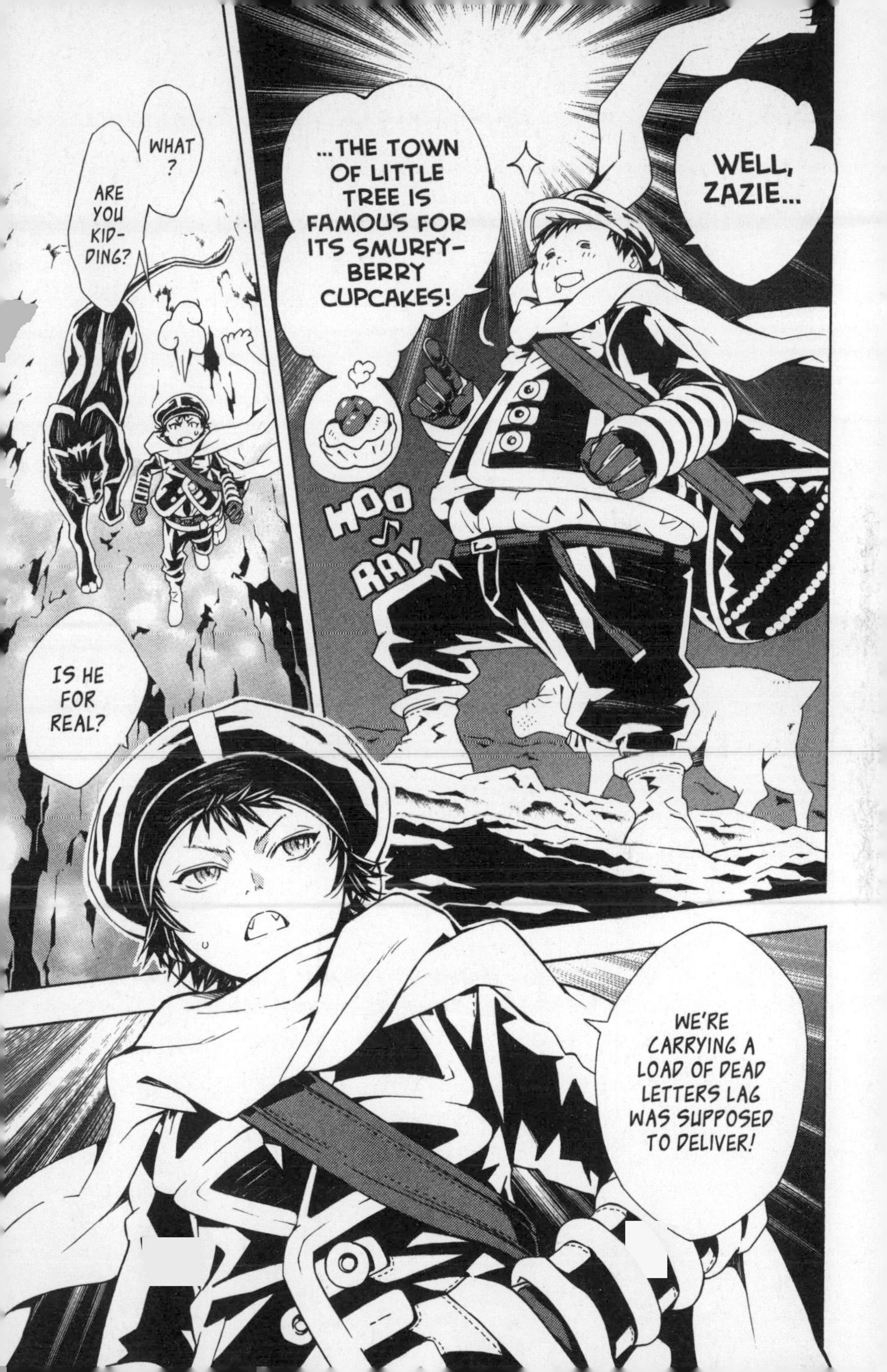
WELL, ZAZIE...
...THE TOWN OF LITTLE TREE IS FAMOUS FOR ITS SMURFY-BERRY CUPCAKES!
HOO ♪ RAY
WHAT?
ARE YOU KID-DING?
IS HE FOR REAL?
WE'RE CARRYING A LOAD OF DEAD LETTERS LAG WAS SUPPOSED TO DELIVER!

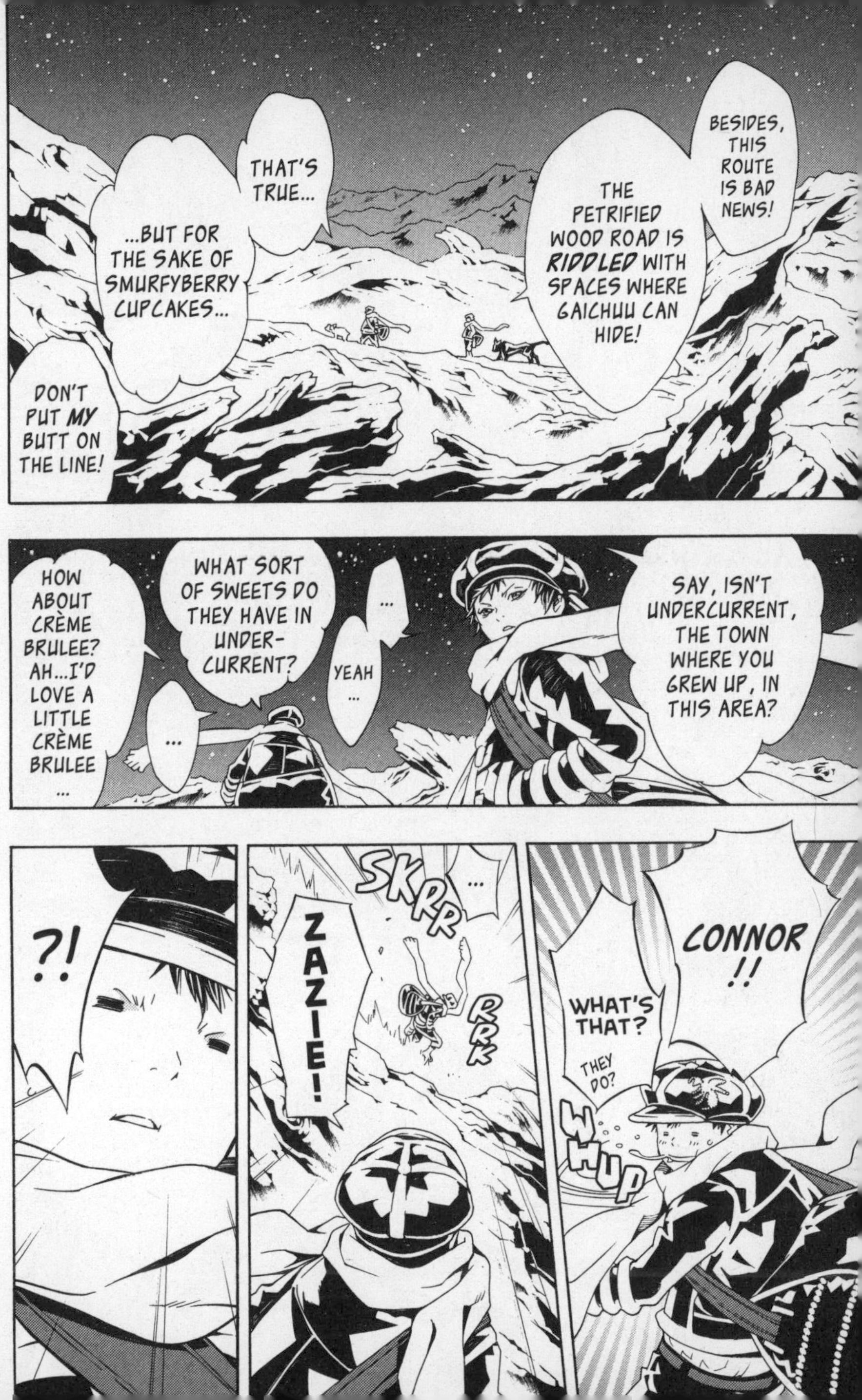
BESIDES, THIS ROUTE IS BAD NEWS!
THE PETRIFIED WOOD ROAD IS *RIDDLED* WITH SPACES WHERE GAICHUU CAN HIDE!
THAT'S TRUE...
...BUT FOR THE SAKE OF SMURFYBERRY CUPCAKES...
DON'T PUT *MY* BUTT ON THE LINE!
SAY, ISN'T UNDERCURRENT, THE TOWN WHERE YOU GREW UP, IN THIS AREA?
...
YEAH ...
WHAT SORT OF SWEETS DO THEY HAVE IN UNDER-CURRENT?
...
HOW ABOUT CRÈME BRULEE? AH...I'D LOVE A LITTLE CRÈME BRULEE ...
CONNOR !!
WHAT'S THAT?
THEY DO?
WHUP
...
SKRR
RRK
ZAZIE!
?!

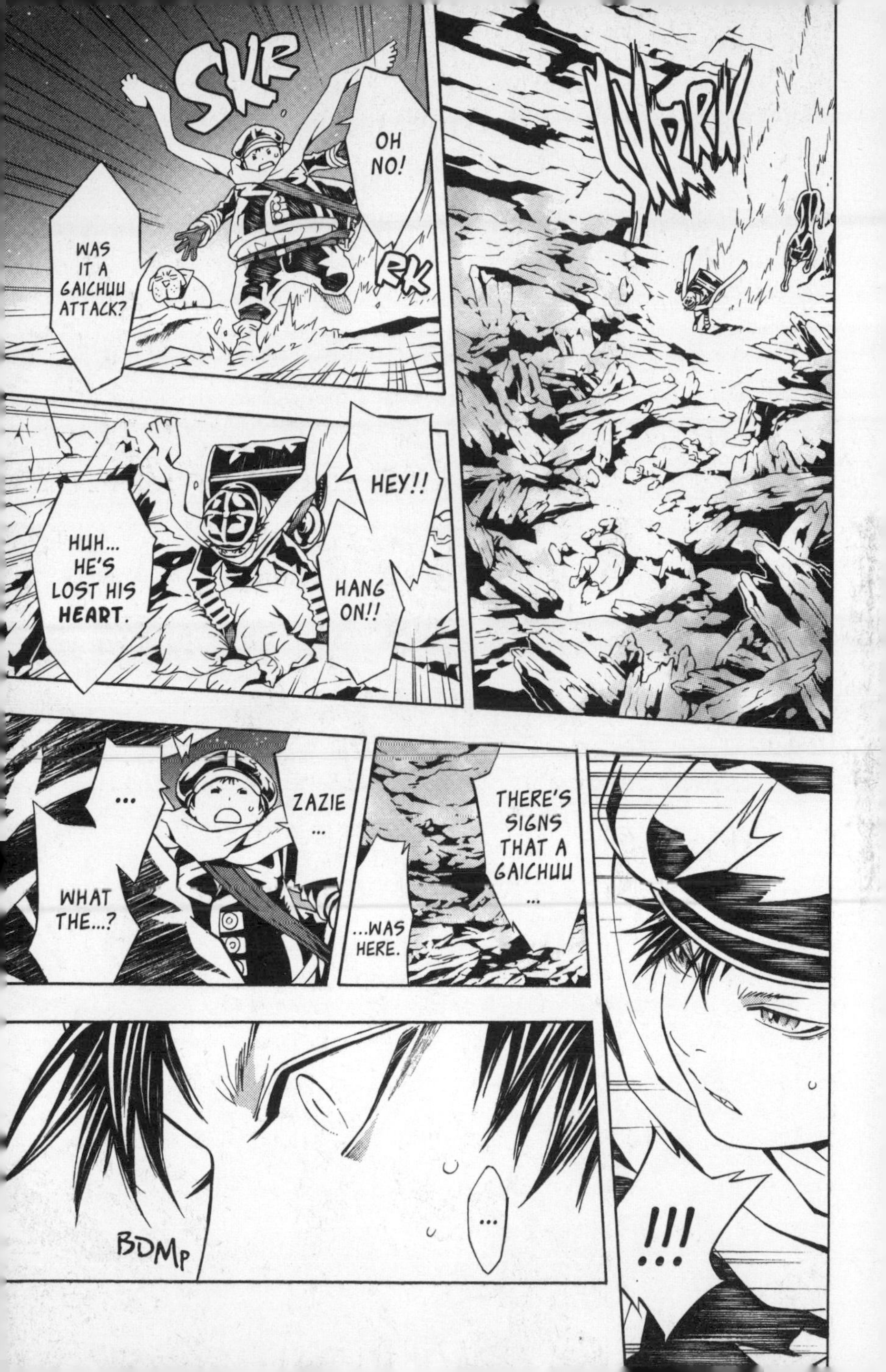
WORK
SKR
OH NO!
RK
WAS IT A GAICHUU ATTACK?
HEY!!
HANG ON!!
HUH... HE'S LOST HIS HEART.
!!!
THERE'S SIGNS THAT A GAICHUU ...
...WAS HERE.
ZAZIE ...
...
WHAT THE...?
...
BDMP

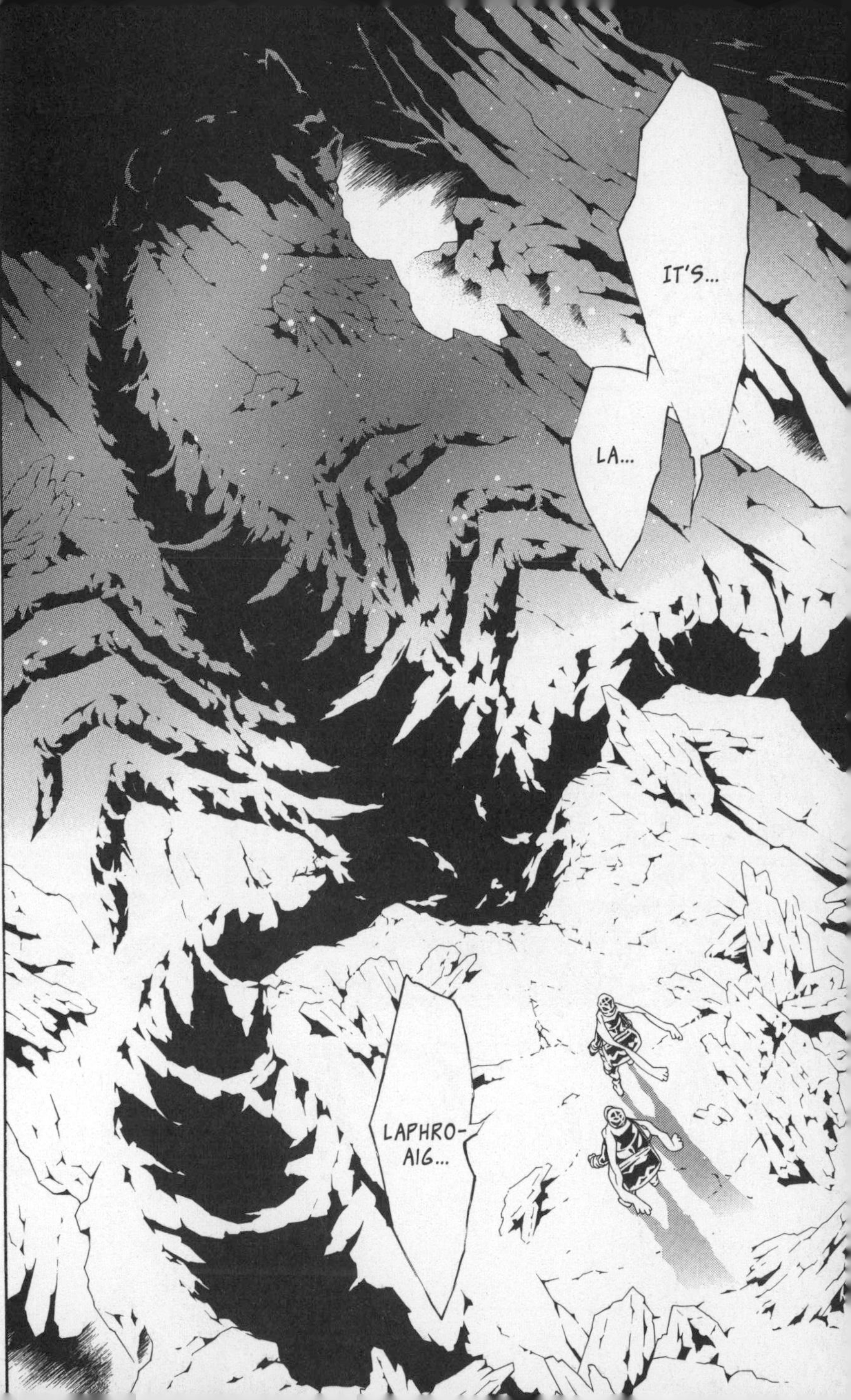
IT'S...
LA...
LAPHRO-AIG...

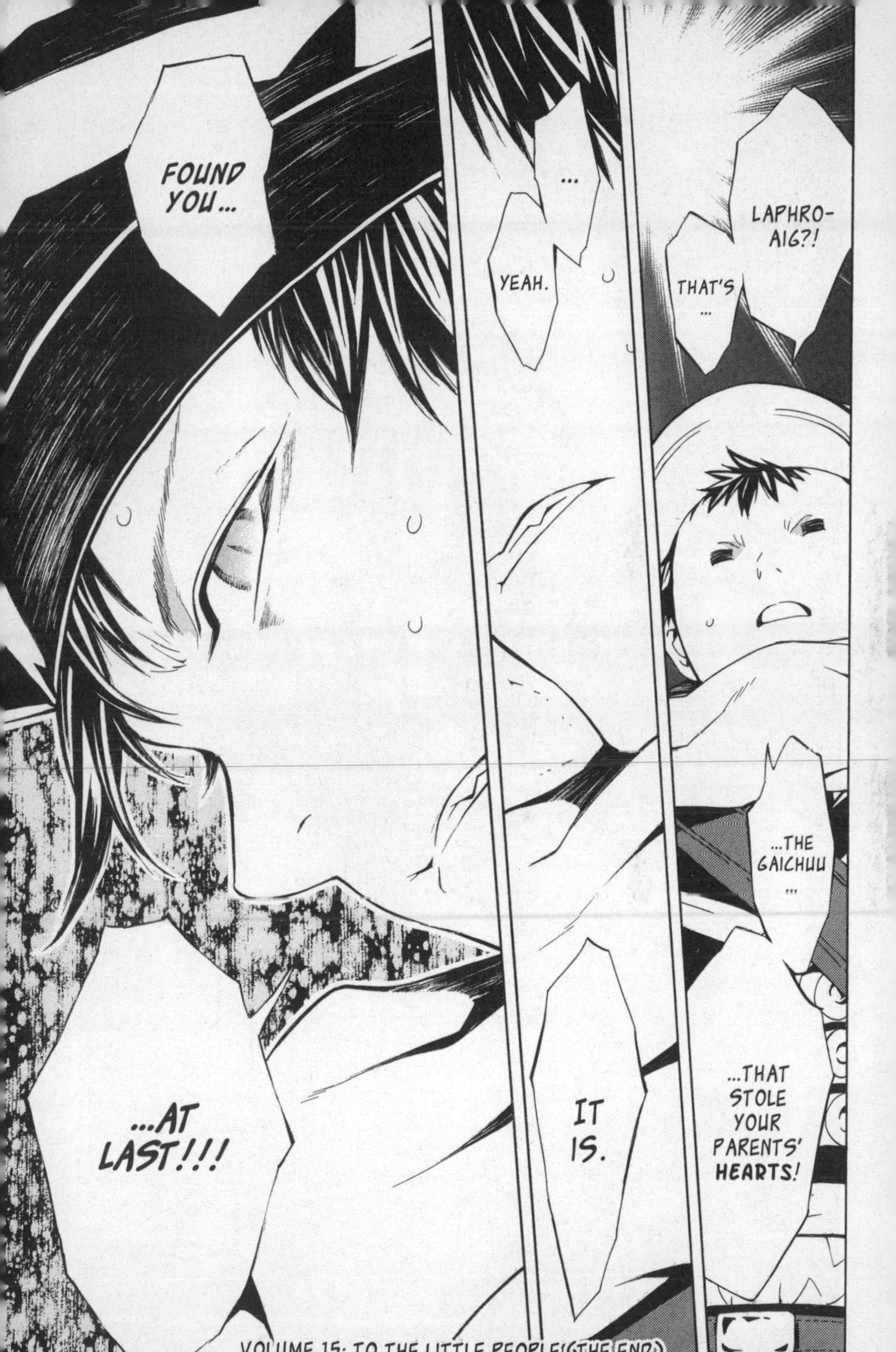
LAPHRO-AIG?!
THAT'S ...
...THE GAICHUU ...
...THAT STOLE YOUR PARENTS' HEARTS!
...
YEAH.
IT IS.
FOUND YOU...
...AT LAST!!!

VOLUME 15: TO THE LITTLE PEOPLE (THE END)

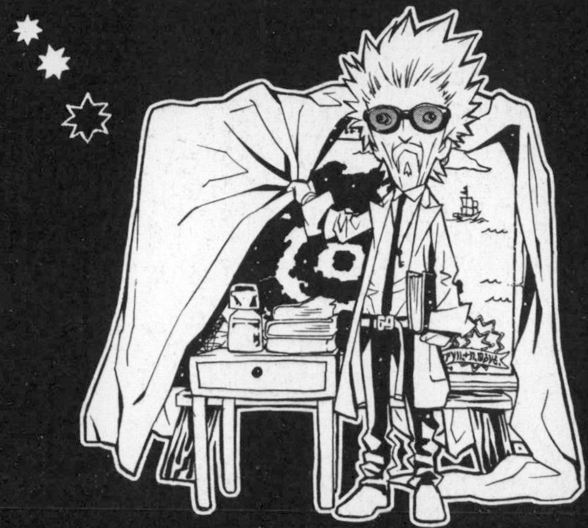

Dr. Thunderland's Reference Desk

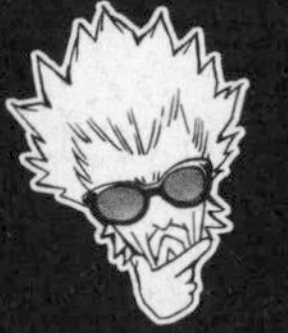

Roda's past and the secret of Lag's birth...whoa! Are you serious?!

Lag is really standing tall, don't you think? To be honest, for a second I felt this was no time for me to complain about not having a turn in the story. Just for a second, mind you. Perhaps, as an elite scientist with a fulfilling career, I should really take the higher ground. After all, I'm very busy at the Beehive, researching all manner of things. But how can I restrain myself while reviewing the events of this volume? Try as I may, it's impossible to suppress my giddy charm. What a dilemma...

■ BEEHIVE GENERAL MEETING

What, me? Behave myself? Stop being so gosh-darn charming? Behave myself, they say...my tears overflow!

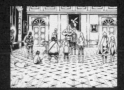

■ LAG SEEING

Oh, Lag! *Sob!* So he's a boy created from many *hearts*. What the heck?! He took solid form when the spirit amber was placed in his body, and he became human, I guess. Hmm... I think I see. Although Lag didn't realize it, the *hearts* of countless people, sent to him from the artificial sun, rest deep inside his own *heart*.

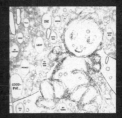

I guess he gets so emotional, and is in sync with the emotions of others, because he contains so many *hearts*. He tunes into other people's feelings as though they were his own. And the Albis part of him came from one of those *hearts*. I don't want to speak carelessly, but...could it be...**Gauche**? *Shhh!* Roda certainly seems to suspect something...

REGRET
SAD
LIES
COURAGE
WHA

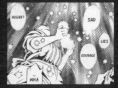

Say...perhaps Lag seems somewhat androgynous because he has the *hearts* of both men and women. No wonder he looked so cute in drag as Lala in volume 8! Even Zazie was taken by him. That Little Red Riding Hood...that kitty cat...*heh heh heh*. Huh? ...I know, I know. Behave myself...

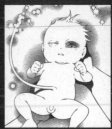

nb: *To the Little People, The Agony of Coming into the World* / a novel by Takeo Arishima (1878–1923). Arishima was a graduate of the Gakushuin Peers' School and a member of Shirakaba, a circle of like-minded writers, along with Naoya Shiga and Saneatsu Mushanokoji. He had two younger brothers, painter Ikuma Arishima and writer Ton Satomi.

FLUTTER
FLUTTER

nb: Lars von Trier / Danish film director. His film *Breaking the Waves* took the 1996 Grand Prix at the Cannes Film Festival, and in 2000 *Dancer in the Dark* won the Palme d'Or.

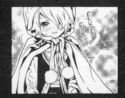

■ EMPRESS

The country of Amberground is ruled by the Empress, who is believed to be descended from God. She is the most powerful person in the world and most elevated of clerics.

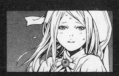

She, in herself, is considered a religion. All of Amberground exists for her sake. And she's Lag's mother, you say?! Are you serious?! This is incredible! Incredible!! *Hff...hff...* I was so astounded that I coughed up a raw oyster I'd had for breakfast. Why did I eat oysters for breakfast? I'm even more puzzled by my diet than the mystery of the Empress.

But even more curious is the content of Anne's letter. Our Empress is a device that keeps the sun from going out?! And the images buried in Noir's dormant memories...what do they mean? *Arrgh!!* There it goes again...another raw oyster! Sea milk!! *Argh*...must... behave myself...

■ CHILDREN BORN ON THE DAY OF THE FLICKER

To learn the secrets of Amberground, Lag must find the four other 12-year-olds who were born on the Day of the Flicker. Together, they should be able to revive all the country's ancient memories. It won't be easy finding them, though. Bah, humbug! But perhaps a Bee is the perfect person to get the job done. Should I go with him? No need? Behave myself? Oh, shut up, will you?

nb: Speed Well / name of a popular Mini Cooper tune-up shop in the 1960s.

nb: Doddodododoudo Dodoudo Dodou / Poem from *Kaze no Matasaburo* (Matasaburo of the Wind) by Kenji Miyazawa (1896–1933), a children's writer and poet born in Hanamaki City, Iwate.

nb: Undercurrent / Popular piano-guitar duet record album from 1963 by jazz musicians Bill Evans and Jim Hall.

So what is the artificial sun, anyway?! What is the Capital? What is Amberground? This is no time to behave myself! I must sally forth!! I must dig deeply into the mystery!! I must bury my face in Aunt Sabrina's mighty bosom!!

...AH
...HA...
HELLO
THERE WERE FIVE CHILDREN, INCLUDING YOU...

Route Map

Finally, I am including a map, indicating the route of Lag's group, created at Lonely Goatherd Map Station of Central Yuusari.

A: Akatsuki B: Yuusari C: Yodaka

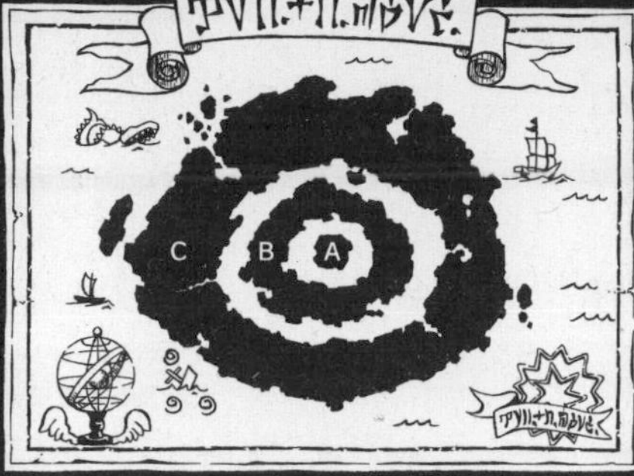
C
B
A

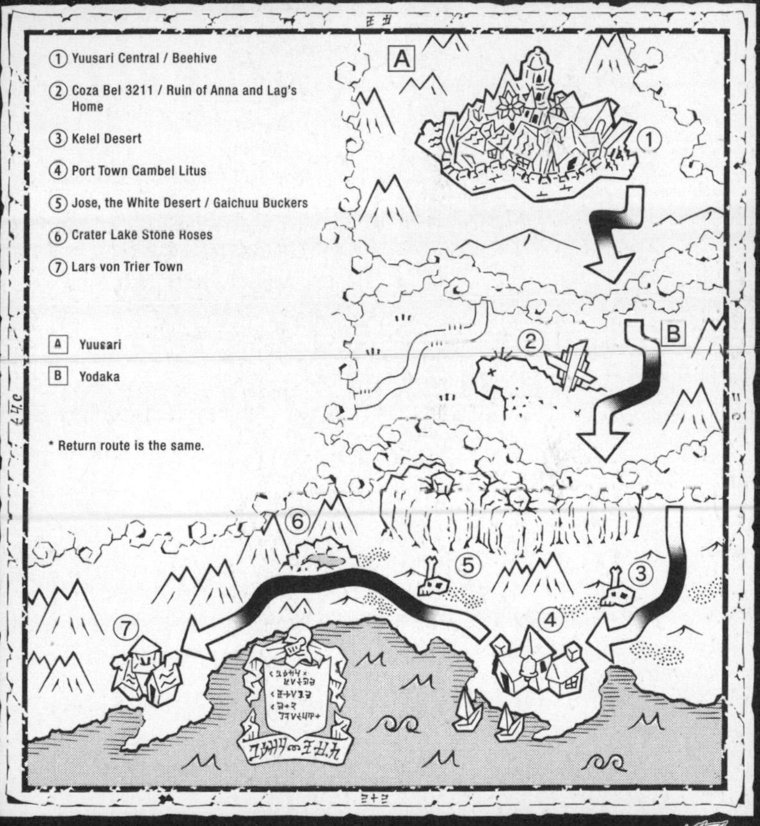
1 Yuusari Central / Beehive
2 Coza Bel 3211 / Ruin of Anna and Lag's Home
3 Kelel Desert
4 Port Town Cambel Litus
5 Jose, the White Desert / Gaichuu Buckers
6 Crater Lake Stone Hoses
7 Lars von Trier Town
A Yuusari
B Yodaka
* Return route is the same.
A
B
1
2
3
4
5
6
7

I have a feeling volume 16 is going to be a Zazie fest! His opponent seems like a powerful one! Is it time for me to rise up at last? Maybe I'll do battle and defeat it! Come on, give me a chance! You can even make me out to be the "bad boy" in the group!

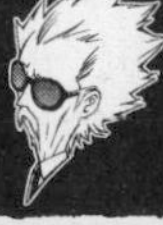

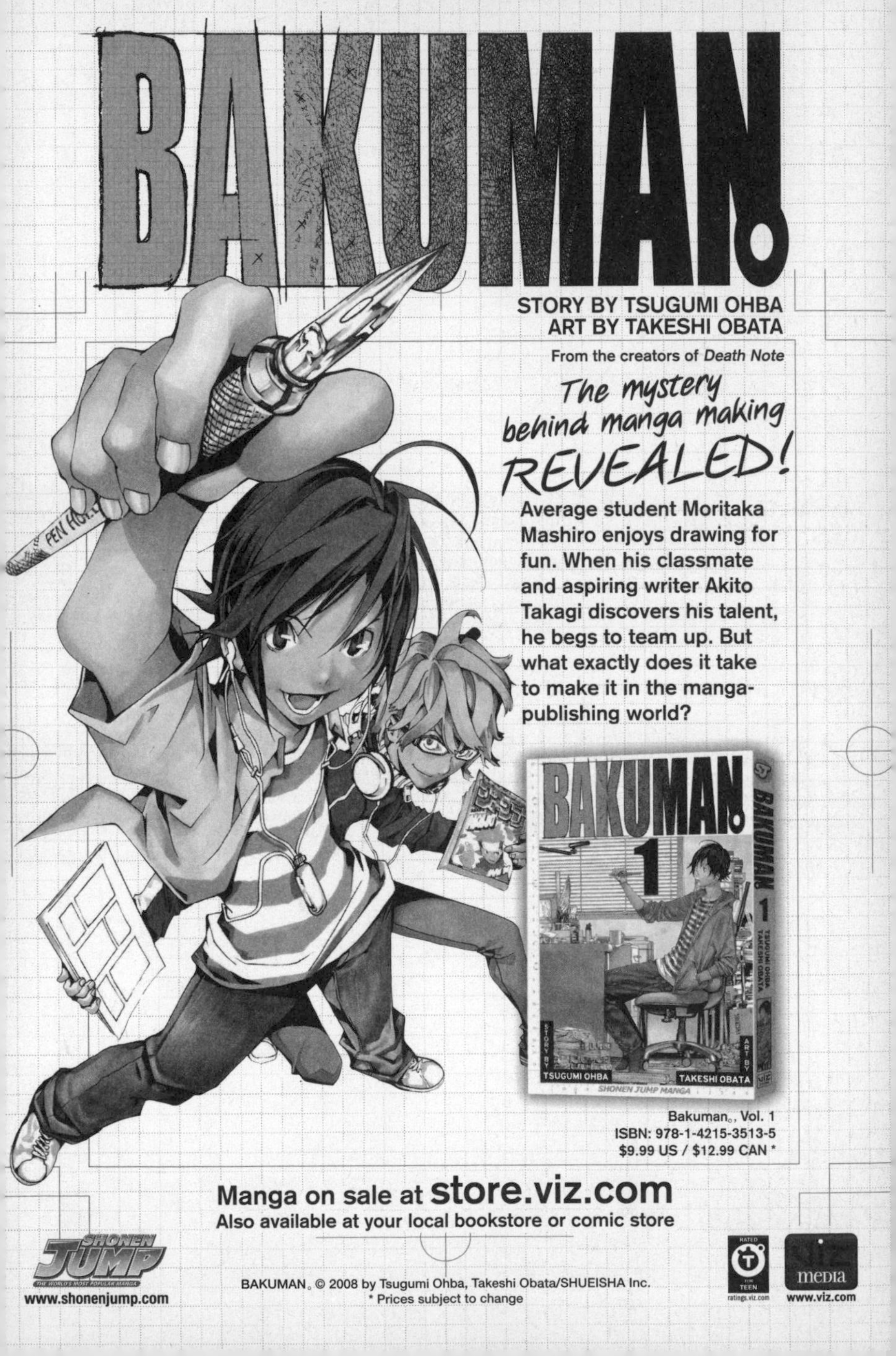
BAKUMAN。
STORY BY TSUGUMI OHBA
ART BY TAKESHI OBATA
From the creators of Death Note
The mystery behind manga making REVEALED!
Average student Moritaka Mashiro enjoys drawing for fun. When his classmate and aspiring writer Akito Takagi discovers his talent, he begs to team up. But what exactly does it take to make it in the manga-publishing world?
BAKUMAN。 1
STORY BY TSUGUMI OHBA
ART BY TAKESHI OBATA
SHONEN JUMP MANGA
Bakuman。, Vol. 1
ISBN: 978-1-4215-3513-5
$9.99 US / $12.99 CAN *
Manga on sale at store.viz.com
Also available at your local bookstore or comic store
SHONEN JUMP
THE WORLD'S MOST POPULAR MANGA
www.shonenjump.com
BAKUMAN。 © 2008 by Tsugumi Ohba, Takeshi Obata/SHUEISHA Inc.
* Prices subject to change
RATED T FOR TEEN
ratings.viz.com
VIZ media
www.viz.com

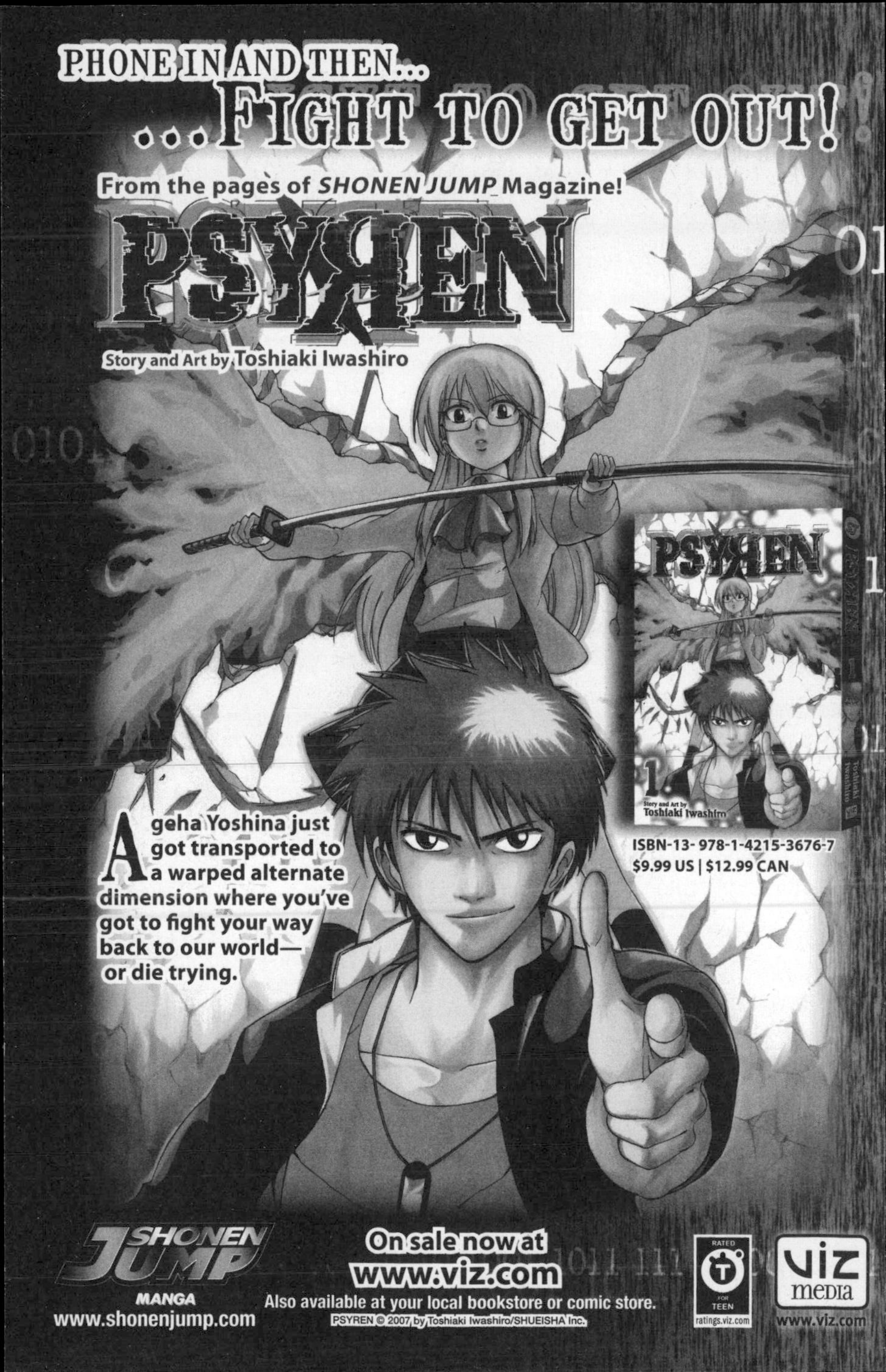

PHONE IN AND THEN...
...FIGHT TO GET OUT!
From the pages of SHONEN JUMP Magazine!
PSYREN
Story and Art by Toshiaki Iwashiro
Ageha Yoshina just got transported to a warped alternate dimension where you've got to fight your way back to our world— or die trying.
ISBN-13- 978-1-4215-3676-7
$9.99 US | $12.99 CAN
SHONEN JUMP
MANGA
www.shonenjump.com
On sale now at
www.viz.com
Also available at your local bookstore or comic store.
PSYREN © 2007 by Toshiaki Iwashiro/SHUEISHA Inc.
RATED T FOR TEEN
ratings.viz.com
VIZ media
www.viz.com

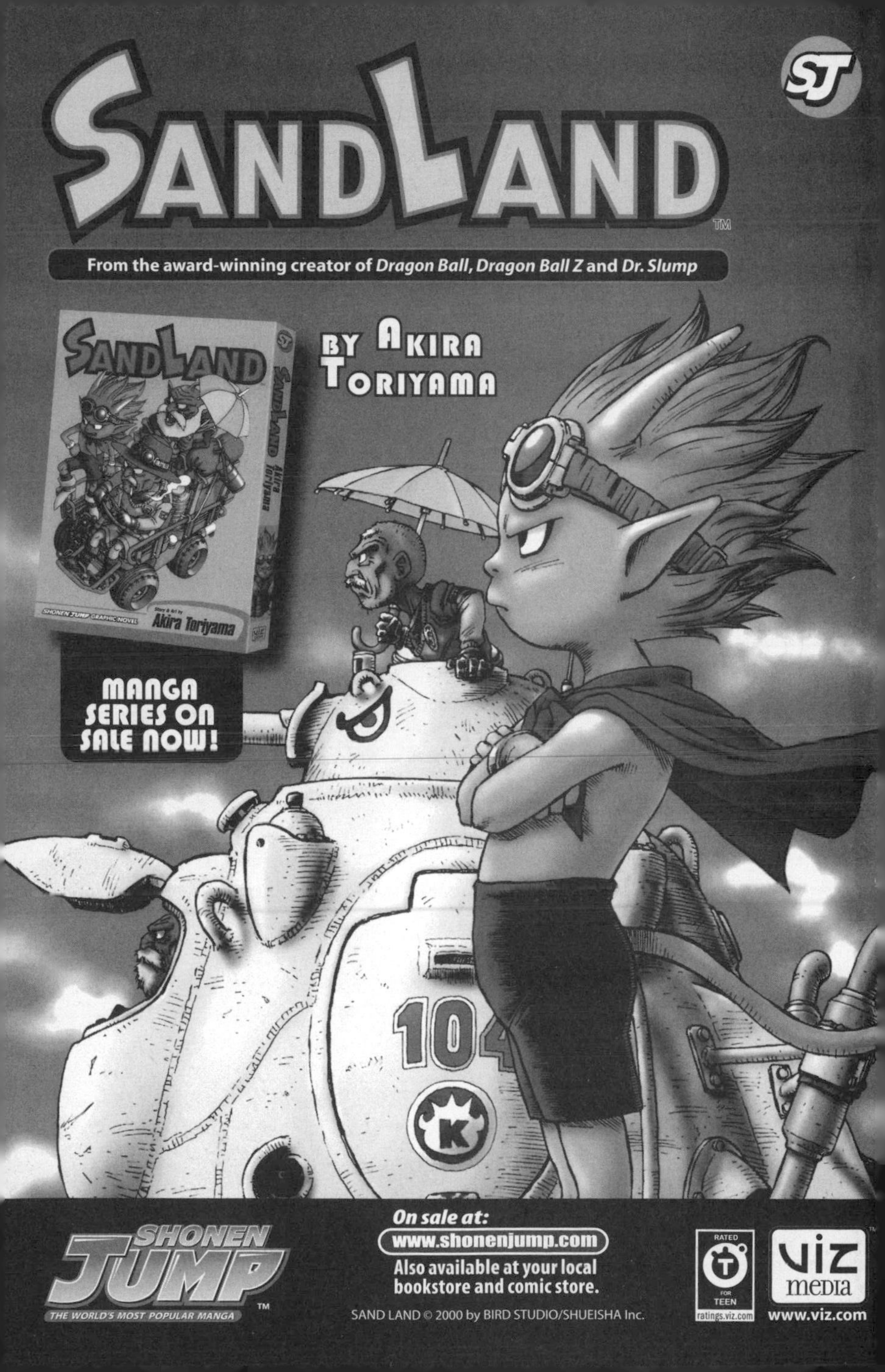

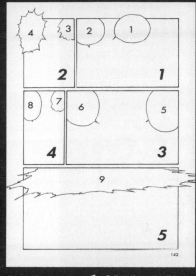

←— Follow the action this way.

THIS IS THE LAST PAGE.

Tegami Bachi: Letter Bee has been printed in the original Japanese format in order to preserve the orientation of the original artwork.

Please turn it around and begin reading from right to left. Unlike English, Japanese is read right to left, so Japanese comics are read in reverse order from the way English comics are typically read. Have fun with it!